Restoring the Right Relationship: The Bible on Divine Righteousness

Mark A O'Brien OP

Restoring the Right Relationship: The Bible on Divine Righteousness

Mark A O'Brien OP

ATF Theology

2014

Text copyright © 2014 remains with the author for all papers in this collection. All rights reserved. Except for any fair dealing permitted under the Copyright Act, no part of this book may be reproduced by any means without prior permission. Inquiries should be made to the publisher.

National Library of Australia Cataloguing-in-Publication entry (pbk)

Author: O'Brien, Mark A., 1945

Title: Restoring the right relationship : the bible on divine righteousness / Mark A O'Brien.

ISBN: 9781922239969 (paperback)
9781922239976 (hardback)
9781922239983 (ebook : kindle)
9781922239990 (ebook : pdf)

Notes: Includes bibliographical references and index.

Subjects: Bible. Old Testament.
Righteousness–Biblical teaching.
Justice–Biblical teaching.

Dewey Number: 224

Cover artwork and linocuts by Yvonne Ashby
Cover design by Astrid Sengkey
Layout by Anna Dimasi

Text Minion Pro Size 11

Published by:

ATF Theology
An imprint of the ATF Ltd.
PO Box 504
Hindmarsh, SA 5007
ABN 90 116 359 963
www.atfpress.com

Contents

Acknowledgments	vii
Preface	ix
Introduction	1
Abbreviations	15

Part One
Divine Righteousness in the Torah/Pentateuch

1. Deuteronomy 32	21
2. Book of Genesis	35
3. Book of Exodus	53
4. Books of Leviticus and Numbers	89
5. Book of Deuteronomy	105

Part Two
Divine Righteousness in the Former Prophets/Historical Books

Introduction	119
1. In The Books of Joshua and Judges	121
2. In The Books of Samuel	137
3. In The Books of Kings	157

Part Three
Divine Righteousness in the Latter Prophets

Introduction	171
1. Book of Isaiah	177

2. Books of Jeremiah and Ezekiel 205
3. Book of the Twelve Prophets 215

Part Four
Divine Righteousness in the Writings

Introduction 227
1. The Psalter 231
2. Book of Job 249

Concluding Remarks 265
Bibliography of Works Cited 273
Indices
 Index of Names, Subjects and Places 295
 Index of Biblical References 301

Acknowledgements

The thought of a book like this was initially sown by a request to write a piece on Justice and Mercy in the Old Testament for the Catholic Social Justice Series (No 64). This happened while I was lecturing at The Catholic Institute of Sydney (CIS). I am grateful to the Australian Catholic Social Justice Council for the opportunity to put some ideas down on paper and have them published as *A God Merciful and Gracious: Justice and Mercy in the Old Testament* (2008). As a result of this I subsequently offered a course on Justice, Mercy and Theodicy in the Hebre Bible/Old Testament [HBOT] when I returned to Melbourne and resumed lecturing at two of the colleges of the MCD University of Divinity, namely Catholic Theological College (CTC) and Yarra Theological Union (YTU). A sabbatical year in Sydney in 2011 provided the opportunity and the time to research the notion of divine righteousness and justice in the HBOT further and to produce a first draft of this book.

The Dominican house in Sydney was full at the time and I am very grateful to Barry Brundell MSC for providing lodgings at the Erskineville presbytery and to the parishioners there for their warm welcome and hospitality during the year. Erskineville had the advantage of being relatively close to Moore College Library, which proved a valuable resource for my research. My thanks to the staff of the library for their assistance. On my return to Melbourne I was able to avail of another excellent research facility and staff at the Dalton McCaughey Library of the United Faculty of Theology (UFT), another college of the MCD University of Divinity.

I am grateful to my Dominican Province for its support over many years of teaching Bible Studies and for assisting me financially during my sabbatical. The MCD University of Divinity also provided a generous research grant. Special thanks are due to those patient students who attended my lectures on righteousness and related topics in the HBOT and contributed many valuable comments and insights.

Finally, I would like to thank Hilary Regan of ATF Press for accepting the book and for assisting me in preparing it for publication, and also to thank Yvonne Ashby for her delightful artwork. The book is dedicated to Antony F Campbell SJ, a long-time friend, mentor and colleague in the field of biblical studies. Without Tony's support and encouragement over the years I would not have been capable of producing this work.

Preface

It may be useful for readers, particularly those not familiar with Hebrew, to have some initial information about the meaning of righteousness and associated terms in the HBOT. The term, as a noun, adjective or verb, is used not only in relation to God but also to human beings, cities, laws, and even inanimate objects such as weights and measures. However, only limited comment will be offered on these other uses, for two reasons. One is that it is beyond the scope of one book to do all of them justice, the other and more weighty reason is the biblical claim that divine righteousness is the source of all righteousness in the created realm. It is only when we know or are taught about the former that we can come to know the latter. This of course is a faith claim and one that is no doubt the product of a lot of reflection and at times vigorous debate. For those who believe in the inspired status of the Bible, God was the guiding spirit throughout this process.

The English term righteousness is not an entirely satisfactory one because it can carry a negative connotation, such as the well-known barb, 'being self-righteous'. This is not the case with the Hebrew term. Some Bibles prefer to use 'justice' or a range of terms (for example the Good News Bible [GNB], The New English Translation [NET]). However, the New Revised Standard Version (NRSV) tends to reserve 'justice' for the translation of another, related, Hebrew term (cf below) and as far as possible to maintain consistency in its use of the term righteousness.[1] A factor that affects choice of translation is the context in which a term occurs: this can alter its meaning to a considerable degree. No translation is perfect or likely to win universal approval.

---

1. Wherever the NRSV varies its rendering of the Hebrew will be noted.

However the consistency that the NRSV generally maintains in its translation of key Hebrew terms in varying contexts inclines me to prefer it for this study. It allows the reader to gauge the particular nuance a Hebrew term may have in this or that context.

The Hebrew term normally translated as righteous is, in its adjectival form *tsadiq*—transliterating the Hebrew script into Roman letters—with the corresponding nouns being *tsedeq* (masculine) and *tsedaqah* (feminine).[2] Scholars debate whether there is any difference in meaning between the two forms of the noun. Some discern little difference or, if this were the case, it belonged to an earlier stage of the language and faded over time.[3] Others argue that the feminine form tends to be used for a concrete application or manifestation of the more abstract notion of righteousness for which the masculine form is preferred.[4] As with most words in Semitic languages, the various grammatical forms are constructed from three core consonants, in this case *ts-d-q*. The various forms of the verb are normally translated into English by employing auxiliary verbs: for example, 'you are righteous', 'he will declare X righteous', 'he will bring about righteousness', etc.

The variety of literary forms and contexts in which these Hebrew terms occur makes it difficult to define their meaning and there is still a degree of scholarly disagreement. Nevertheless their careful work allows a number of important points to be made that will be used as guidelines in the course of this study.[5] In my judgment

---

2. Unlike Hebrew and many other languages English has no grammatical genders for nouns. Transliterations of Hebrew words follow the *General Purpose Style*, as outlined in *The SBL Handbook of Style: For Ancient Near Eastern, Biblical, and Early Christian Studies*, edited by Patrick H Alexander and others (Peabody: MA: Hendrickson, 1999), 28.
3. Cf for example *Theologisches Handwörterbuch zum Alten Testament*, edited by E Jenni/C Westermann (Zürich: Theologischer Verlag/Munich: Chr Kaiser Verlag; 1984), Vol 2, 507–30
4. Mark A Seifrid makes a good case for this distinction in 'Righteousness Language in the Hebrew Scriptures and Early Judaism', in *Justification and Variegated Nomism, Vol 1. The Complexities of Second Temple Judaism*, edited by DA Carson, Peter T O'Brien, and Mark A Seifrid (WUNT 2/140; Tübingen: Mohr Siebeck, 2001), 415–42; see especially 428–29. See also Ahuva Ho, *Tsedeq and Tsedaqah in the Hebrew Bible* (American University Studies Series VII, Theology and Religion 78; New York: Peter Lang, 1991), 24–25, 34–45, 143–48.
5. For a good survey and critique of the literature see Seifrid, 'Righteousness Language in the Hebrew Scriptures', 416–30.

a particularly important one is that a primary sign and presence of righteousness, which has its source in the creator God, is right order in creation/world. Because creation is comprised of myriads of parts, right order means that each part has a relationship to other parts and to the whole and is meant to function in accord with these relationships. Right order in creation—the relationships between the various parts—is, for the HBOT, a dynamic not a static concept; it envisages each part functioning to its fullest capacity in accord with the creator's purpose. A leading advocate of this creation perspective is Hans Heinrich Schmid but his description of *'Gerechtigkeit'* (righteousness) as *'Weltordnung'* (world order) could give the impression that righteousness equals world order whereas if its origin is in God it is surely more than this.[6] Hence Jan Assmann prefers the phrase *'Weltordnung als Gerechtigkeit'*.[7] That is, world order is a key presence or manifestation of the righteousness that has its origins in God. For the HBOT the 'part' of creation that is of primary focus and major concern is of course the human being. It is the creature that most closely resembles the creator (image and likeness of God) and it is also the one that poses the greatest threat to creation and God's purpose for it. The human being's abuse of its relationship with God—its unrighteousness—also affects its relationship with the rest of creation.

The notion of righteousness as right relationship includes norms and laws but is not restricted to them; they mark the boundaries within which a relationship can be productively lived and identify the kind of transgressions (boundary violations) that damage or rupture a relationship. Hence righteousness and associated terms can be applied to the juridical, legislative, and ethical arenas, and include punitive action against unrighteousness, either by God or by

---

6. Hans Heinrich Schmid, *Gerechtigkeit als Weltordnung: Hintergrund und Geschichte der alttestamentlichen Gerechtigkeitsbegriffes* [*Righteousness as World Order: Background and History of the Old Testament Concept of Righteousness*] (Tübingen: Mohr (Siebeck), 1968). For an English version of his basic thesis see 'Creation, Righteousness, and Salvation: "Creation Theology" as the Broad Horizon of Biblical Theology', 102–7 in *Creation in the Old Testament*, edited by Bernard Anderson (Philadelphia: Fortress Press, 1984). (German original in *ZThK* 70 [1973], 1–19).
7. 'World order as righteousness', as reported by Christoph Levin in 'Altes Testament und Rechtfertigung', in *ZThK* 96 (1991/2): 161–76. See 166, note 17.

human beings. But the purpose of such an intervention must be to re-establish righteousness, to restore or create a right relationship. If this is not the case then the elimination of unrighteousness leaves a void, and the biblical understanding of creation is about fullness not emptiness. God's intervention against unrighteousness/wickedness therefore always has in view the establishment of righteousness, evident in the restoration of fully functioning relationships in creation. According to the HBOT this is what God's saving work is about—the elimination of evil/wickedness and the establishment of righteousness/goodness in creation. The story of salvation via God's chosen mediator Israel is therefore an integral part, one could even say the essential part, of the story of creation. The salvation of humanity is good news for all creation. According to Seifrid this explains why righteousness is employed much more frequently in the HBOT in relation to creation rather than to covenant theology. Covenant theology is an essential part of salvation theology, which in turn is an essential part of creation theology.[8] According to Schmid, for Israel as for its ANE neighbours, 'Law, nature, and politics are only aspects of one comprehensive order of creation.'[9] A number of other studies agree on the importance of relationship in the Hebrew notion of righteousness but they tend to associate it primarily with the covenant, and with salvation rather than creation. For example, Jose Krasovec concludes (my translation):[10]

> The Hebrew notion of the righteousness of God (French *la justice de Dieu*) refers to the personal relationship of God to his people in all the situations of its existence. It therefore has a very broad meaning and, according

---

8. Seifrid states that 'the biblical understanding of righteousness has to do in the first instance with the context of creation, not that of covenant,' ('Righteousness Language in the Hebrew Scriptures', 426).
9. Schmid, 'Creation, Righteousness, and Salvation', 105.
10. Jose Krasovec, *La justice (sdq) de Dieu dans la Bible hébraique et l'interprétation juive et chrétienne* (OBO 70; Göttingen: Vandenhoeck & Ruprecht, 1988), 355. Cf also Ho who concludes that both masculine and feminine forms overall 'are concepts in terms of relationships: between man and man according to the customs of society, and between man and God according to a special covenant' (*Tsedeq and Tsedaqah in the Hebrew Bible*, 143); Bruce C Birch, *Let Justice Roll Down. The Old Testament, Ethics and Christian Life* (Louisville, Ky: Westminster/John Knox Press, 1991), 153–55.

to circumstances, it is able to designate victory, fidelity, steadfastness, the rightness of God's act or conduct. God's righteousness is in all cases a positive manifestation of the existence of a personal divinity. Only the righteous can benefit from God's righteousness whilst the unjust find themselves in a situation of judgment in relation to it. The victory of God as saviour is ultimately disclosed in God's subjugation of opposing forces: enemies, the unjust, evil and death.

An aim of this study is to discern where the HBOT places the emphasis in its understanding of God's righteousness—on salvation or creation or both.

Although the Hebrew terminology has a breadth and depth beyond that of its English counterpart it is limited, as is all terminology. Depending on the context other terms have to be employed in association with it or as a replacement for it. Their relationship to one another will therefore vary. A group of words at times closely related to righteous/righteousness derives from another three basic consonants, *sh-f-t*. A noun form, *shofet*, is the common Hebrew term for a judge whose job is to establish *mishpat* (justice) by making a just (*shafat*) decision in a law case. When one considers that law is designed to maintain proper order in society and foster right relationships, then the relationship between terms based on *ts-d-q* and *sh-f-t* can be close and at times difficult to distinguish, particularly when they occur in close proximity, sometimes as a hendiadys (word pair) 'justice and righteousness' (cf 2 Sam 8:15; 1 Kgs 10:9). Another term that is at times difficult to distinguish from *tsadiq* (righteous) and *shafat* (just) is *yashar*. Depending on context this can be translated as 'upright' or 'straight' but there are passages where the context indicates the terms are virtually synonymous.[11] For the purposes of this study the NRSV practice of normally translating *tsadiq* and its derivative by righteous/righteousness and *shaphat* and its derivates by just/justice will be followed.

---

11. For *yashar* with the sense of 'just', in conformity with God's law, see for example 1 Kgs 11:33, 38 14:8; 15:5; with more the sense of 'righteous', see for example Num 23:10; Deut 32:4; 2 Kgs 10:15; Ps 7:10; 11:7; 32:11.

Other Hebrew terms that, depending on context, are also associated with righteousness are *'emet/'emunah* (truth, faithfulness), *shalom* (peace, well-being), *kun* (to be steadfast, reliable), *tam/tammim* (perfect, pure), and *tob* (good). As with combinations of ts-d-q and sh-f-t the meaning of these terms will vary to some extent according to context and this may be signaled in some Bibles by the use of different terms to translate them. Two Hebrew terms that are often used to indicate the opposite of the above are *rasha'* (wicked, rebellious), *shaqar/sheqer* (verb: to lie/noun: deceit).

When discussing the righteousness and justice of God (or human beings) in the HBOT, another cluster of terms needs to be taken into consideration. The reason for this, as will be argued in the course of this study, is that the righteous/just God of Israel is also the merciful and compassionate God who forgives iniquity so that the right relationship between God and human beings can be re-established and flourish (cf Exod 34:6-7)—a purpose to which God is unswervingly committed. The relevant Hebrew terms are *khesedh* (steadfast love/loyalty), *rakham/rakhamim* (mercy/compassion- derived from the Hebrew word for 'womb'), *rakhum* (adjective, merciful), *khanun* (gracious, compassionate), *khanan* (to be compassionate/show favour), *nakham* (to pity/repent/be sorry) *'ahav* (love), *yeshu'a* (salvation). Like the terms listed above, the meaning of these fluctuates according to context. One may say that they tend to refer to attitudes expressed in actions rather than to sentiments or feelings; by the same token, scholars advise that Hebrew thinking did not make a neat distinction between the affective and the active.[12] A significant feature of *khesedh*, *khanan/khanun* and *rakham/rakhamim* is that they are mainly employed to express God's commitment to humanity rather than the reverse, and to do so when human beings are in need or have failed to honour proper relationships. This is particularly the case with *khesedh* which Katharine Doob Sakenfeld describes as a loyalty 'made manifest in concrete action'.[13] As will

---

12. Katharine Doob Sakenfeld, *Faithfulness in Action: Loyalty in Biblical Perspective* (OBT; Philadelphia: Fortress Press, 1985), 131; see also 'Love in the OT', 716 in *The New Interpreter's Dictionary of the Bible I–Ma Volume 3* (Nashville: Abingdon Press, 2008), 713–18.
13. Cf Sakenfeld, 'Love in the OT', 717–18; see also Matthias Franz, *Der barmherzige und gnädige Gott. Die Gnadenrede vom Sinai (Exodus 34, 6-7) und ihre Parallelen*

be noted in the course of this study, these terms frequently occur in conjunction with righteousness and justice and associated terms.

The difficulty in distinguishing clearly between the meanings of these various Hebrew terms is somewhat frustrating yet unavoidable. There are a number of factors that contribute to it. An obvious one is our historical distance from biblical times. Although current knowledge of ancient Hebrew and its historical, cultural and sociological contexts is greatly improved it is still limited. This is evident in scholarly attempts to reconstruct the historical development of Hebrew and the changing meaning of terms over time. They have generated considerable debate. Some are convinced that this can be done with a measure of certainty.[14] Others are skeptical.[15] A second factor is that the Hebrew Bible records only a selection of a larger corpus of oral and written literature that is no longer available. Thirdly, ancient Israelites left no dictionaries that define the meaning of the terms they used. Fourthly, the principal literary forms in the HBOT are narrative (as in the Torah), poetry (as in prophetic books, the psalms and Wisdom literature), and law texts (as in the law codes). One might expect law texts would be consistent and 'systematic' in their use of terminology but the elastic nature of narrative and poetry signals that readers need to be alert to a much more fluid and at times surprising use of terms in these literary forms. This study will strive to be so alert but when it fails more alert readers will hopefully spot the failure and supply their own corrections.

---

im Alten Testament und seiner Umwelt (BWANT 160; Stuttgart: Kohlammer, 2003), 118–19.

14. Ho, for example, argues that one can trace development in the meaning of *tsedeq* and *tsedaqah* (*Tsedeq and Tesedaqah in the Hebrew Bible*). On the more general level Avi Hurvitz claims to be able to distinguish Early Biblical Hebrew (EBH, pre-exilic) and Late Biblical Hebrew (LBH, post-exilic) (cf *The Transition Period in Biblical Hebrew: A Study in Post-Exilic Hebrew and Its Implications for the Dating of Psalms* [Hebrew University: Jerusalem, 1972]).
15. See for example the critique of Hurvitz by Ian Young, 'Is the Prose Tale of Job in Late Biblical Hebrew?', in *VT* 59 (2009): 606–29, and the literature discussed there.

Introduction

As the title indicates, this book is about the righteousness of God and its importance for the HBOT's understanding of the human condition. To propose that righteousness is a central component of HBOT theology is not new. No less a figure than Gerhard von Rad holds that

> There is absolutely no concept in the Old Testament with so central a significance for all relationships of human life as that of *tsdqh*. It is the standard not only for man's relationship to God but also his relationship to his fellows.[1]

Another leading commentator, Hans Heinrich Schmid, argues that the 'righteousness of the world' is 'the fundamental problem of our human existence.'[2] Even though they do not say so explicitly, it is reasonable to presume that von Rad and Schmid identify divine righteousness as the source of human and world righteousness. The more recent commentator, Rolf P Knierim, makes the connection explicit by stating that the 'most fundamental aspect' of the HBOT's teaching is 'Yahweh's universal dominion in justice and righteousness.'[3]

What has not been done so far, and what this book offers, is a study of divine righteousness that follows the arrangement of the tripartite

---

1. Gerhard von Rad, *Old Testament Theology*, vol 1 (London: SCM Press, 1975), 370. (German original 1957).
2. Schmid, 'Creation, Righteousness, and Salvation', 114.
3. Rolf P Knierim, *The Task of Old Testament Theology: Substance, Method, and Cases* (Grand Rapids MI: Eerdmans, 1995), 17. (Originally appeared in *Horizons in Biblical Theology*, 1984).

Hebrew Canon (MT).[4] That is, the Torah provides the foundational revelation or instruction that is then applied and interpreted in the Prophetic Books (Former and Latter Prophets) and the Writings. Accordingly, this study will commence with an analysis of divine righteousness in the Torah and then explore how it is applied and interpreted in a representative selection of texts from the other two parts of the Hebrew Canon. Even though the four-part Greek (LXX) canon—Pentateuch, Historical Books, Wisdom Literature, and Prophets—gives more weight to the future perspective of prophecy by locating it last in the sequence, this future involves the realisation of God's purpose as enunciated in the Pentateuch.

Although there are only seven direct or indirect references to divine righteousness in the Torah, in comparison to the many references in the Prophetic Corpus and the Writings, they are in my judgement strategically located along its storyline.[5] This is an initial sign of their importance. The first occurs in the context of the flood, a paradigm story of human evil corrupting the good order of creation. Genesis 6:9 identifies Noah as 'a righteous man, blameless in his generation; Noah walked with God'. In Genesis 7:1 God declares to Noah that 'you alone are righteous before me'. The clear implication is that Noah's relationship with God is what makes him righteous: in other words, divine righteousness is the measure of his righteousness. The second occurs in association with the destruction of Sodom and Gomorrah (Gen 18–19). It functions within the story of the chosen

---

4. In 2003 Otto Kaiser published a study of divine righteousness entitled *Der Gott des Alten Testaments. Theologie des Alten Testaments 3. Yahwes Gerechtigkeit* (UTB für Wissenschaft; Göttingen: Vandenhoeck & Ruprecht). This work takes quite a different tack to the one proposed here. According to Kaiser the HBOT unfolds divine righteousness within a three-stage eschatological schema (cf 82): there is God's righteous judgement of Israel for its disobedience to the covenant, followed by judgment of the nations, and finally salvation for Israel (and the nations). Support for this schema is drawn from a variety of texts as well as Kaiser's reconstruction of the development of Israel's religious literature and its understanding of its role in the scheme of things.
5. There are forty-one occurrences of righteous/righteousness (adjective, masculine and feminine noun, verb) in the Torah. Four of these, in Lev 19:36, refer to righteous (that is, honest) weights and measures. The adjective is found in Gen 6:9; 7:1; 18:23, 24 [x 2], 25 [x 2], 26, 28; 20:4; Exod 9:27; 23:7, 8; Deut 4:8; 16:19; 25:1; 32:4; the masculine noun in Lev 19:15, 36 [x 4]; Deut 1:16; 16:18, 20; 25:15 [x 2]; 33:19; the feminine noun in Gen 15:6; 18:19; 30:33; Deut 6:25; 9:4, 5, 6; 24:13; 33:21; the verb in Gen 38:26; 44:16; Exod 23:7; Deut 25:1.

people rather like the flood within the story of humanity in Genesis 1–11, setting righteous Abraham and his family (cf Lot in Gen 14) over against an utterly corrupt society. It provides the occasion for God to instruct Abraham about how divine righteousness and justice operate. This is in order that Abraham in turn 'may charge his children and his household after him to keep the way of the Lord by doing righteousness and justice' (18:19).

The third is Exodus 9:27, in the context of God's deliverance of Israel from life-threatening disorder (slavery and oppression). At this one point in the narrative of the plagues only Pharaoh admits that the Lord is righteous whereas he and his people are wicked (*rasha'*). The admission and the surrounding context suggest this is a devious ploy by Pharaoh, nevertheless he ironically proclaims that Israel's God is righteous in bringing the evil of the plagues upon Egypt. The fourth text occurs appropriately within the context of the Sinai covenant. If the exodus delivered Israel from external abuse the covenant laws are designed to protect it primarily from internal abuse—the damaging or destruction of right relationships between its own members. An arena where this is likely to occur is the law court. As part of a series of warnings against improper conduct of lawsuits, Exodus 23:7 has God declare that 'I will not acquit (declare righteous) the wicked' (*rasha'*). God is the righteous judge who will not tolerate abuse of a process that is designed to protect and promote right relationships.

The remaining three occurrences are all in Deuteronomy, a book that renews the people's commitment to the covenant and instructs them on how it is to be lived in the land they are about to enter. The first occurrence is Deuteronomy 4:8, which claims there is no other great nation that has a law as righteous (NRSV 'just') as the one God has entrusted to Israel. The righteousness of the law/torah testifies to the righteousness of the God who has provided it. According to 4:6, if Israel observes the law diligently it will become a wise and discerning people, and be seen as such by others, leading them in turn to know the source of such wisdom and discernment—the statutes of the law. This text reflects in a deuteronomic way two aspects of Genesis 12:1-3; one is Israel as mediator of God's blessing or saving purpose for humanity, the other is the evidence of good in humanity despite its disturbed state. The surrounding peoples will recognise true wisdom and discernment as, according to Genesis 12:3, they will recognise that invoking the name of Abraham ensures blessing The second occurs in the song of Moses (Deut 32) that, as will be shown in the following chapter, draws key aspects of the Torah together and prepares for the story of Israel that follows in the Former Prophets/Historical Books.

Deuteronomy 32:4 is the one text in the Torah that declares God is righteous (NRSV 'just') and upright (*yashar*) in all that God does.[6] The third (Deut 33:21) comprises one of Moses' final blessings for the tribes of Israel (although there is no mention of Simeon) before his death. These provide an important sequel to the prophecy of Israel's failure in the song of Deuteronomy 32. Despite failure the blessing promised to Abraham and his descendants will not be revoked. Israel will play its role in the establishment of righteousness in humanity and creation. The tribe of Gad is blessed because 'he came at the head of the people' and 'executed the righteousness (NRSV 'justice') of the Lord'. While the bulk of these texts are about God's intervention against human evil this is because of the threat that such evil poses to creation, which includes humanity in general and, more specifically, Israel as the chosen people. As Deuteronomy 32:4 expresses it, God is righteous and upright in all that God does.

There are a number of other more indirect yet, in my judgment, no less important features of the Torah that provide solid reasons for a study of the kind undertaken here. One is that the Torah presents its message or teaching via the time-honoured form of narrative (a story of creation and humanity and God's purpose for both).[7] As Robert Alter and others have pointed out, a key factor in the unfolding of the plot of a story is the interaction between its characters—in other words their relationships.[8] Given the findings of scholars consulted in

---

6. Surprisingly, this key text is overlooked by Kaiser in his survey of references to God's righteousness in the Torah and Former Prophets (*Yahwes Gerechtigkeit*, 233-36).
7. Birch, referring to the work of Stephen Crites, states 'that human experience itself is inherently narrative in form' (*Let Justice Roll Down*, 53). For Torah as narrative/story see Thomas Mann, *The Book of the Torah. The Narrative Integrity of the Pentateuch* (Atlanta: John Knox Press, 1988), and more recently Norbert Lohfink, 'Prolegomena zu einer Rechtshermeneutik des Pentateuch,' in *Das Deuteronomium*, edited by Georg Braulik (Österreichische Biblische Studien 23; Frankfurt: Peter Lang, 2003), 11–55, 11. For the close relationship between narrative and law see James W Watts, *Reading Law: The Rhetorical Shaping of the Pentateuch* (The Biblical Seminar 59; Sheffield: Sheffield Academic Press, 1999).
8. Robert Alter, *The Art of Biblical Narrative* (New York: Basic Books, 1981), 114-30.

the Preface that the Hebrew term generally translated as righteousness refers to right or well-ordered relationships, it is reasonable to expect that at least some of the interactions between characters in the various stories of the Torah and Former Prophets—for example God, the ancestors, Israel, prophets and kings—involve the notion of righteousness. This expectation will be tested in a selection of key stories.

An additional significant feature is that the plot of the biblical story of creation and humanity is one of the most common and enduring in storytelling, namely, the conflict between good and evil.[9] In the ANE this plot was exemplified in the myths of a cosmic battle between the good creator god(s) and the gods/forces of chaos and evil. The climax of these stories tells of the triumph of the god(s) of order over the forces of chaos: the generation of this kind of foundational myth was no doubt fueled by the deep human need for a reliable (transcendent) source of good order. The Torah employs several examples of this plot (such as the stories of Noah, Abraham, Moses) but with a major, and challenging, difference to its ANE counterparts. The threat to the good order of creation and society does not come from another god or gods, but from human beings. The Torah's dramatic account of God's battle against the human forces of chaos and evil in creation concludes in Deuteronomy with final victory yet to be won. Moses addresses God's chosen 'warriors' as they are poised to enter the promised land, purge it of evil and establish right order according to the Torah. Heaven and earth are called upon to witness that this is the vocation God has commissioned Israel to carry out (Deut 30:19-20).

The story of Israel's role in God's purpose for creation and humanity continues in the Former Prophets (Hebrew canon) or Historical Books (Greek canon) with most of the books of the Latter or Writing Prophets being located at different points along this trajectory, either via their superscriptions and/or via those addressed in the respective books. The Former Prophets ends with Israel in exile in Babylon (2 Kgs 25), the consequence of its failure to do God's bidding, and about which it had been forewarned in Deuteronomy. The Latter Prophets

---

9. Christopher Booker (*The Seven Basic Plots* [London: Continuum, 2002] describes this the 'Overcoming the monster' story plot. The normal pattern is for the monster (animal, human, divine) to threaten and almost overcome the hero or heroine and their society but be destroyed in a final thrilling battle.

proclaim a future for Israel beyond this disaster because its righteous God remains completely committed to it (maintains *khesedh*) and to the establishment of universal world order or righteousness. In terms of storyline, this is signaled in the books of Ezra and Nehemiah that tell of Israel in the post-exilic, Persian, period in which the prophecies of Haggai and Zechariah are also located. Within this trajectory, the book of Malachi provides a final prophetic reminder of the enduring need to 'remember the Torah of my servant Moses' (4:4 [MT 3:22]) and an assurance that a loyal God will send Elijah on a final mission to save people from 'the great and terrible day of the Lord' (4:5 [MT 3:23]) that will definitively eliminate evil.

The appeal in Malachi to Torah is in line with preceding prophetic books. The Torah storyline and the laws located at strategic points along it provide the foundational guidelines for the prophetic interpretation of Israel's life in the land. This does not mean Torah is a static entity; for those who believe it is the word of God its meaning is always unfolding, particularly through its relationship to prophecy. Moses, who is commissioned to proclaim Torah, is foremost among Israel's prophets (Deut 18:15–22; 34:10) and there is a prophetic thrust to the Torah, evident for example in Deuteronomy 29 – 30 and the song in Deuteronomy 32. This study will examine the relationship between the Torah understanding of divine righteousness and that of the Latter Prophets principally in the book of Isaiah; it contains the most extensive distribution of the relevant terminology. This will be supplemented by shorter considerations of Jeremiah, Ezekiel, and the book of the Twelve (minor) Prophets.[10]

If Moses is foremost among Israel's prophets he is likewise foremost among its wisdom teachers and lawgivers. Torah is identified with wisdom in Sirach 24.[11] The books from the Writings component of the canon that are of particular relevance for this study are the Psalter and Job. The superscriptions attached to many psalms indicate that

---

10. A recent detailed analysis of the relationship between Torah and Prophecy is Stephen B Chapman's, *The Law and the Prophets* (FAT 27; Tübingen: Mohr Siebeck, 2000).
11. According to Alexander A di Lella, Sirach 24:23a is 'one of Ben Sira's most emphatic statements that Wisdom is the Torah of Israel' (*The Wisdom of Ben Sira. A New Translation with Notes By Patrick W. Skehan. Introduction and Commentary by Alexander A di Lella, O.F.M.* (AB 39; New York: Doubleday, 1987), 336.

they are understood to record Israel and David's prayers at various points in their respective stories and to provide guidelines for future prayer. The book of Job is a story about an undated figure and so can be linked to the Bible's story of creation and humanity at any appropriate point. One may also note that the books of Proverbs and Ecclesiastes are incorporated into Israel's storyline by being ascribed respectively to 'Solomon, son of David, king of Jerusalem' and to 'the preacher, son of David, king of Jerusalem'. As with the Prophetic Corpus, this study will examine a selection of Psalms and key texts in the book of Job to try and ascertain in what way they invoke and apply the Torah's understanding of divine righteousness.

Another significant element in the biblical portrayal of divine righteousness is what has been termed by modern scholarship the 'Act–Consequence Dynamic or Connection'. This is a sociological version of the physical law of cause and effect. A good action will have a corresponding good consequence or outcome whereas an evil action will have an evil outcome. The maintenance of right order in creation and society was of enduring concern to the ANE world; as Schmid observes, 'ancient Near Eastern cosmic, political, and social order find their unity under the concept of "creation".'[12] Arrayed against this order are the cosmological forces of chaos that can manifest themselves in any of these arenas and can only be repulsed by appeal to the national creator god, the god of righteousness. Ensuring the continuation of right order involves adherence to the laws promulgated by the god, the regular recitation of sacred texts and performance of rituals, and the launching of holy wars that are authorised by the god who promises victory. The course of a society or individual's life, both in Israel and the larger ANE, was interpreted largely on the basis of the 'Act–Consequence' connection.[13] According to both ANE and biblical belief, the ordered structure of creation, which it is believed the national god establishes and maintains, enables one to see the connection between acts and their consequences (the various relationships).

---

12. Schmid, 'Creation in the Old Testament', 105.
13. See for example, Klaus Koch, 'Is There a Doctrine of Retribution in the Old Testament?', in *Theodicy in the Old Testament*, edited by James L Crenshaw, Issues in Religion and Theology 4 (Philadelphia: Fortress Press, 1983), 57–87.

The problem of course is that the connections cannot be proved in every case: no one can monitor all instances of an individual or a society's life and so a decision has to be made on the basis of limited evidence (for example, a judgement in a court of law). This no doubt at times led to disputes which were resolved on the authority of certain persons (king, priest, prophet, judge) believed to speak on behalf of the national god. As long as people accept the word of the relevant authority, the system will work. A modern secular parallel is the appeal to the umpire to resolve sporting disputes; without this figure of authority a game is likely to descend into chaos.

A prominent feature of mainstream wisdom thinking is the so-called 'two ways', presented in poetic form in Psalm 1—effectively the introduction to the Psalter—and in Proverbs 1. While Proverbs does not use the term Torah as in Psalm 1:2, both speak of walking in the way (*derek*) that leads to life and avoiding the way that leads to death. In Deuteronomy 30:15-20 Moses challenges Israel to choose the way of life (obedience to the Torah) and reject the way of death. As this deuteronomic text in particular makes clear, the theology of the two ways operates according to the Act–Consequence connection. A large number of psalms and the book of Proverbs operate with it, whereas a number of other psalms and the books of Job and Ecclesiastes question it or a certain understanding of it. These point to a vigorous debate in Israelite tradition about the righteousness of God in the face of the evil and suffering that forms an integral and challenging component of the Bible's story of creation and humanity. The debate can also be found in some ANE texts and it is reasonable to suppose that some of these exercised an influence on Israelite thinking.[14] In the 18th century Leibniz coined the term 'Theodicy' to describe this endeavour. This study will consider the theodicy question principally in an analysis of the book of Job.

The Act–Consequence connection is well attested in both Prophecy and Writings. Among the most explicit references in Prophecy are Jeremiah 31:29-30 and Ezekiel 18 that uphold the connection against the bitter jibe 'the fathers have eaten sour grapes and the children's teeth are set on edge'. Many sayings in the book of Proverbs are based

---

14. For a recent survey of ANE literature on theodicy see the section 'Ancient Near East' in *Theodicy in the World of the Bible*, edited by Antti Laato and Johannes C de Moor (Leiden: Brill, 2003), 27–150.

on the connection and serve, among other things, as a motivation to follow Lady Wisdom's school curriculum in Proverbs 10–30. In contrast, the Act–Consequence connection is often not spelt out explicitly in HBOT stories. Yet it is reasonable to expect that it is there, given that many of the stories recount the consequences of good and evil actions. Recent critical study of biblical narrative may offer an explanation for this. As Alter has convincingly shown, one of the characteristic features of biblical storytelling is what he calls the 'art of reticence'.[15] More often than not, key topics are not made explicit in a story or their meaning spelt out. The listener or reader is invited to do this by paying attention to the way a story unfolds its plot and the interaction of key characters, in particular their speeches. Within the framework of the biblical canon, one could argue that the prophetic books at times make explicit what is implicit in Torah stories; that is, they use terms such as righteousness, steadfast love, and compassion to spell out the implications of an aspect of the Torah. If this is the case, then it is wise to follow their lead by focusing, initially at least, on the Torah narrative and then checking how one's findings tally with what Prophecy and the Writings say.

One final factor needs to be mentioned in this introduction and it furnishes a further reason or motivation for the study. This is the debate over whether HBOT theology is primarily a theology of history or a theology of creation.[16] According to von Rad 'Israel's faith is grounded in a theology of history', a presentation of the past that claims to unfold God's saving plan for Israel and the nations.[17] This saving or salvation history is the dominant theological category in the HBOT; creation plays a subsidiary role, providing a foundation or background to the drama of salvation. For von Rad this is indicated in the way the Priestly account of creation in Genesis 1:1–2:4a provides the setting for the Yahwist narrative in 2:4b-25.[18] In contrast,

---

15. Alter, *The Art of Biblical Narrative*, 114–30.
16. The larger context in which this debate has taken place is well chronicled and commented on by Leo G Perdue in *The Collapse of History: Reconstructing Old Testament Theology* (Overtures to Biblical Theology; Minneapolis: Augsburg Fortress, 1994, and in *Reconstructing Old Testament Theology: After the Collapse of History* (Overtures to Biblical Theology; Minneapolis: Fortress Press, 2005).
17. Von Rad, *Old Testament Theology*, vol I, 106.
18. Von Rad, *Old Testament Theology*, vol 1, 140; see also 'The Theological Problem of the Old Testament Doctrine of Creation', in *Creation, Righteousness and*

Schmid argues that 'the doctrine of creation . . . is not a peripheral theme of biblical theology but is plainly the fundamental theme.'[19] The 'righteousness of the world', which is manifested in proper order within creation, is 'the fundamental problem of our human existence'.[20] This is because there is grave disorder (unrighteousness) in creation and the Bible declares that we are primarily responsible for it. The bulk of the HBOT story of salvation is about Israel and its vocation to be the mediator of God's salvation to all humanity, but this does not reduce creation to a subsidiary role. Humanity is an integral part of creation; granted the HBOT's conviction that we are primarily responsible for disorder and division then our salvation means the restoration of right order in creation.[21] As noted in the Preface the biblical notion of order is not a static one; given that it is an integral part of God's creative activity, it is what enables the various elements of creation to flourish to their full capacity.

Whether one sides with von Rad or Schmid, their debate raises important questions about the relationship between time and place. One might be tempted to identify the former with history and the latter with creation but this could imply they are separate entities. We may distinguish them in our discourse but they should not be separated; they are two aspects of the one creation. According to John Barton the HBOT teaches that 'God is responsible *both* for creating the world *and* for directing its subsequent history' (author's emphasis).[22] Moreover God's guidance of history does not commence with the choice of Israel's ancestors, Abraham and Sarah; 'it goes back without a break to the moment of creation itself'.[23] Israel's time and the nations' time in creation—in their generations and their lands—are therefore integral components of a larger march of time, the history of creation. God's purpose in creation will be realised when

---

Salvation, 53-66.
19. Schmid, 'Creation, Righteousness, and Salvation', 111. As noted in the Preface this has been endorsed by the more recent study of Seifrid, 'Righteousness Language in the Hebrew Scriptures', 425-26.
20. Seifrid, 'Righteousness Language in the Hebrew Scriptures', 114.
21. According to Birch, God's creative and redemptive work are linked together in Israel's earliest tradition (for example, Exodus 3) (*Let Justice Roll Down*, 77).
22. John Barton, *Reading the Old Testament: Method in Biblical Study* (new edition, London: Darton, Longman & Todd, 1996), 48.
23. Barton, *Reading the Old Testament*, 49.

(the time aspect) right order between its various components (the place aspect) is established. This also means that all of humanity will come to know God as creator and saviour (restorer of right order in creation). Human knowledge of God is creaturely and operates through the categories of time and place. When everything is in right order then knowledge of God will be universal and complete, in so far as creatures can know their creator.

This line of thinking would suggest that even though particular texts (for example, narratives, prophecies, proverbs) may focus more on creation or more on history the reader needs to relate this to the larger biblical context in which God's purpose is realised; namely creation and its history. All literary forms are limited to a greater or lesser degree and their particular meanings need to be complemented and assessed in relation to the larger context in which they occur. This study will attempt to do so in a limited and selective way. No one study can hope to do justice to all the parts of the canon. Furthermore, this study cannot even hope to do justice to all the parts of the Torah. Instead it will focus on those parts that are judged to be particularly relevant for the understanding of divine righteousness and its implications.

The terminological studies referred to in the Preface are an invaluable resource for the study because they provide some understanding of the meaning of terms within the biblical and broader ANE context. They can function as a kind of sounding board to hopefully fine tune one's appreciation of relevant passages in the Torah and the other parts of the HBOT canon. By the same token, analysis of a story in the Torah can enhance one's understanding of a particular term even though it does not occur in the story.

Analysis to be followed

My analysis is based on the Masoretic Text (MT) as contained in the critical edition BHS, with reference being made to ancient versions such as the Septuagint (LXX) when the sense of the MT is uncertain or corrupt. Historical critical analysis has established beyond doubt that the canonical MT (and the LXX) contains evidence of another kind of story, the story or history of its composition. Although the analysis will take this factor into account where it is judged relevant, it does not attempt to reconstruct the history of the biblical text.

The chapters on the Torah or Pentateuch will focus on its storyline but with due attention to law texts where this is judged appropriate. Laws are also concerned with relationships and their proper order. The distinction and relationship between form and content will be used to identify different kinds of narrative, such as story, anecdote, report, genealogy, etc. They will also be employed to identify different kinds of law texts, such as categorical commands, casuistic laws and paranesis (moral exhortation), and different kinds of poetic texts, such as songs, pronouncements of judgment, prophecies, blessings and curses. The Torah is made up of a wealth of individual literary forms that justify describing it as diversity within unity. There are many individual narratives, law texts and poetry that contribute in various ways to form the larger narrative. The authoritative status of this narrative and its teaching can be seen in the way passages in the Prophetic and Writings corpus invoke it and rehearse aspects of the story.[24]

As is well known, the documentary hypothesis proposed that the Torah was compiled from four existing documents or sources, the Yahwist (J), the Elohist (E), the Priestly (P), and Deuteronomy (D). More recent historical criticism has led to a considerable exodus from the documentary hypothesis, although debate continues as to how the Torah came about.[25] The evidence for a variety of contributors is, in my judgment, convincing although it is unlikely that any one proposal can explain all the textual phenomena and satisfy all critical readers. What is of enduring value in this analysis is its conviction

---

24. The rehearsals vary to a greater or lesser degree, reflecting different contexts and different authors. Examples are Josh 24:2–13; Judg 11:12–28; 1 Sam 12:6–8; Isa 41:8–10; 63:7–19; Jer 2:4–8; 32:16–23; Ezekiel 20; Micah 6:3–5; Psalm 78; 105; 106; Nehemiah 9. There are also numerous briefer allusions to the promise to the ancestors, the exodus, the wilderness wandering, etc. An increasing number of scholars think the Torah is a post-exilic compilation, in which case its authors and editors may have drawn on existing traditions in prophecy and psalmody. Texts such as Deut 6:20–25 and 26:5–9 are thought by some to be early creeds that provided the foundational structure for the gradual development of the Torah story, others would regard them as later summaries.
25. For a recent survey of the debate see Jean-Louis Ska, *Introduction to Reading the Pentateuch* (Winona Lake, Ind: Eisenbrauns, 2006) especially chapters 6 & 7. The most recent defence of the Source Hypothesis is that of Joel S Baden, *The Composition of the Pentateuch. Renewing the Documentary Hypothesis* (New Haven & London: Yale University Press, 2012).

that many stories and collections of stories within the Torah contain their own story or history of composition. Hence, although my analysis will be directed primarily to the present text and in this sense will be synchronic, it will examine the composition of texts where there is good textual evidence for doing so and where it is particularly relevant. Critical analysis may not be able to unravel the details of a text's history fully but the evidence for it testifies to another kind of diversity within unity to be found in the Torah. Given the divinely inspired nature of the Torah, attention to the history of its composition enhances the impression of the Word of God entering fully into the lives of the authors, editors, scribes and communities to whom it was entrusted in its various parts and as a whole. Much the same can be said for Prophecy and Writings.

A more mundane reason for this diversity within unity is the limitations of human beings, even inspired ones. Each culture has a repertoire of literary forms and authors exploit these in creative ways to explain experience, to communicate meaning. But, as noted earlier, there are limits to what one can say via a literary form or any combination of them. Moreover, there is a paradoxical quality about the exploration of a topic via a variety of literary forms. On the one hand, the reader's understanding of the topic is enhanced (the unity factor); on the other hand the variety and diversity of forms introduces a measure of difference. This is particularly the case in narrative or story where a topic is an integral part of the story, its meaning emerging as the plot of the story unfolds. Each story, unless it is a straight repetition, adds another dimension or angle on the topic. Despite the limitations, there are positive sides to this phenomenon. In terms of form, the limitations of a particular form can stimulate new ways of employing it, prompt a turn to alternative forms, or the creation of new ones. In terms of content, the different views about a topic establish a dialectic that can stimulate new syntheses.[26] Texts provide access to but can never fully represent the

---

26. Dialectic can operate at the level of particular texts, as analysed by Michael Fishbane, *Biblical Interpretation in Ancient Israel* (Oxford: Oxford University Press, 1985), or at the level of theologies, with Jon D Levenson proposing a dialectic in the alternation between creation and chaos in the Old Testament (*Creation and the Persistence of Evil: The Jewish Drama of Divine Omnipotence* [San Francisco: Harper & Row, 1988]), or between aspects of Torah and Prophecy, as this study will attempt to show.

person, thing or idea about which they speak; in this sense texts point beyond themselves. The Torah is a text that for believers provides true knowledge about God and God's purpose for creation and humanity; it is not complete because completeness or conclusion is unattainable in this life, but it is sufficient to fuel faith and guide life. If limitation is an inescapable factor in the creation of texts then *a fortiori* it is also the case in the analysis of texts.

Abbreviations

AB	Anchor Bible
AusBR	Australian Biblical Review
Berit Olam	Berit Olam. Studies in Hebrew Narrative and Poetry
BETL	Bibliotheca Ephemeridum Theologicarum Lovaniensium
BKAT	Biblischer Kommentar Altes Testament
BN	Biblische Notizen
BWANT	Beiträge zur Wissenschaft vom Alten (und Neuen) Teastament
BZABR	Beihefte zur Zeitschrift für Altorientalische und Biblische Rechtsgeschichte
BZAW	Beihefte zur Zeitschrift für die Alttestamentliche Wissenschaft
BHS	Biblia Hebraica Stuttgartensia (current critical edition of the Hebrew Bible)
CB	Coniectanea Biblica. Old Testament Series
CBQ	Catholic Biblical Quarterly
CS:BR	Currents in Research: Biblical Studies
FAT	Forschungen zum Alten Testament
FOTL	The Forms of the Old Testament Literature

HBOT	Hebrew Bible/Old Testament
HBT	Horizons in Biblical Theology
HThKAT	Herders Theologischer Kommentar zum Alten Testament
HUCA	Hebrew Union College Annual
JBL	Journal of Biblical Literature
JETS	Journal of the Evangelical Theological Society
JPS	Jewish Publication Society
JSOT	Journal for the Study of the Old Testament
JSOTSup	Journal for the Study of the Old Testament Supplement Series
LXX	Greek Translation of the Old Testament, known as the 'Septuagint'
MT	Masoretic Text of the Hebrew Bible
NCBC	The New Cambridge Bible Commentary
NICOT	New International Commentary on the Old Testament
NRSV	New Revised Standard Version
OBO	Orbis Biblicus et Orientalis
OBT	Overtures to Biblical Theology
OTL	The Old Testament Library
RSR	Revue des Sciences Religieuses
SBL	Society of Biblical Literature
SBLDS	Society of Biblical Literature Dissertation Series
SP	Samaritan Pentateuch

UTB	Uni-taschenbücher
VT	Vetus Testamentum
WBC	Word Biblical Commentary
WUNT	Wissenschaftliche Untersuchungen zum Neuen Testament
ZABR	Zeitschrift für Altorientalische und Biblische Rechtsgeschichte
ZThK	Zeitschrift für Theologie und Kirche

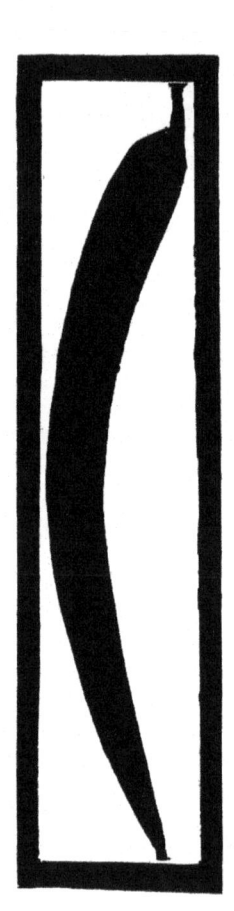

Part One

Divine Righteousness in the Torah/Pentateuch

1

Deuteronomy 32

The first text in the Torah that will be analysed is the song of Moses in Deuteronomy 32:1–43. There are two good reasons for this. One is the already noted fact that 32:4 is the only Torah text that proclaims God is just in all his ways, righteous and upright. This claim applies not just to all that God says and does in the Torah but to all that God will say and do in the future. Another reason is that the song is located at a strategic point in the Torah and exercises an important function in relation to it. This can be seen more clearly by reflecting a little on what we mean by the Hebrew term Torah. Although it covers both the form (formulation) and content (topic) of a piece of legislation it ranges much wider than the English word 'law'. Torah can refer to a particular law, a code of laws, a teaching or instruction, and according to Jewish tradition, the five books of Moses or the Pentateuch. There are a variety of literary forms within the Torah: narrative forms such as stories, genealogies, and reports; poetic forms such as songs and prophecies; and laws and homilies about laws (particularly in Deuteronomy). Each of these can be employed for teaching and instruction as well as for celebration, propaganda, the preservation of traditions, and so on. The same can be said for the five books or Torah as a narrative whole that reaches from creation to Israel camped in the plains of Moab, poised to enter the promised land.[1]

But is the Torah as a whole to be understood primarily as an instruction that enables Israel to live as God's chosen people—which is more the Jewish understanding—or as a narrative/story

---

1. Lohfink says of the Pentateuch, 'Er is eine Erzählung' (it is a narrative); 'Prolegomena zu einer Rechtshermeneutik des Pentateuch,' 42.

that contains such teaching—which would be closer to the Christian understanding?[2] Perhaps it is best to keep both perspectives in view. Thus one can say that the Torah sets out a way of life for Israel and humanity that is progressively revealed in the form of an ongoing narrative in which various law codes are embedded. One can also say that the Torah tells a story of creation and humanity that instructs its listeners and readers as it unfolds. This twofold but related function can also be observed in the connection between the Torah/Pentateuch and the Former Prophets/Historical Books. As the divinely inspired and foundational instruction for Israel, the Torah is set apart from what follows by the division into these two parts of the canon. As the story of humanity and Israel however, the Torah as narrative continues in Joshua and the subsequent books to the end of 2 Kings. The same foundational instruction applies in this continuation of the story as in the Torah.

Even though it is likely the song in Deuteronomy 32:1-43 originated independently of deuteronomic circles, it now forms an integral part of the book and the larger Torah.[3] It is the final word that God commissions Moses to write down and teach the people, just as in the preceding chapters of Deuteronomy he has proclaimed the Torah to the people and written it down. It therefore provides a synthesis or summary of Torah teaching.[4] The song also serves as a

---

2. Cf. Samuel Amser , 'Les documents de la loi et la formation du Pentateuque', in *Le Pentateuque en question. Les origins et la composition des cinq premiers livres de la Bible à la lumiere des recherches récentes*, edited by Albert de Pury (Le Monde de la Bible; Geneva: Labor et Fides, 1989), 235-57, especially 235-44.
3. Paul Sanders concludes that it is of pre-exilic origin, possibly from the pre-monarchical period, and was incorporated into the book of Deuteronomy in the exilic period (*The Provenance of Deuteronomy 32* [Oudstestamentische Studiën 37; Leiden/New York: Brill, 1996]). According to Mark Leuchter it probably originated between the tenth and eighth centuries BCE among northern levitical circles and was later incorporated into the Josianic version of Deuteronomy ('Why is the Song of Moses in the Book of Deuteronomy?' *VT* 57 [2007]: 295-317). In contrast, Eckhart Otto proposes a post-exilic date, between fifth and fourth centuries BCE, (see page 654 of 'Moses Abschiedslied in Deuteronomium 32. Ein Zeugnis der Kanonsbildung in der Hebräischen Bibel', in *Die Torah: Studien zum Pentateuch: Gesammelte Aufsätze* [BZABR 9; Wiesbaden: Harrasowitz, 2009], 641-78).
4. An ancient Jewish sage (Shem-tob) claimed that the song 'contains all the Torah's principles' (cited in Denis T Olson, *Deuteronomy and the Death of Moses* [OBT; Eugene, Or: Wipf & Stock, 1994], 138, n 8). Walter Brueggemann says the song is

bridge between the Torah and the other components of the HBOT canon. According to Eckart Otto, there are clear allusions to passages in Isaiah, Micah and Jeremiah among the prophets, as well as to Psalms and to the book of Proverbs.[5] The song also provides a key motivation for observing the Torah. As Casper Labuschagne notes, in Deuteronomy 32:44-46 Israel is urged 'to take all the words of the *Song* to heart so that they may observe the *law*'.[6] The Torah provides the wherewithal for a fruitful life in the land; the song will serve as a witness against Israel when it (inevitably) fails to abide by it.

Given the integral relationship between song and Torah, the description of God in Deuteronomy 32:4 as 'faithful' (*'emunah*), 'without deceit' (*'en 'avel*), 'righteous' (NRSV 'just') (*tsadiq*) and 'upright' (*yashar*) means that these terms also play an integral and important role in the Torah. This text is the only one in the HBOT where *tsadiq* and *yashar* occur as a word-pair.[7] Also of importance are the two other terms in v 4 that proclaim God's work as perfect (*tamim*) and that 'all his ways are justice (*mishpat*)'. In order to grasp something of the meaning of these terms they need to be read initially within the more immediate context of the song and then within the broader context of the Torah.

A long and complex text such as this may be divided in a number of ways, as a consultation of commentaries will show.[8] My preference

---

'a major theological articulation that is representative of Deuteronomic Theology and indeed of the primary theme of Old Testament Faith,' (*Deuteronomy* [Abingdon Old Testament Commentaries; Nashville: Abingdon Press, 2001], 282-84).

5. Cf Otto, 'Moses Abschiedslied,' 658-62 (links with Isa 1, Mic 5, Ps 18, 72; 74; 78; 82; Prov 8); 666-73 (links with texts in Deutero-Isaiah; Jeremiah); 674-75 (links between the song and Ps 90-92). For Otto, these connections have in the main been created by the author(s) of Deut 32, an indication of its late composition. Leuchter identifies a number of connections between the song and Jeremiah ('Why is the Song of Moses in the Book of Deuteronomy?' 303-5, 314.

6. Casper Labuschagne, on 91 of 'The Song of Moses: Its Framework and Structure,' in *De Fructu Oris Sui: Essays in Honor of Adrianus van Selms*, edited by IH Eybers, CJ Fensham, CJ Labuschagne, WC van Wyk, and AH van Zyl (Leiden: EJ Brill, 1971), 85-98.

7. Psalm 119:137 is a two-part parallelism rather than a straight word-pair ('You are righteous O Lord, and your judgements are right').

8. Among recent commentaries, see Duane Christensen (*Deuteronomy 21:10-34:12* [Word Bible Commentary; Nashville: Thomas Nelson Publishers, 2002], 783-821) who favours a division that, according to him, reveals chiastic structures within

is for the following division: vv 1–3, 4–6a, 6b–14, 15–18 19–27, 28–33, 34–35, 36–38, 39–42, 43. The introductory vv 1–3 are similar to the so-called covenant lawsuit that occurs in books of the Latter Prophets.[9] The lawsuit commences with a summons to the nations and/or all of creation to hear God's case against Israel (cf Isa 1:2; Amos 3:9; Mic 1:2). The case is then presented, followed by a warning or an announcement of punishment. Given the connection between the song and the lawsuit form, vv 1–3 announce that what follows has significance for all of creation. Verse 3 adds a further element that is also found in the Torah: it signals that what follows in the song is effectively a proclamation of the name YHWH (Lord). The primary purpose of God's revelation in both word and deed is so that people will come to know who it is that bears the name YHWH and revere/fear him. It is only in the light of this relationship that all other relationships have their proper place and function.

The main part of the song fills out the brief and blunt contrast between God and people in vv 4–6a. Although the text of v 5a is somewhat corrupt and difficult to clarify, the sense of contrast is clear enough. This, plus the two parallel statements about God in v 4 suggest a corresponding pair of parallel statements about the people in v 5. Verse 4 describes God as 'The Rock' and this metaphor recurs in vv 15, 18, 30, 31. The parallelism in v 4a indicates that here the metaphor refers to the way God acts—'his work is perfect (*tamim*) for all his ways are justice (*mishpat*)'. That is, all God's ways (what God says and does) are a manifestation of the one creative and saving work of God. According to the second set of parallel lines in v 4, this perfect combination of the one and the many reveals YHWH as a God of faithfulness ('*emunah*), without iniquity or deceit ('*avel*), righteous (*tsadiq*) and upright or straight (*yashar*). The impression is that '*avel* serves to reinforce '*emunah*, conveying the sense of God's utter trustworthiness, while *tsadiq* and *yashar* are also virtually

---

the song; JG McConville favours a 7-stanza division (vv 1–3, 4–9, 10–14, 15–18, 19–25, 26–35, 36–43), *Deuteronomy* (Apollos Old Testament Commentary 5; Leicester: Apollos/Downers Grove: InterVarsity Press, 2002), 451. In contrast, George AF Knight provides a more-or-less verse-by-verse commentary (*The Song of Moses. A Theological Quarry* [Grand Rapids: Eerdmans, 1995]).

9. This and other features of the song that will be commented on indicate some prophetic influence on its composition (cf Chapman, *The Law and the Prophets*, 158–64; also Otto, 'Moses Abschiedslied,' 658, 666).

synonymous, making an emphatic statement of God's righteousness. As already noted, this is the only place in the HBOT where these two terms occur as a word pair. Within the context, one could also read the last line of v 4 as drawing together the preceding ones to claim that Israel's righteous God is the one source of all right relationships within creation and humanity. To invoke the metaphor, one could say that God is the bedrock on which all relationships are founded.

As already noted, the Hebrew of v 5a is not clear. If one follows the NRSV version Israel is God's degenerate children who deal falsely; according to the clearer text of v 5b, they are a perverse and crooked generation: in short, full of flaws and cracks, utterly unreliable. The rhetorical question in v 6a expects a negative answer that is supplied in the following verses of the song. Israel has no grounds for disobeying the righteous and loyal God portrayed in v 4.

Verses 6b-9 take up v 4 by reviewing what the Lord has done for Israel from its 'creation', here traced to the beginnings of creation itself. It is an oblique way of claiming that Israel and its vocation are an integral part of God's purpose for the whole of creation.[10] It is not an add-on. Verses 8-9 are a point of debate. Some hold that the apparent acknowledgement of other gods supports an early date for the song.[11] Others disagree, arguing that the text could well reflect a Yahwistic counter to the claims of the Persian god Ahuramazda.[12] Of relevance here is the proclamation in 32:39, 'I, even I, am he; there is no god beside me', which finds a close parallel in the generally accepted exilic Deutero-Isaiah (cf for example Isa 43:10, 13, 25). A common opinion is that this exilic prophecy marks a move in Israelite thinking from

---

10. Following J Luyten, 'Primeval and Eschatological Overtones in the Song of Moses (Dt 32,1-43),' in *Das Deuteronomium. Entstehung, Gestalt und Botschaft*, edited by Norbert Lohfink (BETL LXVIII; Leuven: Leuven University Press, 1985), 341-47. See pp 342-43.
11. It is generally accepted that the MT reading in v 8c 'according to the number of the sons of Israel' does not make sense within the context and should be corrected according to the Qumran MS 4QDeut[j] and the LXX (cf the NRSV translation). Jan Joosten proposes that the Hebrew letters for 'the sons of Israel' can also be read, depending on how one separates them, as 'the sons of Bull El'. If this was the original it would explain both the MT (a misreading or correction) and the Qumran and LXX readings (cf 'A Note on the Text of Deuteronomy xxxii 8*,' *VT* 57 [2007]: 548-55).
12. See for example the discussion in Otto, 'Moses Abschiedslied,' 648-50 and the literature cited.

henotheism (worship of a high god) to monotheism.

Verses 10–14 then testify that God's choice of Israel meant an enduring commitment. This was demonstrated when God found or sustained Israel 'in a desert land, in a howling wilderness waste' (v 10).[13] A key Hebrew term in the phrase 'howling wilderness waste' is *tohu*, the same word used in Genesis 1:2 for the chaos or 'formless void' (NRSV) out of which the creator God brought order. Its presence in v 10 could refer to the 'chaos' of Israel's oppression in Egypt as much or as well as to Israel's wilderness journey.[14] There is some support for seeing v 10 as a poetic reference to the exodus because the image of an eagle bearing its young on its pinions in v 11 is evoked in Exodus 19:4 in relation to God bringing Israel to Sinai. Because of their references to the land and the field, vv 13–14 can be taken as an allusion to the promised land, where God ensures that there is abundant produce for Israel to enjoy. According to the narrative setting of the song however, Israel has yet to enter the promised land. This is another indication of the independent provenance of the song. But the elasticity of its poetry and imagery means that in its present narrative setting, the song can embrace the past from the beginning of creation, the 'present' of the Israel addressed at this point in the narrative, and any subsequent generation or individual that listens to or reads this text.[15] This is so because the author of this song is Israel's God who is the only one who lives forever (v 40) and who therefore is able to provide a Torah that covers past, present and future.

Verses 6b–14 are also replete with different images of God's relationship to Israel and to the nations. God is Israel's 'father', a sovereign ruler who assigns nations to the gods or the sons of the gods, Israel's protector and guardian, as well as a guide on its journey and generous provider in the land. Given the comments in the Preface that the Hebrew term for righteous/righteousness is generally thought to refer primarily to right relationships one can read these

---

13. The translation 'found' follows the MT, whereas 'sustained' follows the Targum (Aramaic translation). The latter reflects more closely the Torah storyline, in particular the journey through the wilderness.
14. Cf. Knight, *The Song of Moses*, 46.
15. Sanders notes that the song, like some psalms, is deliberately vague in its reference to events. A reason for this is that such texts were 'composed with an eye on following generations which might experience similar vicissitudes' (*The Provenance of Deuteronomy 32*, 433). Cf. also Otto, 'Moses Abschiedslied,' 677–78.

images as various manifestations of divine righteousness. By way of contrast, vv 15–18 expose Israel's complete failure to maintain its side of the relationship, as evidenced above all in the charge that Israel 'abandoned God who made him' in favour of 'deities they had never known'. For a listener or reader of the Torah, the song's reference to Israel's apostasy would recall the episode of the golden calf in Exodus 32–34 (cf also Deut 9:8–10:11); at the same time it covers the apostasies that Israel will commit in the land when it becomes prosperous and arrogant, as passages such as Deuteronomy 4:25–28 and 8:11–20 warn.

The contrast between God and Israel recurs in 32:19–27 and 28–33. Verses 19–27 focus on God's response to Israel's infidelities while vv 8–33 focus on Israel's inability to understand, the inevitable consequence of trading knowledge of God for the false knowledge of idol worship. Verses 19–27 portray God as the just judge who is able to accurately assess the crime committed and pronounce the appropriate sentence. So v 19 states that 'The Lord saw it' and then, according to v 20, pronounced the sentence ('He said'). Verses 19–27 thus continue the prophetic covenant lawsuit with which the song commences and, in combination with vv 6b–14, spell out the meaning of v 4a. Verses 6b–14 take up its claim that every work of the Lord is perfect (*tamim*) while vv 19–27 do the same for the claim that all God's ways are justice (*mishpat*). The Lord pronounces a sentence that is in accord with the Torah's requirement for 'sons and daughters' who wilfully disobey or offend their parents (cf Deut 21:18–21; 22:20–21).[16] But vv 26–27 reveal that the just sentence of destruction against Israel for offending 'your father' (v 6b) will not be carried out because of another and more fundamental aspect of the Torah that is now taken into consideration. This is found in texts such as Exodus 6:7 and 7:5 which proclaim that God's purpose is for Israel and the nations to know 'I am the Lord (YHWH)'. This is also the primary purpose of the song as v 3 announces ('I will proclaim

---

16. One can see in these verses a link with prophetic passages in which God summons a foe to bring proud and rebellious Israel down (for example, Isa 5:25–30; Jer 4:5–8). But, as God foresees in v 27 of the song and as later prophetic texts also testify, these nations prove as arrogant as Israel, seeking to destroy it and accumulate booty rather than enact God's punishment, and attributing their power to their own gods instead of the Lord (for example, Isa 10:5–11)

the name of the Lord'). It is therefore essential that the nations be given no grounds for claiming that Israel's demise is a victory for their gods. This would only entrench belief in false gods (cf v 21). For humanity's (and creation's) sake the sovereignty of the one true God must be asserted and acknowledged. The song assures its audience/readership that God weighs the relevant factors of a case and (always) gives a just judgement (*mishpat*). This is in line with the golden calf story in Exodus 32–34 and the spy story in Numbers 13–14 which will be examined below.

Some commentators consider vv 28–33, or at least vv 28–29, to be ambiguous: they could refer to Israel or a foreign nation or both.[17] Perhaps this is intentional; once Israel breaks its relationship with God it effectively becomes, in terms of sense and understanding (cf. v 28), like any other nation that does not know the Lord. A nation that does know would ipso facto understand that what look to be fluctuating fortunes of history are in reality the work of the Rock, the one God who has an enduring and unchanging purpose for creation and humanity (cf also v 4a). For those who know, victory and defeat are manifestations of the just judgements of 'our Rock'. Those who do not know the Rock as their source of life are like Sodom and Gomorrah; they only produce death–dealing poison (vv 32–33).

Verses 34–38 provide the expected counter to this by identifying where true knowledge does reside ('sealed in my treasuries') and what the outcome of this will be. Verses 34–35 could, like the preceding verses, be read as a reference to Israel, or to foreign nations, or to a combination of both. God knows exactly what needs to be done and when it is to be done ('the day of their calamity'). God's victory over hostile forces, whether this is Israel or foreign nations, is the vindication and fulfilment of the divine plan or purpose.[18] Verses 36–38 however clearly refer to Israel or, one could say, single Israel out from among the nations because, despite the overwhelming evidence of infidelity it remains 'his people/his servants'. In God's wisdom

---

17. For example, Christensen, *Deuteronomy 21:10–34:21*, 808. The term for nation in v 28 (*goy*) is normally used in reference to foreigners; hence Israel's adversaries in v 27.
18. Following Knight (*The Song of Moses*, 102–3) who argues that the Hebrew term in v 35 translated in the NRSV as 'vengeance' is better rendered as 'vindication' and the term translated as 'recompense' occurs only here as a noun. Its verbal root means 'to be/make complete'.

this will take place at the appropriate time, when Israel is completely bereft of all the false things on which it has relied and will be able, presumably, to see the folly of relying on gods that are no gods (cf vv 37–38). Within the larger context of the song and the Torah, the term 'servants' has two levels of meaning. On the one hand, the people remain God's servants despite their complete failure: this is a sign of God's unswerving commitment to the chosen people. On the other hand, the call to be God's loyal servants, to live in a righteous relationship with God and with each other, remains as alive and urgent as ever. This is the purpose of the compassion (*khannan*) that Israel's righteous God displays and will continue to display.

Verses 39–42 incorporate the particular 'case' of Israel into a universal proclamation of God's exclusive and sovereign power over life and death. God's power will of course always be executed justly because God is righteous and gives right judgements (v 41). The same two terms translated in v 35 as 'vindication' and 'make complete' reappear here and carry much the same meaning. God's judgements will be vindicated against adversaries; likewise, God's justice will be fulfilled in the punishment meted out to those 'who hate me'. As noted by commentators there are a number of allusions in vv 39–42 to texts in the Torah and the Latter Prophets. For example, the proclamation 'I, even I, am he' recalls the proclamation of the divine name in Exodus 3:7–15 and 34:6–7, and prepares for its recurrence in such texts as Isaiah 43:10, 13, 25. Similarly, the following statement that 'there is no god beside me' recalls the requirement of exclusive worship in the first command of the Decalogue (Exod 20:2–3; Deut 5:6–7) and recurs in similar form in Isaiah 44:6, 8. The claim to exclusive and sovereign power over creation in v 39b ('I kill and I make alive') is similar to Isaiah 45:7.[19] The imagery of the divine warrior at war against adversaries also evokes Exodus 15:3 and prophetic passages such as Isaiah 34:5–6; 63:1–6, and Jeremiah 47:6–7.

The concluding verse of the song (v 43) appears to be somewhat corrupt in the MT and there is considerable variation among the

---

19. Texts such as Deut 32:39b and Isa 45:7 claim that God has sovereignty over all powers in creation, whether good or evil, to counter claims by rival religions and their divinities. The righteous God creates or wields evil forces in order to remove evil from creation, as in the flood story. The book of Deuteronomy requires Israel to do the same (a capital punishment) in order to 'purge the evil from your midst' (cf. 13:5; 17:7; 22:21, 22, 24).

ancient versions such as the LXX, the Samaritan Pentateuch, the Vulgate, and the Dead Sea scrolls (Qumran). The NRSV adds a line from the LXX after the opening line and this gives a reasonable and plausible translation. The opening line exhorts the heavens to praise 'his people',[20] which is presumably a reference to Israel but may include all those who will become God's people by acknowledging and worshipping the Lord. The second line then calls on all 'you sons of God' (preferring the LXX here rather than 'all you gods' in the NRSV) to worship the Lord. The reason for this is then given in the remainder of v 43. God's response to the blood of 'his children' that is shed will vindicate God (as righteous and just in accord with v 4), as will God's action against 'his adversaries'.[21] The NRSV translation adds another line from the LXX ('he will repay those who hate him'). This creates a concentric structure in the last part of the poem (v 43bcde), with references to God's actions on behalf of 'his children' (or 'servants' in the LXX) and 'his people' framing God's actions against 'his adversaries' and 'those who hate him'. It is because of these actions that the heavens are summoned to make glad 'his people', the ones God has delivered from their adversaries. Similarly, it is because of such actions that those delivered, who are also 'sons of God', are called to worship the Lord. Thus the song that began on a highly critical note in relation to God's people ends on a highly positive note.

Those who are called to worship the Lord can only do so authentically when they know the name of the one they worship. Their worship will then be a proclamation of the name of the Lord and in so worshipping they will be at one with Moses and his commitment in v 3 to 'proclaim the name of the Lord'. They will do so because they have learned from the Torah and the song that this puts them at one with God's purpose, not at odds with it. All God's words and actions are in order that people may know 'I am the Lord' (cf Exod 6:7; 7:5). When this takes place everything else will be able to find its right place in the matrix of relationships. The revelation of the divine name includes therefore the revelation of divine righteousness; God's words and actions/works are always right in that they establish the

---

20. Perhaps better 'make glad O heavens' as proposed by Christensen (*Deuteronomy*, 820).
21. As pointed out for the occurrence of the same verb in vv 35 and 41, the closer English translation is 'vindicate' rather than 'avenge'.

right order or relationship between God and creation and between the parts of creation. The consequence of this is that God always intervenes when right relationships are disturbed or threatened. If this were not the case then the understanding of God that the Torah and the song present would be compromised. God's intervention involves a just (true) assessment of the evil that has been perpetrated and the pronouncement of a just sentence or punishment. But each intervention is also judged in terms of its relationship to God's overall purpose. Given that the nations will, like Israel, get things wrong and claim that their divinely commissioned defeat of Israel is the triumph of their gods (v 27), God will act in accord with his overall purpose as stated in the Torah. Israel will be punished as Torah law requires but God will then have compassion (verb, *nakham*) on Israel. This means that its right relationship with God will be restored so that it can resume its mission of living and proclaiming the truth about the divine name to the nations. To be authentic such a proclamation must be in word and deed that is in accord with the Torah; in fact it involves Israel's whole life from one generation to the next (Deut 8:1; 32:47). To borrow a phrase from Genesis 1:26, it means being the image and likeness of God in creation and history.

In short, the song complements the Torah and underscores its authority by rehearsing in a more concise and poetic form the story that it tells about how Israel came to be God's chosen people. But it does more than just rehearse the main lines of the Torah narrative. It also acts as a prophecy of Israel's future with respect to two essential points: its inevitable (and repeated) failure coupled with God's enduring commitment to it as part of the divine purpose for creation and humanity. The way the song ends with the call to the 'sons of God' to worship God is an assurance that this purpose will triumph despite the inevitable failures. What we may call the prophetic thrust of a song from the mouth of Israel's foundational prophet also serves to underline the prophetic nature of the Torah. Although it was proclaimed at Sinai it speaks to and for every generation. The Former and Latter Prophets record how God raised up prophets at strategic points in Israel's subsequent history to remind them of the Torah's enduring, prophetic authority and to show how it applied to their generation. As if to allow for this, the song does not name any particular form of apostasy or when it is to occur, as the Former and

Latter Prophets do, nor does it name enemies to whom Israel will be handed over for breach of the covenant, or lands to which it will be exiled. All this is 'filled in' at the appropriate time by a prophetic voice.

On the basis of these reflections I will now examine how the proclamation in v 4 of the song that 'righteous/just and upright is he' is presented in the Torah narrative and how it relates to God being compassionate or merciful (v 36). Although this is a reading of the Torah informed by the teaching of the song the aim is to discover the way in which its teaching is unfolded in the course of the story that the Torah tells. In doing this the narrative rehearses however imperfectly what Moses urges his audience to do: to listen and re-listen, to read and reread, to tell and retell the Torah and its song to the next generation (cf Deut 6:4–9; 32:46–47). In other words, to absorb the Torah so that it becomes one's constant teacher and companion: according to Psalm 1:2 happy are those whose 'delight is in the law/torah of the Lord, and on his law they meditate day and night'.

The call to keep on keeping the words of the Torah 'in your heart' and to recite them to the children and to talk about them (Deut 6:6–7) has left its legacy, one may say, in that other 'story' of the Torah, the story of its composition that has been unearthed by historical–critical scholarship. Although there has been much debate about which theory best fits the textual evidence, and no doubt there will continue to be debate, the evidence of reshaping and editing is difficult to deny. For example, a favoured story form such as the ancestress in danger is developed into several different versions in Genesis 12; 20; 26. Variants of a story were woven into the main storyline to indicate, according to Antony Campbell, another way of telling the story.[22] The text can thus serve as a 'user base' for developing a rich catechesis. The well-known variations between the law codes provide further evidence that the production of the Torah was a long and involved process. Variations in story and law no doubt also became factors in

---

22. Antony F Campbell, 'The Storyteller's Role: Reported Story and Biblical Text,' *CBQ* 64 (2002): 427–41. Another pertinent aspect of Campbell's hypothesis is that the written text preserves the outline of a story, to be fleshed out in actual storytelling. In doing so, a storyteller would choose one of the options that the written version provided (a combination of main storyline and variants).

the *Wirkungsgeschichte* of the Bible: the history of its reception and use as Sacred Scripture.

Another helpful theory in contemporary study of narrative and storytelling is that it invites the listener or reader to imaginatively enter the world of the story.[23] Our ability to do this is of course limited by our inability to escape our own contexts as twenty first century readers. Contemporary theories of narrative help us to avoid imposing our evaluative criteria on ancient texts and thereby sharpen awareness of our limitations. Another limiting factor is that no study can hope to identify and fully assess all the evidence in the text and the respective contexts within which it should be considered: the ANE context in which Israel lived; the various contexts in which the text was most likely shaped and reshaped; the context of the HBOT canon; the varying contexts of contemporary readers. A selection has to be made; hopefully the selection made here is judicious.

---

23. Cf Perdue's discussion of Northrop Frei and other exponents of narrative criticism in *The Collapse of History*, 234–40.

2

Book of Genesis

As is now widely recognised, the book of Genesis commences with two accounts of creation reflecting different authors or traditions; one is the stately Genesis 1:1–2:4a, commonly attributed to priestly circles, the other is the dramatic story of the man and woman in 2:4b–3:24.[1] Nevertheless there is good evidence to show that they have been combined with a definite purpose in mind. The first concludes with the statement, 'These are the generations (*toledoth*) of the heavens and the earth when they were created' (2:4a). The subsequent narrative traces the *toledoth* of human beings from the first couple in the garden to the second generation of Israelites poised in the plains of Moab to enter another garden, the promised land. A further link between Genesis 1:1–2:4a and the rest of the Torah occurs in 2:4b where the order of the preceding phrase is reversed: 'earth and heavens' instead of 'heavens and earth'. This is not accidental but designed to provide a transition from the first account to the second and beyond.[2] The transition works in two ways. The first is in reference to time; the narrative moves from heavenly bodies that are created to be 'for signs and for seasons and for days and years' to the generations of human beings who live in these seasons, days and years. The second is in reference to place/space; the narrative moves from the cosmic realm to the terrestrial realm in which human beings (and creatures) live.

---

1. According to the source hypothesis, Gen 2:4b–3:24 belonged to an early so-called 'Yahwist' source or narrative. The hypothesis no longer commands the field as it once did, although many still hold to a priestly source or extensive redactional layer.
2. So Mark Smith, *The Priestly Vision of Genesis 1* (Minneapolis: Fortress Press, 2010), 129-31; and Laurence A. Turner *Genesis* (Readings: A New Biblical Commentary; Sheffield: Sheffield Academic Press, 2000), 26.

The carefully constructed link between Genesis 1:1–2:4a and the rest of the Torah provides a context for exploring further connections. An obvious one is the notion of creation as God bringing order out of chaos (cf the *tohu vabohu* ['formless void' in NRSV] and the *tehom* ['deep' in NRSV] of 1:2). Although creation appears quite stylised and unrealistic from a modern scientific point of view, the primary purpose of the text is theological, to portray God as the one who creates a whole in which each part has its place and dynamic role in relation to the other parts. In short, the account crafts an image of God who establishes a right order that is meant to operate throughout the generations of the heavens and earth. The human being is meant to rule over the creatures of the earth in accord with this divinely established order. In doing so it will not only be in a right relationship with creatures—according to the text—but will also, and more fundamentally, be in a right relationship with God. Worth noting here is Claus Westermann's comment on the human being as the image and likeness of God. For him the description 'is valid for all people. God has created all people "to correspond to him," that is so that something can happen between creator and creature . . . The uniqueness of human beings consists in their being God's counterparts . . . Their very existence is intended to be their relationship to God'.[3] Given that being in a right relationship is a key aspect of being righteous then the one whom the human being 'images' must be the righteous one par excellence and the source of all righteous or right relationships.

Another connection between Genesis 1:1–2:4a and the subsequent narrative is forged via the six days of work and the seventh day of rest (the Sabbath): more correctly one should speak of ceasing from the work of the preceding six days.[4] God ceases or turns from the work of creating the heavenly bodies and the creatures of the earth to perform what is effectively another 'work', to bless and make holy the seventh day. The biblical notion of being holy is to be set apart as a sign of or representing God, the one who is wholly other. It is thus wider than our more moral understanding of holiness. Blessing was understood to mediate God's life giving power and so enhance life

---

3. Claus Westermann, *Genesis 1–11. A Commentary* (London: SPCK, 1984), 158.
4. Cf. Smith, *The Priestly Vision of Genesis 1*, 105.

for a good purpose.⁵ Hence the seventh day is set apart as a day that mediates God's life giving power in a unique way. It is not an empty time. The implication of the creation account is that human beings, made in the image and likeness of God, are meant to cease from their work during this sacred time: in doing so they will benefit from its life giving power. In a sense the Sabbath 'works' for them.

Mark Smith observes that 'With this order of time and space, the creation is like a cosmic temple overseen by God for the good of humanity'.⁶ But, the subsequent Torah narrative tells that humanity fails to live in the image and likeness of God. An integral part of God's saving plan for humanity is to restore its image and likeness, and this necessarily involves its right relationship with God. It is little wonder then that the high point of the Sinai covenant is the construction of a sanctuary according to the blueprint that God provides (Exod 25–31; 35–40). The text's claim is that it is as perfect an image of the heavenly dwelling as can be made on earth for God who accompanies and guides the people to the land. Appropriately, Sabbath observance plays a central role in the cult at this sanctuary, the earthly image of God's heavenly dwelling.⁷

Genesis 2:4b–3:24 is often classified as a myth although there is considerable debate about what it is that constitutes a myth. A particularly insightful contribution is Paul Ricoeur's description of myth as a 'symbol of the second degree'.⁸ Symbols of the first degree are terms or images used in an extended or symbolic sense (an example being metaphor); thus 'clean' is used to refer to an aspect of the inner self, 'stained' to its opposite. A myth or symbol of the second degree seeks to bring competing symbols of the first degree into relationship with one another by constructing a story in which there is a dramatic passage from one to the other, from a clean (innocent) state to a stained (sinful) one. The meaning of the less directly accessible realities of life and their relationships can thus be explored via the story form. In keeping with ancient storytelling convention a myth has a cast of characters who can represent or be examples of symbols of the first degree, and their interaction unfolds

---

5. Cf. Jenni/Westermann, *Theologisches Handwörterbuch*, 1, 355.
6. Cf. Smith, *The Priestly Vision of Genesis 1*, 109.
7. It is listed as the first of the 'appointed festivals' in Leviticus 23.
8. Paul Ricoeur, *The Symbolism of Evil* (Boston: Beacon Press, 1969).

in time (on the day the Lord God made the earth and the heavens) and place (a garden). Ricoeur draws attention to the density of the human characters as symbols in the garden story. Thus the woman stands for that which is prone to seduction in humanity. Every man and woman succumbs to temptation 'like' her, just as every man and woman fails in responsibility 'like' the man. In this sense, the mythic form is one way of reflecting on and making sense of reality, the Greek philosophical treatise another way. Each has its strengths and limitations.

Assuming elements in the story function as symbols of more universal realities, we can see that it shares the first account's notion of creation as the establishment of an ordered world (the garden) in which the human being is given a task that mirrors the creative work of God. It is to 'till/serve' (*'abad*) and 'keep/guard' (*shamar*) the garden that God establishes. By doing so it will act in the image and likeness of the creator. However, the human being needs to know how to fulfill this task effectively and in 2:16-17 God provides the requisite knowledge. The combination of permissions and one prohibition (the tree of the knowledge of good and evil) informs the human being that it needs to work within the context or boundary established by God. Within this context human life can flourish. Transgressing its boundary leads to death as 2:17 warns.[9] The presence of the forbidden tree also instructs the human being that its knowledge and therefore its power is finite in comparison to God. This combination of God's initiative on behalf of humanity and its expected response foreshadows the covenant between God and Israel at Sinai.[10]

---

9. A literal translation of the Hebrew is 'dying you shall die'; except for the change from second to third person singular, this is exactly the same as in Exod 21:12-17 (NRSV 'he shall be put to death') and elsewhere. It was most likely a technical phrase that indicated the offender was liable for the death penalty. Whether it was enacted or not would presumably be up to the court and the presiding judge. The close verbal similarity suggests that Gen 2:17 has the same meaning. According to André Wénin, 2:17 warns the human being of the mortal danger involved in transgressing a vital boundary (as it is tempted to do by the serpent). One can only know the true distinction between good and evil from God. The text implies that God intended to teach this and 3:22 is an expression (a regret) that it did not take place ('the human being was to be one like us, knowing good and evil') (cf 'Le précepte d'Adonai Dieu en Genèse 2, 16-17. Narration et anthropologie,' *RSR* 82/3 (2008): 303-18, see especially 311-12.

10. It is worth noting at this point that the two Hebrew verbs in 2:15 not only recall

The ability of a particular myth or story to express or reveal a universal reality is nicely captured in the account of the transgression. It exposes the human being's enduring temptation to transgress boundaries or limitations in the quest for knowledge and power. The serpent claims, falsely as the story subsequently exposes, that doing so will enable the human being to know as God knows. Knowledge is power and knowing good and evil will presumably give the human being the kind of power over the garden (creation) that God enjoys. But the transgression does not yield the desired outcome. Instead of seeing reality clearly human perception becomes distorted, with damaging consequences. Good is seen as evil and evil as good. Whereas they were intimate with each other (naked and no shame), and with God as a friend, they now hide from each other behind fig leaves and from God from behind trees.[11] Same God, same couple, but now seen in a different and distorted light.

This irruption of chaos or breakdown of proper order/relationship is not the result of divine punishment but the consequences of transgression.[12] The story applies the so-called Act-Consequence connection in which good acts are believed to have good consequences and bad acts bad ones. As noted earlier, it is a moral version of the physical law of cause and effect and is used by all societies to a greater or lesser degree. It is a way of making sense of reality, of making what we think are the right connections and is based on the conviction that there is order in creation and one must seek to act in accord with it. The problem of course is that the connection is often difficult to prove. Disputes can arise and one has to appeal to an accepted authority figure or a structure to make the required decision and hopefully settle the matter. This may take the form of a judge and law court, a religious ritual such as the casting of lots, or a prophetic oracle. Within a story God, as a key character and authority figure, normally plays this role as is the case in Genesis 3:14–19.

1:26 but also anticipate the repeated calls, particularly in Deuteronomy, to serve the Lord and keep the covenant laws.

11. David W Cotter makes the interesting observation that 'speech, with which the appearance of human communion had been marked, is here absent' (*Genesis* [Berit Olam; Collegeville: Liturgical Press, 2003], 34).

12. Cf Antony F Campbell, *Making Sense of the Bible. Difficult Texts and Modern Faith* (New York; Mahwah, NJ: Paulist Press, 2010), 23.

God's pronouncement effectively brings order out of the chaos unleashed by the serpent's temptation and human transgression and makes the kinds of connections that reveal God as just/righteous and compassionate. The relationships between the characters—God, the couple, the serpent—cannot return to where they were before the transgression. This would effectively cancel the need for the subsequent story that reveals *how* God goes about restoring right relationships—a key aspect of Torah as instruction. Hence a new order of relationships is decreed that allow for such a story and its theology. In 3:14 the serpent goes from being the craftiest of God's wild creatures to being the one cursed among them and therefore the outsider. It is excluded from any relationship with other creatures, until God's say so (cf the prophecy in Isa 11:8). Verse 15 follows this up with a decree about the relationship between the serpent and the human being, symbolised here by the woman. The decree or sentence means that the serpent will never again be able to tempt humanity—exercise power over it—and so unleash disorder in creation. To be effective, temptation must establish trust even if it is only the illusion of trust. Hostility between woman and serpent rules this out. What is experienced as evil by the serpent is however a good for the other creatures and the couple in the story. They (and the reader) have acquired some knowledge of good and evil.

When the text turns to the woman and the man in 3:16–19 it has to take into account the penalty announced in 2:17; hence the language of punishment rather than curse. Although 2:17 warns of death as the penalty for transgression, to have God carry this out would bring the story of humanity to an abrupt end.[13] It would also not be in accord with the Torah project which needed, in this paradigm example of human transgression, to portray two attributes of God that are crucial for the subsequent narrative, and indeed the whole HBOT. God is the just judge who confronts and punishes evildoers but who is also merciful. Punishment is expressed in God's decree that the couple will suffer evil as a result of what they have done. The woman, at the moment of being creator, of bringing forth life, will experience pain and powerlessness; the man, at the moment of being like God in

---

13. Cf Joze Krasovec, *Reward, Punishment, & Forgiveness. The Thinking & Beliefs of Ancient Israel in the Light of Greek and Modern Views* (Supplements to Vetus Testamentum 78; Leiden: Brill, 1999), 26–30.

bringing forth life from the ground will experience a commensurate powerlessness and pain. In the end both will die and return to the dust. The decree of punishment has a positive side in that it also functions as a torah; it provides instruction about the distinction between good and evil. It is good (right and just) that they are punished for their transgression because it brings home to them (and the reader) the evil they have done. But God is also merciful, waiving the death penalty for which, according to the above reading of 2:17, the couple is liable. Furthermore, God maintains a relationship with them and cares for them, as indicated in the provision of clothing in 3:21. Their relationship with one another also continues even though, like their relationship with God, it cannot be the same as before the transgression.

The theology operating here is somewhat similar to Deuteronomy 32:39 where God says 'I kill and I make alive; I wound and I heal', (cf also Isa 45:7 'I form light and create darkness, I make weal and create woe'). As already noted, such texts have to claim God's sovereign power over evil otherwise it has power over or independently of God. Where necessary, God will bring about or 'create evil' as part of God's just rule over creation. The evil may well be experienced by the wicked as terror and chaos, depending on how depraved their perception of reality is but, according to biblical thinking, it is all under the control of the creative hand of God. For the ones who see the distinction between good and evil clearly, it is right and just that evil be so punished. Also, as with other texts in the Torah such as Exodus 32–34 and Numbers 14, the relationship between punishment and mercy/compassion in Genesis 3:1–19 is justified by appeal to divine authority (God's decree).

The next pertinent text is the flood story in Genesis 6–9. It is preceded by the cryptic account in 6:1–4 about the sons of God (or 'the gods') having children of women. As a result of this 'boundary violation', the just God intervenes, as in the garden story, to establish order via an authoritative pronouncement. The offspring of this union will not be gods but mortals with a limited life span (120 years).[14] It effectively constitutes a second attempt to join human and

---

14. Following Anthony Phillips who states that v 4 'refers specifically to the sentence passed on the monstrous offspring of these illicit divine/human relationships, and not on mankind in general' (*Lower than the Angels. Questions Raised by*

divine, earth and heaven. The third is the story of the tower of Babel in 11:1-9. The implication is that the union of human and divine can only take place on God's initiative and in the way God decrees. As will be seen, these are the criteria that govern the account of the Sinai covenant and the construction of the desert sanctuary.

As for the flood story itself, critical scholarship has uncovered convincing evidence that two versions have been preserved in the text. One commences in 6:5-7 with God's judgement that the human being's wickedness has become so great that God resolves (in grief not in anger) to destroy all living things. The other commences in 6:11-12 with God's judgement that the earth was corrupt and that 'all flesh had corrupted its way upon the earth'. In the former God unleashes a storm that lasts 40 days (7:12) and causes a flood; in the latter a cosmic flood that lasts 150 days (7:24). The present text therefore offers two ways of telling the story. What both versions agree on, and what the present text preserves, is that the flood is not a return to pre-creation chaos, as some commentators argue, but the perfectly controlled wielding of forces in creation to remove chaos—represented by destructive wicked humanity and the living things that it has corrupted.[15] The flood lasts a certain length of time, rises to a certain level in order to destroy all flesh (fish of course are not mentioned) and then subsides. There is no impression of the flood being a threat to the ark.

In 6:7 God resolves that such universal wickedness must be eliminated, a good act that will of course be experienced as evil by the wicked. But, as with the couple in the garden, there needs to be a factor that allows the story of humanity to continue; hence the rather abrupt introduction of Noah in 6:8 who 'found favour (*khen*) in the

---

Genesis 1-11 [Oxford: Bocardo & Church Army Press, 1983], 41).
15. In his *Creation and the Persistence of Evil. The Jewish Drama of Divine Omnipotence*, Jon D Levenson states on page 10 that humanity's injustice threatens 'to cause the world to revert to the primordial aquatic state from which it had emerged' but appears to revise this interpretation when commenting on Isa 54:7-10, 'Here, as in the story of Noah in the Torah, even the chaotic waters are at the beck of YHWH' (page 21). A more recent example is Joseph Blenkinsopp, *Creation, Un-creation, Re-Creation: a discursive commentary on Genesis 1-11* (London/New York: T&T Clark, 2011), 141. The eruption of chaos in creation would mean that these destructive forces are no longer under God's control, which is clearly not the case in the flood story. A key point of the story is to emphasise God's complete control over creation.

eyes of the Lord'.[16] Noah provides a narrative opportunity for the Torah to again show that God is a just and merciful judge; in this case, as the one who is always able to separate the good from the wicked. Genesis 6:9 supplies the reason for the Lord's favour/compassion—it is because Noah is righteous (*tsadiq*). This is the first occurrence of the term in the Torah. The verse goes on to state that being righteous means that Noah is blameless (*tamim*) because he walked with God (the notion of relationship). In 7:1 God tells Noah that he is righteous, a verse that directly follows the report in 6:22 that Noah did all God commanded him. The implication one can draw from these texts—within the context of the Torah—is that Noah is righteous because the one with whom he walks is the righteous one par excellence. God displays the divine righteousness by showing favour to Noah and his family.

Apart from stating that Noah obeyed God's instructions for the ark and its purpose, the story does not spell out the nature of the path in which Noah walked, the law of God that he followed. The authors of the Torah could hardly locate the Decalogue or other law code at this point in the story because it would rob the Sinai covenant of its impact, particularly in relation to Israel. Nevertheless, some law is presumed otherwise there is no basis for praising Noah and condemning the rest of humanity.[17] One group of texts that point in this direction is the command in Genesis 1:28 and the post-flood 'revision' of it in 9:1–7. The first commands that the human being is to increase and multiply, fill the earth and subdue it, and have dominion over living creatures.[18] The second establishes a 'new' order that is

---

16. The Hebrew noun *khen* (favour) is derived from the verb *khanan* (to show favour/have compassion). Depending on the context, the verb is similar to *nakham* which can mean to have pity/compassion, as in Deut 32:36, or to repent/be sorry, as in Gen 6:7, where God regrets/repents of having created humanity.
17. One answer is the 'natural law' advocated by patristic and medieval commentators, a component of God's eternal law that governs creation. The Torah laws are a historical revelation that enables Israel and all who accept them to live in accord with the natural law.
18. Being in the image and likeness of God, the human being is presumably meant to 'subdue' and 'have dominion' over the earth and living creatures as God does. This means ensuring that right order is maintained; cf. Andre Wénin, 'La question de l'humain et l'unité du livre de la Genèse,' in *Studies in the Book of Genesis*, edited by A Wénin (BETL 155; Leuven: Leuven University Press/Peeters, 2001), 3–34; especially 5–6.

appropriate for the human being, the inclination of whose heart is 'evil from youth' (8:21). But it is an interim order while God seeks to teach the human being, via the Torah narrative and laws, to distinguish clearly between good and evil ways and to walk only in the former as Noah does.

This suggests that the law codes proclaimed in the Sinai covenant are not something entirely new nor specifically Israelite. They reveal key components of God's teaching that is there, has always been there as part of the right order of life, but the wickedness of humanity blinds it from seeing, accepting, and living by it.[19] The proclamation of the law at Sinai is an integral part of God's purpose for humanity, providing the wherewithal for human beings to know good and evil and become like Noah, blameless and righteous. Another text that points in this direction is the Sabbath. God establishes it as part of the created order to be of benefit for the human being. Yet it is introduced to the Israelites in Exodus 16 as something that they know nothing about. The Decalogue version in Exodus 20:8–11 explains that keeping the Sabbath will enable them to live within the created order in the way the creator intends. It is therefore a key element in the restoration of Humanity's right relationship with God and creation.

The singling out of Noah introduces another important theme that will recur in the subsequent Torah narrative, namely the relationship between the one (or the few) and the many. The presence of one good person or community in the midst of an evil multitude is a narrative way of affirming that there is a core of goodness in humanity no matter how evil it may appear, and via this one (or few) God will triumph over the many or bring salvation to the many—depending on the plot of the particular story. God shows favour to the righteous Noah by delivering him and his kin from destruction. This involves a just judgement by God that Noah is innocent/blameless (cf. Gen 6:9; 7:1). What is more, when Noah offers proper sacrifice after the flood (8:20), God makes another just and compassionate decision—a promise never again to destroy every living creature (8:21). What is striking about the reason given in 8:21 is that it is the same reason

---

19. Something similar may lie behind the remark in Gen 4:26 that, in Enosh's day, people began to invoke the name of the Lord. The completely corrupt humanity in the flood story no longer knows God's name, except for Noah. After Noah (9:26), no figure invokes the name of the Lord until Abraham.

given for the flood in the first place, namely the evil inclination of the human heart (6:5). This is confirmed by the subsequent story of Noah's drunkenness and its impact on his family (9:20-27), and by the story of the tower of Babel. The clear implication is that of themselves human beings are incapable of maintaining a right relationship with God and with one another. Only God can make this possible and God undertakes to do so via the one chosen people (12:1-3).

Within the story of Israel's ancestors, Abraham and Sarah (Gen 12-25), there are two passages that develop the Torah teaching on righteousness in important ways, Genesis 15:1-6 and 18:16-33. According to the first text Abraham believes God's promise that his descendants will be like the stars of heaven. He has just complained that he is childless (his wife Sarah is barren) and that 'a son of my house' (so not his own progeny) will be his heir. In short, Abraham sees himself in a situation of complete powerlessness vis-à-vis the future and the promise of descendants like the stars of heaven could seem quite preposterous. But the text says that 'he believed the Lord and the Lord reckoned it to him as righteousness' (v 6).[20] The point of this episode is that a right relationship with God is founded primarily on faith; an acknowledgement of complete dependence on God and trust in God's word.

Is there a point beyond which, according to biblical thinking, one cannot or even should not believe? There is no way within the realm of faith that one can provide a definitive answer to this question. However, the 'aqedah or 'binding of Isaac' story in Genesis 22 invites one to 'test the waters' in a radical and challenging way. Here Abraham is called to obey a command/revelation that appears to contradict the promises of descendants and land that he has thus far received from God. Abraham obeys the seemingly absurd word and in 22:15-18 the angel informs him (and the reader) that this is the right faith response; it is the kind of relationship with God that advances God's purpose of bestowing blessing on his descendants and ultimately on all nations.

---

20. The subject of the verb 'reckoned' is simply 'he' in the Hebrew and could refer either to the Lord or to Abraham. Daniel A Klein does not think the ambiguity can be resolved satisfactorily (cf 'Who Counted Righteousness to Whom? Two Clashing Views by Shadal on Gen 15:6,' in *Jewish Biblical Quarterly* 36 [2008]: 28-32). Despite this most translations read it as a reference to the Lord, as in the NRSV, rather than to Abraham.

Granted this is a fair reading of the story there is some commonality between its theology and the challenging question of the satan in the book of Job; 'does Job fear (trust) God for nothing' (1:10)?

The importance of right faith and the difficulty human beings have living it is highlighted by the location of Genesis 15. It is preceded and followed by stories which show Abraham failing to trust God's promise of progeny; there is his sojourn in Egypt 12:10–20 where he trades Sarah his wife for his own safety, and Genesis 16 where Sarah in a sense squares the ledger by ordering him to beget her a child by the surrogate Hagar. One senses here an instance of the competition and conflict between man/husband and woman/wife decreed in Genesis 3:16. It is only in the climactic story of Genesis 22 that Abraham is able to trust God above all else and to learn that all else flows from this.

The second text, Genesis 18:16–33, forms the prelude to another account of God eliminating evil and disorder in creation (the land)—Sodom and Gomorrah. The text unfolds in two stages. In vv 16–19 the reader is granted access to a soliloquy from God. It begins with a rhetorical question that invites the reader to supply an answer, in this case given by the helpful NRSV translator at the beginning of v 19 (not in the Hebrew). God will not conceal the divine plan from Abraham because he is the chosen mediator of it. To do so would also imply that the relationship between them is not righteous, God is withholding or concealing knowledge from him. The soliloquy then recalls (cf v 18) Abraham's vocation in Genesis 12:1–3, the first words that God speaks to him. The initial Hebrew verb in v 19 is 'to know' but the MT has a pronoun suffix that creates a somewhat awkward sequence. It can be translated literally as 'I know/have known him in order that . . .' The NRSV translates this as 'I have chosen him that . . .' A number of ancient versions have 'I know that . . .' which looks like an attempt to clarify the MT. The MT and NRSV make the instruction of Abraham's descendents a reason why God chose him; the versions simply state that God knows Abraham will do this. It may be best therefore to follow the *lectio difficilior* of the MT that a key component of God's purpose as announced in 12:1–3 is that Abraham may know about righteousness and justice so that he can instruct his descendents to do so. In order that Abraham and his descendents can mediate universal blessing to all nations they need to know about and adhere to righteousness and justice. In order to do this, they must themselves know and obey the source of righteousness and justice.

The story of Sodom and Gomorrah provides an appropriate setting for such a crucial instruction. In 13:13 the inhabitants of Sodom are singled out as great sinners and now (18:20) the outcry against both cities has reached God who comes to investigate. The image of a completely corrupt society recalls the wicked humanity of the flood story while God's personal inspection recalls the story of the tower of Babel. This suggests the Sodom and Gomorrah story serves as a kind of paradigm for the relationship between Abraham/Israel and the nations that will unfold in the course of the Torah. It also provides a crucial teaching about Israel's vocation as adumbrated in the ancestor Abraham. It is pretty clear that the visit of the three to Abraham and Sarah is linked narratively and theologically to the visitation and judgement of Sodom and Gomorrah. That is, the vocation and mission of Abraham (and Israel) are an integral part God's overall purpose for humanity, represented here by the two cities.

The exchange between Abraham and God contains three main points. The first is Abraham's question about the respective fate of the righteous and the wicked (*rasha'*) in the cities. This is also meant to be an abiding concern of his descendents (listeners and readers are to take note). But while genuine concern is one thing, making the correct distinctions between righteous and wicked (between good and evil) and discerning what should happen as a result is another thing. Knowing how to do this is the second point and it unfolds in the discussion between God and Abraham, where God is cast as the teacher answering the pupil's questions.[21] This in its turn develops two aspects of the distinction and their implications. One is contained in the question whether the righteous should share the fate of the wicked (vv 23, 25). God does not respond to the question, perhaps to signal to the character Abraham and to readers that the answer should be obvious. A positive answer would impugn the theology of a just God who rewards the good and punishes the wicked. Within the Torah storyline this has already been illustrated in the case of Noah.

---

21. Cf Michael Widmer *Moses, God and the Dynamics of Intercessory Prayer* (FAT; Tübingen: Mohr Siebeck), 295 (citing an unpublished dissertation by MacDonald). Others think Abraham is the teacher and God as pupil. See for example p. 51 of Thomas M Bolin 'The Role of Exchange in Ancient Mediterranean Religion and Its Implications for Reading Genesis 18-19*,' *JSOT* 29.1 (2004): 37-56, and the views cited in n. 44.

The other aspect is whether the wicked city should be spared on account of the righteous in its midst. This is another example of the relationship between the one (or few) and the many. Can the righteous few save the many wicked? The dialogue ends with God stating that the city will be forgiven for the sake of ten righteous inhabitants. Two points emerge from this. One is that God's compassion for the many on account of the few is made in the name of justice (cf v 25b). In making such a judgment God displays righteousness, the purpose of which is to enable the city, along with the ten righteous ones within it, to re-establish proper order. A second point is that the text does not give the impression that ten is the cut-off number below which God will not forgive. The dialogue simply comes to an end and God and Abraham go their respective ways. But, given that God keeps assuring Abraham as he reduces the number of righteous from an initial fifty to ten, does the text imply that God will even forgive the city for the sake of one righteous person, as is the case in Jeremiah 5:1?

Despite God's replies to Abraham the reader is left somewhat uncertain as to which of the above two criteria (or both of them) is to be applied to Sodom and Gomorrah. Is it that the righteous will be spared while the wicked will be destroyed? If so, who is the righteous one(s), Lot or Abraham? Given that the HBOT does not provide a neat definition of righteousness and that human righteousness is limited, one may also ask what kind of righteousness is needed to win divine pardon. The portrait of Lot in the story is somewhat ambiguous but he is perhaps no less righteous than Abraham in the earlier chapters of Genesis. However, Genesis 19:29 states that when God destroyed these cities, God remembered Abraham and spared Lot and his family. Is this because of Abraham's righteousness in trusting God's word in 15:6, even though the following account of the birth of Ishmael exposes him acting contrary to that trust? Can one say that the story is (also) an application of the rule that many wicked can be forgiven because of a few righteous (ten or one)? Sodom could not be delivered because there was not even one righteous person there. As is often the case biblical narrative is somewhat reticent. The reader is challenged to think and make a decision—sound catechetical technique. In making a decision or judgement, one can appeal to the larger context of the Torah as well as other parts of the biblical canon.

For example, within the larger context of the Torah the spy story in Numbers 13-14 illustrates the case where the righteous/loyal ones—Joshua and Caleb—are spared the fate of the wicked (14:36-38), as also does Numbers 16. Within the prophetic corpus it is the principle repeatedly invoked in Ezekiel 14:12-20. A paradigm case of the wicked being spared because of a righteous person is the golden calf story in Exodus 32-34; loyal Moses is able to win a reprieve for apostate Israel. The biblical claim is that in each case the judgement delivered by God is just.

Lest the listener or reader think that the nations are all wicked like Sodom and Gomorrah and entirely dependent on the mediation of Abraham and his descendents, the Torah provides a timely caution in the story of Abraham and Abimelech in Genesis 20. As in 12:10-20 Abraham acts in a disloyal (unrighteous) way towards his wife and towards the people among whom he sojourns by passing her off as his sister. As a result the king takes her, presumably to become his wife. According to Deuteronomy 22:22 to lie with another man's wife is a capital offence in Israel and is what lies behind God's threat in Genesis 22:3.[22] The deuteronomic text requires the execution of the man and the woman, but here only Abimelech is threatened because Sarah is a victim not a perpetrator. In his defense, Abimelech claims that he and his people (who passed on Abraham's lie) have been duped. In a somewhat ironic echo of Abraham's question in 18:23, Abimelech asks in 20:4, 'Lord, will you destroy an innocent (NRSV; MT *tsadiq*, righteous) people'? and claims that he has acted with integrity and in innocence. God acknowledges Abimelech's righteousness by informing him that he has protected him from touching her—he has not actually lain with her and so breached Deuteronomy 22:22. What is striking about this tale is that God acknowledges Abimelech and his people's righteousness without any ministry on the part of Abraham; in fact Abraham has abused it. Does this text affirm that non-Israelites, rather like Noah, can be righteous and blameless, at least in some things, without knowing the laws of the Torah? Or, that when Israel fails the nations in its ministerial role, God will not. By the same token, the story also affirms that God does not abandon

---

22. Cf Christoph Levin, 'Gerechtigkeit Gottes in der Genesis,' in *Studies in the Book of Genesis*, edited by A Wénin (BETL 155; Leuven: Leuven University Press/ Peeters, 2001), 347-57, especially 355.

the chosen ones even when they fail. Abraham's ministerial or intercessory function is maintained via his prophetic prayer (20:7, 17). It is interesting to note that the one who fails in his relationship with his wife must now become God's mediator/servant on behalf of all the women of Abimelech's house.

The story of Abraham revolves around his relationship with God and the promise of an heir, his relationship with Sarah and Hagar, and with foreigners. He is the chosen mediator of God's blessing to all families of the earth (12:3). In each of these relationships Abraham is portrayed as a flawed character who, because of fear or the desire to control others, has a distorted perception of reality. He struggles to know the distinction between good and evil, at times doing evil (for example, in relation to Sarah) for the sake of what he perceives as good—for himself (the perceived threat of foreigners which turns out to be erroneous in both 12:10–20 and 22). God is portrayed as loyal to the chosen one, instructing him by word and deed to learn the way of the Lord. By the end of the story, he can act rightly in relation to the promise of an heir (Gen 22) and in his relationship with foreigners (in the purchase of a burial plot for Sarah in Genesis 23). The story of Abraham expresses the hope that the one good person/nation can bring blessing to the many and in this way unite the many as one.

The final text in Genesis that is of relevance to this study is the story of Joseph and his brothers in 37–50. Three episodes draw attention. The first concerns Joseph's response to the wife of Potiphar who propositions him (Gen 39). He refuses to transgress the boundary of marriage and usurp the place of his master who is her husband, not only because this would create conflict and disorder but primarily because it is a 'great evil' and a 'sin against God' (39:9).[23] Unlike many of the characters in Genesis 1–11 and in the story of his ancestors Joseph knows how to distinguish between good and evil (the same word for evil as in the garden story—3:5). This is because, unlike them, Joseph's loyalty to God is the measure of his relationships with others. It enables Joseph to become the wise one as the Pharaoh himself recognises in 41:38–39. The second is the intriguing manner in which Joseph exercises power over his brothers in Egypt. Words and actions that are experienced by the brothers as an evil inflicted by a cruel tyrant are, as things turn out, an integral part of Joseph's

---

23. Cf Wénin, 'La question de l'humain,' 15–16.

plan to achieve reconciliation in his family. Had he immediately welcomed them and revealed himself to them, would the brothers have undergone such a transformation as the story depicts?[24] They needed to come to know the wrong that they had done to Joseph and their father, and their own experience of evil enables them finally to see what is good and what is evil.

One could say that Joseph acts in the image and likeness of God who punishes wickedness (inflicting evil) for the sake of good (to establish right relationships). Joseph sums it up in 50:20; 'Even though you intended to do harm (evil) to me, God intended it for good, in order to preserve a numerous people'. Yet, and this engages the third episode, Joseph is not righteous in all his relationships. In the light of Judah's climactic speech in 44:18–34, Joseph is exposed both to his brothers and to the reader as putting his father's life in danger to satisfy his demand to see Benjamin in Egypt.[25] Joseph had insisted on it despite the brothers' warning that Jacob would die as a result (44:22). Although Joseph is portrayed as a righteous one he is, like his ancestors, flawed to some degree. The question of righteousness, of God as its source, of humanity's need for it, and of God's resolve to establish it is one that pervades the book of Genesis.[26]

---

24. Cf Wénin, ibid., 28.
25. On this see my 'The Contribution of Judah's Speech, Genesis 44:18–34, to the Characterization of Joseph,' *CBQ* 59 (1997): 429–47.
26. In the words of Levin, 'Das Motiv der Gerechtigkeit Gottes durchzieht des Buch Genesis vom Sündenfall bis zur Josefsgeschichte' ('Gerechtigkeit Gottes,' 355).

3

Book of Exodus

The story of the 'exodus' shares a number of features with the flood story and the more general story plot of the battle against evil (in Booker's terminology 'overcoming the monster').[1] Evil and chaos envelop a key component of God's creation (Israel) and threaten to destroy it.[2] God delivers Israel by wielding the forces of creation in an ordered/righteous way (cf the Pharaoh's acknowledgement in 9:27). Moses plays an analogous role to Noah in the flood, the one who is loyal to God and mediates salvation for the people. The threat to God's purpose in creation is definitively removed when the 'monster' is destroyed in the sea (15:1–18); a liberated Israel can now be led to its right place (the land) and there fulfill its purpose within creation. To facilitate this the covenant at Sinai establishes the boundaries within which a right relationship between Israel and God, between Israelites themselves, and with others, can flourish.

At this point the story brings to the fore a powerful and disturbing theme that has been adumbrated at points in the story of the exodus.[3] The Israelites in the story (and the reader) may think that the greatest obstacle to God's saving purpose is an enemy outsider like Egypt. But the golden calf episode exposes the insider (the chosen people) as the greatest obstacle and God's enemy. This provides another echo of the flood story where the greatest threat to right order in creation is not a hostile divinity (as in ANE myths) but humanity itself. It is its own and God's worst enemy. Despite this, the Torah proclaims

---

1. Cf Booker, *The Seven Basic Plots*, 21–50.
2. Israel is not 'created' as God's people in the book of Exod according to 3:7 it is already so.
3. For example, in Israel's loss of faith at the sea (Exod 14:10–12), in their complaints on the journey to Sinai, in the Amalekite episode (Exod 17:8–16).

that God remains committed to living among the people of Israel in the sanctuary (constructed in Exod 35–40) and to leading them to the land. The book of Exodus makes a massive faith claim about God's commitment to Israel—and thereby to all humanity—which is underwritten by a number of texts in the subsequent narrative (a key one being the spy story in Num 13–14) and, as was pointed out earlier, by the song in Deuteronomy 32.

But before embarking on an analysis of pertinent texts within Exodus it is worth checking its connections to the book of Genesis and the portrayal of righteousness and associated terms there.[4] According to Genesis the establishment of righteousness or right relationships in humanity depends on true knowledge. Without it one only has a distorted perception of reality that leads to disordered relationships, as the garden story outlines. God is the only reliable source of it. Genesis provides a final and telling example of this in the story of Joseph and his brothers. The Pharaoh recognises the God-given wisdom of Joseph and therefore the one who can deliver Egypt and indeed the whole earth from the great famine (41:57).[5] Likewise, when Joseph's brothers acknowledge they have done him and their father a great wrong, relationships within the family can begin to be restored. The family accepts Joseph's plan to move to Egypt where, according to the opening verses of the book of Exodus, it flourishes and multiplies. But when 'a new king arose over Egypt, who did not know Joseph' (Exod 1:8) things change dramatically. The new Pharaoh plans to oppress Israel, kill all the new-born boys but spare the girls. This is a bizarre policy even for an oppressive regime; it will effectively eliminate the slave workforce that the regime plans to exploit.[6] It is a classic example of the distorted perception of reality that occurs when one repudiates the source of divine wisdom and its

---

4. I refer to the present text of the Torah; it may well be the case, as some recent studies of the composition of the Pentateuch have proposed, that the connection between the stories of the ancestors and the story of Israel in the book of Exodus is late (for a discussion of the literature see Ska, *Introduction to Reading the Pentateuch*, 196–202).
5. Gordon J Wenham also notes how Joseph's wise rule echoes the command to the human being in Gen 1:28 (*Torah as Story. Reading the Old Testament Ethically* [Old Testament Series; Edinburgh: T&T Clark, 2000], 26).
6. The policy requires that all males eventually born to the girls who are spared be killed as well.

truth (the sense of 'who did not know Joseph'). The opening verses of Exodus signal that, whatever the origins of the component parts of the present text, they have been carefully assembled to advance the Torah's theological agenda.

The question of knowledge and its link to power comes to the fore when Moses first approaches Pharaoh about letting the people go to worship the Lord. Pharaoh retorts 'who is the Lord, that I should heed him and let Israel go? I do not know the Lord' (5:2). For ANE rulers as for modern ones, to know a rival meant knowing his or her power and whether it was a threat to one's own. Knowledge is a form of power. God assures Moses that 'the Egyptians shall know that I am the Lord, when I stretch out my hand against Egypt' (7:5). The divine power displayed in the plagues will make the Egyptians know who really is in charge of creation and history. Knowledge of God and God's ways is also of central importance for Israel; the difference here being that the exodus will enable Israel to know 'that I am the Lord, *your* God, who has freed you from the burden of the Egyptians' (6:7). Although the plagues are part of God's plan to deliver Israel, their ultimate purpose is to reveal the Lord as God.[7] One could say that the best thing for Pharaoh and the Egyptians, who are bent on death and destruction, is that they come to know who is God. True knowledge of God enables one to see the source of all life; without it any society will inevitably, in the biblical view, descend into chaos and evil.

A striking and, for the modern mind, troublesome feature of the plague narrative is God's hardening of Pharaoh's heart so that he refuses to set Israel free. Not every reference to this motif attributes it to God's initiative and this may be a sign that different traditions have been combined, whether one identifies them as J, E and P versions, as in the classic source hypothesis, or as non-P and P 'histories', as in the recent commentary by Thomas Dozeman.[8] Nevertheless, the fact that it occurs in the present text and, furthermore, that it is stated as an integral part of God's plan (cf 4:21; 7:3) invites the reader to consider

---

7. Hence the refrain accompanying each plague, that Pharaoh 'shall know I am/who is the Lord' (cf 7:17; 8:10, 22; 9:14, 29; 10:2).
8. See Thomas B Dozeman, *Exodus* (The Eerdmans Critical Commentary; Grand Rapids MI: Eerdmans, 2009). A clear presentation of the source hypothesis as applied to the plagues can be found in the commentary of Brevard S Childs, *The Book of Exodus. A Critical, Theological Commentary* (Louisville Ky: Westminster Press, 1974), 130-41.

its function in the narrative.⁹ At first glance there would seem to be a contradiction between instructing Pharaoh via the plagues that the Lord is God and God hardening his heart. The former implies freedom to respond to the challenge (true knowledge cannot be imposed) while the latter overrides that freedom. Commentators have wrestled with this conundrum and suggested various answers.¹⁰ My own suggestion is that some idea of the relationship between human freedom and divine causality can be gained by turning to the distorted perception of reality as presented in the garden story.

As noted above, Exodus 1–15 belongs to 'the battle against evil' or 'overcoming the monster' story plot, with a cast of good (God, Moses) and bad characters (Pharaoh, Egyptians).¹¹ A new Pharaoh repudiates Joseph's God-given wisdom; the result is a distorted perception of reality with an evil outcome, the oppression of Israel. His opposite number, God, counters with the same call or challenge made to Israel and all humanity: to know that the Lord is God (cf 7:5). Once this is done evil can be overcome and order and peace established. But according to the HBOT the encounter with God or God's word usually triggers two kinds of reactions; one is acknowledgement of the Lord, the other is resistance. This is not something which applies only to Pharaoh: in Exodus 32:9; 33:3, 5 God attributes the golden calf apostasy to Israel's stubbornness ('stiff of neck'; cf also Deut 9:13 and 16) and 29:19 (MT 29:18) warns against future stubbornness of heart.¹² The difference is that whereas Moses is able to intercede on

---

9. Texts that state God hardened Pharaoh's heart are Exod 9:12; 10:20, 27; 11:10. Even some that attribute the hardening to Pharaoh add 'as the Lord said', presumably a reference to 4:21 and 7:5 (cf 7:13, 22; 8:15 ([MT 8:11]; 8:19 [MT 8:15]; also in 9:12). The only two that contain no such reference are Exod 8:32 (MT 8:28) which has 'Pharaoh hardened his heart', and 9:7 'the heart of Pharaoh was hardened'.
10. A good discussion and survey of opinions can be found in Childs, *The Book of Exodus*, 170-75.
11. Cf. Booker, *The Seven Basic Plots*, 21-50. Exodus 1–15 is not a 'holy war' story, at least not in the sense in which this term is applied to the war stories in Joshua and Judges. There divine power is manifest in the way a small force of loyal Israelite troops triumphs against impossible odds. In Exodus, oppressed Israel is not (yet) God's victorious army.
12. The Hebrew adjective (*qasheh* = hard, stiff) in Exod 32:9 and Deut 9:13, 16 has the same root as the verb used in Exod 7:3 to describe what the Lord will do to Pharaoh's heart and to summarise Pharaoh's own hardness in 13:15.

Israel's behalf and Israel repents of its apostasy, Pharaoh is obdurate in resisting the power of the God that he comes to know.

In the story Pharaoh never denies that a wonder or plague has taken place. As well there are his evasive responses and pleas to Moses to have a plague cease. He is portrayed as a character who knows he is up against a more powerful rival yet tries to maintain control of events.[13] It provides further evidence of his distorted perception of things, rejection of true knowledge and the source of this true knowledge. One can link this to the hardening of heart motif. Pharaoh thinks he is making his own decisions and is therefore in control of events but the only one who is really in charge, and must be so for the good of creation and humanity, is the Lord. In an ironic touch by the narrator, at the very point at which Pharaoh thinks he is in charge he is not and doesn't know it—perhaps a mocking allusion to his statement in 5:2 'I do not know the Lord'. The hardening motif ensures the deliverance of Israel and, more importantly, reveals that there is only one Lord of creation and history.

Within this context a particularly ironic text is the already noted 9:27 where the Pharaoh, after the plague of hail, confesses 'This time I have sinned; the Lord is in the right (literally; 'is the righteous one'), and I and my people are in the wrong' (literally; 'are the wicked/guilty ones'). Taken by itself, this would seem to signal that God's prophecy in 7:5 is fulfilled and the plagues have achieved their aim: Pharaoh now knows that the Lord is 'the righteous one', and this enables him to know who he and his people really are, 'the wicked ones'. It also suggests that he is prepared to cede control to the Lord who alone has power to deliver Pharaoh and his people from the evil that entraps them. But the context, particularly Moses' response in 9:30 ('I know that you do not yet fear the Lord God'), indicates this is another ploy by the character Pharaoh. The irony of course is that devious Pharaoh actually (for the reader) proclaims the truth, not only about the Lord but about the plagues as well—they are a manifestation of God's

---

Deuteronomy 29:19 (MT 29:18) uses another term *sherirut* in combination with heart. The majority of references to the hardening of Pharaoh's heart employ the verbs *kabed* (be/make heavy) and *khazaq* (make firm/harden). Cf Childs, *The Book of Exodus*, 170-71.

13. Following Moshe Greenberg, *Understanding Exodus* (New York: Behrman House, 1969), 181, cited in Mann *The Book of the Torah*, 95.

righteousness. God wields the forces of creation, as at the flood, in order to remove the disorder and destruction of Egyptian oppression. Does the context invalidate the prophecy of 7:5? Not if one notes the difference between it and 6:7—'You shall know that I am the Lord *your* God'. In 9:27 Pharaoh acknowledges the Lord but not as *his* God.

In keeping with God's prediction in 3:19-20, Pharaoh is eventually 'compelled' by the mighty hand of the destroyer (12:23) to let the people of Israel go (cf 12:29-32). There is the recognition of divine power but no submission; instead he issues a command ('rise up, go away') and demands that the Israelites bless him for doing so (literally; 'and you shall also bless me'). The impression given is that once the Israelites are dismissed the status quo will resume as before. But in this paradigm story evil, as represented by Pharaoh, needs to be 'conquered' by the forces of good in order to meet the requirements of Torah and its theological message. Hence there is one more account of God hardening Pharaoh's heart (14:4)—whereas Pharaoh thinks he is changing his mind (14:5)—leading to the dramatic destruction of the Egyptian host in the sea.[14] According to 14:10, Pharaoh leads the army in pursuit of Israel but the text refers only to the destruction of 'the entire army of Pharaoh' (14:28). The inclusion of Pharaoh in the death toll is implied but not specified. According to 14:25 the Egyptians recognise the identity and power of the one fighting against them: 'Let us flee from the Israelites, for the Lord is fighting for them against Egypt'. This verse evokes the prophecy of 7:5 in the same sense as 9:27. The Egyptians' attempt to flee indicates there is no submission to the Lord as *their* God and so they are destroyed as an enemy hostile to both God and Israel. The Israelites, witnessing God's 'great work' against the forces of evil, express fear (reverence) and belief (14:31), and in the song that follows proclaim it as a sign of the Lord's 'steadfast love/loyalty' (*khesedh*) for Israel (15:13). Within the context one could describe this *khesedh* as God's unswerving resolve or commitment to establish righteousness or right order. The song concludes by proclaiming that the only universally valid and right rule is that of the Lord (15:18).[15]

---

14. Reading 14:4 and 5 in combination; they were probably originally parts of once independent sources (J and P) or different versions of the deliverance at the sea.
15. Cf Erich Zenger, 'Le theme de la 'sortie d'Égypte' et la naissance du Pentateuque,' in *Le Pentateuque en Question*, 301-31, especially 315.

There is no indication that Israel's enslavement in Egypt is a punishment for sin, the normal explanation employed by the Former and Latter Prophets to account for the Assyrian (for northern Israel) and Babylonian (for Judah) exiles. Several reasons can be offered for its absence. A general one is that the 'overcoming the monster' plot normally portrays the good characters in dire straits from which they are ultimately delivered. A second reason that relates more specifically to the Torah is that Israel's oppression is revealed to the ancestor Abraham in Genesis 15:13.[16] Hence it is an integral part of the vocation of being the chosen people and therefore part of God's plan to bring salvation to humanity. In this sense, the evil experience of oppression by an enemy is a good—for the chosen people who remain loyal to God in the face of persecution/suffering and are delivered. The oppressor is either also saved or eliminated (no longer able to oppress). Both outcomes testify that the Lord is God. There is a thematic link here with the so-called 'suffering servant' poems in Isaiah 42:1-4; 49:1-6; 50:4-9 and 52:13-53:12. The final poem proclaims that the suffering of the righteous servant (named as Israel in 49:3) 'will make many righteous' (Isa 53:11). The Torah and book of Isaiah are painting with a broad brush and do not, and indeed cannot, within the limitations of a particular narrative and prophecy, anticipate or respond to the details of each generation's experience or the experience of each individual. This is done to some extent in the lament psalms, the lamentations in the book of Jeremiah and the book of Lamentations. Their questions, laments and attempts to provide an answer expose the limitation of Torah and prophecy, but by continually returning to them and drawing on them they also testify to their enduring authority.

A third and related point is that the opening chapters of Exodus provide two indications that God is present to the people in their affliction.[17] One is the episode of the midwives who fear God and are blessed with families (Exod 1:21). The other is in 2:24 that reports God

---

16. Although Gen 15:13 clearly has the Egyptian oppression in view, it speaks of 400 years whereas the story in Exodus unfolds in the reign of two Pharaohs. The only text in Exodus that supplies a specific chronology is 12:40 which claims Israel was in Egypt for 430 years, a number that presumably includes the time taken to become a multitude and the period of oppression.
17. In disagreement with Dozeman (*Exodus*, 66) who writes of the absence of God as a character in the story, in contrast to Genesis.

heard the groaning of the Israelites and remembered the covenant with the ancestors. The use of the Hebrew verb to remember here (*zakar*) within the context of the covenant recalls Genesis 8:1; 9:15, 26 and 19:29. In the first God remembers Noah in the flood, in the second and third God promises to remember the covenant with creation, and in the third God remembers Abraham and delivers Lot from the destruction of Sodom and Gomorrah. These texts, and Exodus 2:24, do not therefore refer to God remembering something forgotten up to that point but signal that God acts in accord with a promised covenant (Gen 8:1) or an established covenant (Gen 9:15, 16; 19:29; Exod 2:24). Moreover, God's action will take place in a time and manner that demonstrates God's loyalty to the respective covenant. It is also worth noting that Exodus 2:23 reports that the people 'groaned under their slavery, and cried out' but without specifying that their cry was directed to the Lord. Does this mean that the people had lost their knowledge of God during, or because of, their prolonged oppression?[18] If this is the case, an essential aim of God's deliverance from oppression is to restore this knowledge.

The third major player in the drama of the exodus story is of course Moses, the one who mediates God's salvation to the many.[19] Exodus 2:11–22 is a lesson in how human actions, even well-intentioned ones such as those of Moses are presumably meant to be understood, lead to chaos and disorder without a right knowledge of God and a right relationship with God. Moses thinks he is at one with his people but his violent intervention leads to rejection by them and pursuit by the Egyptians. In an ironic allusion to his future role in Israel, a Hebrew slave asks 'Who made you a ruler and judge over us'? Moses has to encounter the just judge before he can have true knowledge of himself and his role in 'judging' Israel. This is signaled in the question he asks at the burning bush, 'Who am I that I should go to Pharaoh' and God's reply 'I will be with you'.[20] The dialogue between Moses

---

18. Cf. Dozeman, *Exodus*, 92–93.
19. The portrait of Moses in Exodus has understandably attracted much scholarly attention, particularly about its provenance. Does it have ancient roots or is it, as John Van Seters proposes, an exilic construct that drew on prophetic traditions (*The Life of Moses. The Yahwist as Historian in Exodus–Numbers* [Louisville: Westminster/John Knox, 1994], see ch. 2)? As noted earlier, the focus of this study is the meaning of the present text rather than the process of its composition.
20. Following Mann *The Book of the Torah*, 83.

and God in Exodus 3-4 unfolds important aspects of the relationship between knowledge, faith and power. Moses thinks that in order for the people to believe in him they need to know the name of the one who has sent him. The faith relationship between Moses and Israel depends on his own faith in God, which is based on his knowledge of God (the divine name) and of God's purpose. The accompanying signs reveal the power that has been entrusted to Moses, the same power that will be revealed in the confrontation with Pharaoh.[21]

The series of objections voiced by Moses in his encounter with God is designed either to emphasise that his call and commission is not his initiative and that he is an unworthy candidate (a common motif in prophetic call narratives), or to forge a link with the earlier Torah theme of the difficulty human beings have correcting their skewed perception of reality. Perhaps both, but his appeal to the people's likely skepticism and his inability as a speaker suggest that he is unwilling to accept things on God's terms—shades of Abraham, at least in the early part of his story.

Moses' final attempt to escape his call comes after the disastrous initial encounter with Pharaoh in Exodus 5. Moses blames God (5:22-23); the worse situation of the people shows that God has blundered badly in choosing him. This kind of accusation can be a cop-out, as in the case of Adam in Genesis 3:12 who blames God for putting the woman with him. It can also be a genuine cry of bewilderment and pain as in the lament psalms. The Exodus text may be delicately poised between both.[22] From the point of view of Torah theology God's plan to deliver Israel cannot be described as 'evil' (the Hebrew verb in 5:22), as Moses claims. This is a distorted perception of things. The text offers no direct response to his accusation or, one might say, responds to it with an assurance that it is all part of God's saving plan. Pharaoh's arrogant rejection of God's demand is the foreordained

---

21. Cf 123-24 of Franz Polak, 'Theophany and Mediator. The Unfolding of a Theme in the Book of Exodus,' in *Studies in the Book of Exodus: Redaction—Reception—Interpretation*, edited by Marc Vervenne (BETL 126; Leuven: Leuven University Press, 1996), 113-47.
22. Pharaoh's rebuff may appear inexplicable in light of God's promise to deliver Israel; on the other hand Moses may be deflecting the supervisors' desire that God will judge him responsible for what has happened. If so, Moses two attempts thus far to make judgements on behalf of Israel have backfired badly (2:13-14; 5:1-9).

moment ('now you shall see') for the mighty deeds that God will perform in liberating Israel.

One further element in the call and commissioning of Moses that is significant for the notion of a righteous God is the cryptic episode in Exodus 4:24-26. Here God seeks to kill 'him' (from the context more likely a reference to Moses than his son Gershom) but Moses' foreign wife Zipporah saves him by cutting off her son's foreskin and touching Moses' 'feet' (often a euphemism for genitals) with it. The comment by the narrator at the end of v 26 indicates that this is to be understood, at least in part, as a rite of circumcision. Why does God seek to kill Moses? The context may help.[23] The preceding passage is almost equally cryptic, providing a condensed summary of what is to come in the narrative. Moses is to work the signs for Pharaoh who will, because God is to harden his heart, refuse to let Israel go and worship. Moses is to then inform him that because he refuses to let the Lord's firstborn son go, his own firstborn son will die. The death of the firstborn males of Egypt is subsequently narrated in the context of the Passover where Israel is instructed to touch (same verb) the lintels of the two doorposts of their houses with the blood from the slaughtered lamb. This will ensure that they have obeyed the Lord's instructions, are therefore loyal servants of the Lord, and their firstborn sons will not be killed along with the Egyptian firstborn. The subsequent command that Israel 'set apart to the Lord' all the firstborn of its livestock and redeem all firstborn sons serves as an ongoing memorial of this deliverance (13:11-16).

When 4:24-26 is read in relation to this it indicates that although Moses has been transformed by his encounter with God from an Egyptian on the run to God's messenger to Israel there is one sign of his former life remaining on him: he is uncircumcised and as such cannot be a full member of the community of Israel. It also places him under the same threat of death as the Egyptians. He is saved by his Midianite wife who recognizes the God of Israel and knows what needs to be done. Zipporah belongs to a select group of those who deliver Israel (Hebrew midwives in 1:15-20) and Moses (his sister and the daughter of Pharaoh when a baby [2:1-10]; Zipporah when he is her husband [4:25-26]), or who bring blessing upon Israel

---

23. My interpretation here draws in part on Dozeman's careful attention to the larger context (*Exodus*, 154-56).

(Moses' father-in-law Jethro who relieves him and the people of a burdensome form of judging [18:17-18]; Balaam in Num 22-24). The actions of the daughter of Pharaoh and of Zipporah and Jethro signal that the flow of divine blessing is not all in one direction, from Israel to the nations. There are foreigners who constitute a threat to Israel and there are foreigners who bring blessing to Israel. The blessing they bring is of course the blessing that God has revealed through Israel. This is demonstrated clearly in the case of Jethro, who pays homage to Israel's God in 18:10-11. Israel's mediation of divine blessing is meant to engage outsiders; they are not to remain passive recipients but to become active and creative like Israel. In doing so they become truly Egyptian, Midianite, etc.

Although Israel is to be the chosen mediator of divine blessing to others it can also become the major obstacle to it. This is a development of a motif in the story of the ancestors, it features in the lead up to the Lord's victory at the sea and becomes an important motif of the wilderness journey. Despite the assurance provided by the Lord's overwhelming power over the forces of Egypt in the plague narratives, at the first sight of the advancing Egyptian army Israel's faith turns to fear (Exod 14:10-12).[24] They accuse Moses (and God) of doing evil in bringing them out of Egypt. In effect this is another example of the distorted perception of reality: good is seen as evil (leaving Egypt) and evil as good (remaining slaves in Egypt). Faith in God and Moses as God's servant is restored when Israel sees the dead Egyptians on the shore (14:30-31), but keeping a firm grasp on reality is a constant challenge, as the subsequent narrative of the journey to Mt Sinai testifies. The people to whom God has been revealed as all knowing and all powerful in the exodus quickly loses faith in God's presence and power when faced with the new and unknown—the wilderness. Three accounts of Israel murmuring against God and Moses (15:22-26; 16; 17:1-7) are followed by a victory over Amalek (17:8-16) and Jethro's arrival in the Israelite encampment (18). This narrative sequence signals that Israel is a greater obstacle to the

---

24. The presence of the 'murmuring' motif here has fuelled debate as to whether the victory at the sea is the climax of the exodus story or the commencement of the wilderness wandering story. For a discussion of the historical critical debate see Childs, *The Book of Exodus*, 254-64; and with more focus on the present text Dozeman, *Exodus*, 347-51. It does not affect the point being made here.

realisation of God's purpose than a foreign power such as Amalek. As if to drive this message home, the final story of the journey to Sinai casts a foreigner—Jethro—as more perceptive than Israel. He learns all that God has done for Israel and comes to pay homage to this God and to be of service to Moses and Israel.

The narrative of the Sinai covenant testifies (Exod 19-24) to God's loyalty to a people who, judging by the preceding narrative, would appear an unlikely choice. It commences by linking what God proposes for Israel to what God has already done for Israel (cf Exod 19:3-6). The covenant is therefore the next stage in the unfolding of God's plan for humanity and creation. It establishes a context, a 'real world', within which Israelites can live a right relationship with God and with each other and carry out their vocation. As in the garden story, the boundaries of this covenant context or relationship are set by God and are by definition right and good. Any other context creates a 'false world' that has only evil consequences. Israel's role, like that of the couple in the garden story, is to 'obey my voice and keep my covenant' (19:5). On the basis of this, a number of things follow. Israel becomes 'my treasured possession' among the nations in order to serve as 'a priestly kingdom' and 'a holy nation'. These last two epithets appeal to elements of priestly lore to describe Israel's vocation. Like a priest, but as a whole nation, it is to mediate and foster the relationship between God and humanity.[25] Like a priest, but once again as a nation, it will be 'holy', that is, set apart and so known as designated by God for this ministry. This divine plan for Israel to minister to the nations is another version of the relationship between the one and the many and, as will be seen, appears in various forms in other books of the HBOT. Although there is a conditional element in the covenant ('if you obey my voice') the emphasis is on God's initiative, what God has provided and what God will provide. In keeping with the encounter between God and Moses in Exodus 3-4, Israel's knowledge of its identity and vocation is intimately bound up

---

25. Cf Dozeman, *Exodus*, 446. However, Arie van der Kooij argues that the phrase 'priestly kingdom' refers to Israel being ruled by priests and derives from the time of Josiah when leading priests in the temple had a powerful influence ('A Kingdom of Priests: Comment on Exodus 19:6', in *The Interpretation of Exodus: Studies in Honour of Cornelis Houtman*, edited by Riemer Roukema (Contributions to Biblical Exegesis and Theology 44; Leuven/Paris/Dudley, MA: Peeters, 2006), 171-79.

with its knowledge of God. In summary form God recalls what was revealed in the conflict with Egypt and in the subsequent journey to Sinai (19:4). Israel is provided with the necessary knowledge to make an informed and free commitment to 'be the community of righteousness'.[26]

Modern critical scholarship has established that the covenant narrative is based on ANE treaties; nevertheless it has been carefully shaped to advance Torah theology. A key difference between them is that whereas ANE treaties are generally made between rulers (a sovereign and a vassal) the covenant is established between God and each adult Israelite male. According to Joshua Berman, in the biblical understanding 'the subordinate king with whom God forms a political treaty is, in fact, the common man of Israel'.[27] This gives added meaning to the statement in 19:6 that Israel 'shall be for me a priestly kingdom'. An example of biblical reshaping of ANE treaties is 23:17 which commands 'three times a year, all your males shall appear before the Lord God'. ANE treaties required the vassal to 'appear' before the sovereign on designated occasions as a sign of loyalty. In the biblical understanding each Israelite male takes the place of an ANE vassal or dependent ruler. Each adult Israelite male, and therefore, according to the biblical understanding of corporate personality, all Israel is freed from being a slave of Pharaoh to become a servant of God.[28] The difference is that, according to the biblical claim, obeying the covenant laws will ensure these servants of God are truly free. God's laws ensure right relationships with God, with one another, and with creation.

These relationships, or perhaps better, interrelationships, are outlined in the Decalogue in the form of apodictic laws and their accompanying motivations (Exod 20:1–17). The introductory statement identifies who God is ('I am the Lord your God') and who

---

26. As expressed by Mann, *The Book of the Torah*, 100.
27. Joshua A Berman, *Created Equal. How the Bible Broke with Ancient Political Thought* (Oxford: Oxford University Press, 2008), 41. A number of references in Deuteronomy points to the (later) inclusion of women as subjects of the law. In contrast to Exod 20:17, Deut 5:21 separates the wife from a neighbour's 'house', while other deuteronomic laws legislate the same protection (cf 15:18) or penalty (22:20–22) for a woman as for a man.
28. The same Hebrew word (*'ebed*) is used for both servant and slave. Translation depends on context.

Israel is (the people brought 'out of the land of Egypt, out of the house of slavery'). Israel's identity derives from God ('who brought you out of the land of Egypt'). The commands that follow instruct/inform the people how to relate to their God, to each other, and to creation (the Sabbath observance and the reason for it).[29] What we would call the sacred and secular or social laws of the Decalogue operate in unison. An Israelite who is loyal to God according to the Decalogue stipulations will, as a matter of course, be loyal to his neighbour according to the Decalogue stipulations. Similarly, an Israelite is loyal to his neighbour primarily because of loyalty to God. Otherwise any claim to be loyal to God and the covenant is a sham. Because the Decalogue functions as a prologue or introduction to the laws that follow in Exodus 21-23, this interrelationship is operative for all the laws of the covenant.[30]

A pointer to this is that the Decalogue contains a condensed version of a larger structure that can be identified in the Sinai narrative as well as in the book of Deuteronomy. It is widely accepted that this structure draws at least in part on ANE treaties that have three main elements; the identification of the suzerain and what he has done for the vassal, a proclamation of the stipulations or conditions of the treaty or covenant, a statement of the benefits (blessings) that will flow from loyalty to it and sanctions/curses that will be imposed for breach of it.[31] In the Sinai narrative, the first element is supplied by 19:3-6, the second element by the Decalogue and 'covenant code', and third element by 23:20-33. This tripartite structure also occurs in Exodus 20:2-6, where v 2 is the first element, vv 3-5a the second, and vv 5b-6 the third. These final verses contain the sanction (v

---

29. 'The self-introduction indicates that the entire Decalogue is a revelation of the divine name Yahweh' (Dozeman, *Exodus*, 479).
30. Much the same can be said for the place of the Decalogue in the book of Deuteronomy. This is so whether one judges the Decalogue was an early law code or a late addition or a summary of law (for a discussion of the positions see Dozeman, *Exodus*, 469-72). Another indication of the Decalogue's importance is that it is delivered by God directly to the people; it is only as a result of their request that Moses acts as mediator (Exod 20:20-21).
31. ANE treaty texts generally include the provision of copies for the participants and the name of witnesses (the national gods). The Sinai narrative refers to two tablets of law and Deut 31:9 reports that Moses wrote down the law. Leviticus makes reference to the writing down of laws. The biblical texts do not name witnesses.

5b) for breach of covenant law and blessing for adherence to it (v 6).[32] According to Jeffery Tigay, the term 'jealous' in 20:5a (*qanna'*) often refers to the 'fiery passions' of love and anger.[33] The husband in Numbers 5:14 who is jealous of his wife for alleged infidelity is a case in point. This is no doubt a reasonable interpretation and gains support from Hosea's marriage metaphor, even though the term is not used there to describe God's attitude to unfaithful Israel.

Within the context of Exodus this divine jealousy also, or perhaps more likely, refers to God's overriding concern that Israel and all peoples know 'I am the Lord'. All else depends on this, in particular right order in society. The worshippers of idols are those 'who reject (literally 'hate') me' in 20:5b. The attempt to replace the Lord with a false god can only lead to chaos and disorder and must, for the sake of truth and salvation, be removed.[34] The terms of the sanction do not specify whether it is because the first generation hates God or because each generation does. Nor does it say what kind of negative experience will be identifiable as punishment: there is no mention of an Israelite court being involved, the presumption is that only God can make a judgement in such cases. It is a highly rhetorical piece and its likely primary aim is to motivate people to shun the practices condemned. This motivational thrust is even more evident in v 6 where the assurance of steadfast love (*khesedh*) for those who love (*'ahab*) God forms a dramatic contrast to the punishment for hating God.[35] What is significant about this text is that God's steadfast love is bestowed on those who do the right thing in terms of the covenant—they show they are committed to the cause of establishing right order in society and creation and God's steadfast love is an expression of the divinity's unswerving commitment to them. God's *khesedh* provides the assurance that the faithful will enjoy the benefits that

---

32. Cf Polak, 'Theophany and Mediator,' 135. The connection with treaty alliances is also recognised by Watts, *Reading Law*, 108.
33. Jeffrey Tigay, *Deuteronomy* (JPS Commentary; Philadelphia: Jewish Publication Society, 1996), 65.
34. The command may originally have prohibited an image of the Lord (singular in verse 4a) and was subsequently reshaped to refer to images of false gods (plural in v 5a).
35. On the motivational function of rhetorical texts such as blessings and curses/sanctions, see Watts, *Reading Law,* 46-47.

righteousness brings. Blessing for the faithful and punishment for the wicked both reveal the nature and purpose of God.[36]

Because of their location in the Decalogue, the motivational clauses in Exodus 20:5b–6 (and Deut 5:9b–10) constitute a kind of template that is applied and adjusted in a variety of contexts. Examples within the Torah are Exodus 34:6–7 and Numbers 14:18; there are also numerous examples in the Latter Prophets and Psalms. Because Exodus 20:5b–6 (Deut 5:9b–10) establishes the principle that God is the one who blesses or punishes justly in each instance, each of the subsequent examples can claim that their particular application or interpretation is a manifestation of God's righteous rule of creation. The ratio of three to four generations of punishment to a thousand generations of steadfast love would appear to serve a number of aims. One is to appeal to divine authority to set a limit to the baneful consequences of evil acts (three or four generations of those who hate God), otherwise such baneful consequences of evil would become too much to bear. It is also a way of signaling God's mercy. A third is that the promise of enduring steadfast love to those who love God provides a powerful motivation to keep the covenant.

The blessing/sanction clauses in Exodus 20:5b–6 and 23:20–33 effectively form a frame around the Sinai covenant laws; they thus apply to all the laws, both sacral and social. A specific example of a sanction for breach of a sacral law is the ban (*kherem*, NRSV 'shall be devoted to destruction') in 22:20. An Israelite who worships another god becomes like the wicked nations in the land that are placed under the ban (cf Num 21:2–3; Deut 7:2, 26; Josh 6:17–18, 21; 10–11; 1 Samuel 15). Within the storyline the apostate nations are cast as a presence of evil in the land and God is utterly committed to removing such evil and providing a good land, like the good creation of Genesis 1. Hence, any Israelite who repudiates God shares the fate of the wicked nations. Specific examples for breaches of social laws occur in 22:21–24, 27 and 23:6–8.[37] What is striking is the motivational

---

36. The rather vague or general nature of the sanction in 20:7b probably has much the same aim, to focus attention on another key aspect of the knowledge of God, the divine name.

37. Exodus 22:24 warns that God's wrath will burn against those who abuse the powerless (widows and orphans). Like the ban this is an expression of God's commitment to eliminating sin and evil and establishing proper order in society. In the words of Stephen Butler Murray 'the wrath of God affirms that the love

clause attached to each case; like 20:5b–6, they emphasise that God will intervene personally to punish the lawbreakers. Two reasons are given. One is to protect those who are powerless and are therefore vulnerable to those with power. This power—the freedom that comes from being a member of the covenant community—should be used to empower others not to oppress them. The other, and more important reason, is to protect the true knowledge of the nature and purpose of God. Maltreating aliens is not the way God treated Israel as an alien in Egypt (22:21–24). Fleecing the poor is not being compassionate as God is compassionate (22:27). Perverting justice distorts the relationship that is supposed to exist between Israel's earthly court and the heavenly one where judgements are always righteous (23:6–8).[38] The heavenly judge will expose this kind of disorder by not declaring the guilty righteous (23:7). Just how this will be done is not spelt out in the legislation.

A number of commentators propose that the blessing and sanction clauses attached to many biblical laws indicate that the purpose of the law is not simply to ensure compliance but to inculcate an ethos, a right understanding and attitude to life.[39] Another way of saying this is that the Torah teaches how to acquire good habits and avoid bad ones; that is, to become virtuous. This makes sense, given that the overall thrust of the Torah is to show how human beings are able to be in the image and likeness of God, to be creative within the context that

---

of God will not tolerate evil, nor will the love of God provide amnesty toward that which is evil'. This would be 'a love without conviction or commitment' (*Reclaiming Divine Wrath: A History of a Christian Doctrine and Its Interpretation* [Bern: Peter Lang, 2011], 261).

38. Cf Walter J Houston, *Contending for Justice. Ideologies and Theologies of Social Justice in the Old Testament* (Library of Hebrew Bible/Old Testament Studies 428; London: T&T Clark, 2007), 115.

39. An important study here is Eckart Otto's *Theologische Ethik des Alten Testaments* (Theologische Wissenschaft 3,2; Stuttgart: Kohlhammer, 1994). Otto traces the development of a theological ethic in his reconstruction of the history of HBOT law. He notes a shift from blessings and curses/sanctions to paranesis (moral exhortation, as in Deuteronomy), a growing emphasis in later codes (Deuteronomy and the Holiness Code in Leviticus 17–26) on community solidarity (page 85), a commitment to righteousness (88–89) exemplified in compassion (84). God's actions on Israel's behalf enable it to share in God's holiness and be the mediator of divine holiness to all (cf Lev 19:17–18, 33–34) (257).

is appropriate for humanity.[40] Individual laws teach one to make the right distinction between good and bad behaviour, but individually and as a whole they also point to God as their source. Their ultimate purpose is to foster a right relationship with God.

That this is the case emerges also from a consideration of the Sinai narrative which can be read as an extended theophany or series of theophanies—manifestations of God. Exodus 19 commences with a spectacular *son-et-lumière* on the mountain, with thunder, lightning, smoke and an earthquake. This however proves to be a preliminary to a much more important kind of theophany—God's words, spoken first to all the people and then, at their request, to Moses. But this proclamation of the covenant stipulations, and the accompanying ritual and meal in Exodus 24, prepare in their turn for the third and most important kind of theophany—God dwelling among the people in a sanctuary (25:8). This amounts to a crossing of the boundary between divine and human that is expressly forbidden in the book of Genesis. It can only take place when God decrees and on God's terms and the text claims that both of these occurred at Sinai. God dwelling among the people is the goal of all that precedes in the Torah storyline. The book of Leviticus, with its instructions about how Israel is to conduct itself before the all holy God in its midst, effectively forms the centre of the Torah.

But the preparations for this event are interrupted by the golden calf apostasy in Exodus 32–34.[41] It is a well-established hypothesis that this is a complex piece, the work of a number of hands.[42] Nevertheless it is a story, the basic structural components can be identified in the initial setting of Israel at Mt Sinai, the critical factor that drives the story forward (Israel's apostasy), the climax or crisis of the story

---

40. Wenham sees Old Testament ethical thinking exemplified above all in the 'imitation of God' (*Story as Torah*, 105).
41. The analysis follows my article 'The Dynamics of the Golden Calf Story (Exodus 32-34),' *AusBR* 60 (2012): 18–31.
42. There are of course disagreements over the identification and extent of particular contributions. For a recent survey of the literature see Dozeman, *Exodus*, 688–700 (on Exod 32), 719–20 (on Exod 33), 734–39 (on Exod 34, in particular vv 6-7). Comparative texts are the version in Deut 9:7–10:11 and 1 Kgs 12:26–32 which reports that the first king of northern Israel, Jeroboam, set up bull calves in Bethel and Dan as rival shrines to the Jerusalem temple.

(God's intervention), and the resolution (renewal of the covenant).[43] It is remarkable that those responsible were able to integrate their contributions within the framework of this story so that it functions as part of the larger Torah storyline. Their achievement is all the more remarkable when one considers the following factors.

The story is located at a strategic point in the narrative, immediately after the covenant at Sinai where the terms of the foundational relationship between God and Israel are outlined. This has implications for a number of other relationships, especially between God and Moses, between Moses and Israel, between Israelites themselves, between God and the nations, and between Israel and the nations. These in turn have implications for the fulfillment of the promises to the ancestors, for how Israel is to carry out its God given mission, and for key notions such as truth and falsehood, reward and retribution, repentance and forgiveness. According to texts in the Sinai covenant such as Exodus 20:5b and 23:20-33, apostasy will reap a fearful response from God.[44] Yet, as with earlier examples of human failure and its retribution—for example, the garden story, the flood story—there needs to be a way out of a 'crisis' such as apostasy otherwise the whole Torah enterprise grinds to a halt and its authors and editors have effectively put themselves out of a job.[45] God's choice of Israel cannot be a mistake that must be erased; this would impugn the theology that the authors and editors of the Torah were committed to promoting. Hence the story of Israel has to continue

---

43. The constitutive elements of the story form, as identified in recent narrative criticism, are summarised by David N Gunn, 'Narrative Criticism' in *To Each Its Own Meaning. An Introduction to Biblical Criticisms and Their Application*, edited by Steven L McKenzie and Stephen R Haynes (Louisville, Ky.: Westminster/John Knox, 1993), 171-95. On p. 180 Gunn states 'Plot may be conceived as a simple model of exposition, conflict, climax, and resolution.' See also Booker, *The Seven Basic Plots*. 17-18.
44. Exod 22:20 is somewhat different in that it requires the presumably loyal covenant community to eliminate a member who is guilty of sacrificing to another god. Texts in Deuteronomy such as 4:26; 7:4 are even more severe than the Exodus texts cited, warning Israel that God will ensure it disappears from the land if it engages in worship of other gods.
45. As Francesca Aran Murphy sagely points out, the Bible is a comedy not a tragedy. Despite all the troubles and failures it promises 'all's well that ends well' (*The Comedy of Revelation. Paradise Lost and Regained in Biblical Narrative* [Edinburgh: T&T Clark, 2000]).

beyond the golden calf apostasy but in a way that is in accord with Torah requirements.

In my judgement those responsible for Exodus 32–34 achieved this via the skilful application of Torah criteria in a variety of forms—narrative, speech, law, comment. This enabled them to account for the sin of apostasy and incorporate it within the overall Torah storyline. It involved a reshaping of what we might call the 'standard' story form in which a key point of interest is *whether* the crisis will be resolved to the question of *how* it will be resolved.[46] The story thereby becomes more a catechesis or instruction, a move that enhances its location and function within the Torah. It also allows for considerable expansion of the storyline as it unfolds how the crisis is resolved. In the golden calf story, for example, this component effectively runs from 32:7 to Moses reporting the renewal of the covenant to the people in 34:32. It is here that one finds the dynamics of Exodus 32–34, an intricate and at times taut interplay between various elements. Not all of them can be examined here in detail. Hopefully the selection made is sufficient for the task in hand and the omissions are not critical.

Exodus 32–34 can be divided into the following sections: the report of Israel's apostasy in 32:1-6; first dialogue between God and Moses in 32:7-14 about its implications; report of Moses' intervention in 32:15-29; second dialogue between God and Moses in 32:30-34 (35); God's assessment of the people and their reaction in 33:1-6; report of the tent of meeting in 33:7-11; third dialogue between God and Moses in 33:12-23, presumably at the tent; God's instructions for Moses to bring two new tablets of stone up the mountain and Moses' compliance in 34:1-4; theophany in 34:5-9; renewal of the covenant and its stipulations in 34:10-28; report of Moses' return to the people in 34:29-35.

Israel's apostasy in 32:1-6 has been described as 'the nearest equivalent to the concept of original sin.'[47] Interestingly, there is a parallel with the sin in the garden story in that it arises because of a distorted perception of reality. The forty days during which Moses is on the mountain leads the people to conclude, wrongly, that he has

---

46. Other examples of this shift of focus are the garden story, the flood story and the murmuring stories in the wilderness, in particular the spy story in Num 13-14.

47. Cf M Aberbach and L Smolar, 'The Golden Calf Episode in Postbiblical Literature,' *HUCA* 39 (1968): 91-116 (as quoted in Dozeman, *Exodus*, 685).

abandoned them. The reader knows the people have no justification for this complaint because in 24:12-14 Moses instructs the elders to wait until he and Joshua return from the mountain where God is, while 24:17 reports that the people were able to see continually the fire of God's presence on the mountain. The reader also knows from the intervening narrative that God and Moses have been busy about Israel's welfare. But, as the garden story 'teaches,' human beings have a fatal tendency to distort the good order of relationships that God (and here Moses) has established. Moses, who 'brought us up out of the land of Egypt' has failed his role as leader and, by implication, so has his God. Hence they are justified in replacing them. Also, as in the garden story, acting on such flawed and false knowledge has divisive and chaotic consequences. Aaron is appointed leader in place of Moses, a disastrous move (cf Exod 32:2-4), while the people's covenant relationship with their creator and saviour is transferred to something they (and Aaron) have created. Aaron appears to try and retrieve the situation in a confused way by proclaiming a feast to YHWH. Is the bull calf meant to be an image of YHWH? For their part the people claim the thing they have made is in fact 'your gods who brought you up out of the land of Egypt' and engage in revelry.[48] It is a mocking, sarcastic portrait of the people and their priest.

The intense dialogue that follows in 32:7-14 tackles the implications of this crisis for Israel's relationship with God and Moses. Within the larger context, the people's sin is clearly a breach of the first two commands of the Decalogue, and for such a breach there is the accompanying sanction in 20:5b. As noted earlier 20:5b-6 functions as a kind of template or paradigm that is applied to a variety of situations in a variety of ways in the subsequent story of Israel. In 32:10 God pronounces or judges that the people are stiff necked and so worthy of destruction: coming from God this is by definition a just verdict. Being stiff necked or stubborn could be likened to hating and, according to 20:5b, those who hate God will be punished. An unusual feature of God's words is the reference in 32:7 to the people as 'your

---

48. The plural reference to 'your gods' fits the context of 1 Kgs 12:26-32 and its two calves rather than the single calf of the Exodus narrative. In terms of characterisation it may be meant to indicate the utter confusion that results from such sin; at the level of Torah, it may be a signal for the reader that the two texts are to be compared when reflecting on apostasy.

people' rather than 'my people', as occurs in 3:7, 10; 4:22 (my son); 6:7. This implies the people are no longer God's but still Moses' people. One might ask why a narrator would have God say this when 32:7 clearly indicates that God knows the people have rejected Moses? A number of answers are possible but I would suggest that this, along with the offer in 32:10 to make Moses the father of a new and 'great nation,' is part of a divine initiative that provides the opportunity or challenge for Moses to profess loyalty both to God and to the people even though they are apostates. These are two essential relationships in which Moses is engaged and, as commentators have noted, they form the foundations of the prophetic vocation.[49]

One might also ask why the all-knowing God of the story needs to put Moses to the test, as it were, in this way. Two reasons can be offered. One is that although God knows Moses' loyalty this needs to be 'revealed' to the reader as part of the story plot. Once this has been done Moses can function within the story as God's representative to the people. As already noted, stories of crisis and conflict within the Bible require someone or a group (a faithful remnant) that proves faithful and mediates God's salvation for the wicked many, otherwise the story cannot advance God's purpose or plan for humanity and creation. It must contain stories that point to the eventual triumph of good over evil otherwise its claims for God and God's purpose are compromised. Another reason is the Bible's portrayal of relationships between God and human beings as dynamic—we are called to be active participants in the work of salvation, not passive recipients. This means commitment in word and deed to God and God's purpose, particularly in times of crisis.

Moses displays such commitment in the second part of the dialogue (32:11–14). His loyalty to the people is shown by the way he does not deny they are his people despite their apostasy, nor accept the offer of becoming the 'father' of a new and great nation in v 10. His loyalty to God is evident in his concern for God's reputation among the Egyptians, an allusion to the recurring refrain in the plague narrative that Pharaoh and the Egyptians 'shall know that I am the Lord.' For the Egyptians (or anyone) to conclude that God acts 'with evil intent'

---

49. For example, as Jack R Lundbom states 'The true prophet is one who speaks for Yahweh and leads people in Yahweh's way' (*The Hebrew Prophets: An Introduction* [Minneapolis: Fortress, 2010], 146).

promotes a distorted perception and needs to be corrected. If God fulfills the promises to Israel's ancestors of descendants and land then the nations have no case. The dialogue ends with God changing his mind about consuming Israel (32:14). To have God revise an earlier decision through the intercession of a loyal servant such as Moses serves the plot of the story in that it points to its positive outcome and provides scope for telling how it comes about. It also enhances the dynamic and positive nature of the relationship between the two and fuels hope among the faithful in the efficacy of intercessory prayer.

Exodus 32:7-14 effectively appeals to Israel's role in a divine plan that involves the promise of descendants and land as well as God and Israel's relationship with the nations (represented here by Egypt). Moses' intercession invites a comparison with the one by Abraham in Genesis 18. There God does not appear to rule out the prospect of pardon for Sodom for the sake of fewer than ten righteous citizens, and the story concludes with the report that Lot was delivered because God 'remembered Abraham' (19:29).[50] These factors prompt one to ask whether in our text God spares Israel because of the intercession of righteous Moses (parallel to Abraham) or because there are some righteous ones still in Israel, or perhaps a combination of both. The description of Israel's apostasy does not support the second or third as the reason, hence the first is the likely one. A danger with this theology is that it could encourage a somewhat cavalier attitude to sin, punishment and forgiveness. That is, God is committed to the terms of the ancestral promises and to maintaining the divine reputation among the nations, whether Israel is loyal or not—they are essential components of the divine plan of salvation. Furthermore, the intercession of a leader like Moses will gain forgiveness even for Israel's worst breach of the covenant.

The subsequent narrative seeks to counter such a view by the way it depicts Moses exercising leadership of the people (32:15-29) and God responding to a key aspect of Moses' role as leader, that of intercessor (32:30-34:9). His leadership is immediately to the fore in 32:17-18 where it is Moses, not Joshua, who knows what the people are up to in the camp. His smashing of the tablets, presumably near the camp, is a sign to all that they have broken the covenant, a gesture that

---

50. As noted earlier, the dialogue between God and Abraham in 18:23-33 does not establish the number ten as the bottom line.

recalls God's word in 32:8, 'they have been quick to turn aside from the way that I commanded them.' He then singlehandedly destroys the calf. If it had divine power it would, as Pharaoh attempted in the plague narrative, oppose or resist God's representative. Moses makes the people drink/consume the powdered calf to show that the divine power they attributed to it was simply a figment of their distorted imagination.

Following these authoritative actions Moses turns his attention to Aaron (32:21-24). He shares Moses' relationship with God, being designated his assistant in the confrontation with Pharaoh (cf 4:14-17) and in the Sinai covenant (19:24). He and his sons are to be consecrated priests to minister before the Lord in the sanctuary that is to be built (Chapters 28-29).[51] Although Aaron, according to 32:5, is not guilty of the sin of apostasy he has failed to act as God and Moses' representative while they are on the mountain (cf. 24:13-14), and has allowed chaos and disorder to erupt.[52] The description in 32:25 of Israel running wild to the 'derision of their enemies' may, like Moses' earlier concern about the divine reputation among the Egyptians, refer to Israel's reputation among its adversaries.

Within this context of seeming total corruption the question arises; is there anyone who is loyal to God and Moses? The dramatic scene in 32:25-29 supplies a positive answer. In response to Moses' call 'all the sons of Levi' obey and execute three thousand. The scene may, as many propose, be an addition to the narrative: within the context of 32:3 that states all the people were involved the reader is left unsure whether the Levites repented of their part in the apostasy or had not taken part in it. Moreover, the executions create some tension with God's resolve in 32:14 not to destroy the people. Despite some unevenness the scene nevertheless plays an important role in the narrative. It teaches that relationship with God must take priority

---

51. Even though it is quite probable that the golden calf story originated independently of the surrounding priestly material in Exod 25-31 and 35-40, my comment is made in terms of the present narrative sequence.
52. Exodus 24:14 also mentions Hur as a representative. The lack of any reference to him in the calf story is an example of how biblical narrative focuses on what is relevant for the plot and ignores elements that are judged unimportant or would unduly complicate it if introduced. The focus on Aaron the priest provides a link with the surrounding narrative about the tent sanctuary and the priestly ministry there.

over all others. And so the Levites side with God and Moses 'at the cost of a son or a brother'. Such loyalty identifies the Levites as worthy of having a privileged relationship within God's saving plan, of being ordained 'for the service of the Lord' (32:29). Presumably this includes the flawed Aaron who is himself a 'son of Levi' as is Moses (cf 6:14-25). The text can thus be read as an example of another side of the relationship between the one and the many: in this case, the loyal Levites save the one disloyal Levite, Aaron. Some commentators see 32:25-29 as an enactment of divine punishment and even link it to the earlier scene where Moses makes the people drink water contaminated by the powdered calf. It is a case of trial by ordeal similar to the one described in Numbers 5:11-31. The three thousand executed by the Levites are those that the ordeal (drinking the powdered water) exposes as (the key) perpetrators.[53] In my opinion there is insufficient evidence in the text to support this proposal. As already noted Exodus 32:3 states that 'all the people' took part in the apostasy. The purpose of 32:25-29 is to provide a graphic teaching about the primacy of loyalty to God and its reward; however the deaths do testify to the gravity of the sin and raise the question how, granted that God has decided not to destroy the people, a right relationship can be restored and what Moses' role in it might be.

In keeping with the garden and flood stories the people cannot simply and immediately return to the situation before the apostasy. This would trivialize both their relationship with God and the nature of their sin. It would also imply that Moses' role is redundant. How does his relationship to the people relate to the one between them and God? These issues are addressed initially in Exodus 32:30-34 and developed in the remainder of the story. In 32:30 Moses informs the people that he will approach God in the hope of making atonement for 'your great sin'. Dozeman reads 32:32-33 (Moses' proposal and God's response) as installing a theology of individual guilt and salvation in place of the corporate theology that operates in the earlier chapters of Exodus and elsewhere in the HBOT. For example, the righteous Joseph is able to unite his family and save the world from starvation,

---

53. For example, Dozeman, *Exodus*, 699. Christopher Begg provides a thorough discussion of the issues in 'The Destruction of the Calf (Exod 32,20/Deut 9,21)', in *Das Deuteronomium: Entstehung, Gestalt und Botschaft: Deuteronomy: Origin, Form and Message,* edited by Norbert Lohfink (BETL 68; Leuven: University Press, 1985), 208-51.

whereas the evil of Pharaoh afflicts his people as well. Unlike Joseph, Moses cannot atone for the many because, as v 33 states, God punishes each sinner for his/her sin.[54]

The weakness with this reading is that it does not pay sufficient attention to the context. This second dialogue between God and Moses in 32:30–34 needs to be read in conjunction with the first in 32:7–14. There God proposes a plan and Moses counters with an alternative; here their roles are reversed. Moses proposes that if his request for the people to be forgiven is not acceptable to God then he should be eliminated. He is not offering himself in place of a people destined for destruction because God has already resolved not to destroy them in 32:14.[55] Rather, the thrust of the text is about leadership. Moses is effectively proposing that God appoint a new leader. In a modern context his ultimatum could look like an exercise in brinksmanship but in the biblical context it is an expression of his commitment to restoring a right relationship (through forgiveness) between God and Israel. Moses thinks that if God rejects his proposal this is a sign that he is failed leader, unable to intercede effectively for his people in their relationship with God. There is an intriguing and perhaps ironical allusion here to God's proposal in 32:10 to make Moses the leader of a new people; here Moses proposes a new leader for the people.

As Moses countered God's proposal in 32:7–14 by appealing to key aspects of the divine plan, so God now counters Moses' proposal by appealing to other key aspects. Exodus 32:33 is the first of what one could call three 'codes of divine conduct' in this story; the other two are 33:19 and 34:4–7. Each is an application and interpretation of an element or elements of the template text in 20:5b–6. The first draws on the punishment clause in 20:5b and has two applications here. One is to Moses whom God will not replace because his loyalty is evidence that he is not a sinner: in the words of 20:5b he is not one of 'those who hate me'.[56] Rather than be replaced he is commanded to lead the

---

54. Cf Dozeman, *Exodus*, 700, 712.
55. Cf Widmer, *Moses, God, and the Dynamics of Intercessory Prayer*, 333.
56. The image of a book in 32:32–33 may reflect the practice of recording the names and tasks of officials in ANE royal courts as a sign of their legitimacy and authority. If one were dismissed from office his/her name would be erased. Martin Noth saw a connection with the 'book of life' in Ps 69:28 in which the names of the righteous are inscribed (cf *Exodus* [Philadelphia: Westminster

people with the angel of 23:20-23 as guide. The second applies to the people. The references to 'the day' of visitation/punishment and 'their sin' in 32:34 are vague enough to include the golden calf apostasy and any future sin either as a people or as individuals.[57] No sin escapes the scrutiny of the divine judge who alone decides the appropriate day to 'visit' or punish the guilty in accord with 20:5b. The report in 32:35 that God struck the people is equally vague and it is not preceded by any announcement from God to the people. It may point to what is in store for the people on the day of God's visitation: a taste of things to come as it were. A plague can bring death or serve as a warning, as is evident in the plagues of the exodus story. Here it would seem to function as the latter.

Up to this point, all the dialogue has been between God and Moses but, if the relationship between God and Israel is to be restored and once again become dynamic, the people need to be informed and respond. To meet this need there is a second speech by God to Moses in 33:1-3 the content of which is then passed on to the people in vv 4-6. Because of their breach of the covenant it is not fitting that God address the people directly as is the case with the Decalogue (20:1); hence they are brought into the loop in this indirect manner. They learn that God is committed to the promise of land made to their ancestors (cf 'place' in 32:34), but they also learn that God will not journey with them. This is because they are 'stiff-necked' (cf 32:3) and so will inevitably sin and again stir the consuming wrath of God, as in 32:7-10. While these are indeed 'harsh words' (literally 'evil word') they are, coming from God, a just judgement that informs Israel of the truth. But they are made in the context of two positive statements by God toward Israel, one being the commitment to the promises, the other the order in 33:5 for Israel to strip off its ornaments and to wait until God decides 'what to do to you'. The story of the golden calf commences with the people refusing to wait on God and Moses, and taking matters into their own hands: they are now challenged to do the opposite. The implication is that if they obey there will be a positive outcome.

Press, 1962], 251).
57. The Hebrew verb *paqad* carries the basic sense of 'visit' or 'pay attention to' as well as the applied sense of 'punish'.

The words and actions of Moses earlier in the story have shown that the biblical notion of a right relationship is a dynamic one that grows when one partner responds appropriately to the challenge or command of another. The report in 33:6 of the people obeying God's directive is the first point in the narrative where they act in a correct way in their relationship with God. The implication is that a restoration of this relationship can now take place but, given the importance of Moses' role in the unfolding of this story, it is only fitting that it comes about through his mediation.

The tent of meeting provides a locus of the divine presence that matches the liminal state of Israel's relationship to God at this juncture in the story. Instead of on top of Mt Sinai the divine presence is now 'outside the camp' where the apostasy took place but visible to the people and accessible, although it is not stated that any of them enters the tent. According to 33:9 only Moses does so. Whenever he enters the tent and the pillar of cloud appears the people worship the Lord, a contrast to their earlier worship of the calf. In place of rebellious impatience they now patiently await what God has in store for them. Their attention to the actions of Moses shows that they accept his role as mediator and the initiatives that he takes.

Significantly, the third dialogue in the story between God and Moses, which takes place at the tent of meeting (33:12–23), focuses on correct knowledge and its implications for the key relationships that this story deals with. These are between God and Moses, between God and the people, and between Moses and the people, each of them being an aspect of the covenant at Sinai.[58] The dialogue is in two sections, vv 12–17 and 18–23. The first commences by resuming the preceding dialogue in which Moses is commissioned to lead the people to the land. The provision of 'my/an angel' (cf 32:34; 33:2) recalls 23:20–23 and Moses now requests to know who this will be. This is necessary so that a proper relationship can operate between them and that the journey to the land is conducted in an orderly manner. Moses justifies

---

58. James Muilenburg concludes from his study of knowledge within this passage that it 'implies the personal inward relationship' between Moses and God (cf 188 of 'The Intercession of the Covenant Mediator (Exod 31:1a, 12–17)', in *Hearing and Speaking the Word: Selections from the Works of James Muilenburg*, edited by TF Best (Scholars Press Homage Series; Chico, Calif: Scholars Press, 1984), 170–92.

the request by appealing to the right relationship between himself and God, as stated by the latter (v 12b).[59] It is notable that Moses reports God saying 'you have found favour (*khen*) in my sight'. This is very similar to Genesis 6:8 which reports that Noah 'found favour in the sight of the Lord'; the reason for this being given in 7:1—Noah alone of his generation was righteous. Hence one could say that the reason Moses has found similar favour is because he, like Noah, is righteous; his righteousness is evident above all in his conduct in the golden calf crisis.[60]

The last part of Exodus 33:13 indicates that Moses is not making this request for his own advantage but for the nation that is 'your people'. As has already been noted there are two sides to the Mosaic (and prophetic) vocation, namely, being at the service of God and of the people. The preceding dialogue, especially 33:5, signals that God has something positive in mind for Israel that relates to their journey Moses has been commanded to resume. Granted this, it is important to know the manner of God's relationship to Moses and Israel on this journey. One might think the promise of an angel in 33:2 meets this need but this angel's task is to go 'before you', marking out the journey. Moses seeks something more that cannot be denied to one who enjoys God's favour—namely, to know God and God's ways. This leads God to assure Moses that 'my presence (literally, 'my face') will go *with* you and I will give you rest' (33:14). Moses knows that this promise assures him and the people not only that they have found favour with God but also that their unique status as the chosen people will be made known to all the nations (33:16; cf 32:12-13). Israel is able to resume its role in the divine plan of universal salvation. Moses' request is granted (finds favour) because God knows Moses (v 17).

In light of the preceding dialogue it is not surprising that Moses asks to see God's glory (33:18). If God grants this further request then Moses (and the reader) are assured that the Sinai covenant has been fully restored. According to 24:15-18 the glory of the Lord settled

---

59. Even though there is no source text to check Moses' quotation, within the context one is meant to take it as a record of what God said to him at some point. Otherwise, he is making a fraudulent claim that would negate his petition, and this is obviously not the case.
60. But, like Noah's subsequent overindulgence, Moses later stumbles at the waters of Meribah. As Ps 143:2 says, 'no one living is righteous before you'.

on Mt Sinai, the cloud covered the mountain and Moses entered the cloud. Seeing God's glory at this point would therefore signal that Israel is restored to full covenant relationship with God. The request is granted but in a way that provides an important torah or instruction about divine glory and in what way the human being, represented by Moses, can experience it. To see the fullness of God's glory is to see God's face (cf 33:18, 20, 23) and this is not available to the human being. There are boundaries or limits to human experience and knowledge of the divine—the relationship between human beings and God—and these need to be protected by God for their welfare.[61] Moses' experience will therefore be limited to a theophany or manifestation of three aspects of divine glory: a parade of all God's goodness that will 'pass before you', a proclamation of the divine name, and of the 'code of divine conduct' (33:19).

One should note that these are not new revelations; they are present in somewhat different form in earlier Torah texts. Genesis 1:31 describes all of God's work in creation as 'very good', the divine name is revealed to Moses in Exodus 3:15, and the code of divine conduct is, like 32:33, an application of the template text in 20:5b–6, in this case 20:6.[62] The implication is that while Moses' experience of God is unique, as is every experience of the divine, it is of the one Lord of creation and history. It is also, as is every experience of the divine, not exclusively for Moses but an integral part of God's purpose for humanity and all creation. Hence Moses' encounter takes place within the context of the renewal of the covenant between God and Israel and Israel's vocation as a covenant people. The renewal involves the preparations in 34:1–4, the fulfillment of the promised appearance of God to Moses in 34:5–7, and the covenant and stipulations in 34:11–26. Although all this is reported as taking place only between God and Moses on the mountain, the narrative subsequently states that

---

61. Although Exod 24:10 states that Moses and others 'saw the God of Israel' on Mt. Sinai, the immediately following text focuses on what was under God's feet. Exod 33:11 states that God spoke with Moses 'face to face', that is, on intimate terms (so Dozeman, *Exodus*, 726-27).

62. While the terms for compassion (*khnn*) and mercy (*rkhm*) do not appear in 20:6 they are closely related to its reference to steadfast love (*khesedh*), as shown by the way this term occurs in conjunction with the adjective 'merciful' (and related term 'gracious') in the version of the code of divine conduct in 34:6-7.

Moses reported to the people 'all that the Lord had spoken with him on the mountain' (34:32).

The code of divine conduct in Exodus 34:6-7 should be read in conjunction with the preceding versions, namely 20:5b-6; 32:33 and 33:19.[63] It endorses them but in a manner appropriate to the context of covenant renewal after transgression.[64] This leads to the sequence of statements in 20:5b-6 being reversed. The covenant is renewed because of God's merciful (*rakham*) and gracious (*khannan*) nature—as proclaimed earlier in 33:19—that accepts a wayward people, and because God is utterly committed to the chosen people and the purpose for which they are chosen. The terms that express this commitment or loyalty are steadfast love (*khesedh*) to the thousandth generation—quoting 20:6—and faithfulness (*'emet*). Taken in isolation the references in 34:6 to God as merciful and gracious could give the impression that this is how God behaves no matter how bad Israel is. The following 'slow to anger' (or 'forbearing of anger') warns against such an assumption; there is a limit although it is not spelt out. Taken together, the sense could be that the anger of God is displayed in concert with God's mercy and compassion, as for example when God strikes down an evildoer or people threatening the helpless (22:21-24). In 20:6 God's steadfast love or covenant loyalty is directed to those 'who love me and keep my commandments'. There is no such specification in 34:6-7a; it claims that God keeps steadfast love for the thousandth generation (or 'thousands'). But, are these thousands only those who love and obey God (20:6) or those who are forgiven 'iniquity and transgression and sin'? If the latter were the case it would apply to just about everyone.

The subsequent statements appear to be formulated—at least in part—to counter such an understanding. The merciful and compassionate God who forgives is also the righteous judge who always brings the guilty to account.[65] There is little point having a

---

63. As John Van Seters notes, Exod 34:6-7 'is hardly adequate by itself as a confession of the deity's total relationship to humanity or to this people' (*The Life of Moses*, 351).
64. As it stands the subject of the verb 'proclaimed' in 34:5 and 6 could be the Lord or Moses. Nevertheless, the fact that God is the speaker in 32:33 and 33:19 and that Moses bows down and worships at this encounter with the divine (v 8) point to the Lord as the subject.
65. Widmer states that 'YHWH's visiting of Israel's iniquities is not inconsistent with

forgiveness clause in this code of conduct if there is no guilty party to forgive. The second part of v 7 adds the rider that God will by no means 'clear the guilty' but will visit the iniquity of the parents on the children to the third and fourth generation. In the wake of the calf apostasy, this is a vital clause, a motivation not to repeat that sin. The most likely sense of the verb 'visit' in this context is that God will 'examine/assess' the iniquity or sins of each person.[66] It is widely recognized that the Hebrew term for iniquity (*'avon*) can include punishment or the consequences that follow a particular transgression. One can therefore read the second part of 34:7 as an assurance that God will assess or examine the sins/iniquity of each person and his or her descendants in each of the generations listed before distributing mercy or punishment.[67] This aligns it more closely with 20:5b and 32:33. In short, one's understanding of 34:6-7 is enhanced by comparing it with the preceding versions of the code of divine conduct in 20:5b-6; 32:33; 33:19. The location of Exodus 34:6-7 in the context of Moses' passionate appeal on Israel's behalf may explain why it tends to be the version of the divine code of conduct invoked in subsequent texts. A notable case within the Torah is the spy-story in Numbers 14; others are Joel 2:13; Jonah 4:2; Psalms 86:15; 103:8; 145:8; Nehemiah 9:17; 2 Chronicles 30:9; less explicitly Psalms 111:4; 112:4; 116:5; Nehemiah 9:31. A version more in line with Exodus 20:5b-6 is Nahum 1:3, within the context of a prophecy of Nineveh's doom.

Exodus 34: 8-9 provides further evidence of Moses' solidarity with the people and his continuing intercession of their behalf. In asking for their forgiveness Moses, like God, displays a true knowledge of his people, describing them as 'stiff-necked', a signal that, despite gestures of repentance (33:6), there is an ongoing propensity for rebellion.

His fundamental covenant loyalty' (*Moses, God, and the Dynamics of Intercessory Prayer*, 183 and summary on 202). Also Matthias Franz, *Der barmherzige und gnädige Gott. Die Gnadenrede vom Sinai (Exodus 34, 6-7) und ihre Parallelen im Alten Testament und seiner Umwelt* (BWANT 160; Stuttgart: Kohlammer, 2003), 187 ('In der Endfassung ist das barmherzige Wesen Jhwhs der Grund für den neuen Bund').

66. See the discussion in Widmer, *Moses, God, and the Dynamics of Intercessory Prayer*, 199-201, and Franz, *Der barmherzige und gnädige Gott*, 141-43.

67. The addition of 'the children's children' to the formulation in 20:5b adds to this sense of careful examination of each line of descent.

Erik Aurelius and John Van Seters have noted a parallel here with the flood story where humanity's evil inclination is the reason why God unleashes the flood (Gen 6:5-7) but also the reason why God vows never to do so again (8:21). Exodus 34:6-7 is a measure of the Torah's conviction of God's unconditional commitment to Israel and humanity despite their inability to change.[68]

Although the law code in 34:11-26 may have originated independently it fits the context of the golden calf apostasy well.[69] It teaches how Israel is to be exclusively devoted to God. Within the larger context it serves as a restatement of key elements in the Decalogue (20:2-17) and the Covenant Code (20:22-23:33).[70] Apostate Israel is called to maintain the same loyalty to God demanded in these earlier codes and will be challenged at each step of its subsequent journey to stay loyal to the covenant that God has renewed and to its role within God's saving purpose. All the divine epithets invoked in 34:5-7; that God is merciful, gracious, steadfast in love and faithful, forgiving sin and punishing the guilty after examination (visiting), testify to God's commitment to this relationship and its ultimate purpose—that the whole world may come to know 'I am the Lord' (cf 33:19; 34:5).

With the covenant renewed the narrative can resume preparations for God's dwelling among the people (Exodus 35-40). The construction of the sanctuary provides an opportunity for the people to be active and creative in their relationship with God and with one another. As long as they follow the blueprint provided by God and keep the divinely ordained rhythm of six days' work and Sabbath rest (35:2-3) they will be acting in the image and likeness of God as described in the account of creation (cf 31:16-17).[71] The subsequent narrative

---

68. Cf Erik Aurelius, *Der Fürbitter Israels. Eine Studie zum Mosebild im Alten Testament* (CB 27; Stockholm: Almqvist & Wiksell, 1988), 124-25; Van Seters, *The Life of Moses*, 353.
69. Franz proposes the plausible thesis that the present text is a combination of a tradition that emphasises divine appearance to which 34:6-7 belonged (T_S; Gottesschau Tradition), and one that emphasises divine laws to which 34:11-26 belonged (T_G; Gebotstradition) (cf. *Der barmherzige und gnädige Gott*, 158-62).
70. According to Childs, for the redactor of the present text 'The laws in ch. 34 represented a convenient abbreviation of both these collections of laws on which the covenant is to be renewed' (*Exodus*, 608). The respective laws to which Childs refers are the Decalogue and the Covenant Code. Cf also Dozeman, *Exodus*, 741-42.
71. Blenkinsopp (*The Pentateuch. An Introduction to the First Five Books of the Bible*

reports how the men and women, in contrast to their behaviour in the golden calf story, contribute to its construction in accord with instructions. God enables the finest artistic work by bestowing 'skill and understanding' (36:1-2).

The construction completed, God 'descends' the mountain of revelation to dwell among the people (40:34-38). This intimate entry of the divine into the human realm is nicely captured in the way the vertical symbolism of Mt. Sinai is rendered horizontal in the sanctuary and its cult, as outlined by Mary Douglas:[72]

Mt Sinai	Animal Offering	Tabernacle
Summit or head, cloud like smoke, God came down to top, access for Moses (Exod 19:20-2)	Entrails, intestines, genital organs (washed) at the summit of the pile	Holy of holies cherubim, ark, and testimony of covenant
Perimeter of dense cloud, access restricted to Aaron's two sons, and seventy elders, (Exod 19:1-9	Midriff area, dense fat covering, kidneys, liver lobe, burnt on altar	Sanctuary, dense clouds of incense symmetrical table and lampstand, restricted to priests
Lower slopes, open access	Head and meat sections, access to body, food for people and priest	Outer court, main altar, access for people
Mountain consecrated (Exod 19:23)	Animal consecrated (Leviticus 1-7)	Tabernacle consecrated (Leviticus 16)

[New York: Doubleday, 1992] 218), and more recently Dozeman (*Exodus*, 762) identify a number of texts that parallel passages in the creation account (cf. Gen 1:31 and Exod 39:43; Gen 2:1 and Exod 39:32; Gen 2:2 and Exod 40:33; Gen 2:3 and Exod 39:43).

72. Mary Douglas, *Leviticus as Literature* (Oxford: Oxford University Press, 1999), 79.

The impression gained from reading Exodus 25–31; 35–40 is that the sanctuary is a point in the story of creation that recaptures the union between heaven (represented by the top of the mountain) and earth (represented by its base) of the first creation account. It is a place in the disturbed post-flood creation where God and the people can meet. Because the sanctuary is portable it can also be any place where God decides (in the pillar of cloud) to stop on the journey to the land. Because it is the manner of God's presence among the people on their journey, there is the implication that another form of divine presence may be established once the people enter and occupy the land. The story of Israel to this point has presented them as a fractious 'stiff-necked' people who are nevertheless capable of repentance (33:4–6). They have made a completely distorted image of divinity in the golden calf. But, by following God's instructions they have constructed a perfect symbol of divine presence in the tent sanctuary. How will they conduct themselves before God in their midst? The book of Leviticus undertakes to instruct Israel in the right and proper way.

4

Books of Leviticus and Numbers

The Book of Leviticus

It has long been recognised that the book of Leviticus is priestly literature, that it was most likely put together in the post-exilic period, and that it was incorporated into the emerging Torah at a late stage. This tended to create an impression that it is of lesser importance than other parts of the Torah. More recent focus on the present text has resulted in something of a reversal; a growing tendency to see it as a key piece within the Torah, even its centerpiece.[1] It provides instructions that are central for the relationship between God and Israel, between Israel and creation (represented by the land), between Israelites themselves, and between Israel and the nations. The instructions are to enable each of these relationships to function and develop in a proper manner. As an integral part of a larger Torah narrative Leviticus also needs to be read against the background of the preceding narrative and the presentation provided there of each of these relationships.

The term 'holy' (*qadesh*) permeates the book of Leviticus. It is generally agreed that the basic meaning of holiness in the HBOT is to be 'other' or 'separate', also 'to be whole'. God is the holy one par excellence because God is utterly 'other', separate from anything in creation, a whole that is not comprised of parts. However, Walter Kaiser argues that the holiness of God can also express 'the righteousness and goodness of Yahweh and that became the basis

---

1. Cf for example, Watts, *Reading Law*, 59; also 98 of F García López, 'La place du Lévitique et des Nombres dans la formation du Pentateuque,' in *The Books of Leviticus and Numbers*, edited by Thomas Römer (BETL 215; Leuven; Dudley, MA: Peeters, 2008), 75–98.

for the morality and ethics taught in the Old Testament'.[2] On this understanding holiness, depending on context, could refer to how a person, animal or thing represents or points to the divinity (the other) in some way; it could also describe a person's moral status (being in a right relationship with God and neighbour).

These two senses of holiness should not be separated because a relationship is always with someone or something that is 'other'. Building a right relationship involves respect for appropriate boundaries or differences and avoidance of, or dismantling of, inappropriate ones. An intimate relationship between human beings can only be established when the 'otherness' of each is honoured.[3] Hence the relationship between a human being and God as the utterly 'other' or holy one is the ultimate or foundational relationship and must of course be founded on God's righteousness. In the book of Exodus Moses is instructed to build a dwelling for God in the midst of the people. The book of Leviticus is devoted to fostering a proper and intimate relationship between Israel and the all holy one who is now in its midst. All other relationships are based on and draw their legitimacy from this foundational one. Hence the 'rules of engagement' need to be outlined carefully and followed faithfully.

Although Leviticus most likely stems from priestly circles it is not primarily about priests. It commences with an address to all Israel, signaling that all are called to be holy. The cultic regulations that follow are likewise addressed to all Israel; the specific instructions for the priests only commence in 6:9. This universal call to holiness is a prominent feature in Leviticus 19, which has itself been identified as the 'central turning point' of the book and as a centerpiece of HBOT ethical teaching.[4] While this is true one can add that ethical and

---

2. Walter C Kaiser Jr, *Toward Old Testament Ethics* (Grand Rapids: Zondervan Publishing House, 1983), 143.
3. The statement in Gen 2:24 that man and woman 'become one flesh' does not contradict this. It is an expression of the intimate union that marriage is meant to bring about between two individuals. This union enhances the uniqueness of each partner.
4. As the 'central turning point' see page 7 of Jacob Milgrom's *Leviticus. A Book of Ritual and Ethics* (A Continental Commentary; Minneapolis: Fortress Press, 2004) and his outline there of the structure of the book. As a centrepiece of ethical teaching see Otto, *Theologische Ethik*, 242. Otto also points to a number of connections between Leviticus 19 and the Decalogue.

cultic conduct are closely connected in Leviticus. Each contributes in its divinely designated way to the holiness of the relationship between God and Israel. The chapter commences with a call to all Israelites that 'You shall be holy, for I the Lord your God am holy' before providing a (selective) list of the 'others' towards which they are commanded to relate in a godlike (holy) way—people, animals, things, land and its produce. The godlike, holy or 'other' nature of these relationships is underscored by the repeated refrain 'I am the Lord' after each command. Of particular note for this study are vv 15 and 36 where the term *tsedeq* (righteousness) occurs. Verse 15 forbids partiality towards the poor or deference to the great in matters of dispute; it is only on the basis of a relationship of righteousness (NRSV 'with justice') in each case that just judgements will be made. Verse 36 may reflect a more technical use of the term *tsedeq* to designate 'honest' forms of measurement but one can see the same principle in operation. God demonstrated righteousness in relationship with Israel by delivering it from slavery in Egypt. How could any Israelite therefore treat another dishonestly in business relationships? To tip the scales ever so slightly in one's favour is disloyalty to God. An implication of v 36 is that the relationship between God and Israel touches all areas of life, even those that may appear least significant.

Each part of creation plays its divinely designated role in fostering the foundational relationship between God and Israel, reminding it at every turn of the need to be holy before the all holy one. Certain people (priests), actions/events (that one initiates or that happen to one), animals (clean and unclean) and things are 'set apart' on God's authority so that the relationship can function effectively. A graphic example of this is Numbers 16 where a rebellious group of Levites claims that all should have equal access to the presence of God in the sanctuary because 'all the congregation is holy' (16:3). But there are various categories of holiness and an aim of the Torah is to instruct Israel and the reader in this. While the congregation is holy because it has been chosen by God (cf Deut 7:6) this does not mean everyone has access to the presence of God in the sanctuary. Some are 'set apart' (designated as 'holy') on God's authority for this role. As Moses states in 16:5, God chooses 'who will be allowed to approach him' in the sanctuary—namely Aaron the priest and his descendants. Those who reject this instruction end up with a fatally distorted perception of relationships.

What is good for the relationship between God and Israel is also good for all other relationships that Israel has or may develop—among themselves, with foreigners, the land and its produce, the animal kingdom. While the teaching about some of these may seem strange to modern readers, they make sense within the context of Leviticus. For example, unclean or 'detestable' (NRSV) animals are not 'dirty' in our sense of the term. According to the garden story there are divinely designated boundaries (the commands about access to the trees) that mark out the environment within which the human being can flourish and outside of which it cannot. In line with this Leviticus permits the use of certain animals for food and for the sacrificial cult while prohibiting others. Both categories are 'set apart' in an appropriate manner, thus both are holy in that they play their designated roles in the relationship between God and Israel.[5]

The Israel addressed in the book of Leviticus is the one guilty of the golden calf apostasy. Even though it has been called to mediate God's blessing to the nations, this 'original sin' exposes it as flawed like the rest of humanity portrayed in the Torah narrative. According to Genesis 9:1–5, God permits Noah and his descendants to eat of all animals in creation which will live in fear and dread of the human being. This reflects the disorder in the relationship between humanity and creation that human beings unleashed through their transgressions. Leviticus announces two developments in relation to this post-flood scenario. One is that only certain animals (mainly the domesticated herbivores such as sheep, cattle and goats) can be used for food; the rest are set apart. Fear and dread in the animal kingdom is diminished. The second is that Israel can now kill designated animals as part of the sacrificial cult. According to the faith claim of Leviticus, the proper performance of the cult is not only an appropriate way to honour God as 'the other' but it also heals and restores Israel's relationship with God when this has been damaged through intentional or unintentional sin.[6] What in Genesis 9:1–5 is

---

5. Mary Douglas states that the dietary laws in Leviticus are 'like signs which at every turn inspired meditation on the oneness, purity and completeness of God. By rules of avoidance holiness was given a physical expression in every encounter with the animal kingdom and at every meal' (*Purity and Danger*, London: Routledge & Kegan Paul, 1966), 57.
6. The common Hebrew term for sin (*khattah*) carries the basic sense of 'missing the mark'. Hence it can refer to a culpable breach of a covenant law or an inadvertent breach of a ritual law, such as touching a dead body.

effectively a sign of the disorder and death that human beings bring into the world becomes, according to Leviticus, a means of restoring right order and blessing.[7] As with the notion of righteousness, the Torah implies there are levels of holiness or, perhaps better, stages in the growth of holiness. God's initiative in establishing the Sinai covenant renders Israel holy or set apart to a degree, as does the renewal of the covenant with a repentant Israel. Without it there could not be a real relationship. But, as noted in the analysis of the golden calf story, relationships are dynamic and meant to grow towards perfection, to be healed when damaged and to be restored when broken. The overall thrust of Leviticus and its contribution to the notion of righteousness is well summed up by Mann:[8]

> Leviticus offers not only a way in which righteousness may be followed, but also a way by which *un*righteousness may be remedied. It holds before Israel the command, 'You must be holy', but also the promise, 'atonement shall be made for you' (16:30). The new way of righteousness now includes a way out of sin.

Leviticus, like other books in the Torah, is part of a larger whole, and the Torah itself is part of the larger story of Israel and humanity. While the book calls Israel to be holy in the image and likeness of God's holiness, it does so within the context of a flawed and sinful society and a still troubled post-flood creation. Even though the fear and dread of humanity in the animal kingdom is diminished, certain ones are slaughtered for food and for sacrifice. The relationship between humanity and creation as envisaged in Genesis 1:28-29 is not yet in sight. This raises the question whether the sacrificial cultic system of Leviticus is meant to continue if and when Israel (and the rest of humanity) achieves the holiness and righteousness desired by God. In the eschatological vision of Isaiah 2:2-4, the nations do not come on pilgrimage to Zion to sacrifice but to be taught by God. Nor does

---

7. For a fuller treatment of the connection between Leviticus and the early chapters of Genesis see Suzanne Boorer, 'The Earth/Land ('*eretz*) in the Priestly Material: The Preservation of the "Good" Earth' and the Promised Land of Canaan Throughout the Generations', *AusBR* 49 (2001): 19-33.
8. Mann, *The Book of the Torah*, 121.

the portrait of a restored city and people in Isaiah 4:2–6 mention the restoration of the sacrificial cult. In contrast, Ezekiel 40–48 provides a 'law of the temple' (43:12) and plans for a new temple, replete with sacrifices, so that the people may hopefully, finally, put away their abominations that resulted in the exile and learn to live with God in their midst. While the majority of rabbis hoped for a reestablishment of temple sacrifices in the (messianic) age to come a minority held that the sacrifices 'apply only in this world, but the practices of charity and civil justice apply both in this world and in the next'.[9]

The Book of Numbers

Even though the book of Numbers has long been recognised as a compilation from disparate traditions, there is presumably some organisational principle or principles behind it. Denis Olson makes a good case for accepting two major sections in the book: Numbers 1–25 recounts the wilderness journey of the exodus generation and its demise, while 26–36 recounts the emergence of a new (conquest) generation that will inherit the land as long as it does not follow the ways of its parents.[10] The first part opens with a census of the military strength of Israel in preparation for the conquest of the land. The second part (26) also commences with a census, one that reveals no surviving members of the first one. They have all died in the wilderness in accord with the sentence God pronounced against them for their conduct in the spy story of Numbers 13–14 (cf 14:29). This story is therefore a key feature of Numbers 1–25 and of the book's overall structure.[11] It represents Israel's most serious rebellion after the golden calf apostasy in Exodus 32–34 and the most serious one within the book of Numbers itself. Like Exodus 32–34 it makes an important contribution to the Torah's presentation of the relationship

---

9. So Abraham Joshua Heschel, *Heavenly Torah As Refracted through the Generations* (London: Continuum, 2005), 695.
10. Denis T Olson, *The Death of the Old and the Birth of the New. The Framework of the Book of Numbers and the Pentateuch* (Brown Judaic Studies 71; Chico, CA: Scholars Press, 1985).
11. Cf Olson, *The Death of the Old and the Birth of the New*, 143. Even though some disagree with Olson's understanding of the structure of the book, the importance of the spy story is acknowledged. See for example the recent study by Won W Lee, *Punishment and Forgiveness in Israel's Migratory Campaign* (Grand Rapids, MI: Eerdmans, 2003), 217.

between God and Israel and, because of this, of a number of other key relationships that featured in the golden calf apostasy—between God and Moses, between Moses and Israel, between God and the nations, between Israel and the nations.

Numbers 13-14 tells of Israel's third 'murmuring in the wilderness' after the departure from Sinai. The first one is the brief report in 11:1-3 of Israel complaining about its misfortunes, the second is the story in 11:4-35 where the people complain about the food provided and Moses in turn complains about the burden of the people. God's response is to briefly bestow a portion of Moses' spirit on 72 elders, a sign of the power of the spirit that he himself has received. These murmurings involve all the people, as does the spy story. Between 11:4-35 and the spy story there is the account of Aaron and Miriam's challenge to Moses' unique relationship with God (Numbers 12). While their 'murmuring' against Mosaic leadership is different to the preceding episodes that involve all Israel it provides a suitable prelude to the spy story and the leadership role that Moses plays in it.

The murmuring stories in Numbers form part of a longer narrative thread in the Torah; depending on one's assessment of the evidence the thread can be traced back to the account of the victory at the sea (cf Exod 14:10-14) or to the episode involving bitter water in the wilderness of Shur (15:22-26). But, whereas Israel is punished for its murmuring in the book of Numbers this is not the case in Exodus. The difference is presumably due to the Sinai covenant that comes between these two narrative blocks.[12] Once Israel is invited into an intimate relationship with God and accepts there are consequences. With rights or privileges (cf Exod 19:3-6) come responsibilities (cf the Decalogue in Exod 20:1-17 and the 'Covenant Code' in 21:22-23:33) and the prospect of blessing for obedience, punishment for disobedience (Exod 20:5b-6; 23:20-33). The murmuring stories in Numbers take place within this context. A reader of the Torah expects Israel to be punished for its rebellion in Numbers 13-14 and this focuses attention on the nature of the punishment and what it reveals about God. The reader also expects the story to explore the relationship between punishment and mercy, given that the option of destroying Israel is ruled out in Exodus 32:14, as it has to be for the story of Israel (and humanity) to continue.

---

12. Following Dozeman, *Exodus,* 350; and Olson, *Numbers* (Interpretation; Louisville: John Knox Press, 1996), 63.

As with the preceding examples, the murmuring motif in the spy story involves a failure or unwillingness to trust and follow God's saving plan as revealed to Moses. Within the context of the Sinai covenant, such a response is culpable. Once true knowledge is rejected it has to be replaced—the void needs to be filled—and according to the Torah this inevitably involves a skewed perception of the reality in question. In this case it is the promised land and its inhabitants. In a clear echo of the first creation account (Gen 1:31), Joshua and Caleb describe the land accurately as 'very good' (Num 14:7), but the other spies see it as a land 'that devours its inhabitants' rather than provides life (13:32). This is akin to denying creation is good. Joshua and Caleb also give a true picture of Israel as an invincible army with God at its head (13:30; 14:8–9). In contrast, the other spies see themselves and Israel like grasshoppers facing giants. Given their preceding claim that the land devours its inhabitants, to speak of them as invincible giants is absurd. The author mocks the spies and an Israel that accepts such a contradictory report about the land.

When relationships start to unravel an almost inevitable consequence is to play the blame game, as Israel does in 14:2–3. Not surprisingly, it also skews this badly. God has brought the people to this point in the journey not to give them the land but to 'fall by the sword'. As God's designated leaders and intermediaries, Moses and Aaron are also to blame. Given the context of the Sinai covenant and all that God has done for Israel, the one who is really to blame is Israel itself. As in the preceding stories of Israel's journey through the wilderness, the real enemy is not outside (the giants) but within. The seriousness of the situation is further underscored by the proposal to 'choose a captain, and go back to Egypt' (14:4). Not only is this a rejection of 'captains' Moses and Aaron but also of God and God's plan. At least in the golden calf story, Israel felt that it needed someone (gods) 'who shall go before us' (Exod 32:1). Here the people play God, choosing a leader and following their own plan.

A dialogue follows between God and Moses in 14:11–35 that parallels the earlier ones between them in the golden calf story. In verse 11 God puts a question to Moses: will any amount of signs bring 'this people' (within the story, the exodus generation) to change their ways? God, as presented in the golden calf story, knows that they cannot or will not, at least not in a lasting manner, having declared they are a 'stiff-necked' people and telling Moses that 'when the day comes for punishment, I will punish them for their sins' (Exod 32:34). Moses has personally experienced this rebelliousness in the murmuring stories of Numbers 11-12. The fact that he does not answer God's question in 14:11 implies he knows the answer and accepts it. In 14:12 God proposes a way out of the impasse—replacement of the exodus generation with a new nation and Moses as its founder and leader. This is the same kind of proposal made in Exod 32:10 and, as there, it is the point at which Moses acts as intercessor. One senses that the authors/editors of the text drew on the practice of advocates in royal and law courts in Israel and in the wider ANE—but with appropriate changes to serve the Torah's purpose.[13] It is significant that in neither instance does Moses question or try to change God's judgment about what is evil and what is good. According to the Torah this is not the role of a loyal advocate or intercessor because it would impugn its portrayal of God, casting Moses as a lawyer arguing the rights or wrongs of an action with God. The role of an intercessor comes into play after judgement has been made with its accompanying reward/ blessing or retribution/punishment. This is the area where a plea can be entered on behalf of those sentenced. But, in deference to the sovereign's authority and power, negotiations take place around an initial proposal that he or she makes and it is the sovereign who has the final say. Such is the case in this passage. An advocate like Moses will of course seek to be loyal to the two relationships involved in such a negotiation—his relationship to the sovereign (God) and his relationship to Israel.

As in the golden calf crisis, Moses responds by foregrounding the primary (and ultimate) reason for all that God says and does—that all may know God and God's righteous purpose. In doing so Moses expresses his complete commitment to God and God's purpose. Another parallel with the golden calf crisis is that Moses does not take up God's proposal in 14:12; it is a sign of his complete commitment to the people. There is however an added element in Moses' response

---

13. For a recent discussion and assessment of theories about the composition of 14:11-25, see Aurelius, *Der Fürbitter Israels*, 130-41. He notes that most analysts regard the advocacy scene as an expansion by one or more deuternonomistic editors (132). Nevertheless, the present text has been carefully put together to advance a complex yet important theology, which is the focus of my analysis.

that addresses the particular context of the spy story. The Egyptians will circulate an evil report about God to the inhabitants of the land, this will lead them to conclude—another distorted perception—that God did not have the power to bring the people through the wilderness to the land and therefore killed them (14:16).[14] In short, it will be interpreted by the nations not as a punishment for Israel's infidelity but as a lack of divine power—that the Lord is not a god. As in the description of the unfaithful spies, one senses a mocking tone here. It paints a contradictory and bizarre picture of a god who can wield divine power to bring people out of Egypt but then kills them because he runs out of steam. Moses does not say God's sentence in 14:12 is wrong, rather it will be perceived by the nations in this completely distorted and evil way and thereby impede God's purpose that all may know 'I am the Lord'. How can the sentence against Israel be presented in a way that advances God's purpose and prevents the nations construing a false understanding of divine power? The criteria for doing so have been provided in what I described as the 'code of divine conduct' texts—namely Exodus 20:5b–6; 32:33; 33:19 and 34:6–7. Exodus 20:5b–6 serves as a kind of template that the other passages apply in various ways to varying situations. The Torah claim is that in each case the application is just and merciful.

Numbers 14:18 refers to the version in Exod 34:6–7, which is understandable: like the spy story it is about Israel's rejection of God, it also provides the basis on which God renews the covenant with Israel and maintains it despite their ongoing murmuring. God is indeed slow to anger, gracious and forgiving and steadfast in love to a stiff-necked people. Hence Moses concludes his response in Num 14:13–19 with a plea that God display that same steadfast love by forgiving Israel also this time.[15] But as the character Moses knows—and the reader needs to remember—the terms of the covenant renewal in 34:11–26 are as demanding as the Decalogue and remind Israel that the Lord is a jealous God (cf 34:14), a clear allusion to 20:5a and its

---

14. The Hebrew of 14:13–16 is somewhat awkward; the sense given here follows the discussion in Baruch A Levine, *Numbers 1-20. A New Translation with Introduction and Commentary* (AB 4A; New York: Doubleday, 1993), 365–66.
15. Even though the Exodus text does not actually have the word 'forgive', Num 14:19 implies that Moses understands the covenant renewal as an act of forgiveness in accord with Exod 34:7a.

warning of punishment for 'those who hate me' in 20:5b. Although 'hate' and 'despise' are different verbs in Hebrew their meaning is similar, as indicated by their occurrence in a synonymous parallelism in Proverbs 5:12. The question in Numbers 14:11 is how long can Israel continue to despise God before punishment is decreed? These contextual and textual factors impinge on the reply that God gives to Moses.

An intriguing feature of 14:18 is that although Moses invokes Exodus 34:6-7 he does not cite the full text. The Numbers' version lacks the following phrases: 'a God gracious and merciful', 'and faithfulness', 'and sin', 'keeping steadfast love to the thousandth generation', and 'and the children's children'. The shorter Numbers' version has two sets of three statements:[16] the first set is about God's steadfast love and forgiveness, the second about God's judgment of the guilty and the visiting of parents' iniquity on their offspring. The result is a text evenly balanced between forgiveness and punishment. The reason for this may be that the earlier texts are God's words whereas in Numbers 11:18 Moses makes an appeal on the basis of God's words. The evenly balanced nature of the verse acknowledges that God is the one who decides the relationship between forgiveness and punishment, their respective 'distribution' in each instance. This was the case in the golden calf story and, one may presume, will also be the case here.

God's reply is to forgive the people as Moses asked (14:20), that is, to forgive them within the terms of 14:18 and its links to Exodus 34:6-7 and the template text in the Decalogue. It also means to forgive them for the sake of advancing the divine purpose as Moses outlines it in Numbers 14:13-16. Moses, as a loyal servant of God and advocate of the people, has faithfully presented the issues that need to be taken into account. The details of God's forgiveness are set out in 14:21-35. That this is the definitive ruling on the fate of 'this people' is indicated by the divine oath with which v 21 commences, and with which v 28 also commences.[17] It is made within the context of God's

---

16. As indicated by the accent markers in the Masoretic text. Some versions (LXX, Samaritan Pentateuch, Targum Onkelos) have 'and faithfulness' 'and sin' but given the well-balanced MT text, these may be attempts to align Numbers more closely to the Exodus version.
17. Cf Widmer, *The Dynamics of Intercessory Prayer*, 312.

unswerving resolve 'that all the earth shall be filled with the glory of the Lord'. It is the divinely decreed and therefore just way in which this people will contribute to and promote God's universal purpose.

Verse 22 takes up God's opening words in vv 11-12, indicated by the reference to the people who have seen all the signs that God has done and yet refused to obey. It also takes into account Moses' reply and prayer. This people have had the privilege of being the first—within the Torah narrative—to see God's glory, the same glory that is to fill the whole earth. Having repeatedly misrepresented and repudiated the God of glory thus far it is clear they are not going to change. It would run counter to God's purpose and be a distorted judgement on God's part to let them see the sign of divine glory they have just rejected—the conquest of the land. God therefore swears that none of 'those who despised me shall see it' (v 23). They will die in the wilderness and their children will inherit the land. The people are not struck with a deadly pestilence in accordance with v 12, or killed 'all at once' in accordance with v 15. Instead God will provide for them in the wilderness (the forty years) until they die. In this sense the covenant relationship continues.[18] The subsequent narrative bears this out; the reader has to wait until the second census in Numbers 26 to learn that the exodus generation has finally disappeared (26:65-66).

In 14:12 God proposed to start afresh with Moses and a new nation. Instead, God now decrees there will be a new generation who will see the fulfillment of the promises, as their conquest of the land in the book of Joshua testifies.[19] God also proposed in 14:12 to disinherit the people. One can say that this happens in so far as they do not enter the land and receive their allotment. But the inheritance does pass to their children and so remains within their clans and tribes. Numbers 14:21-35 is effectively an implementation of 14:12 in the light of Moses' intercession, in particular v 18. God brings order

---

18. Lohfink proposes that 14:21-25, when compared with 14:12, can be seen as a manifestation of divine grace (see page 118 of 'Darstellungskunst und Theologie in Dtn 1,6-3,29,' *Biblica* 41 [1960]: 105-34).
19. Olson (*The Death of the Old and the Birth of the New*, 191-96) points out that the motif of the passage of generations, the death of the old and the birth of the new, continues beyond the Torah in the Prophets (for example, Hos 2:23; Isa 42:9; Jer 31:31-33; Ezek 37; Zech 10:7-9) and the Writings (for example, Pss 95:8-11; 96:1-2).

out of the chaos unleashed by the rebellion and aligns relationships in a way that is appropriate to the situation. To underscore this, God's pronouncement makes special provision for the faithful spy Caleb (v 24).[20]

The preceding Torah narrative has drawn attention at strategic points to the need for right knowledge in order to form and foster right relationships. In 14:26–35 God instructs Moses and Aaron to inform the exodus generation that the forty years in the wilderness is to be a period of instruction, both for them and their children.[21] The people's complaint and perception of God and God's purpose in 14:1–4 is a tissue of distorted/twisted desires and fears—it would be better to die in Egypt or the wilderness than to be brought into the land to die (14:2); why is God bringing us into the land to fall by the sword (14:3); our wives and little ones will become booty there (14:3). God now announces that what eventuates over the next forty years will serve as a correction of each one of these skewed perceptions. They will learn that it is not better to die in the wilderness or Egypt; they are places of death whereas the 'very good land' is life. Secondly, they will learn, as the subsequent conquests of East-Jordan in Numbers 21 confirm, that God is not bringing Israel into the land to die by the sword but to conquer it. Thirdly, they will learn that they are wrong to think their children will become booty; instead their children will conquer the land and take their enemies' towns as booty. Even the forty-year wandering in the wilderness will serve as a form of instruction, recalling the 40 days' of the spies' reconnoitre that God authorised yet the people rejected. In bearing their iniquity over this period they will come to 'know my displeasure' (14:34).[22] One can see in 14:21–35 a parallel to the garden story in that both texts combine

---

20. As noted earlier this text, along with 14:38, can be seen as a response to Gen 18:25—God will not destroy the righteous with the wicked.
21. The shift of focus is signalled by a new introduction in 14:26 that includes Aaron alongside Moses. According to Noth it is part of P with additions (for a breakdown of the text see Campbell and O'Brien, *Sources of the Pentateuch. Texts, Introductions Annotations* [Minneapolis: Fortress Press, 1993], 81–82).
22. The NRSV's 'displeasure' does not catch the strong sense of opposing/frustrating in the Hebrew. As the wicked generation repeatedly opposed God's purpose, it will come to know that God opposes and will frustrate its every evil purpose (for a discussion see Widmer, *The Dynamics of Intercessory Prayer*, 319).

divine punishment, that informs or instructs the offenders about the error of their ways, with providential care (God clothing the couple in Genesis 3:21 and God providing for the exodus generation in the wilderness for forty years).[23]

The parents are to bear their own iniquities (14:34) while their children are to 'suffer for your faithlessness' (literally 'bear your harlotries/infidelities', 14:33). This is an application of the clause in 14:18 that God visits the iniquity of the parents upon the children to the third and fourth generation. Here too however, Moses' intercession results in an appropriate application that advances God's purpose as well as taking into account his plea. This is indicated by the term 'harlotries/whoredoms'. The parents' complaint about the fate of their children in 14:3 gave the (false) impression that they were devoted to them and their welfare. The children will learn that their parents' conduct was actually a betrayal—of their relationship to God and through it of their relationship to their children. A spouse who is unfaithful (a harlot) in a marriage relationship is also unfaithful to the children of the relationship. This will be a painful burden for the children to bear but one that will hopefully motivate them not to repeat the infidelities of their parents. The conduct of the Reubenites and Gadites in Numbers 32 indicates that the new generation has learned the lesson; hence they will 'know the land' (14:31). One might think that all of this would drive home to the exodus generation the evil nature of their rebellion and lead to repentance. But, as God knows this stiff-necked people, it is not going to happen and indeed it doesn't, as the subsequent narrative makes clear. In 14:39-45 the people ignore a warning from Moses that God is not with them and attempt an invasion of the land that ends in defeat.

A final point to be made about Numbers 14:21-35 concerns divine power. In 14:13-16 Moses expresses concern that, if God destroys Israel in the wilderness, the inhabitants of the land will see it as a lack of divine power. A god who cannot exercise power over life and death in the wilderness is not the god of the wilderness and certainly incapable of being the god of the land where the inhabitants dwell. The Lord corrects this distorted perception by decreeing the life and death of the exodus generation in the wilderness and by appointing their children as witnesses. They will see their parents live and die in

---

23. Noted by Widmer, *The Dynamics of Intercessory Prayer*, 326, n. 188.

the wilderness and so be able to testify that it is all in accord with the divine decree. The children will in turn enter and occupy the land, thereby testifying to God's power over the land and its inhabitants. This advances God's avowed purpose that 'all the earth shall be filled with the glory of the Lord' (14:20). The various relationships that the text deals with—between God and Israel, between God and Moses, between the generations of Israelites, between God and the nations, between Israel and the nations, between God and the land and between Israel and the land—are all ordered in a way that manifests God's righteous relationship with creation and humanity.

Given that God knows all things one might well ask what is the point of a text like this with its emphasis on Moses' intercession and its efficacy. In answer I would restate the comment made in the analysis of Exodus 32–34 about the dynamic nature of the Torah's understanding of God's relationship with human beings. A relationship between human beings is authentic when all participants are active and contribute. This must also be the case in a relationship between God and human beings otherwise it will not be truly human and therefore not a real relationship between them. God knows this better than us and therefore provides a context within which the human being can contribute actively. Even though God knows all things, the human contribution is real and effective as the texts show by portraying God hearkening to Moses' intercession and making changes, all of course within a certain boundary or framework that respects the divine initiative. While the relationship is real it is not between equals. The Torah's portrayal of the relationship between God and Moses is also designed to fuel faith among listeners and readers that their relationship with God is real and dynamic, to encourage them to pray (cf the Psalms) and to assure them that their prayers will be heard.

5

Book of Deuteronomy

The book of Deuteronomy is now generally linked by critical scholarship to the reform of king Josiah in the late seventh century BCE (cf 2 Kgs 22–23). It is thought the decline of Assyria provided 'deuteronomic reformers' with an opportunity to promote the exclusive worship of Israel's God via a policy of centralised worship in the Jerusalem temple and an accompanying reform of law. To enhance its authority the work was attributed to Moses, the great leader of hoary antiquity. According to Martin Noth, this reform became the prologue and interpretative key to Israel's first major historical work compiled during the exile.[1] It told the story of Israel's conquest of the land, the troubled period of the judges, the emergence of the monarchy, and the decline and demise of the northern kingdom of Israel and the southern kingdom of Judah. This 'Deuteronomistic History' was an earlier version of Deuteronomy, Joshua, Judges, Samuel and Kings. Deuteronomy subsequently became attached to the emerging Pentateuch while the remainder of the history was edited, supplemented and then divided into the books that make up the canonical Former Prophets or Historical Books.

While there is ongoing debate over Noth's hypothesis, few would deny the presence of deuteronomic language and theology in the Former Prophets. The location of Deuteronomy at the end of the Torah immediately before the Former Prophets accords well with the way Moses' speeches recall Israel's past in order to prepare it for the future. It is a book that looks back as well as forwards, it also provides a narrative link between the storyline of the Torah and that of the

---

1. Martin Noth, *The Deuteronomistic History* (JSOTSup 15. second edtion; Sheffield: JSOT Press, 1981/1991), German original 1943.

Former Prophets/Historical Books. Deuteronomy is a complex book and historical critical analysis helps explain something of its inner complexity as well as the differences between it and the preceding Tetrateuch, especially Exodus and Numbers. For the purposes of this study only a selection of texts will be commented on and the focus, as with preceding examples, will be on the present text rather than its composition.

The book can be divided into the following major parts. A narrative introduction in 1:1–5 is followed by Moses' first discourse to the people assembled 'beyond the Jordan in the land of Moab' (v 5). This discourse (1:6–4:40) covers the demise of the exodus generation, the subsequent conquest of trans-Jordan by the new 'conquest' generation, and concludes with an exhortation to obey 'the statutes and ordinances' (4:1) and the consequences of disobedience. A narrative section follows, comprising a report of the establishment of cities of refuge (4:41–43) and an introduction (4:44–5:1a) to a second major discourse of Moses on loyalty to the terms of the Horeb covenant (5:1b–26:19): the two key laws texts within this block are the Decalogue in 5:6–21 and the so-called 'Deuteronomic Code' in 12–26. Deuteronomy 27 reports instructions by Moses and the elders of Israel, and by Moses and the Levitical priests about the blessings and curses to be proclaimed when Israel crosses the Jordan into the land. Deuteronomy 28 provides a detailed list of blessings and (mainly) curses. Deuteronomy 29:1 (MT 28:69) is a narrative introduction to Moses' third major discourse in 29:2–30:20. In it Moses proclaims the terms of a new covenant set 'in the land of Moab' which, within the context of Deuteronomy, incorporates what has been proclaimed beforehand in relation to the Horeb covenant.[2] Deuteronomy 31–34 reports the installation of Joshua as Moses' successor, the writing down of the law, the song in 32:1–43 and the reasons for it, and Moses' blessing of the tribes in 33. The book concludes with a report of Moses' death and burial outside the land (34:1–12).

Apart from the song in Deuteronomy 32 with which our analysis of righteousness in the Torah began, the portions of the book of

---

2. So McConville, *Deuteronomy*, 401 and Lohfink 'Prolegomena zu einer Rechtshermeneutik des Pentateuch', 32–33. See also the detailed discussion in Paul A Barker, *The Triumph of Grace in Deuteronomy* (Paternoster Biblical Monographs; Carlisle, UK/Waynesboro, GA: Paternoster Press, 2004), 112–16.

particular import are Moses' account of the spy episode in 1:19-45, the golden calf episode in 9:7-10:11, and the covenant 'in the land of Moab' in 29-30. Even though Deuteronomy's origins were most likely independent of the Tetrateuch at least to some degree, it now forms part of the Torah storyline and contributes to its overall meaning and purpose. Its understanding of the key relationships that have been commented on so far therefore needs to be taken into account—the relationships between God and Israel, between God and Moses, between Moses and Israel, between God and the nations, between Israel and the nations, and between Israel and the land. Because these relationships are integral parts of God's one saving plan for humanity and creation, reflection on one has implications for the others.

As with the preceding books Deuteronomy can be read at more than one level; the level of the characters in the book such as God, Moses and the two generations of Israel, of the author/narrator who steps forward at times to provide an explanation (for example, 2:10-14) or additional information (for example, 10:6-9), and of the Israelite listener or reader (any subsequent individual or generation). But Deuteronomy differs from the preceding books by explicitly including subsequent individuals and generations alongside the ones addressed in the book. This occurs in two ways. One is implicit, employing the rhetorical artifice of the second person form of address ('you' singular and plural) throughout Moses' discourses. The second explicitly unites past, present and future; in proclaiming the covenant in the land of Moab Moses states that he is not only making it with the conquest generation ('you who stand here with us today') but also 'with those who are not here with us today' (29:15). As McConville notes, the effect of this is that 'Israel in all its generations stands in principle once again at Horeb, confronted with the covenant commands as if about to be given for the first time'.[3] For Deuteronomy, Israel is meant to live throughout all its generations according to the terms of the Horeb covenant made with its ancestors. As already pointed out, although the covenant 'in the land of Moab' (29:1; MT 28:69) has Israel's future life in the land in mind it does not invalidate or replace the Horeb covenant; it is effectively the Horeb covenant as it is to be lived in the land. Deuteronomy also signals this in the way it refers to 'the commandments, the statutes and ordinances' that

---

3. McConville, *Deuteronomy*, 124.

God communicates to Moses at Horeb after the proclamation of the Decalogue. They are for Israel's life in the land (5:31) and are therefore the law of the Moab covenant.[4] Indeed all that God has done for Israel in Egypt and in the wilderness has had this aim in mind; that Israel 'may know that I am the Lord' (29:6), that it may 'diligently observe the words of this covenant', and that 'you may succeed in everything that you do' (29:9).

All this demonstrates, according to Deuteronomy, that God has been completely loyal to Israel and has initiated the kind of relationship that will enable it to fulfill its divinely ordained role in the land. According to 11:12, 'the Lord your God looks after' this land from one year's end to the next. The land is now the 'garden' that God entrusts to Israel's care. Israel is to take the conduct of the owner as its model, one 'who is not partial and takes no bribe, who executes justice for the orphan and the widow, and who loves the strangers' (10:17-18). In 16:18-20 instructions are given for the appointment of judges and officials to ensure that 'Justice, and only justice, you shall pursue'. In 10:9 Israel is exhorted to 'love the stranger, for you were strangers in the land of Egypt' (10:19). Deuteronomy 24:13 asserts that if each one cares for his/her poor neighbour then 'it shall be righteousness before the Lord your God' (NRSV 'it will be to your credit'). As an expression (and celebration) of its commitment to the terms of the Horeb covenant, Israel is to worship God at 'the place that the Lord your God will choose as a dwelling for his name' once it is living in the land in safety and free from the threat of all its enemies (12:10-12).[5] One could say that Israel will be playing its true role in the divine scheme of things when it is the one nation living in the one land according to the one 'righteous' Torah (4:8 NRSV 'just'), worshipping the one God at the one place that God will choose. If it does this it will live a fruitful life in a blessed land (11:13-15) and have a powerful impact on the nations who will recognise its uniqueness and acclaim 'Surely this great nation is a wise and discerning people!'

---

4. As Barker notes (*The Triumph of Grace*, 113), 'The same stipulations apply to both'.
5. In his message to king Hiram of Tyre in 1 Kgs 5:1-6 Solomon claims that these 'conditions' for the establishment of centralised worship have finally been met in his reign. This identifies 'the place' in Deuteronomy as the Jerusalem temple that Solomon subsequently constructs.

(4:6). If it does not then just retribution will follow, as Deuteronomy is at pains to point out, in particular in the graphic description of curses in chapter 28.

However, as the Tetrateuch narrative testifies and as Deuteronomy 9:6 reminds, Israel has consistently shown it is rebellious and disloyal. Deuteronomy incorporates this factor into its theology of reward (blessing) for loyalty and retribution (punishment/curse) for disloyalty in a way that explains why Israel is still God's people and about to enter the land.[6] The two most serious instances of disloyalty in the preceding narrative are the golden calf apostasy and the spy mission and, understandably, these are the focus of attention.

The spy story is incorporated within the deuteronomic reward-retribution equation via the demise of the exodus generation and the emergence of the conquest generation, in line with Numbers 14. A striking feature of Deuteronomy's take on the golden calf episode in 9:7–10:11 is the absence of retribution/punishment. This has attracted a lot of scholarly attention, the most recent contribution being that of Vincent Sénéchal.[7] According to him scholarly analysis has proposed five reasons for the absence. One is that Deuteronomy 9:7–10:11 is to be read within a trajectory that reaches to 2 Kings 17 which claims the retribution implied in the deuteronomic text came to pass in the exile of the northern kingdom; a second is that the requirement is dealt with satisfactorily in the spy episode (1:19–46); a third is that the absence of retribution is due to Moses' role as Israel's intercessor; a fourth is that it is designed to fuel the faith of readers in a difficult time, such as the exile (a historical–critical explanation); and a fifth is that it is a way of including the children of the exodus generation and indeed each generation of listeners and readers ('you') in the transgression.[8] That is, all share in the sin of Israel and therefore merit retribution; it is only through God's compassion ('The Lord was unwilling to destroy you'—10:10) that Israel continued and continues as God's people. After a detailed analysis of text and context, both

---

6. As pointed out earlier, the reward–retribution schema appeals to divine authority (via a prophetic word or some other form of mediation) to identify instances of the Act–Consequence connection, particularly when these are disputed.
7. Vincent Sénéchal, *Rétribution et intercession dans le Deutéronome* (BZAW 408; Berlin/New York: Walter de Gruyter, 2009).
8. For a summary see Sénéchal, *Rétribution*, 254–62.

from a diachronic and synchronic perspective, Sénéchal's preference is for the second and fifth options.⁹

This is a well-reasoned analysis but I do not think it gives sufficient weight to the importance for Deuteronomy of Moses as Israel's advocate or intercessor. According to 9:18, 25 and 10:10 Moses interceded for Israel on Mt Horeb for forty days and nights. This emphasis on his intercessory role and its success may well explain the absence of any reference to Exodus 34:6-7 in Deuteronomy 9:7–10:11. Deuteronomy is well aware of the criteria by which God distributes reward and retribution because it repeats the foundational proclamation of it made in Exodus in the context of the Decalogue (cf Exod 20:5b-6 and Deut 5:9b-10, also 4:24; 6:15; 7:9-10). But it does not invoke it in order to give full play to Moses' intercessory role—a powerful example of the one righteous person being able to save the wicked multitude. This in turn provides a likely explanation for the absence of any intercession by Moses in the spy episode (1:19-46), in contrast to the version in Numbers 13-14. According to Deuteronomy's version of the episode, God was angry with Moses on account of the people (1:37) and forbade him to enter the land. Moses was no longer righteous in the sight of God and therefore unable to intercede for the people as he did at Horeb.

A difficulty with any explanation of the spy episode in Deuteronomy is the vague nature of 1:37 which is not made any clearer in the subsequent references to it in 3:26 and 4:21—what was the reason for God's anger against Moses? Some have seen these texts as an example of corporate or collective responsibility; Moses 'as leader suffers the consequences' of the people's rebellion.¹⁰ Others argue that, in order to promote its theological and rhetorical purposes, Deuteronomy has compressed elements from two incidents in the book of Numbers— the spy story in 13-14 and Moses' and Aaron's failure at the waters of Meribah (20:2-13).¹¹ There is another possible explanation;

---

9. Cf Sénéchal, *Rétribution*, 431–33, although the reader will find them referred to there as the first and fourth options. The reason for this is that Sénéchal's analysis leads him to discount the first option listed above and to weigh the merits of the remaining four. Of these he considers the first and fourth more persuasive but with a final preference for the fourth.
10. So Christensen, *Deuteronomy 1:1–21:9*, 32; also Sénéchal, *Rétribution*, 155. This is effectively a reversal of the impact of the one on the many.
11. McConville, *Deuteronomy*, 71. Deuteronomy 32:48-52, which refers to Num

Deuteronomy imputes guilt to Moses for accepting the people's initiative and proposal in 1:22-25 rather than relying on God's initiative and instructions.[12] Does Moses' version of the spy episode indirectly admit that he should not have trusted the stubborn exodus generation (cf. 9:27) as his account of their subsequent rebellion bears out (1:26-29)?

Whatever the case, God's refusal to let Moses enter the land has two important implications in Deuteronomy. One affects the relationship between God and Israel. Because Moses will not enter the land, Israel will not have anyone to intercede on its behalf as at Horeb. No provision is made in Deuteronomy for another advocate like Moses; Joshua's role is to lead the people into the land (1:38; 3:28) and although 18:15-22 envisages a future prophet like Moses there is no mention of him acting as an intercessor for sins such as the golden calf apostasy. Neither Leviticus nor Deuteronomy authorises the clergy to intervene for Israel in such a case. Indeed, to have the ongoing availability of such advocacy would make this 'stubborn' people arrogant or complacent or both. The absence of Moses and any replacement for him in the land effectively serves Deuteronomy's larger purpose of establishing its Torah as the only (the right) way to live in the land as the people of God. Moses speaks Deuteronomy's version of the words of God to the people assembled in the plains of Moab; these words, which are also Moses' words, are then written down and entrusted to the care of the Levitical priests, to be proclaimed to the people every seventh year (31:9-12). In this way Moses remains Deuteronomy's ever present and faithful advocate, promoting its authority and the need for Israel to accept it and live by it.

The second implication concerns the relationship between God and Moses. In 1:37 Moses is forbidden to enter the land and 3:26

20:2-13 and 27:12-14 as the reason why Moses is to die outside the land, is commonly regarded as a priestly addition to the book. If however Deut has compressed Num 13-14 and 20:2-13 in Deut 1:19-46, then 32:48-52 could have singled out Moses' 'second' failure in order to identify the location of his death, 'the mountain of the Abarim'.

12. This interpretation is recognised as a possible one ('perhaps') by Jeffrey Tigay, *Deuteronomy. The traditional Hebrew text with the New JPS translation, commentary* (The JPS Torah commentary; Philadelphia: Jewish Publication Society, 1996), 19.

shows that he cannot intercede for himself any more than he can for the exodus generation in the spy episode. Despite this, he is still able to function as God's spokesperson, as long as he discharges this duty faithfully—which Deuteronomy presents him doing. For this he is rewarded before his death by being given a privileged view of the land from Mt Nebo. According to 34:1, God 'showed him' the whole of the promised land. Although Moses did not enter it, Deuteronomy implies that God answered his request in 3:25 to see it and that he saw it in a way no other human being ever had or ever will see it; being shown the land personally by God is to see it, as it were, through God's eyes. Not even the first ancestor to see the land, Abraham, saw it in this way (cf Gen 13:14).

The deuteronomic portrait of Moses provides another instance of the juxtaposition of punishment and compassion, or retribution and reward, observed in Exodus 32–34 and Numbers 13–14. The Torah's claim is that God distributes them in a way that is appropriate to each case and thereby brings order out of failure and disorder. Each case is unique and requires a number of factors be taken into consideration; God does not assign reward or retribution mechanically but justly/wisely. Like any text the Torah is limited and can only present a selection of cases to illustrate and validate principles. As Olson notes, 'Humans, including Moses, are given only a partial disclosure of the divine'.[13] Yet the claim is that what is revealed is sufficient for Israel to fulfill its vocation. In the words of Deuteronomy 29:29 'The secret things belong to the Lord our God, but the revealed things belong to us and to our children forever, to observe all the words of this law'.

Deuteronomy does not tackle the golden calf apostasy or the spy story only to remind Israel of its past failures. It also sees them as typifying its future. The link between the two is clear in 9:4–6 where Moses warns Israel not to think that God is bringing it into the land because of its righteousness since it has shown itself to be a stubborn people, prone to rebellion as the subsequent account of the golden calf apostasy demonstrates. Even Moses' first discourse contains a grim prophecy of Israel's failure and exile from the land (4:25–28).[14]

---

13. Olson, *Deuteronomy and the Death of Moses*, 179.
14. The NRSV has 'if you act corruptly'; a more literal rendering captures the predictive thrust of 4:25: 'When you beget sons and sons of sons and are old in the land and act corruptly by making an idol...'.

This does not mean however that living in the land according to the Torah is simply unrealistic or unattainable; this would impugn the theology of God and God's purpose that Deuteronomy and the larger Torah promote.[15] Hence, Deuteronomy 26 requires each Israelite to make an annual pilgrimage to the place that God will choose in order to dedicate the first fruits of the land to God and to rejoice in God's blessing of land and people. The celebration of the land's bounty will be a sign of God's ongoing commitment and loyalty to Israel (26:5–9) and a reward for the loyal Israelite's commitment to justice in society (26:12–15).

Nevertheless, because Moses speaks with prophetic authority Israel will at some stage fail and his prophecy is borne out in the subsequent story of Israel in the land in the Former Prophets. But Moses' prophecy is not restricted to these instances. All listeners and readers are to take note. When failure occurs God will punish the evildoers in accord with the terms of the covenant curses as graphically described in Deuteronomy 28, in particular those of defeat and exile. Nevertheless, God will remain loyal to Israel and restore it to the land when it 'seeks' (4:29) or 'returns' (30:2) to God. Furthermore, God will 'circumcise your heart and the heart of your descendants so that you will love the Lord your God' (30:6). While Deuteronomy never softens its call to loyalty to the covenant, it recognises that the fulfillment of Israel's vocation—and God's universal plan of salvation—ultimately depends, as did its beginning, on the divine initiative.[16]

Deuteronomy frequently invokes the promises to the ancestors whether in terms of covenant (cf 4:31; 7:8; 8:18; 29:13, 25) or the promise of land (cf 1:8, 21, 35; 4:1; 6:10, 18, 23, etc). Within the context of the Torah narrative, these recall the earlier promises to the ancestors of land, of becoming a great nation, and of being the mediator of God's blessing to all the families/nations of the earth (cf Gen 12:1–3; 18:18; 22:17–18; 26:4; 28:14; Num 24:9). Even though the blessing/salvation of the nations is not mentioned explicitly in the deuteronomic passages, one can assume it is included. Israel's

---

15. The Former Prophets claims that the deuteronomic vision was realised at two points in Israel's life in the land; in the conquest and settlement of the land (Josh 24:31; Judg 2:7) and in the first part of the reign of Solomon (1 Kgs 4:20–21, 25).
16. What in Christian terms is called grace; this is the emphasis of Barker's study *The Triumph of Grace*.

imminent emergence as a nation on the world stage necessarily involves its relationship with other nations. This invites the reader to link the ancestral promises to Deuteronomy's understanding of the nations and how Israel's conduct in the land advances or hinders its mission among them.

At certain points Deuteronomy speaks of nations and their cults that pose a powerful and seductive threat to Israel's commitment to its mission. In order for Israel to fulfill its mission it is essential that it knows and remains faithful to the Lord. The cults of false gods threaten knowledge of the true God and of Israel as the 'image' of the all holy God; hence they are to be eliminated (7:2-6). Once Israel clears the land of 'wicked' nations and their false gods and lives according to the terms of the Horeb covenant there will be a positive or blessed outcome. The nations will exclaim 'Surely this great nation is a wise and discerning people' (4:6). But if Israel succumbs to the evil influence of the nations God will appoint them as agents of Israel's punishment (cf 4:27-28; 28:33-34, 48-57). But what Israel experiences as a terrible evil will be revealed as part of God's universal saving purpose; according to 29:25 the nations will acknowledge that Israel is being punished 'because they abandoned the covenant of the Lord, the God of their ancestors'. In short, Israel's punishment will prompt the nations to confess that Israel's God is the Lord, the one sovereign over creation and history (cf 29:26-28). But all this can also serve as an important learning experience for Israel 'if you call them to mind among the nations where the Lord your God has driven you' (30:1). It will lead Israel to repent and return to God and to be restored to the land in order to continue its mission. But lest a reader or listener forget that the nations are as prone to evil as Israel, 30:7 envisages there will be nations who are not changed by its punishment but take advantage of it. They are like those condemned in a number of prophetic texts for overstepping their mandate to be God's agents of Israel's punishment and indulging in violence and oppression.[17]

The HBOT's understanding of Israel's relationship with the nations is not presented as a systematic theological treatise but in dramatic stories, prophecies and poems. One should therefore not expect a completely homogeneous and integrated picture. On the one

---

17. Cf Isa 10:5-11; 37:22-29; Jer 50:11-20; Ezek 27; Obadiah; Nahum; Zeph 2:8-10.

hand, Israel is chosen to be the mediator of God's blessing to all the families of the earth. The ones that bless Israel will be blessed, the one/ones that curse Israel will be cursed.[18] Within the Torah storyline, the prophecy of Balaam (Num 24:9) announces to the nations in the person of king Balak of Moab the promise first made to Abraham in Genesis 12:3. Those that resist Israel's entry into the land and seek to destroy it are therefore repudiating God's saving purpose and, as a sign of God's sovereign power and commitment to this purpose, they themselves will be destroyed.

Although the prophecy is directed to Balak (and the nations), within the storyline its main function is to advance the Torah's theological strategy. Because all the earth belongs to the Lord, the claims made by nations about their boundaries and their spheres of influence are flawed and must give way to the sovereign will of the Lord who has the good of all creation and the proper course of history in mind. As the song of Moses claims (Deut 32:8-9) it is the sole prerogative of the 'Most High' to assign each nation's share of the earth. Deuteronomy 2:1-25 claims this has already taken place with Israel's kin, the Edomites, Moabites and Ammonites. The 'fact' that God has assigned these nations their lands lends weight to the Torah's claim about Israel's portion and 'justifies' the removal of those nations that resist it.[19] By the same token, Deuteronomy 2:1-25 also infers that Israel is forbidden to encroach on any other nation's divinely designated territory or to initiate hostilities against it. This is a very limited take on complex historical realities but it serves two aims. On the one hand it seeks to include the nations within the Torah's theological framework of blessing/reward and curse/retribution. On the other hand it provides a glimpse of how the nations are to live together in their designated allotments and some hope that this can be realised.

All those who fight against Israel in the book of Joshua are therefore wicked and fall within the category of the nations that have

---

18. Genesis 12:3 refers to the one who is cursed whereas Num 24:9 uses the plural.
19. Judges 11:12-28 also deals with the distribution of land among the nations. Jephthah urges the Ammonite king to stay within the land that his god Chemosh has given, and the overall thrust of this exchange is that any nation attempting to take what the Lord has given Israel will be punished. The text is not monotheistic but henotheistic, with the Lord as the high god who maintains right order among the nations in their lands.

repudiated the divine plan announced to them in Numbers 24:9. In order that God's name be known in all the earth and that salvation reach the ends of the earth such obstacles must be removed. In contrast, those who accept Israel as the blessed people of God, namely Rahab and her family in Joshua 2 and the Gibeonites in Joshua 9, are saved. These two hardly constitute by themselves a sufficient context for portraying Israel's mission among the nations and the unfolding of God's universal purpose. There needs to be many other nations to whom Israel mediates God's blessing, otherwise the whole biblical enterprise would look pretty flimsy. Perhaps it is for this reason that Deuteronomy 4:6 speaks of 'the peoples' that will be impressed by Israel's obedience to God's law and 29:24 speaks of 'all the nations' that will see the hand of the Lord in Israel's affliction. In a similar way prophetic texts such as Isaiah 2:2-4 and its parallel in Micah 4:1-4 foresee 'the nations' coming to Zion to be taught God's ways. On the other side of the coin, deuteronomic texts such as 4:27-28; 28:49-52 and prophetic passages such as Isaiah 5:26-30; Jeremiah 5:15-17 claim that God will engage foreign nations as agents of Israel's punishment. By the same token, if the nations overstep their God-given brief they will, like Israel, be punished (cf the woe oracle against Assyria in Isa 10:5-19). Texts such as these aim to assure Israel and any reader that the vicissitudes of history are not chaos and disorder; God is in charge, everything has its meaning and all is unfolding according to the divine purpose.

Much of this deuteronomic and Torah theology is captured in poetic form in the song of Moses in Deuteronomy 32, the text with which our study commenced. However, it may be useful for the reader to link the way the Torah narrative ends in Deuteronomy with the way it begins in Genesis. Thomas Mann expresses the connection well:

> With this description of the new community of God (Deuteronomy), the Pentateuch has reached its true end—its *telos*—its goal and purpose. The Pentateuchal narrative renders a new world. But as it was 'in the beginning', so it is now; while that world exists as a reality in terms of what God has done, it exists only as a possibility in terms of what Israel will do. The Torah ends very much the way it began. Just as God placed

the earth before Adam and Eve and offered it to them as their dominion, so God places the land of Canaan before Israel and offers it to them. Just as God provided for Adam and Eve a commandment, obedience to which would mean continued blessing, but disobedience to which would entail a curse, so God has blessed Israel as his special people, but warned them of the curse that leads to death. Just as Adam and Eve could be genuinely human only in responsibility to the divine will, so Israel can be God's holy nation only in responsibility to God's *torah*.[20]

In other words, God has established a right relationship with Israel that will enable it to play its role within God's righteous purpose—the restoration of proper order in humanity and creation/land in the wake of the story of human sin and disorder in Genesis 2–11. God has demonstrated unswerving commitment (steadfast love or *khesedh*) to this purpose, evident in the way God has distributed punishment and compassion when Israel has failed, providing instruction about the nature and seriousness of the failure, coupled with a renewed call to obedience to the (covenant) relationship. The Torah not only claims to provide an authoritative account and interpretation of humanity and Israel's story to this point on the edge of the land but also a prophecy for the future. Subsequent prophets endorse its veracity and proclaim its realization in Israel and humanity's ongoing story. Both Torah and prophecy are selective, as they have to be; human words, even inspired ones, cannot embrace all experience. The biblical claim however is that the selections faithfully represent the whole.

---

20. Mann, *The Book of the Torah*, 161.

Part Two

Divine Righteousness in the Former Prophets/Historical Books

Introduction

The Torah concludes with Israel poised to enter the promised land and live there according to God's law. The chosen people and their land will become a sign of the order that God has in store for all humanity and creation. The 'Former Prophets' tells the story of Israel from its entry into the land until its exile from the land (cf 2 Kgs 17; 25).[1] Granted that this is the continuation of the Torah's storyline one would expect the interpretative criteria employed in the earlier story would also be employed here. That is, Israel's initial success and ultimate failure would be presented as the consequence of fidelity and infidelity to the Torah. That this is the case is indicated by two strategically located passages in the Former Prophets. The book of Joshua commences with God's assurance to Moses' successor that as long as he is 'careful to act in accordance with all the law that my servant Moses commanded you' (Josh 1:7) all will be well. Toward the end of the Former Prophets Huldah prophesies disaster 'for this place and its inhabitants' in accord with 'all the words of the book that the king of Judah has read' (2 Kgs 22:16)—that is, the book of the law found in the temple (22:8).

As noted in the reflections on Deuteronomy, Martin Noth proposed that an earlier version of Deuteronomy served as the prologue and interpretative key for an account of how Israel obtained the promised land and ultimately lost it. During the Babylonian exile an author/redactor combined existing material and his own compositions to construct what Noth entitled 'the Deuteronomistic History'. He

---

1. 2 Kings 17 reports the conquest and exile of the northern kingdom of Israel by the Assyrians; 2 Kgs 25 the conquest and exile of Judah by the Babylonians.

identified the principal compositions of 'the Deuteronomist' in two kinds of texts. One is the speeches of leaders (for example, Moses in Deut 1-4; Joshua in chapter 23; Solomon in 1 Kings 8) and prophets (for example, Samuel in 1 Sam12; Ahijah of Shiloh in 1 Kgs 11:31-39; Elijah in 1 Kgs 21:20-24; Isaiah in 2 Kgs 19; Huldah in 2 Kgs 22:15-20). The other is commentary at strategic points; for example, to introduce the account of the judges (Judg 2:11-19), and to conclude the account of the northern kingdom of Israel (2 Kgs 17:7-23). In the post-exilic period, Deuteronomy became part of the emerging Torah and the remainder of the history was edited and divided into the books of the Former Prophets. Whether or not one agrees with Noth's hypothesis it does point to sustained theological reflection in the development of the canon, particularly the stages that produced Torah and Prophecy. The Former Prophets was, like the Torah, not only shaped to give an account of Israel's past—incorporating existing material in the process—but also to provide instruction or catechesis for listeners and readers. The model for this latter role was of course the Torah itself. The Former Prophets effectively endorses Torah teaching and like the Torah does so via the narrative portrayal of key relationships—between God and Israel, between God and Israel's leaders, between Israel and its leaders, and between Israel and the nations. The following analysis will try to illustrate this in a limited way via selected passages in the books of Joshua, Judges, Samuel and Kings.

1

In the Books of Joshua and Judges

The Book of Joshua

The terms 'righteous' and 'righteousness' do not occur in the book of Joshua and, after reading its stories of the conquest, one could be forgiven for concluding 'with good reason'. To a modern reader the divine command to utterly destroy another nation smacks of 'ethnic cleansing' or genocide. Nevertheless, if one takes the literary and theological context of the larger Hebrew Bible/Old Testament into account, as well as its ANE context, some appreciation can be gained of the presence of such stories and their contribution to the theology of divine righteousness.

There can be little doubt that one of the most pressing questions in the wake of the two exiles—of the northern kingdom of Israel circa 722 BCE and the southern kingdom of Judah circa. 587 BCE—was 'why' they had happened. For those committed to faith in Israel's God it would have been unacceptable that Assyrian and Babylonian gods had triumphed over the God of Israel.[1] The only acceptable answer was to assert that God had delivered the two kingdoms into the hands of their enemies as punishment for infidelity.[2] Various forms of this assertion or faith claim gradually found their way into the

---

1. It is difficult to determine when Israel (as a whole or an influential group) became monotheistic and which parts of the HBOT reflect this. Deuteronomy is a passionate advocate of it whereas priestly literature seems to presume it (there is only one injunction against idols in Lev 19:4). While many think priestly literature was later than deuteronomic, a number reverse the order (for a discussion see Ska, *Introduction to Reading the Pentateuch*, 159–61).
2. According to Kaiser, there was a move from initial bewilderment at the exile, to reflection on why it happened, to the recognition and acceptance of sin, guilt and God's just punishment (*Yahwes Gerechtigkeit*, 99).

Torah, Prophecy and Writings; the process no doubt drew on various aspects of Israel's tradition. It sought to preserve the people's belief in God and their relationship with God—the essential component of their national identity—and fuel hope that the period of punishment would come to an end.[3] The assertion meant of course that the God who has power to dispose of lands and people must also be the one who assigned them in the first place. This stimulated reflection on why God chose Israel and gave it the land. Reflection and debate about such issues would have been aided by prophetic preaching, by recourse to aspects of Israel's tradition enshrined in story, song and law, and by the challenge posed by the propaganda of conquering nations. What came to be the accepted and authoritative response is now enshrined in the Torah and Prophecy components of the canon.

Within the book of Joshua, a significant passage in this regard is 21:43-45, located at the end of the account of the conquest of the land and its distribution among the tribes of Israel. It makes three claims: that the Lord gave Israel the land in accord with the oath sworn to their ancestors ('fathers' 21:43; cf 1:6); that, also in accord with the oath sworn to their ancestors, the Lord gave Israel victory over their enemies so that they enjoyed 'rest on every side' (21:44; cf 1:5); that all the promises made to the house of Israel came to pass (literally, 'there did not fall/lack a word from all the good word the Lord had spoken'; 21:45). The first two are specific (land and conquest) whereas the third is general (every word). Within the context of the 'Deuteronomistic History' hypothesis Joshua 21:43-45 can be linked to passages in Deuteronomy, for example 1:8; 6:10 (with respect to the land) and 12:8 (with respect to rest from enemies). However, within the canonical context it can include all the promises of the Torah.[4] In claiming that God fulfilled all the promises made to the house of Israel, Joshua 21:45 is effectively also proclaiming God's unswerving commitment (*khesedh*) to the goal of establishing right order in the land. This becomes a sign on earth of divine righteousness.

---

3. E Theodore Mullen, Jr proposes that a key function of the 'Deuteronomistic History' was to forge an ethnic identity for Judah/Israel that could withstand the potentially destructive impact of the exile. It was one among a number seeking to do much the same thing at this time (*Narrative History and Ethnic Boundaries. The Deuteronomistic Historian and the Creation of Israelite National Identity* [SBL Semeia Studies; Atlanta Georgia: Scholars Press, 1993]).

4. A pointer in this direction is the general nature of the third claim ('every word') and the phrase 'house of Israel' which does not occur in Deuteronomy.

Thus the gift of the land is the fulfillment of the promise to Israel in a number of deuteronomic texts, in Exodus texts (cf 3:8; 6:8; 12:25; 13:11; 23:20-33; 32:34; 33:1), and in Genesis texts in the promises to the ancestors (cf 12:1; 13:15; 15:18; 28:13).[5] It includes the fulfillment of the promise to the ancestors that their descendants would become a great nation, the one that inherits the land (cf Gen 12:2; 13:16; 18:18; 22:17; 28:14; 46:3; Exod 32:13; Deut 1:10 [fulfilment]). The God-given victory over enemies in the book of Joshua and the resulting rest from war is in fulfillment of a number of passages in Deuteronomy (for example, 7:1-2; 12:8-10 [rest from enemies]; 19:1), and of the promise to the ancestors in Genesis 22:17; 27:29. The Torah and the book of Joshua also contain additional explanations or reasons for the conquest. It is instructive to outline the more important ones because they provide further theological reflection on key relationships—between God and Israel, between God and the nations and between Israel and the nations. Genesis 12:3; 18:18; 26:4; 27:29c; 28:14 and Num 24:9 proclaim that Abraham and his offspring are chosen to bring God's blessing to 'all the families/nations of the earth'. While the Genesis texts emphasise blessing for all nations, 12:3 contains a curse clause against 'the one' who curses Abraham, and in Genesis 27:29c and Numbers 24:9 this curse is in the plural.

First, the blessing side of the equation. There are only two families/nations in the book of Joshua that can be described as receiving the blessing promised to the ancestors, namely Rahab and her family in Joshua 2, and the Gibeonites in Joshua 9. Although this may look like slim pickings in comparison to the many hostile nations destroyed, their strategic location in the narrative points to their thematic and theological importance. Each forms a prelude to a major section of the conquest narrative, and each is delivered from the ensuing destruction because of a profession of faith in the Lord and of Israel as the chosen nation destined to conquer the land (cf Josh 2:8-11; 9:9-11, 24). This sets them apart from the other (wicked) nations in the book of Joshua (cf 2:2-3; 9:2-3). Rahab and the Gibeonites

---

5. According to Deuteronomy 2, God gave the descendants of Esau (Edomites) and Lot (Moabites, Ammonites) their lands. Ishmael is not mentioned here perhaps because his lands (as given in Gen 25:18) do not border Israel's, whereas those of Edom, Moab and Ammon do. Genesis 17:20-22 promises a great nation for Ishmael but the covenant is to be established with Sarah's son Isaac.

may be intended to evoke in a way the theme of the one/few and the many. They constitute a sign that, despite appearances (the many hostile nations in the book of Joshua), many will eventually come to be blessed through Abraham and his offspring.

Douglas Earl has proposed an intriguing contrast between Rahab and Achan. Rahab is the complete outsider who through her profession of faith and loyalty (*khesedh*) to the spies in Joshua 2 becomes an insider to whom the Israelites show loyalty; she is the one in right relationship with God and with Israel and so is blessed. In contrast Achan is the insider/Israelite who is disloyal to the covenant relationship with God and with Israel and is placed under the ban/curse. In effect he becomes an outsider like the wicked nations.[6] An equally intriguing feature in the Gibeonite episode is that they initially lie to Israel to protect themselves but, when their lie is exposed, their profession of faith is seen to be genuine (9:24) and so they are spared. One can perhaps see in the relationship between the Gibeonites and Israel a kind of allegory of Israel's relationship with God. The Gibeonites behave like devious Israel while Israel is obliged to act like its loyal God. As God remains committed to Israel despite its behaviour, so Israel is committed by its oath to the cunning Gibeonites (9:4, 18–19).[7] Even though Israel gets to play a god-like role here it is less than perfectly executed. Joshua makes peace with the Gibeonites, the people partake of their provisions, and an oath of protection is sworn. God is not consulted beforehand (cf 9:14–15, 18). The contrast between Rahab and Achan, and Israel's inept handling of the Gibeonites exposes some fragility in Israel's relationship with God and with foreigners that could crack under pressure—as the subsequent narrative in Judges bears out.

The ones who are referred to in the Torah as cursing Israel impugn its God and are equated in the book of Joshua with the nations to be destroyed. Like corrupt humanity in the flood story, the citizens of Sodom and Gomorrah, the Egyptian army at the sea, the Midianites who seduced Israel in the plains of Moab (Num 25; 31), they are a

---

6. Douglas S Earl, *Reading Joshua as Christian Scripture* (Journal of Theological Interpretation Supplements 2; Winona Lake, Ind.: Eisenbrauns 2010), 149–50.

7. Is there also a hint of how Israel oscillates between blessing/reward and curse/retribution in its relationship with God in the way the Gibeonites are cursed (by Josh 9:23) and subjected to slavery yet enjoy the blessing of life in the land?

threatening presence of evil that has to be removed. If God is not depicted in the narrative as resolved to eliminate them then the Torah claim that God's aim is to establish right order is inconsistent and compromised. The destruction of the wicked nations is carried out according to the *kherem* or 'ban'—a motif in the 'holy war' stories that requires an enemy be completely 'devoted to the Lord for destruction' (Josh 6:17).[8] This ensures the evil is completely eliminated which is the good and just thing to do. The narrative does not address questions of ethnic cleansing, violence, human rights, and so on; the nations function as ciphers for the evil that needs to be destroyed.[9] On occasion women and/or livestock are exempt from the ban (for example, virgins in Num 31:18; livestock and spoil in Josh 8:27) but these are for Israel's benefit rather than a humanitarian gesture to the enemy. God's decree that certain things are exempt from the ban presumably renders them good—an example of the argument from authority. God's purpose in all this is to 'create' a 'very good land/ earth' (Num 14:7) devoid of evil, a mirror image of creation in Genesis 1. This means that any subsequent eruptions of evil in society and the land cannot be blamed on God or a residue of wicked foreigners. Israel alone is guilty of fouling its nest.[10]

The fulfillment of the promises of land and conquest of enemies also needed to be linked to Israel's relationship to God. The loyalty to God of the ancestors and the conquest generation must have been a key factor in the success of the conquest, if not loyalty/obedience would lose much of its motivational power. Hence another promise fulfilled in the book of Joshua is the conquest of the land as a reward

---

8. For reflections on the development of the holy war tradition in Israel and associated scholarly literature see Lohfink, 'The Strata of the Pentateuch and the Question of War,' in *Theology of the Pentateuch. Themes of the Priestly Narrative and Deuteronomy* (translated by Linda M Maloney; Edinburgh: T&T Clark, 1994), 173–226.
9. Cf Susan Niditch on the ideology of the ban as God's justice (*War in the Hebrew Bible. A Study in the Ethics of Violence* [Oxford: Oxford University Press, 1993], 56–58).
10. For this reason Deuteronomy warns Israel not to pursue relationships with foreigners and their false cults (cf 6:14; 7:2–3; 9; 10:16; 13:1–18). In the view of Lev 18:24–28 the previous inhabitants defiled the land and the Lord 'visited' (*paqad*) upon it its iniquity and it vomited them out. In this way the land was cleansed. If Israel follows the practices of these nations the land will in turn vomit it out (cf also 20:22).

for loyalty to God. This promise first occurs in Genesis 22:18 where Abraham is promised that, because of his obedience, his offspring will triumph over their enemies and bring blessing to the nations; it is reiterated more in terms of gift in 26:5. In Exodus 23:20-22 Israel is urged to be attentive to the guiding angel and his voice in order to enter the land and conquer it. The good spies Joshua and Caleb warn Israel in Numbers 14:8-9 that it will only enter the land 'if the Lord is pleased with us'. In 14:24 Caleb is promised an inheritance in the land for his loyalty. Deuteronomy 4 opens with Moses' exhortation to Israel to obey the 'statutes and ordinances' so that it may 'live to enter and occupy the land' (cf also 6:18; 11:22-25). Not only the occupation but also Israel's entire life in the land is seen in Deuteronomy as a reward or consequence of obedience to the law (cf 6:1-3; 11:8-9, 21). Reward for loyalty, like retribution for disloyalty, always operates within the larger context of God's overall righteous purpose.

It is no surprise therefore to find Joshua being reminded in 1:7 of the need 'to act in accordance with all the law that my servant Moses commanded you' so that 'you may be successful wherever you may go'. In 1:16, the people in their turn promise Joshua 'All that you have commanded us we will do'. Joshua 24:31 declares that 'Israel served the Lord all the days of Joshua and all the days of the elders who outlived Joshua' (cf also Judg 2:7). Israel's loyalty was in accord with the 'book of the law of Moses' proclaimed at a ceremony between Mt Gerizim and Mt Ebal in Joshua 8:30-35 (MT). The ceremony is located elsewhere in the LXX and the Qumran manuscript 4QJosh[a]; in the LXX it comes after 9:2 and in 4Josh[a] before 5:2. This suggests the passage is a later addition. Its location in the MT makes good sense despite the fact that one has to allow for an unreported return to camp at Gilgal for the setting of the Gibeonite episode (9:6). It portrays Joshua and Israel reaffirming their commitment to the law of Moses with its blessing and curses; fidelity to it enabled the evil of Achan's transgression to be purged from Israel's midst and the curse of defeat to be turned into the blessing of victory. The engraving of the law of Moses on stone and its public proclamation (8:32, 34) establishes the land as the Lord's and the Lord's law as the law of the land; only the Lord is to be worshipped in this land according to the law of Moses.[11] Joshua 8:30-35 marks the completion of the first stage

---

11. Cf J Gordon McConville & Stephen N Williams, *Joshua* (The Two Horizons

of the conquest narrative and introduces the second stage in which there are no further setbacks.[12]

After the successful conquest and distribution of the land to the tribes, the book ends with another assembly at Shechem. Joshua, following his predecessor and model Moses, reviews all that God has done for Israel and urges the people to 'revere the Lord' (24:14). Somewhat surprisingly, he then tells them that they are unable to serve their jealous Lord who will punish their (inevitable) transgressions (v 19). As in Deuteronomy this second person address is meant to reach all generations of Israelites. The faithful generation assembled at Shechem commit themselves to serve the Lord and v 31 states that they remained committed. According to vv 25-26 Joshua sets 'a statute and an ordinance' for the people and writes them in 'the book of the law of God'. While this phrase is not found in Deuteronomy, it is difficult to accept that this book and its contents are to be understood as different to or in competition with the Torah. It may signal that Joshua, who has faithfully meditated on the law in accord with 1:8, is able to provide 'a statute and ordinance' that will help the people, like him, to 'be careful to act in accordance with all that is written in it'.[13] The location of this assembly at Shechem is strategic; it recalls 8:30-35 because Shechem is between Mts. Gerizim and Ebal. It also recalls Deuteronomy 11:29-30 (Shechem) and 27:1-26 (Gerizim and Ebal). Joshua and the people fulfill the requirements of Deuteronomy.

Old Testament Commentary; Grand Rapids, Michigan: Eerdmans, 2010), 44; also Jean-Louis Ska, 'Josh 8:30-35: Israel Officially Takes Possession of the Land,' in *'Gerechtigkeit und Recht zu üben' (Gen 18, 19): Studien zur altorientalischen und biblischen Rechtsgeschichte, zur Religionsgeschichte Israels und zur Religionssoziologie. Festschrift für Eckart Otto zum 65. Geburtstag,* edited by Reinhard Achenbach and Martin Arneth (Beihefte zur ZABR 13; Wiesbaden: Harrassowitz, 2010), 308-16.

12. Richard D Nelson suggests that the LXX location provides an object for what the kings 'heard' in 9:2, thereby linking their reaction to news of Ai's destruction (*Joshua* [Interpretation; Louisville, Ky: Westminster John Knox, 1997] 117). The Qumran location portrays Joshua fulfilling the requirement in Deut 27:2 that 'on the day' Israel enters the land it is to enact the ceremony described. This however requires that Israel decamped from Gilgal by the Jordan to Mts Gerizim and Ebal, a journey that is not reported in the text (for a discussion of the different sequences, see Earl, *Reading Joshua as Christian Scripture,* 116).

13. Following Ernst Axel Knauf, *Josua* (Zürcher Bibel Kommentare AT 6; Zürich: Theologischer Verlag, 2008), 198.

Given the conviction that God gave the land, the author(s) of Joshua were obliged to depict Israel as faithful otherwise it could not function as a sign of God's presence and purpose.[14] There is no neutral ground in the Torah's understanding of the covenant relationship with God: one either demonstrates loyalty by keeping the law and reaps its reward or disloyalty by breaching it and reaping its retribution. Hence to have a disloyal Israel occupy the land would contradict Torah theology. This is a case where theology drives the shaping of the story. Two additional reasons may lie behind the way the book of Joshua tells the story. One involves propaganda: it helps to persuade audiences and readers of the veracity of God's promises and to foster the conviction that obedience to the Torah is the only way to life. Moreover, the kind of loyalty displayed by the conquest generation is possible for any generation; this may be designed to counter a charge that what the Torah demands is unrealistic and impossible (cf Deut 30:11-14). The other involves consistency. The conquest generation's success 'across the Jordan' under Joshua is in line with its earlier success in 'trans Jordan' under Moses (Deut 2-3). Thus Joshua completed what Moses began.

Even though fidelity and its rewards needed to be the dominant theme, Israel's theologians were able to keep the retribution side of the equation in view, and to do so without unduly complicating the storyline or compromising the notion of a successful conquest. This is evident in the account of Achan's theft of the 'devoted things' that were under the 'holy war' ban (6:18; cf Deut 7:25-26). In a reversal of the one saving the many, the guilt of one afflicts the whole nation in the form of defeat at Ai. According to Deuteronomy, Israel is to be the one people of God living the covenant relationship according to the one Torah; hence the transgression of one ruptures the covenant bond—as God informs Joshua in 7:11. But the story is shaped to showcase the correct behaviour of Joshua and Israel in response to the crisis; their fidelity to God's instructions enables the guilty Achan to be identified in the trial by lot and he and his family are destroyed (7:6-26). The account provides a three-pronged catechesis: it emphasises that God's decrees must be obeyed at all times (the example being the ban); it warns that the infidelity of one can threaten the covenant

---

14. As McConville notes, 'if idolatry wins out in Canaan, then where in the world is Yahweh to be known and worshipped?' (McConville & Williams, *Joshua*, 114).

relationship of all (an example of the one and the many); it assures a positive outcome for those who follow God's injunctions. Right relationships with God are contrasted sharply with their opposite in the figure of Achan. Despite this the Achan episode, as noted, creates a sense of fragility and foreboding, particularly in relation to the warnings of failure in the Torah. Will Israel in due course become like Achan?

The Book of Judges

The introduction to the book of Judges (1:1–3:6) is complex and most likely the work of several hands. A full investigation of its composition is beyond the scope of this study but the following comments will hopefully provide a reasonable if limited explanation of how the various parts relate together.[15]

According to Joshua 24:31 Israel served the Lord all the days of Joshua and of the elders who outlived him. Given this, one would presume that after his death Israel obediently undertook to conquer the remaining nations as per his words in 23:4–5. A list of these nations is provided in 13:1–7. But the stories of war in Judges 3:7–16:31 clearly presume they were not conquered. These factors needed to be accounted for in terms of Torah criteria and one can see this in the way the present text has been arranged. Judges 1:1–36 reports that Israel did set out to conquer the remaining nations after the death of Joshua but was unable to complete the job.[16] An angelic messenger in 2:1–5 proclaims that this is because the people have failed to obey God's command. The implication from 2:2 is that Israel has made a covenant with the inhabitants of the land and not destroyed their altars—a breach of Deuteronomy 7:2–5. But there is no explicit

---

15. For a discussion of the literary evidence and indications as to how the text may have been composed see Campbell and O'Brien, *Unfolding the Deuteronomistic History. Origins, Upgrades, Present Text* (Minneapolis: Fortress Press, 2000), 170–76.
16. One could include the nations in Josh 13:13 and 16:10 that were not driven out, and those in 15:63 that were unable to be driven out. It is intriguing that Joshua is not mentioned in association with these texts. Are they meant to foreshadow Judg 1:1–36? According to Judg 1:21 the Benjaminites did not drive out the Jebusites from Jerusalem whereas according to Josh 15:63 it was the people of Judah who did not do it. Judges 1:29 is close to Josh 16:10 but there is no reference to 13:13 in Judg 1:1–36.

accusation of apostasy. Because of Israel's disobedience God resolves not to drive the remaining nations out in order that they shall be Israel's adversaries and their gods a snare.[17] This prepares for their presence and role in the subsequent stories. Israel responds to the angel's message by weeping and sacrificing to the Lord (2:4-5). Like the preceding accusation these verses are general but they could be read as a sign of repentance and a commitment to remain faithful to God.

Given this reading of 1:1-2:5 one can offer an explanation of 2:6-10. From a compositional point of view it looks to be what is called a 'resumptive repetition', a literary device to return to the main storyline (Josh 24:28-31) after an insertion, in this case 1:1-2:5.[18] If this is the case it means that the hand responsible for 2:6-10 made the insertion. The combined text can be read as an assertion that, except for the disobedience of 2:2, which was not apostasy, the conquest generation remained faithful to God after the death of Joshua. This is in line with an aspect of the Torah, namely that no one is completely innocent or righteous, not even Abraham, Moses, Joshua (cf Josh 9) or the conquest generation. According to 2:10 and following, it was the next generation (and their descendants)—'who did not know the Lord or the work that he had done for Israel'—that proved unfaithful by committing the 'original sin' of apostasy (2:11-13). Judges 2:11-3:6 is probably the work of more than one hand but, in terms of the present text, it can be read as an application of the angel's speech in 2:1-5 to this far more serious situation. The following elements of the speech recur in 2:11-3:6 but in a more explicit and developed manner—Israel's transgression, God's response, Israel's punishment, the role of the nations. Each element involves of course a relationship. According to 2:11-13, 19 Israel not only commits apostasy but does so repeatedly and flagrantly, an ancient example of a recidivist. God's response is to punish Israel by handing it completely into the power of its enemies so that it is in 'great distress' (2:14-15)—a dramatic

---

17. The MT term translated as 'adversaries' in the NRSV is unusual, a literal rendering would be 'to your sides/on your flanks', implying that they will always be around as a rival. The same term occurs in Num 33:55 and Josh 23:13.
18. On this literary technique see Burke O Long, 'Framing Repetitions in Biblical Historiography', *JBL* 106 (1987), 385-99.

escalation of the scenario in 2:3.[19] Yet, in accord with 2:1b and the Torah, God does not sever the relationship with Israel and in due course 'raises up' leaders who deliver from oppression.[20] What we might call God's righteous purpose in doing this is underscored by the way these deliverers also function as teachers (of Torah; cf 2:17). Israel is given every opportunity to 'know the Lord' and change its ways but it doesn't, as Moses foresaw and warned in passages such as Deuteronomy 4:25-31; 29-30 and the song in 32.[21]

Israel's recidivism leads in turn to a recasting of the role of the surrounding nations—conveniently available thanks to 1:1-36. Judges 2:20-22 decrees that, because of Israel's flagrant transgression of the covenant, God 'will not repeat/continue' to drive out the nations that remained when Joshua died.[22] God is reported doing so in 1:1-36 up to a point but now no longer (cf 1:2, 19, 22). The nations still remaining will henceforth provide a test of Israel's loyalty to God (2:21-22; 3:4). In accord with 2:14 every failure of the test will be met with defeat at the hands of these nations. Within this context one can offer the following comment on Judges 3:1-2. The remaining nations were originally meant to provide subsequent generations of Israelites with the same experience of war as their fathers—namely, loyalty leads to victory—but now they will provide quite a different experience of war—disloyalty spells defeat and oppression by enemies. The just nature of these decrees and provisions is borne out by the report in 3:5-6 of Israel intermarrying with the nations and worshipping their gods, and in the way the subsequent narrative of Judges unfolds. The focus on Israel's transgressions and their consequences effectively puts on hold the theme of Israel as the mediator of divine blessing for

---

19. This connection is also noted by Mann, *The Book of the Former Prophets* (Eugene, Or.: Cascade books; 2011), 55.
20. According to Susan Niditch, the basic sense of the term 'judge' is that of 'decision maker'. The judge makes decisions about war in which he or she (cf Deborah) functions as a military leader, as a ruler, at times as a prophet (again Deborah), and as an administrator of justice (*Judges* [OTL; Louisville/London: Westminster John Knox, 2008], 1-3.
21. The NRSV translation of Deut 4:25 has 'if you act corruptly' whereas the Hebrew reads literally 'and you act corruptly', like the preceding clause 'and you are old/long in the land'. The verse is effectively a prophecy or prediction of what Israel will do, like 29-30 and 32.
22. Reading Judg 2:22 as a continuation of God's speech in 2:20-21, in contrast to the NRSV.

the nations: it can only function in this capacity when it is itself in a right relationship with God as was the case with the faithful conquest generation, as illustrated in the cases of Rahab and the Gibeonites. Israel can only pass on what it has itself received.

The only occurrence of righteousness in the book of Judges is the feminine plural form in the song of Deborah (5:11), in reference to God. The phrase is frequently translated in English as 'the triumphs/victories of the Lord'. However, in her recent commentary, Susan Niditch translates it as 'the justice-bringing acts of Yhwh' and comments that the verse, like 5:6–7 and 5:13, portrays the Israelites as 'the military and political underdogs'.[23] One could combine these translations to say that God's victory overturns the existing order by delivering Israel from unjust oppression by the Canaanites (cf 4:3). The agents of God's punishment have overstepped their mandate and acted unjustly, reaping in turn a just punishment by way of defeat in battle.[24] There is a similar kind of argument in the prophets, for example in Isaiah's condemnation of the Assyrians (10:5–19). In an act of mercy/compassion God punishes oppressive nations so that Israel may once again be provided with an opportunity to carry out its God-given task—to live in the land according to the requirements of the Torah—which, according to the book of Judges, it seems incapable of doing.

Passages such as Judges 3:9, 15; 4:3; 6:6; 10:10 imply that enemy oppression does lead Israel to recognise its sin in so far as it calls on God for deliverance from oppression. Judges 10:10–16 reports that Israel confessed its sin and put away the foreign gods. But the change doesn't last; with the death of the last 'minor judge' in 12:15 Israel relapses once more (13:1). Repeated disloyalty to God has repercussions for the good order of Israelite society and it gradually unravels as the narrative unfolds. There is the violence unleashed by Gideon's son Abimelech in Judges 9 who seeks to be king on his own terms—a complete reversal of the requirement in Deuteronomy 17:14–20. There is the civil war between Ephraimites and Gileadites in Judges 12 in the wake of Jephthah's victory, while the story of Samson has no report of Israel crying to the Lord for deliverance.

---

23. Cf Niditch, *Joshua*, 68, 79.
24. The narrative does not report whether and how the nations are informed of their task.

Even the loyalty of a number of the deliverer judges is found wanting. Barak does not trust the prophetic word of Deborah (4:4–10), Gideon makes an ephod that ensnares his family and Israel (8:27), Jephthah makes a foolish vow that leads to the death of his daughter (11:30–40), and the last judge in the book, Samson, fails to deliver the people from Philistine domination.[25]

The final section of the book, Judges 17–21, makes no mention of deliverer judges. Given that Samson failed to deliver Israel from the Philistines and that it remains under their hegemony until 1 Samuel 7, it is reasonable to presume this is the broad context for Judges 17–21. Yet there is no report of Israel crying to God for deliverance as before. Instead the reader is informed near the beginning of this section (17:6) and at its end (21:25) that 'In those days there was no king in Israel; each man did what was right (*yashar*) in his own eyes'. Two other passages refer to the absence of a king in those days (18:1; 19:1). These comments are distributed across the two stories that make up Judges 17–21; the first is that of Micah and a Levite in 17–18 and the second that of another Levite and his concubine in 19–21. The two stories may well be of independent provenance and older than the book of Judges in its final form. My interest is in how they function in relation to the comments or refrains in 17:6; 18:1; 19:1; 21:25 and in relation to the larger book of Judges.

It is surely significant that each story commences with an individual—Micah in 17:1 and a certain Levite in 19:1—who sets out to do what is right in his eyes, and initially at least looks to a reader to be doing what is indeed right. Micah returns stolen money to his mother and the Levite seeks to be reconciled with his concubine. Yet each character quickly becomes corrupted or exposes a corrupt side—Micah's establishment of a shrine and a priest for his own benefit (17:13), and the Levite's self-indulgence (19:4–9). As each story unfolds other characters become corrupted or are exposed as equally corrupt as Micah and the Levite.

EA Mueller argues that the characters in Judges 17–18 breach several of the commandments, namely making an idol, dishonouring a parent (mother), taking God's name in vain, killing, lying, and

---

25. According to Mann 'it is never really clear that Samson delivers Israel from the oppression of the Philistines' (*The Book of the Former Prophets*, 80).

coveting.[26] Whether one agrees with this assessment or not, the sense of increasing confusion about right relationship with God and between Israelites is difficult to avoid—particularly when read against the background of Torah stipulations. The story ends with the Danite tribe kidnapping Micah's Levite, stealing his idol and setting it up as a rival shrine to 'the house of God' in Shiloh (18:30–31). As well they effectively implement the ban against Laish without any authorisation from God. The impression is that doing what is right in one's own eyes in this story means doing it independently of or without reference to God, with the inevitable consequences (as portrayed in the story).[27] Thomas Mann entitles his section on Judges 19–21 as 'Rape, Murder, and Mayhem'.[28] The Levite lies in order to goad the tribes of Israel into avenging a rape and murder in which he is complicit. In an ironic twist the story concludes with them effectively advocating what they had initially set out to avenge—the rape of women—by approving the abduction of the maidens of Shiloh (21:19–21). This is designed to restore the tribe of Benjamin (21:3) and thus preserve Israel's unity but, as the story clearly implies, it is a bogus unity involving lies and deception (21:22).

It is difficult to escape the impression that Judges 17–21 is about the breakdown of proper relationships in Israelite society and the disorder and chaos this unleashes.[29] Within such a context the term *yahsar* (right) in 17:6 and 21:25 assumes a certain ironic tone. Each character or group in the story may do what he or they think is right ('in his own eyes') but the outcome reveals a completely distorted perception of reality. This can only lead to disorder and chaos. Within the larger context of the book of Judges one may ask whether this is the 'end-game' of what Judges 2:10 announces, the emergence of an Israel that 'did not know the Lord or the work that he had done

---

26. Cf E Aydeet Mueller, *The Micah Story: A Morality Tale in the Book of Judges* (Studies in Biblical Literature; New York: Lang, 2001), 3, 14, 35 (cited from Mann, *The Book of the Former Prophets*, 89).
27. This is of course an interpretation; for a different one see Niditch, *Judges* 210-11.
28. Mann, *The Book of the Former Prophets*, 89. According to Phyllis Trible 'Such internal anarchy produces violence and vengeance, as the narratives about the tribe of Benjamin amply demonstrate' (*Texts of Terror: Literary Feminist Readings of Biblical Narratives* [OBT, 13; Philadelphia: Fortress Press, 1984], 65).
29. Cf Barry Webb, *The Book of the Judges. An Integrated Reading* (Eugene, Oregon: Wipf & Stock, 2008), 199; for a different reading, cf Niditch, *J*, 210-11.

for Israel'. There is a sense of increasing loss of knowledge of God and the ways of God in the stories of the deliverer judges that bears full fruit in these final chapters of the book.[30] No report of enemy oppression occurs in Judges 17–21. As noted, this can be explained by the ongoing Philistine oppression from 13:1. But these chapters may also be hinting at the same theme as in the golden calf story, that the greatest obstacle to God's purpose is not an external enemy but the enemy within Israel—its continued infidelity.

Four times Judges 17–21 notes that 'in those days there was no king in Israel' (17:6; 18:1; 19:1 21:25). Depending on the context in which one reads these statements they take on a somewhat different meaning. Read within the context of Judges 17–21 they could imply that if Israel had had a king 'in those days' such disasters would not have occurred. But what kind of king does the text have in mind? Presumably not like Abimelech in Judges 9 because his murderous rule created much the same kind of internal mayhem as recounted in Judges 19–21. Do the statements anticipate the reign of Saul, or of David and Solomon? But Saul fails as a king and David and Solomon are censured for infidelity and for bringing trouble on Israel. Perhaps it is the ideal outlined in Deuteronomy 17:14–20 which requires a king to be completely devoted to the Torah. Such a king will do what is right in God's eyes, not his own.[31] But, as already noted, the teaching of the Torah is that no one person or society is completely righteous in God's eyes (cf Ps 143:2).

---

30. Cf Webb, *The Book of the Judges*, 198, 200–1. For a detailed examination of the 'echoes' of the stories of the judges in chapters 17–21, see Gregory TK Wong, *Compositional Strategy of the Book of Judges: An Inductive, Rhetorical Study* (Supplements to Vetus Testamentum 111; Leiden/Boston: Brill, 2006), 79–141.
31. Wong (*Compositional Strategy of the Book of Judges*, 212–23) proposes, from a comparison of the Judges' passages with 2 Chr 15:3–6, that the term 'king' refers to God. Whether one agrees or not, this illustrates how the meaning of terms can vary according to the contexts in which they are read.

2

In the Books of Samuel

1 Samuel 1–7

The opening verse of 1 Samuel clearly echoes Judges 17:1 and 19:1 (a certain man from the hill country of Ephraim) prompting the question; are we in for more tales of woe? Initially this indeed looks to be the case; there is division within the family of Elkanah and a less than adequate proposal to resolve it. The fertile Peninnah provokes the barren Hannah (1:6, a verse that is not in the LXX) while Elkanah assumes that what will ease Hannah's distress is complete devotion to him (1:8, 'Am I not worth more to you than ten sons'?). Another example of what is right in one's own eyes? Peninnah's provocation is all the more disturbing if, as 1:6 implies, it is because she knows the Lord has closed Hannah's womb. Given that she sees this as punishment for some misdemeanor, Peninnah is taunting Hannah as a sinner. As the story unfolds this is exposed as a false perception. The closing of Hannah's womb is a divine initiative—unknown to her—that challenges her to trust God and remain loyal despite the signs to the contrary, which she does. She turns in prayer to God for a son, not for her own benefit but to advance God's cause. Hannah is the one faithful Israelite who is able to be a mediator of God's blessing for the fragmented society portrayed in the book of Judges. The description of her son's vocation in 1:11 recalls that of Samson in Judges 13:3–7, a hint that he will accomplish what Samson failed to do, deliver Israel from the Philistine oppression. God answers her prayer and in thanksgiving Hannah sings a song (2:1–9) that celebrates her 'victory' as an integral part of God's just rule of all humanity and creation. The statement in 2:2 that 'there is no Rock like our God' recalls the same image in the song of Deuteronomy 32; it is its first occurrence after that deuteronomic text and is taken up again in David's song in 2 Samuel 22—celebrating the 'day' of his deliverance from 'the hand of all his enemies, and from the hand of Saul'. God alone is the one firm foundation because God alone has all knowledge (2:3b), power over human life (2:6) and over creation (2:8c), is utterly loyal to 'his faithful ones' (2:9), and will judge all the earth (2:10b).[1] The song begins with the exaltation of an Israelite (Hannah) and it ends with the exaltation of another (the king/anointed). The implication is that what God has begun with Hannah will reach its fulfillment with the establishment of 'his king/his anointed'.

The first story that confirms how God, according to the song, overturns the existing disorder is about the house of Eli. It juxtaposes reports of Samuel's growth and ministry before the Lord (2:11, 21b, 26; 3:1) with reports of the wickedness of Eli's sons (2:12-17), their father's inability to change them because of their refusal to listen (2:22-25)—a remark that recalls Judges 2:17—and the advent of a prophet who pronounces doom for the house (2:27-36).[2] Eli's sons serve themselves instead of God and God's people (2:12-17), a gross abuse of their priestly vocation and of the cultic relationship between God and the people. What is worse, their actions foster a false notion of God and God's relationship with the people. This evil must be eliminated and an unnamed prophet announces that the promise of an eternal priesthood for the house of Eli is revoked in favour of a 'faithful priest' whom God will raise up to minister on behalf of 'my anointed one', presumably a reference to the same royal figure as in Hannah's song (cf 2:10c, 35). The death of Eli's sons will be a sign of the truth of this prophecy and this is duly reported in the war

---

1. The verb translated as 'judge' in 2:10 is *din*; although it may earlier have had a somewhat different meaning to the more common verb to judge (*shaphat*) in time they became virtually synonymous (so Jenni/Westermann, *Theologisches Handwörterbuch*, 446-47).
2. The sons' refusal to listen to Eli in 2:25 is followed by the statement that 'it was the will of the Lord to kill them' (literally: 'because the Lord delighted in/wanted to kill them'). The implication is that the Lord has hardened their hearts in order to bring about their doom, as God does with Pharaoh. Eli's sons think they are in control of their father and the liturgy but the only one who is really in control of the course of history, and must be so for the good of creation and humanity, is the Lord (cf Campbell, *1 Samuel* [FOTL VII; Grand Rapids/Cambridge: Eerdmans, 2003], 49). The prophecy places their demise within God's overall saving purpose.

with the Philistines (4:11). A second sign of the truth of the prophecy is that Eli subsequently receives the same message via Samuel in 3:11-18. Samuel thus replaces Eli and his house as God's established representative (3:20).

The subsequent account of the decline of the Elide priesthood and the violent end of some of its members (for example, the priests of Nob in 1 Sam 22:6-19), as well as the emergence of a 'faithful priest' (Zadok in 1 Kgs 2:27, 35), reveals the impact of the retribution announced by the unnamed prophet and by Samuel. There is an element of compassion; the house of Eli is not wiped out and will continue to have some priestly function, but only with the permission of and in complete dependence on the 'faithful priest' (2:36).[3] In a telling reversal of the arrogance and greed of Eli's sons, future members of this house will have to beg for priestly sustenance from the faithful priest (and his house). As well as these links with the subsequent story of Israel there are also links with the preceding story. One is explicit; when Eli drops dead at the news that his sons have been killed in the war the text reports that 'he had judged Israel for forty years' (4:18). The story of the judges continues in the book of Samuel but Eli is more like Samson who failed to deliver Israel from the Philistines. The second is that the sins and death of Eli's sons recall the similar fate that struck the sons of Aaron in Leviticus 10:1-3 for performing an improper liturgy. The extreme nature of the penalty in each case emphasises the importance of the priests' role in the relationship between God and Israel.

The second story about overturning or reversing the existing disorder is the war with the Philistines in 1 Samuel 4-7. The people's presumption is that the presence of the ark will guarantee victory but it doesn't—another example of the distorted perception that occurs when one operates without true knowledge of God. The Philistines are afflicted with much the same malaise: they think they have captured the ark and their god therefore has power over Israel's God, but the subsequent story of the ark in Philistine territory reveals this is not

---

3. For further proposals that seek to correlate elements in the prophecy with the subsequent narrative, see Campbell and O'Brien, *Unfolding the Deuteronomistic History*, 224-25, and more recently Campbell, *1 Samuel*, 53-54. The continuing but impoverished situation of the Elides as prophesied in 1 Sam 2:36 may have in mind Josiah's reforms in 2 Kgs 23:5, 9.

the case. The God of Israel has absolute power over the Philistines and their god Dagon. This of course reveals Israel's defeat as divine retribution for sin, namely the people's (arrogant) assumption that God is on their side and on their terms (4:3). This situation is reversed in 1 Samuel 7.

Samuel's establishment as prophet, plus the return of the ark to the edge of the land in 1 Samuel 6:13-7:2, signals something new is in store. Whatever it is will be on God's terms, depicted graphically in the death of those who presume to know what they can do when the ark arrives at Beth-Shemesh.[4] As a result the ark is lodged at Kiriath-jearim for 'a long time, some twenty years' but it is somewhat uncertain whether this refers to the time between the ark being lodged there and its next move in 2 Samuel 6, or to the time between being lodged and Samuel's initiative in 1 Samuel 7:3. The latter reading would better accommodate the report that the people lamented after the Lord. Samuel's intervention seeks to engage an attitude among the people that is like the cry of distress in the book of Judges. There it leads to God raising a deliverer to free the people from foreign oppression, and much the same thing occurs here. The people put away the foreign gods and confess (7:4-6) their sin, the Philistines mass for attack, Samuel invokes God's help and the Philistines are routed, the hand of the Lord being against them 'all the days of Samuel' (7:13). Like Deborah before him, Samuel the prophet is also a judge who 'judged Israel all the days of his life' (7:15).

1 Samuel 7 affirms that the judge form of government, as established by God and faithfully implemented by the people and their leader, promotes the good of the people as effectively as any other. Israel is able to maintain proper relationship with God and within the society, and to be free of enemy oppression. One could say that it is not so much the organisation that is to blame but the people who operate it. The key of course is the Torah that teaches the way in which God desires relationships to be established and ordered, the way in which people are to behave. In this way the various limited and in themselves flawed forms of human organisation can

---

4. As the NRSV notes indicate, it opts for the LXX version of 1 Sam 6:19 rather than the Hebrew (MT). Proof is not available but, in my judgement, the MT is closer to the initiative taken by Uzzah in 2 Sam 6:6-7 for which he was also struck down.

function properly. Nevertheless, the preceding narrative in Judges and 1 Samuel raises the spectre that Israel will yet again relapse into apostasy, just as Moses prophesied in Deuteronomy 31:26-29. This indeed happens in the subsequent account of the emergency of the monarchy; in both 8:7-8 and 10:17-19 Israel's demand for a king is described as tantamount to apostasy.

1 Samuel 8-12

This is a complex section of 1 Samuel, generating considerable debate among historical-critical analysts as to how it was compiled and the likely sources from which it was compiled. In *Unfolding the Deuteronomistic History* Campbell and O'Brien propose that it was compiled principally from two traditions or strands.[5] One is a 'prophetic strand' (identified principally in the story of the anointing of Saul), the other an 'assembly strand' (identified in the account of three assemblies, at Ramah in chapter 8, at Mizpah in 10:17-25, and at Gilgal in 11:14-12:25). The former reflects a more pro-monarchical tradition, while the latter a more anti-monarchical tradition. While no one theory is likely to account for all the textual phenomena or convince all readers, this seems a reasonable and defensible one. The more synchronic analyses of Robert Polzin and David Jobling focus on the internal dynamics of the present text and the interaction between text and reader.[6] These have provided valuable insights and challenges for the necessarily limited reading of the text proposed here. It is my contention that the two strands were carefully combined to claim that kingship in Israel is founded—like the covenant relationship in the Torah—on proper relationships between the various players. These are God, Samuel, his sons, the people, and the king.

Two things strike one on a reading of 1 Samuel 8; one is that the conduct of all the human players is sinful or at least questionable in some way, the other is that despite this there is no announcement of divine punishment, in particular for the people who are effectively

---

5. Campbell & O'Brien, *Unfolding the Deuteronomistic History*, 229-30.
6. Cf Robert Polzin, *Samuel and the Deuteronomist. A Literary Study of the Deuteronomistic History. Part Two. 1 Samuel* (San Francisco: Harper & Row, 1989); David Jobling, *1 Samuel* (Berit Olam. Studies in Hebrew Narrative & Poetry; Collegeville, Mn: The Liturgical Press, 1998).

accused by God of apostasy in 8:7-8. Even though historical critical analysis would almost uniformly regard these verses as an addition they are presumably meant to play an important role in the portrait of the people. To take Samuel's sons first: their crime is a clear case of social injustice; they abuse their rights as judges and fail in their responsibility to the people. Nevertheless neither God nor Samuel decrees punishment for them, as one might expect in the light of the preceding storyline. Perhaps the punishment 'clause' may be contained indirectly in God's instruction to Samuel to 'set a king over them' (8:22). This implies the removal of the sons from the office of judge. One could think that they get off lightly compared to the sons of Eli but Eli's own remark to his sons in 2:25 is worth noting. Despite some variation between the versions, the thrust of the verse is that 'another' (or God in the MT) can intercede 'if one person sins against another' but when the offence is against God directly (as is presumably the case with the sons' abuse of the cult) no such intercession is possible[7] Given that Eli's statement is to be taken as an authoritative statement in the narrative, the social injustice of Samuel's sons is not as serious as the cultic abuse of Eli's.

The case is not so clear with Samuel. A number of scholars hold that he breached the charismatic nature of judgeship by appointing his sons as judges.[8] This can be read as an attempt to establish a dynasty of judges/rulers, implying that he has his own and his family's welfare at heart rather than Israel's. Against this view however are two pieces of evidence from the book of Judges. One is that, according to the book of Judges, the charismatic nature of judgeship only applies to those whom God raises up to combat an enemy. This is not the case in 1 Samuel 8; as 7:1 states, 'the hand of the Lord was against the Philistines all the days of Samuel'. A second is that one can read the appointment of the sons as a sign of Samuel's concern for the people rather than self-interest. According to the book of Judges, whenever a judge dies and the people are bereft of leadership they relapse. Samuel therefore appoints his sons in the hope of overcoming this problem.

---

7. The MT has 'God' as subject, the LXX has 'they shall pray for him', while a Qumran MS has 'someone'.
8. Cf Jobling, *1 Samuel*, 63; Christophe Nihan, 'L'injustice des fils de Samuel, au tournant d'une époque. (Quelques remarques sur la fonction de 1 Samuel 8,1-5 dans son context littéraire),' *BN* 94 (1998), 26-32, see especially 29.

A more likely failure on Samuel's part is that he did not rebuke his sons, something that at least his predecessor Eli did.⁹ Even though it is possible to read the initial encounter between Samuel and the elders in 8:4–6 as the first news that he has of his sons' misdemeanors it seems unlikely. Given his portrayal in the preceding narrative as the judge and prophet of all Israel, it is hard to read 8:6 in this sense and not as his reaction to the request/demand—to have a king—which he sees as 'evil'. This is more in keeping with his subsequent prayer to God and God's reply. Granted there is a measure of failure in Samuel's responsibilities as judge (and prophet), one would expect some punishment to be forthcoming. While none is directly decreed one may argue that it is contained indirectly in God's command that he listen to the people in all that they say. The implication is that Samuel has not been listening and has things skewed. He thinks the people are rejecting him and his sons as judges whereas in fact, according to God's assessment—which by definition is correct—they are rejecting God as their King (8:7–8). Samuel needs to learn and so is reminded/corrected that his relationship with the people is based on the foundational relationship that he and the people have with God. It is because the people have rejected their relationship with God that he has in turn been rejected.¹⁰

1 Samuel 8 concludes with God commanding Samuel to listen to the people and make them a king, but surprisingly, he dismisses them instead. Is this a sign that Samuel is resisting God's directive?¹¹ Two things need to be taken into account in assessing the likely sense of 8:22; one is that the Hebrew verb for making a king is different to

---

9. One might appeal to Samuel's old age (8:1) as an extenuating circumstance, and that the elders may be excusing him because of this (8:4). However, Eli is also portrayed as an old man who nevertheless rebukes his wicked sons.
10. This is an attempt to relate the two references to Samuel's rejection by the people in 8:7–8. Even though Campbell (*1 Samuel*, 102) is probably right to regard the second as the work of a pedantic editor, it presumably has a function within the narrative.
11. A Graeme Auld asks 'Is Samuel playing for time? Or is he even refusing to take the divine instruction forward'? (*I & II Samuel. A Commentary* [OTL; Louisville: WJK, 2011] 95). Bruce C Birch thinks that Samuel's recalcitrance is one possible reading, another is that 8:22 is a way of ending an episode in order to move the story forward (cf 1029 of 'The First and Second Books of Samuel. Introduction, Commentary, and Reflections' in *The New Interpreter's Bible, Volume Two* [Nashville; Abingdon, 1998] 947–1383).

the preceding verb 'set' (*sim*) and implies something different to what the people have in mind.[12] The second is that Samuel's dismissal of the people l is the first time in the assembly that he takes charge of proceedings. It is a sign that he has regained the initiative but this is only as a result of heeding God's instructions. The verse can be seen to have two functions in the narrative; it recounts the end of the assembly at Ramah but it also indicates that what follows will reveal God's choice of a king through the mediation of a Samuel now attuned to God's word.

The clearest case of sin in 1 Samuel 8 concerns the people; according to 8:7-8 their demand for a king is a rejection of God as King and tantamount to apostasy. What God communicates privately to Samuel here he proclaims publicly in the subsequent assembly at Mizpah (10:17-19). The people's rejection of God and Samuel is underscored by the report in 8:19 that they refused to listen to Samuel's warnings about the ways of the king they have in mind—a warning that God instructed Samuel to communicate to the people. In light of this what is striking is the apparent absence of retribution on the model of the book of Judges—apostasy reaps foreign invasion and oppression by an enemy. One reason may be that 1 Samuel 7:13 states that the Philistines were subdued 'all the days of Samuel'. Another reason may be that the people's demand to 'set' (*sim*) a king over us' recalls the legislation in Deuteronomy 17:14-20. According to this text when Israel has possession of the land and is settled in it and says 'I will set (*sim*) a king over me like all the nations that are round about me', it may do so as long as it is a king that God chooses and is not a foreigner. Moreover, as the passage unfolds it becomes clear that the kind of king envisaged in this legislation is anything but 'a king like all the nations'; rather he will be a model Israelite, completely devoted to imbibing and living the teaching of the Torah.[13] There is therefore nothing wrong with the desire to have a king as long as these criteria are fulfilled.

---

12. It is the *hif'il* or causative form of the verb 'to be a king' (*malak*).
13. This interpretation of Deut 17:14-20 is developed in more detail in my 'Deuteronomy 16.18-18.22; Meeting the Challenge of Towns and Nations,' *JSOT* 33.2 (2008), 155-72, and is in disagreement with Serge Frolov who argues that in 1 Samuel 8 'the request for a king is filed in full accordance with Deuteronomy' (*The Turn of the Cycle. 1 Samuel 1-8 in Synchronic and Diachronic Perspectives* [BZAW 342; Berlin/New York: Walter de Gruyter, 2004], 188). Note how Deut 17:18-20 (for the king) reflects 6:1-9 (for the people).

However, the people are at fault in the following areas. Firstly, their desire for a king is a reaction to division (the elders/people versus Samuel and his sons) and not an expression of the unity signaled by the 'I' of Deuteronomy 17:14. Second, there is no reference to God's choice in their demand; according to 8:5 they want a king to govern them like all the nations and in 8:19 they add the requirement of a king who will fight their battles.[14] The attitude driving this is exposed by God's judgement in 8:7-8; it is a rejection of God as their King, a sin like apostasy. But the narrative can be read as implying the people are not entirely responsible for their situation; it is, at least in part, due to the misconduct of Samuel's sons and perhaps also of Samuel himself. In other words, the situation is not the same as the golden calf apostasy or the apostasies in the book of Judges and necessitated a different distribution of the manifestation of divine anger/retribution and compassion. This is unfolded in the following chapters.

The final figure to be considered in 1 Samuel 8 is the king. No person is identified or named in the chapter; instead 8:11-17 provides a description of the kind of rule that the king demanded by the people will establish. It will not resolve the disorder unleashed by Samuel's sons but only exacerbate it.[15] The people have complained to Samuel about the misconduct of his sons, but the way of the king (*mishpat hammelek*) they choose will lead to such misery that they will cry out—as their ancestors did in Egypt (cf Exod 2:23)—but God will not answer 'in that day' (1 Sam 8:18). The people remain unrepentant and so God commands Samuel to make them a king. In the wake of what has been narrated so far, one would expect this king not to be the people's choice and to establish a way or rule that is not like that of the nations but in accord with Deuteronomy 17:14-20. For God to allow or approve any other kind of king would imply an unrighteous relationship with the people and with Samuel.

The second assembly—at Mizpah—is preceded by the story of the anointing of Saul as God's choice to be king, a story that is most likely drawn from the 'prophetic strand'. The assembly itself commences with Samuel proclaiming God's assessment of the people's demand;

---

14. One could read 8:5 as a reason for the demand being evil in Samuel's eyes and his recourse to God.
15. As indicated by the repeated use of the verb 'take' (*lqkh*) in 8:11-17, in contrast to its single occurrence in the description of the injustice of Samuel's sons (8:3).

they have repaid God's loyalty with disloyalty and rebellion. It is effectively the same message that God communicated privately to him in 8:7-8. Despite this God, as in preceding instances, remains loyal to the people and chooses Saul to be their king (cf 10:24). The people's acceptance marks a change from their earlier recalcitrance, although at this point there is no acknowledgement of their sin in demanding a king. Moreover, 10:23-24 leaves one somewhat unsure whether their acceptance of Saul is because he is God's choice or because he is the big man. That is, he meets their expectations of a king like all the nations. In a further 'answer' to the people's demands, Samuel tells them the way of the kingdom (*mishpat hammalukah*, NRSV 'rights and duties of the kingship') and writes it in a book as a sign of its enduring validity. This will enable God's chosen one to avoid the disastrous way of the king (*mishpat hammelek*) described in 8:11-17.

As with the assembly at Ramah, the account of the assembly at Mizpah leaves some things unresolved; more is expected. As well as this 10:26-27 reports division among the people with some worthless fellows (literally 'sons of Belial') asking 'How can this man save us'? Their question is answered by Saul's victory over the Ammonites in 11:1-12 and his pardon of the worthless fellows. Saul is here cast as a king who recognises he is merely the earthly representative of the real King who gives the victory, and that he should do as God does. His compassion towards the worthless fellows is in accord with God's compassion towards rebellious Israel. This is seen by Samuel as an opportunity to 'renew the kingship' and so he calls for an assembly at Gilgal. This provides the setting for Samuel's third address which outlines how the troubled relationships between God and the people, as described in the preceding chapters, can be healed and flourish in the new era of kingship.

From a formal point of 1 Samuel 12 comprises three speeches by Samuel in 12:1-3, 6-17, 20-25, punctuated at two points by reports of the people's reaction (12:4-5, 18-19). Each of Samuel's speeches presents an assessment or judgement; in the first Samuel invites the people to judge his own conduct thus far, in the second he judges the people's conduct, and in the third he assesses their future prospects.[16] In 12:4-5 the people declare 'before the Lord' that Samuel is innocent

---

16. Cf Campbell, *1 Samuel*, 118-19.

of any wrongdoing; in 12:18-19 Samuel calls on God to confirm his judgement of the people by a sign that in turn prompts the people to acknowledge their sinfulness in 'demanding a king for ourselves'. In sum, the chapter combines reviews of the past with respective declarations of innocence (Samuel) and guilt (people), confession of guilt (by the people), followed by instructions about how the people can avoid repeating the failures of the past.

The closest parallel to 1 Samuel 12 would appear to be Exodus 33-34 and to a lesser extent Deuteronomy 29-30, both of which deal with renewal of the covenant after its rupture by the people. These renewal texts can be linked to the foundational account of Israels covenant in Exodus 19-24, and Joshua 24. The components that 1 Samuel 12 shares with Exodus 33-34 are: the presence of a covenant mediator (in this case Samuel); a review that exposes the people's misconduct; an expression of the people's repentance; restatement of the stipulations that govern the covenant relationship; promise or restatement of blessing for obedience and punishment for disobedience. These components are shaped in each case to advance the story and its theology/meaning. Given the importance of assessment/judgement in 1 Samuel 12, a key function of it as a covenant renewal is to have the people acknowledge that they have been unfaithful in their relationship with God and with Samuel in demanding a king 'like all the nations'.[17] On the basis of this confession and repentance a right relationship with their righteous God and God's prophet can be re-established and they can faithfully live their vocation in the new era of monarchy.

Analysis of 1 Samuel 12 is complicated by the fact that its review of the past does not tally with the preceding narrative. There is no reference to the misdeeds of Samuel's sons, the lists of enemies and judges in 12:9-11 do not match those in the book of Judges, and the threat from Nahash (12:12) is not what triggers the demand for a king in 1 Samuel 8. Of these the least problematic are the differences

---

17. Cf David Toshio Tsumura, *The First Book of Samuel* (The New International Commentary on the Old Testament; Grand Rapids, Mich: Eerdmans, 2007), 314-15; and Ralph W Klein (*1 Samuel* [second edition; Word Biblical Commentary 10; Nashville, Tenn: Thomas Nelson, 2008], 120) recognise covenant renewal features in 1 Samuel 12 but also stress its uniqueness. For Campbell (*1 Samuel*, 126) the chapter's genre is well nigh indefinable.

between 12:9-11 and Judges. Despite them the version in 1 Samuel 12 captures well the repeated pattern of apostasy and deliverance in the book of Judges. As for the misdeeds of Samuel's sons, the emphasis on Samuel's innocence in 12:1-5 may be an oblique way of distancing him from their crimes. Samuel's reference to his sons as 'being with you' also implies they no longer exercise any authority as judges. However, Samuel's speech and the people's response make no mention of his apparent failure to rebuke them.

The identification of the Nahash crisis as the trigger for the people's demand was probably motivated by two factors. One is that this military threat is more in line with the review in 12:6-11 than the issue of social injustice. A second is that it enabled the author(s) of 1 Samuel 12 to link the demand for a king with Samuel's indictment of the people in 10:17-19. This invokes God's private word to him in 8:7-8 in order to charge the people that their demand for a king who 'will fight our battles' is in reality a rejection of God (as King) who has delivered them from all their foes since the exodus. Within this context the formulation of 12:12 claims that the threat of Nahash showed the people had not really changed their attitude; despite this God, in keeping with all his 'righteous deeds' (*tsedaqah* in the plural; NRSV 'saving deeds'), responded to their demands by setting a king over them who, as 1 Kings 11 recounts, delivered them from Nahash. This is another example of the storyline being adjusted to meet the exigencies of the theological point that the author(s) wants to make.[18]

A further point to note about the review is that God's righteous actions cover both deliverance from enemies and oppression by enemies when Israel sins. Punishment is an integral component of God's righteous relationship with the people because its purpose is to provide the knowledge (the people are at fault) that leads to repentance and conversion (12:10).[19] As noted earlier, there is no announcement

---

18. In *Unfolding the Deuteronomstic History*, 247, Campbell & O'Brien present three options to explain the discrepancy between aspects of 1 Samuel 12 and the preceding narrative: it is a different version of the same tradition perhaps based on uncertain recall of its elements; it reflects a different tradition; the text is a selection of elements from the past. The interpretation I have presented here is a variation of the third option; the text draws on selected elements from the preceding narrative. Jobling states that here the character Samuel 'adjusts the story a little' (*1 Samuel*, 67).
19. RP Gordon (*I & II Samuel* [Exeter: Paternoster, 1986] 127) observes that the

or report of divine punishment in the wake of the people's demand that, according to 8:7-8 and 10:17-19, amounts to a rejection of God (apostasy). The sign of the thunderstorm in 12:17-18 can be read as filling this gap. It not only confirms Samuel's judgement, it also brings home to the people the seriousness ('your great evil') of their sin and the punishment it deserves.[20] The implication for the people is that their merciful God has withheld the punishment, a realisation that prompts 'all the people' to repent and beg Samuel to intercede on their behalf. Such is the way this narrative distributes divine punishment and mercy.

Samuel provides reassurance that the Lord 'will not cast away his people' (12:20).[21] He then outlines how divine loyalty is to be matched by the people's loyalty to God and, as one would expect, this is in line with Torah theology. The punishment of which the storm was a sign and which God has withheld will nevertheless be executed if the people and their king 'still do wickedly'. As in the golden calf story, God displays mercy towards Israel in order that it may once again face the challenge of loyalty to the covenant relationship. According to 12:22 the ultimate reason why God does not cast Israel aside is the same for all God's doings; it is for 'his great name's sake' (12:22). Israel is the people chosen to mediate God's name and the knowledge of God to the world; it is only on the basis of this that the human being can escape the trap of distorted perceptions and its chaotic consequences. If Israel remains faithful (12:24; *'emet*) to its vocation God will do great things for it as God has already done (12:24). The text is not specific about the 'great things' (NSRV: literally 'what he has made great with you') but within the context it is reasonable to take them as a reference to the era of the kings that has commenced. As a loyal servant and mediator between God and Israel, Samuel assures the people of his own commitment to maintaining a right relationship

---

    phrase 'all the righteous deeds of the Lord' 'takes account of the fact that God's covenant faithfulness involves disciplinary, as well as salvific, acts (for example v 9)'.

20. Israel is invited to compare itself with a ripe crop during the harvest when farmers would hope and pray for fine weather. A violent storm would destroy the crop.
21. There is a similar play on the meaning of fear (*yare'*) in 12:18, 20, 24 and Exod 20:18-20. The people react in fear (are afraid) in 12:18, Samuel instructs them not to fear (be afraid) in 12:20 but to fear (revere/obey) the Lord in 12:24.

with them and with God in the form of prayer and instruction on the good and right (*yashar*) way (12:23). In disagreement with some commentators, the era of the kings is not presented in 1 Samuel 8–12 as a tragedy or sin.[22] As with the judges the emphasis is on the conduct of the human participants rather than on the institution. As long as the king and people remain loyal to God, kingship can contribute to the welfare of Israel and God's purpose just like judgeship. It is regarded as an acceptable option in Deuteronomy 17:14–20, as long as the model outlined there is followed. The implication is that God can operate just as effectively through one institution as the other.

The Story of Israel Under Prophets and Kings

According to 1 Samuel 12:18, 'all the people greatly feared the Lord and Samuel', a text that echoes Exodus 14:31.[23] Samuel is now a Moses like figure who represents the authoritative voice of God for both king and people. Moreover, the message he proclaims is in keeping with the Mosaic Torah. Because his speech in 1 Samuel 12 is a paradigmatic one for the future of Israel under the leadership of the king, subsequent prophets will presumably continue Samuel's role, both in relation to the king and the people. It is reasonable therefore to describe the narrative that continues through to the end of 2 Kings as the story of Israel under the prophets and kings. In order to illustrate this I will now look at a selection of passages in the storis of Saul, of David, of Solomon, and of the divided kingdoms of Israel and Judah.

On Saul

According to 1 Sam 13:13, obedience to God's command in 10:8 would have won Saul a 'kingdom over Israel forever' but he fails to wait the seven days in Gilgal as instructed until Samuel arrives.[24] As

---

22. Polzin speaks of the 'story of Israel's tragic romance with kingship' (*Samuel and the Deuteronomist*, 79); according to Jobling, Samuel (with whose view he sides in his reading) 'attempts to dissuade YHWH from just such a disastrous course' (*1 Samuel*, 65).
23. Noted by Walter Brueggemann, *First and Second Samuel* (Interpretation; Louisville, Ky: John Knox Press, 1990), 94.
24. As Klaus-Peter Adam points out, Saul observed one part of the command—in that he waited seven days—but not the second part—until Samuel arrived

if to underscore this and confirm Samuel's prophecy, in the following war story Saul lays a curse on Israel (according to 14:24 a 'very rash act') that causes the army to act rashly (14:32) and endangers the life of his heir apparent, Jonathan. Is there an implication here that the disorder in Saul's relationship with God has an impact on Israel's social order? In the subsequent conflict between David and Saul, Jonathan recognises David as God's appointee and sides with him against his father. Jonathan has a correct perception of the ways of God and accepts there will be no Saulide dynasty ruling over Israel. Saul disobeys a divine command for a second time in the war against the Amalekites (1 Samuel 15). God is portrayed entering the fray directly this time, expressing regret to Samuel for having made Saul king (15:10-11). Samuel confronts Saul and announces that God has rejected him as king (15:23).[25] Through disobedience Saul has forfeited not only God's promise of an enduring dynasty but also his own reign as king. Kingship and dynasty will now be transferred to David.

Does God's regret and sorrow (15:35) mean that the anointing of Saul was a mistake? Not according to Torah theology. God does right in choosing Saul, who nevertheless fails, just as God does right in choosing Israel who also fails repeatedly. All God's choices are by definition right but for a right relationship to be established, the ones chosen must be free to accept or reject. God's sorrow is an expression of the complete commitment that God brings to every relationship. By the same token, each relationship is part of God's equally complete commitment to bringing about world order/salvation. How is a failure such as Saul's included in this? One way is by becoming a 'word of the Lord' about Saul, a word that is a divine revelation and so a teaching for all generations of believers. As a teaching it is perhaps significant that 15:26 states Saul is rejected 'from being king over Israel', it does not state that Saul is himself banished from any relationship with God.

(see 149 of 'Saul as a Tragic Hero: Greek Drama and Its Influence on Hebrew Scripture in 1 Samuel 14,26-46 (10,8; 13,7-13a; 10,17-27),' in *For and Against David. Story and History in the Books of Samuel*, edited by A Graeme Auld and Erik Eynikel [BETL 232; Leuven: Peeters, 2010], 123-83).

25. Samuel's poem in 15:22-3 recalls, on a thematic level, 8:7-8, 10:17-19; 12:9-12, linking disobedience with divination and stubbornness with idolatry.

On David

The story of David commences in much the same way as that of Saul: David is anointed to become king and, like Saul in the war with Nahash the Ammonite, triumphs over the Philistine giant Goliath. David's stated purpose in this battle is that 'all the earth may know that there is a God in Israel' (1 Sam 17:46), an echo of statements in the Torah such as Exodus 7:5; 8:11; 9:14; 14:4, 18; Numbers 14:21. David's dedication to God's purpose enables him to eventually bring peace and unity to warring Judah and Israel (2 Sam 5:1-5) and to administer 'justice and righteousness to all his people' (8:15).[26] He is able to do what Saul failed to do—deliver Israel from 'the hand of their enemies all around' (1 Sam 10:1; cf 2 Sam 7:1). David completes the conquest of the land, defeating the hostile nations that remain (cf Josh 13:2-6; 23:4-5). A further sign of David's positive role in the unfolding of God's purpose is the report of kings seeking 'right' relationships with him and Israel (cf Hiram of Tyre in 2 Sam 5:11 and Toi of Hamath in 8:9-10). Like Rahab and the Gibeonites in the book of Joshua these nations provide evidence of Israel as the mediator of God's blessing to all the families of the earth.

The reports of David's unification of Israel and Judah and his righteous rule, along with his recognition by foreign kings, frame two central components of the story in which the divine initiative is to the fore: the account of the ark coming to Jerusalem in 2 Samuel 6 and the promise of an enduring dynasty in 2 Samuel 7.[27] Each advances God's purpose with David the king and with Israel. But each also serves as an instruction for David (and the reader) that God's plan unfolds in God's way. David's plan to bring the ark to Jerusalem shows his devotion to the Lord but is brought to a sudden halt by God's slaying of Uzzah for taking hold of the ark (6:6-7). This prompts David to ask 'How can the ark of the Lord come into my care?' The answer is given

---

26. According to Moshe Weinfeld, the administration of justice and righteousness was seen as a primary goal not only of Israelite but also of ANE kings (*Social Justice in Ancient Israel and in the Ancient Near East* [Minneapolis: Fortress Press/Jerusalem: Magnes Press, 1995). Psalm 72:1-2 prays for the gift of righteous rule for the king.

27. On the centrality of 2 Sam 7 see for example Brueggemann, *First and Second Samuel*, 259, and more recently, Mann, *The Book of the Former Prophets*, 188. In my opinion 2 Sam 6 and 7 go together, as is indicated by 7:1-2.

by a subsequent report that God blessed the house of Obed-edom where the ark was lodged after the Uzzah incident (6:12). The whole episode serves as a signal to David that God decides when the ark is to come to Jerusalem.[28] In 2 Samuel 7 David plans to build a house for the ark but is informed via the prophet Nathan that God has other plans. According to vv 9b–17 these are: to make a great name for David like the name of the great ones of the earth, to grant Israel rest from all its enemies, to establish an enduring house/dynasty for David, to have his son build a house for God's name.[29] If this son commits iniquity God will punish but not take away his steadfast love or commitment (*khesedh*). Each of these is in accord with and develops promises proclaimed earlier in the storyline—the great name for Abram (Gen 12:2), rest from enemies (Deut 12:10), dynasty as the exaltation of the power of the Lord's anointed (1 Sam 2:10b), a dwelling for the name of the Lord (Deut 12:11 and passim). David's reply shows that he now sees and accepts he is part of a larger divine purpose: 'Thus your name will be magnified forever' (7:26; cf also 7:23). As stated in the Torah, all that God does is ultimately in order that 'you may know I am the Lord'.

2 Samuel 11–12 exposes another side of David. Here he behaves like a king of the nations, taking (*lqkh* 11:4; cf 1 Sam 8:11–17) for himself Bathsheba the wife of Uriah the Hittite and then having him murdered.[30] Although there is debate about the nature of David's affair with Bathsheba and its legal implications, there is no doubt about David's murder of Uriah along with a number of other innocent soldiers (2 Sam 11:23–25), and the death penalty attached

---

28. Cf Campbell, *2 Samuel* (FOTL VIII; Grand Rapids, MI: Eerdmans, 2005), 66–67. In 1 Sam 6:19 the Lord executes seventy for not rejoicing at the return of the ark; according to the MT version they looked inside it, presumably breaking a taboo.
29. Within the framework of Torah theology, the promise of dynasty applies to royalty the promise to Abraham of descendants down the generations (Gen 12:1–3; 15:5), and the promise to Israel of descendants living in the land as long as it remains faithful (Deut 6:2). Israel's occupation of the land through the generations is presented in 6:3 as the fulfillment of the promise to the ancestors. From a historical point of view dynasty was an inseparable part of monarchy in the ANE, as indeed it still is in the modern world.
30. There may be a foreshadowing of this 'other' side of David in the account of his pillage of towns and massacre of their inhabitants in 1 Sam 27:8–12. In both episodes David kills in order to deceive; there it is the Philistine king Achish, here it is his own people.

to such a crime (cf Exod 21:12; Deut 19:11-13).[31] There are a number of parallels between God's response to David's sin and God's response to Israel's sin in the golden calf story. This is not unexpected given the key role that David is called to play in the story's unfolding of God's plan. God's initial response to Israel's worship of the calf is that it deserves destruction—a just judgement (Exod 32:7-10). In a similar way, God judges rightly that David's crimes deserve death, implied in the prophet Nathan's statement 'you shall not die' (2 Sam 12:13b). In response to Moses' intercession, and subsequently the people's repentance, the covenant is renewed. Israel's relationship with God continues. Yet this does not cancel punishment for sin as the code of divine conduct in Exod 34:7 signals. God does not clear the guilty but decides what kind of punishment is due, and for how long. Similarly, David confesses his sins and the sentence of death is commuted ('you shall not die'). The relationship between God and the Davidic dynasty continues but, as the pronouncement in 2 Samuel 12:11-12, 14 signals, God is the one who alone has sovereignty over life and death, not David.[32] The death of the child provides a chilling lesson of this for David. As Moses was unable to have God reverse the decree that he would not enter the land (Deut 3:23-28) so David is unable to move God to reverse the decree about the child (2 Sam 12:20-23). But also, as with Moses, the refusal has the right effect; David emerges chastened and humbled before his God.[33] It is not without

---

31. The legislation on adultery in Lev 21:10 and Deut 22:22 presumes mutual consent but 22:25-27 recognises a special case (in the country) that should presume non-consent by the woman, in other words a case of rape. Only the man is to be executed. The fact that Bathsheba is not charged with any crime or threatened with any punishment in the text would seem to imply rape rather than adultery (cf. Campbell, *2 Samuel*, 103-4). In contrast Randall C Bailey describes it as 'a co-partnership' (*David in Love and War. The Pursuit of Power in 2 Samuel 1-12* [JSOTSup 75; Sheffield: JSOT Press, 1990], 88).
32. Thilo Alexander Rudnig sees the child's death as an addition that applies the Act-Consequence connection to correct the impression in an earlier version of 2 Sam 12:1-15 that David is forgiven his sin and escapes retribution. The connection is thereby defended but restricted to the death of the child, in place of David ('"Ausser in der Sache mit Uria, dem Hethiter" (1 Reg 15, 5): Jahwes und Davids Gerechtigkeit in 2 Sam 10-12,' in *For and Against David*, 273-92, see especially 275-83.
33. Gillian Keys sees David's 'humility before Yahweh' as an important theme in 2 Sam 12-20, parallel to the theme of the weakness of David (*The Wages of Sin. A Reappraisal of the 'Succession Narrative'* [JSOTSup 221; Sheffield: Sheffield

significance that, according to 23:3, at the end of his life David affirms that the rule of the Lord is righteous.

2 Samuel 12:10-12 invites comparison with 7:14-15.[34] The former is effectively an example of generational retribution—David's sin has repercussions for the whole dynasty—whereas the latter applies individual retribution, restricted to Solomon's own misdemeanours. It is God who will decide, in accord with divine righteousness, what form the 'sword' of retribution will taken and when. 2 Samuel 12:11 provides a graphic example: God will raise up trouble within David's own house and give his wives to his neighbour—presumably a foreshadowing of Absalom's revolt. But, as 7:14-15 indicates, not every instance of 'trouble' that afflicts the dynasty will be a sign of David's punishment. Solomon, and presumably other members of the dynasty, will be punished for their own sins. If the text did not contain this proviso then the seriousness of sin and its evil impact would be compromised. What is common to both of Nathan's prophecies is that the promise of an enduring dynasty is not revoked because of the sins of its members. One could say that the two prophecies effectively incorporate the story of the dynasty within a theological framework that is in line with the Torah. That is, God's loyalty to the dynasty despite its failures mirrors God's loyalty to disobedient Israel; both are a sign of God's steadfast love/commitment.

Richard G Smith proposes that the theme of the 'Court History of David' (2 Sam 8:15b-20:26) is 'the fate of justice and righteousness during David's reign'.[35] David establishes them in 2 Samuel 8:15b,

---

Academic Press, 1996], 148).

34. The link between the two texts can be seen by comparing their formulation—in 7:15 'My steadfast love *will not depart* from him'; in 12:10 'The sword *will not depart* from your house' (cf. David T Lamb 'The "Eternal" Curse: Seven Deuteronomistic Judgement Oracles against the House of David,' in *For and Against David*, 315-25; especially 315). It is generally accepted that the Hebrew phrase *'ad 'olam'*, used to describe the enduring nature of the Davidic dynasty, does not normally mean 'forever' or 'eternity' in the English sense but rather 'a very long time' (cf. Jenni/Westermann, *Theologisches Handwörterbuch*, volume 2, 228-43, 230 'fernste Zeit'). 2 Samuel 12:10 can also be taken as God's reply to David's remark about the random sword in 11:25. The sword that God wields always strikes its target and in the manner God intends.

35. Richard G Smith, *The Fate of Justice and Righteousness During David's Reign: Rereading the Court History and its Ethics according to 2 Samuel 8:15b-20:26* (Library of Hebrew/Old Testament Studies 508; New York: T & T Clark, 2009).

abuses them in 11–12, and reaps the consequences in 13–20. This is an attractive thesis but the course of justice and righteousness in the narrative is, in my judgement, set within the framework of Nathan's prophecies. Neither position can be demonstrated because 2 Samuel 13–20 does not refer explicitly either to the justice and righteousness of 8:15b or to the terms of Nathan's prophecies. If one removes 12:9-10 the subsequent narrative can be read as the consequences of David's injustice towards Bathsheba and Uriah.[36] But once one factors in the word of God it provides the key to reading 2 Samuel 13–20, as well as the subsequent account of the dynasty in Kings. Such a reading is more in keeping with the overall story of Israel as the unfolding of God's initiative and purpose. It also offers a better context for explaining how David is presented in these chapters. Although at times an inept or irresponsible father of his 'house', he remains loyal to God throughout and, in the crisis of Absalom's coup, acknowledges that it is God's purpose rather than any plans of his own that determine the outcome (cf. 2 Sam 15:24–29).

---

36. Steven L McKenzie proposes that 2 Sam 10–12 is a late (post-Dtr) addition to the books of Samuel that dramatically changes the portrait of David in the subsequent narrative 'from positive to negative' (313 of 'Ledavid (for David)! "Except in the Matter of Uriah the Hittite"', in *For and Against David*, 307–13).

3

In the Books of Kings

On Solomon

The story of Israel under the prophets and kings reaches another important stage in the succession of Solomon. A key text is David's farewell speech to Solomon in 1 Kings 2:1-9 which is in two parts; vv 1-4 are about Solomon's loyalty to God while vv 5-9 are about Solomon's loyalty to David. An understanding of the relationship between the two is important for the story of Solomon and the subsequent story of the Davidic dynasty.

1 Kings 2:1-4 assures Solomon of blessing and prosperity as long as he remains loyal to God 'as it is written in the law of Moses'. In v 4 David appeals to a word from God that is not reported in the preceding narrative.[1]. Despite this it has an important function, bringing elements of the preceding narrative to bear on what is to follow. In order to give it the requisite authority it is presented as a word of God to David. The elements in question are the Torah, the dynastic promise of 2 Samuel 7, and the prophecy of the sword in 2 Samuel 12:10. Although Nathan's prophecies are meant to cover the whole story of the dynasty it is important that their content be reiterated at this axial point in the story and linked to the larger Torah agenda. Hence the call to Solomon and his descendants to walk before the Lord with all their heart—a clear evocation of Torah texts such as Deuteronomy 6:5; 30:6, 10. The promise of an enduring dynasty is reiterated in the corresponding promise of 1 Kings 2:4, 'there shall not fail you a successor on the throne of Israel'. Though not explicit

---

1. Cf also Bathsheba's appeal in 1:17 to an oath that David swore but which is not reported in the preceding narrative.

the threat of the sword is reflected in the way continued occupation of the throne of Israel is dependent on complete fidelity by members of the dynasty; failure will be punished by its loss which would almost inevitably involve war.

The phrase 'throne of Israel' is not in 2 Samuel 7 and the only other occurrences are in 1 Kings 8:20, 25; 9:5 and 10:9, all within the context of the united kingdom of Israel and Judah. This allows one to see that 2:4 draws 2 Samuel 7 and 12:10 together and at the same time 'redraws' them to cover the subsequent story of the Davidic dynasty up to and beyond the schism in the united kingdom (1 Kgs 12). 1 Kings 9:4-5 explicitly applies the conditional promise about the future of the throne of Israel to Solomon. As well as this 1 Kings 2:4 identifies punishment with the 'rod of men' in 2 Samuel 7:15 with loss of the united kingdom, and that it is a loss (a rod/sword?) that will afflict 'your heirs'. That is, the throne of Israel will remain 'cut off' from the dynasty.[2] As with 2 Samuel 12:10, the text does not say the dynasty will end, only that it will not retain the throne of Israel. This covers the post-schism story of the dynasty.

The torah component of 1 Kings 2:1-4 also brings it into line with the promise and warning that Moses proclaims to Israel in the plains of Moab (Deut 29-30). While the sword always hangs over David's house this is, as already noted, presumably with reference to disobedience. As long as David's heirs remain loyal to God according to the terms of the law of Moses (the Torah covenant), his house is assured of the throne of Israel. This is the same kind of assurance Moses makes to Israel in the plains of Moab. Solomon initially seems to rise to the challenge and he and the kingdom enjoy blessing and advance key aspects of God's plan of salvation, as the conquest generation of Israel does in the book of Joshua. There is security and prosperity in the land (4:21-34; MT 5:1-14). Because both the conditions of 2 Samuel 7 and Deuteronomy 12:10 are fulfilled Solomon (1 Kgs 5:1-6) discerns that the time has come to build the house for the name of the Lord.[3]

---

2. The NRSV of 1 Kgs 2:4 is 'There shall not fail you a successor on the throne of Israel'. The Hebrew verb translated as 'fail' is *karat* (to cut/cut off). The verb can refer to making/cutting a covenant or to being cut off from the people (for example, Exod 12:15, 19; Lev 7:20, 21).

3. The implication of the ark coming to Jerusalem in 2 Sam 6 is that God identifies it as the place to which Deut 12:11 refers. The ark is lodged in the completed temple

Hiram, king of Tyre, acknowledges that this is the work of the Lord and willingly agrees to Solomon's request for material to build the temple (5:7-12). King Solomon, 'this great people', and the temple become symbols of the knowledge and presence of God among the nations, a God who is present in the temple not just for Israel but 'so that all the peoples of the earth may know your name and fear you' (cf. 8:41-43). In 8:56 Solomon proclaims that not one of all God's promises spoken 'through his servant Moses' has failed to come true. This expresses much the same sentiment as Joshua 21:43-45 at the conclusion of the conquest and settlement. While Solomon celebrates the just and wise rule of God, the queen of Sheba, an outsider, celebrates the just and wise rule of Solomon in 1 Kings 10:6-10. She concludes her visit by proclaiming that because 'the Lord loved Israel forever' he has set Solomon on the throne to execute justice and righteousness (10:9; cf 2 Sam 8:15). Solomon is an integral part of God's plan to establish world order and, as long as the justice and righteousness that he executes is God's, the plan will advance. But there is another side to the Solomon presented in the narrative.

As noted, 1 Kings 2:5-9 is about Solomon's loyalty to his father; there is no mention of God. David commands Solomon to ensure that Joab and Shimei pay for their disloyalties. He is also commanded to show kindness to the sons of Barzillai, the one who showed loyalty to David during the Absalom crisis. In terms of the present text of the Torah and Former Prophets, the plot to bring down Joab and Shimei raises questions. Is this in accord with the law of Moses referred to in 2:1-4? In placing these demands on Solomon, is David the old man falling back into bad old habits—assuming control of events on his terms? If Solomon obeys, he may be loyal to his father but is he being loyal to God and to Israel? Can one say that Solomon is excused of guilt because he is effectively coerced by his father? This is hard to accept when one reads how readily or even ruthlessly he disposes of his brother Adonijah (2:13-25).[4]

---

in 1 Kgs 8:1-11.

4. The relationship between texts that portray the good and wise Solomon and others that appear to be more critical has been a source of much debate. Historical critical scholarship tends to assign the respective texts to different authors. This may be the case, at least in part. Two more recent studies prefer a more synchronic approach. Eric A Seibert argues that the negative tones are the work of royal scribes who subtly subvert even as they praise the king (*Subversive*

Further questions about Solomon's loyalty to God are raised by the report of his marriage to the daughter of Pharaoh, which is in breach of Deuteronomy 7:3. Subsequently, 1 Kings 9:10-14 reports a rift between Solomon and Hiram, 9:15-22 his policy of forced labour, and 10:14-29 his enormous wealth and trade, above all in chariots and horses—explicitly forbidden by Deuteronomy17:14-20. At the end of 1 Kings 10 a reader may well ask whether Solomon has done what the queen of Sheba believes he was commissioned to do. Has he failed in his relationship with his people and his God? In one sense this dark side of Solomon aligns him with other leading characters in the story of Israel. No one is depicted as perfectly just and righteous; all face challenges and all fail to some extent. Solomon breaks the deuteronomic code for a king by multiplying foreign wives (11:1-2); as Deuteronomy17:17 warns, these will turn a king's heart away. He not only commits the sin of apostasy by worshipping their gods but also the requirement of centralised worship by building high places for them. The consequence of this—loss of the 'throne of Israel'—is announced twice in the narrative, first in 11:9-13 which is God's third and final 'appearance' to Solomon, and secondly in the prophecy of Ahijah of Shiloh in 11:31-38.

Although the schism is accounted for in passages such as 1 Kings 2:4; 8:25; 9:4-5, Israel's theologians needed to explain why this did not happen during the reign of Solomon—as an appropriate form of punishment. According to 1 Kings 11:12 it was 'for the sake of your father David', a rather cryptic statement that cries out for further elaboration. This is supplied in the extensive prophecy of Ahijah of Shiloh in 11:29-39. Here David is invoked as a model of loyalty to God that wins a reprieve for his disloyal son Solomon. This poetic piece appears to be drawing something of a parallel with the earlier

---

Scribes and the Solomonic Narrative. A Rereading of 1 Kings 1-11 [Library of Hebrew Bible/Old Testament Studies 36; New York/London: T&T Clark, 2006]). Christina Duncker proposes a somewhat similar view, that the narrator/scribe's principal tool in portraying Solomon was irony. He is gradually turned into an Israelite Pharaoh (*Der andere Salomo. Eine synchrone Untersuchung zur Ironie in der Salomo-Komposition 1 Könige 1-11* [Frankfurt: Peter Lang, 2010]). In contrast, Marvin A Sweeney thinks that texts like 1 Kgs 2:5-9 are explicit and condemnatory 'Such a portrayal undermines both David and Solomon and indeed the house of David as a whole' (*I & II Kings. A Commentary* [Louisville/London: Westminster John Knox Press, 2007], 61).

narratives about Moses. A key factor in God's decision not to destroy Israel in the wake of the golden calf and spy crises is the chosen leader's loyalty. He remains completely committed to God and people, despite God's proposal to start again with him as the founder of a great nation (cf Exod 32:10; Num 14:12). As a result, punishment is deferred or modified and Israel is able to continue as God's people and eventually inherit the chosen land.

On the Kingdoms of Israel and Judah

One could say that David is to Solomon and the dynasty what Moses is to Israel. God will not tear the kingdom apart in Solomon's day 'for the sake of my servant David and for the sake of Jerusalem, which I have chosen'.[5] Unlike Solomon, David kept God's commands (11:33-34). Hence the schism is deferred until his son's day although he will, also because of David, get to rule over Judah. According to 1 Kings 11:14-25, there is a measure of divine retribution during Solomon's reign, but it does not amount to the rupture of the united kingdom. The narrative also assigns a measure of responsibility to Solomon's son, Rehoboam. In the account of the schism in the kingdom (1 Kgs 12) he rejects the wise counsel of the elders and acts arrogantly in relation to the people. The rebellion that follows serves as a fulfillment of Ahijah's prophecy and as retribution for Rehoboam's folly. In effect the narrative seeks to incorporate the apparent course of events (the schism occurred in the time of Rehoboam) within the Torah's reward/blessing—retribution/punishment schema and, as with earlier examples, to justify the distribution by appeal to prophetic (divine) authority. Because the respective judgements are from God they are just and have authority.

The appeal to David's loyalty in 11:33-34, 38 and other passages may seem somewhat contradictory, given his conduct in the Bathsheba/Uriah episode.[6] Nevertheless, a further comparison

---

5. Jerusalem here parallels the promised or 'chosen' land in the Torah.
6. According to Solomon's claim in 1 Kgs 3:6 David walked before God in 'faithfulness (*ʾemet*), in righteousness (*tsedaqah*), and in uprightness (*yishrah*) of heart'. Other similar passages occur in the story of Solomon (8:25; 9:4); in the subsequent story of the dynasty (14:8; 15:3, 5, with reference to the Uriah affair); and in briefer form in 15:11b; 2 Kgs 14:3; 16:2b; 18:3b; 22:2.

with the Torah may allow one to see a connection. As noted in the preceding chapter, although none of the leading characters in the Torah is fault free God continues to treat them as loyal servants. David failed badly but, when accused, confessed his guilt, was forgiven and accepted his punishment. In this sense David remained loyal to God when confronted with his transgressions, which is not the case with Solomon. According to 11:40 Solomon sought to kill Jeroboam in the wake of Ahijah's prophecy. Far from repenting of his apostasy, he added to it the sin of attempting to subvert God's word. Shades of Israel in the spy story (Num 14:10). Another sign of David acknowledging the sovereignty of God in all things is the account of the entry of the ark into Jerusalem (2 Samuel 6). In this sense David promoted the exclusive worship of the Lord in Jerusalem whereas Solomon grossly polluted it. In the eyes of the theologians responsible for the narrative in Kings, David displayed two key attitudes that set him apart as a model for all subsequent kings—loyalty to the one true God, and worship of God in the chosen place (Deut 12:10-11). The only two subsequent Judean kings who are judged comparable to David are Hezekiah (2 Kgs 18:3-5) and Josiah (2 Kgs 22:2; 23:8-9), and this is for the same two reasons—their complete devotion to God and their promotion of centralized worship by removing the 'high places'.[7] A number of other Judean kings are compared favourably with David except for the failure to remove these rival/alternative shrines.[8]

The narrative also holds David up as the model in assessing the right or wrong conduct of northern kings. Jeroboam is promised the same enduring dynasty as David, as long as he conforms to the model and does what is 'right' (*yashar*) in God's eyes (11:38).[9] But he

---

7. According to 2 Kgs 23:13 Josiah defiled the high places of foreign gods erected east of Jerusalem by Solomon. These represent the two sins of Solomon that brought on the schism; namely, apostasy and repudiation of centralized worship in the Jerusalem temple. The text implies that Josiah restored what God initially established through David and Solomon.
8. Cf Asa (1 Kgs 15:11-14); Jehoshaphat (1 Kgs 22:43-4). The same charge about the high places is made against Jehoash (2 Kgs 12:3-4); Amaziah (14:3-4); Azariah (15:3-4); Jotham (15:34-35), but these texts do not make it the exception to their Davidic like rule.
9. The occurrence of *yashar* (right) and *tsadiq* (righteous) in texts which present David as the model of conduct suggests that they are practically synonymous terms (cf righteous/righteousness in 1 Kgs 3:6 [noun]; 8:32 [adjective]; and

commits the same apostasy as Israel does with the golden calf (1 Kgs 12:28–30; cf Exod 32:4).[10] The prophet Ahijah proclaims the end of his dynasty in 14:7–14 because he failed to 'be like my servant David'. All the subsequent kings of Israel are condemned for complicity in the apostate cult established by Jeroboam. A series of prophecy-fulfillment schemas is employed to account for the passing of each northern dynasty, forming a marked contrast with the prophecy of an enduring dynasty for David, despite the sins of a number of Judean kings.

The long peroration on the end of the northern kingdom in 2 Kings 17:7–23 condemns the people as willing accomplices in Jeroboam's sin. As in Judges 2:17, they refused to listen to the voice of God's prophets, abandoned the covenant laws, followed the practices of the nations around them, and perpetrated horrific crimes such as making 'their sons and daughters pass through the fire' (2 Kgs 17:17; cf also 16:3; 21:6; 23:10). According to 2 Kings 17:19 Judah is infected by Israel's corruption. The story of the northern kingdom is effectively the undoing of all that Israel is called to be and do according to the Torah, to Joshua's speeches in Joshua 23 and 24, and to Samuel's speech in 1 Samuel 12. God intervenes to clean up the mess, as the theology of a just and righteous God requires, and this involves removing the source of pollution. Israel is exiled from the land, ending up in the situation of punishment/curse that Moses warns about in the book of Deuteronomy. Yet if it follows his instructions and 'returns' to the Lord with all its heart, then he promises that 'the Lord your God will bring you into the land that your ancestors possessed, and you will posses it' (Deut 30:1–5).

The exile of the northern kingdom could be accounted for within the terms of Torah theology as the just retribution for the sins of its kings and people; the explanation is given added authority by use of the prophecy-fulfillment schema. Matters were not so straightforward

---

right in 9:4; 11:33, 38; 15:5, 11; 22:43; 2 Kgs 14:3; 16:2b; 18:3. The term *yashar* is applied to the assessment of kings without reference to David in 2 Kgs 12:3; 15:3, 34, 22:2.

10. Even though Jeroboam's establishment of cult centres (with bull calves) in Dan and Bethel may historically have been designed to bolster the independence of his new kingdom by providing it with centres for the worship of Israel's God, within the present text 12:28 casts him as an apostate who promoted the cult of false gods (cf Exod 32:4); cf. Sweeney, *I & II Kings*, 176–77.

when it came to 'explain' the fate of the Davidic dynasty in Judah. Additional factors had to be taken into account, such as the promise of an enduring dynasty despite the threat of the sword (2 Sam 12:10), and the claim that Jerusalem is the chosen city and the temple as the place where, according to 1 Kings 9:3, God has 'put my name there forever (*'ad 'olam*); my eyes and my heart will be there for all time'. It has already been pointed out how the promise of an enduring dynasty and the prophecy of the sword over the house of David were incorporated within Torah theology in 1 Kings 2:1-4 and associated texts. In a similar way, passages such as Solomon's negotiations with Hiram of Tyre about the construction of the Jerusalem temple (5:1-12), the lodging of the ark there (8:1-11), the dedication prayer (8:14-53), and God's response in (9:1-3) show a parallel move to incorporate the ark, the chosen city and its temple into the name theology of Deuteronomy. The ark as a symbol of the throne of God is not denied (cf 2 Sam 6:2; 1 Kgs 8:7-9) but according to 8:9, the only thing inside it are the tablets of the Horeb/Sinai covenant. Each of these theological components could be maintained in their Torah form as long as the Davidic dynasty continued to rule Judah in Jerusalem and the temple continued as a place of worship, despite failures to remove the high places. The challenge was to explain them in relation to the Judean exile. As well there was a need to explain the implications of all this for the people.

To maintain continuity with what is told of the northern kingdom, the account of Judah's demise also needed to be framed within a prophecy-fulfillment schema that incorporates the above components in a way that conforms to the Torah. All the northern kings and their kingdom are condemned because of the sin of Jeroboam and their willing complicity in it. The Baal worship of the house of Omri/Ahab can be incorporated in this explanation and prophecy-fulfillment schema because it is another sin of apostasy. As Sweeney notes, the same kind of condemnation could not be applied to the Davidic dynasty because of its loyal founder and because a number of Davidic kings 'are judged to be righteous (for example, Asa, Jehoshaphat, Hezekiah, Josiah, etc.)'.[11] The blame for the Judean exile is laid on Manasseh (2 Kgs 21:1-18); this may have been because he was historically a thoroughly bad egg but when one reads the

---

11. Sweeney, *I & II Kings*, 426.

quite different account in 2 Chronicles 33 it is difficult to avoid the conclusion that history gives way to theology where appropriate or necessary. A plausible reason for the Kings' account of Manasseh is that it enabled Israel's theologians to show how the end of Davidic rule over Judah was in accord with a key Torah text, namely Exodus 20:5b and associated passages in Exodus 34:7; Numbers 14:18; Deuteronomy 5:9b. The iniquity of the fathers (here Manasseh) is visited on the children (the subsequent kings and their subjects) until the third and fourth (generation).[12] The reigns of all four kings are either violently terminated or dominated by foreign powers. The fourth generation kings are Jehoiachin and Zedekiah who are both taken into captivity (2 Kgs 24:12; 25:7).[13] 2 Kings 25:21b also states that 'Judah went into exile from the land'. The people share the fate of their kings. Thus the story of Israel from beginning to exile concludes with what one might call the definitive example of divine retribution 'to the third and fourth generation' for breach of the Decalogue, especially its prohibition of the worship of other gods. It was pointed out earlier that Nathan's prophecy of the sword in 2 Samuel 12:10 also applies a generational form of sin–retribution: the sins of David afflict his house. Hence this account of the end of Davidic rule over Judah can also be seen as confirmation of this prophecy.

Because of the role of the Davidic dynasty, the fate of the people of Judah, Jerusalem and the temple needed to be linked to it in a way that is also in accord with the Torah. Two texts address this need. The first is the account of the many evils of Manasseh; it culminates in 2 Kings 21:7b–9 with the accusation that Manasseh and the people paid no heed to God's promise that the temple, Jerusalem, and the land as

---

12. As proposed by Bernard M Levinson, *Legal Revision and Religious Renewal in Ancient Israel* (New York: Cambridge University Press, 2008), 56, and Jeremy Schipper 'Hezekiah, Manasseh, and Dynastic or Transgenerational Punishment', in *Soundings in Kings. Perspectives and Methods in Contemporary Scholarship*, edited by Mark Leuchter and Peter–Klaus Adam (Minneapolis: Fortress Press, 2010), 81–105, especially 97–98. As Schipper notes (99), the formulation of Exod 20:5b and Deut 5:9b 'does not specify whether "the sons upon the third and fourth" refers to three or four sequential generations or three or four individual children'. This allows it to be applied in either way.
13. The four generations after Manasseh are Amon son of Manasseh (2 Kgs 21:18b), Josiah son of Amon (21:26b), Jehoahaz son of Josiah (23:30b), and Jehoiachin son of Jehoiakim (24:6). Jehoiakim/Eliakim is another son of Josiah (23:34) and the last king of Judah is Zedekiah/Mattaniah, Jehoiachin's uncle (24:17).

the people's home would endure as long as king and people obeyed the law of Moses. Their disobedience, like that of northern Israel in 2 Kings 17:7-23, amounts to a complete reversal of all that the people are called by God to be according to the Torah. This provides the context for the second text, a divine decree as to how retribution is to be distributed in relation to the dynasty, the people, the city and the temple. The importance of this decree for the theology being promoted and the complexity of relationships involved resulted in a series of prophetic proclamations/words of God rather than a single text.[14] The first is the word of God proclaimed by 'his servants the prophets' in 21:10-15. This is followed by Huldah's prophecy in 22:17, and a third and final word of God in 23:26-27. 2 Kings 24:2b-3 and 13b report the fulfillment of God's decree. These reports occur in the reigns of the third (Jehoiakim) and fourth (Jehoiachin) generations of kings.

2 Kings 21:10-15 proclaims doom for Judah (people) and Jerusalem. Jerusalem will suffer the same fate as the capital of the northern kingdom, Samaria. A dish wiped and turned upside down is completely clean and empty. As an image of Jerusalem's fate it implies that the city site will be completely razed and cleared—in preparation for a new one?[15] Such imagery raises the question of the fate of the temple in the city. Its destruction is implied here but it is only made explicit in 23:27b. As for the people of Judah they, like the people of the northern kingdom of Israel, will be handed over to their enemies—all in accord with the Torah and in line with similar decrees of punishment in the preceding story of Israel. The absence of any mention of the dynasty also raises questions and expectations. One can point to two reasons for this. One is the promise to David of an enduring dynasty (2 Sam 7) which Nathan's prophecy of the sword in 2 Samuel 12:10, as noted, does not cancel. The fact that the doom of the dynasty is not pronounced indicates that whoever completed the narrative remained committed to this promise. The report of Jehoiachin's release from prison may have been a factor

---

14. As many commentators have argued, the present text is probably the culmination of the careful work of a number of editors/redactors.
15. The image of a measuring line used to ensure the complete destruction of Samaria and Jerusalem is reversed in Zech 5:1-5 (MT 5:5-10) with its vision of a man with a line measuring the dimensions for the new/rebuilt city of Jerusalem.

in this. Though bereft of power, the dynasty is still there. What its future is to be is in God's hands. The second reason follows from this. Because of their commitment to the dynastic promise or their unwillingness to pronounce on its fate in light of the report about Jehoiachin, Israel's theologians distribute divine retribution (and reward) on each member of the dynasty in the way they recount each reign. This could be done without difficulty for Amon, Jehoahaz, Jehoiakim, Jehoiachin and Zedekiah. Amon comes to a violent end while the rest are under the hegemony of the Babylonians in one form or another. Each is judged to have done 'evil in the sight of the Lord' (cf 21:20; 23:32; 23:37; 24:19) and reaped the appropriate retribution.

Manasseh and Josiah however are a different story. Perhaps the reason why no retribution is pronounced against Manasseh directly is because he has the longest reign of any king (fifty-five years) and, according to the text, rules undisturbed by foreign or internal strife. The Kings' account seems to have proved quite unsatisfactory to the Chronicler who rewrote it in order to fit Manasseh's long rule into his theology of individual reward and retribution. God punishes Manasseh for his sins, but he repents and remains faithful and so enjoys the reward of a long reign (2 Chron 33). This comparison with Chronicles provides a clue to understanding the Kings' account. Whereas Chronicles is focused more on Manasseh's personal piety, the Kings' account aims to explain the exile and the lead up to it in relation to the Torah. According to the account of his reign, Manasseh so corrupted Judah that it became a willing accomplice in his evil. This brought the retribution of the exile, the destruction of city and temple, and the end of Davidic rule. In a sense this terrible legacy is also Manasseh's own punishment. Policies aimed at securing the future of the Davidic dynasty and Judah spell their demise (an example of the distorted perception of reality, seeing evil as good and vice versa). When one also takes into account that the narrative is not simply a record of the past but an interpretation of it and a teaching/ torah about it, this becomes an important and valuable feature.

The account of Josiah's reign reveals the ingenuity of Israel's theologians as well as the limitations of their theology—and indeed any theology—to explain the complexities of experience/reality.[16]

---

16. Campbell and O'Brien judge that the account of Josiah reveals 'the deconstruction of the dtr theology of reward and punishment' (*Unfolding the Deuteronomistic*

According to Exodus 20:5b and related texts, transgenerational punishment to the third and fourth (generation) will fall on 'those who hate me'. The judgement formulas for Josiah in 22:2 and 23:25 testify that, unlike Manasseh and the other kings, he was completely devoted to the Lord. He is therefore the exception that proves the rule and this is taken into account in Huldah's prophecy. Because of his penitent and humble heart he will be spared the sight of Judah's end. In this sense, his death at the hands of Pharaoh Neco is what we might call a blessing in disguise. The reign of Josiah could thus be incorporated within the prophecy–fulfillment schema that 'explains' the exile but there is some evidence that its author(s) sensed its limitations and that his violent death needed to be explained also in relation to the sin–retribution schema. In the report of him going to meet Neco (23:29) the Hebrew verb '*qara*" can mean 'he met' in the English sense of the term but it can also mean 'he went against' in a hostile fashion or 'attacked' as in war (cf Exod 1:10; Num 20:18, 20; 21:23, 33; Deut 1:44; 2:32; 3:1). Does the verse imply that Josiah took an initiative against Neco that he should not have taken without divine authorisation via a prophetic word? If this is the case, Josiah's death is a sign of divine retribution as well as mercy. According to the narrative, it is retribution for an unauthorised initiative; according to Huldah's prophecy, it mercifully preserves him from witnessing the end of Judah.

But perhaps one can relate them by proposing that Josiah conforms to the axiom of Psalm 143:2 that 'no one living is righteous before you'. Something of a parallel can be observed in the portrayal of his illustrious predecessor Hezekiah. According to the judgement formula in 2 Kings 18:5 Hezekiah is a model king but is censured by Isaiah for feting a Babylonian delegation (20:12–19). Like Josiah he takes an initiative—in contrast to his earlier behaviour—and gives them the grand tour. In response Isaiah prophesies that initiating a relationship with Babylon on one's own terms will not lead to blessing but disaster. In this way both Hezekiah and Josiah, good and loyal though they are portrayed to be, are nevertheless responsible in their respective ways for troubles that follow. The explanation claims authority by being encased within a prophecy-fulfillment schema.

History, 459). The reader can judge from my comments here whether 'limitation' may be a better term than 'deconstruction'.

An important feature of the Kings' account is its linking of Huldah's prophecy with the discovery of the 'book of the law (Torah)'. Whether the book was an earlier version of Deuteronomy or not, within the present text the Torah is clearly the point of reference. In one sense, the discovery of a book that is read and its laws then implemented conveys the impression of a 'return' to the past. However, Huldah's speech emphasises that this book is not just law/instruction but also prophecy, a word of God that is being fulfilled. As voiced by Huldah, it decrees God's allocation of reward and punishment for Josiah and his generation even as the reform is implemented. The role of Huldah recalls that of Samuel in 1 Samuel 8. The people approach him with what looks to be a reasonable request but God 'exposes' their real reason to Samuel (and the reader). In the Kings' passage the people join in the covenant (2 Kgs 23:3) and Passover (23:21-23) but Huldah's prophecy exposes their real status as the same idolaters led astray by Manasseh (21:7-9, 11). The implication is that despite their participation they do not or are unable to repent as Josiah does (22:19). The comment in 24:20 bears out the truth of Huldah's prophecy against them.[17] On this reading Josiah's reform does not fail; rather the Torah succeeds as it always does in identifying the cause and locus of either reward or retribution. Judah, like the northern kingdom of Israel, like past generations of Israelites, fulfills Moses' prediction of failure and its consequences. But just as it is certain that Israel will at some stage(s) fail its God, it is even more certain that God will have compassion on Israel and return it to the land when it repents and seeks God (Deut 4:29-31; 30:1-5). In this way punishment is a sign of God's steadfast love and righteousness; its purpose is to teach Israel to know the wrong turn it has taken and the

---

17. An additional point to note about Huldah's prophecy is that it refers several times to 'this place'. The term recalls the requirement in Deut 12:5, 11 that Israel worship only at the place God will choose as a dwelling for the name. In 1 Kgs 8:29 this is identified as the Jerusalem temple. However, 2 Kgs 22:16 would seem to indicate that in Huldah's prophecy it means the city (cf 'on this place and its inhabitants') or perhaps both city and temple. Whatever the case, 23:27b specifies that the temple will also be destroyed and this appears to revise or revoke the promise of 1 Kgs 9:3 that God's name would dwell there forever ('*ad 'olam*). But the final say on this may be 2 Kgs 24:20 which states that the Lord expelled Jerusalem and Judah 'from his presence'. This implies that although God rejects 'this city' and the house built for 'my name' (23:27), God's presence in the land and sovereignty over it continues.

right way that will lead it back to God. Its purpose is also to teach the nations and bring them to know and confess that the Lord is God. According to Deuteronomy 29:25-28 and 1 Kings 9:8-9 they will recognise the hand of the Lord in the devastation of people, land and temple.

This analysis of the story of Israel under the prophets and kings shows that it is incorrect to describe the Sinai/Horeb covenant in the Torah as conditional and the covenant or promise to David as unconditional—at least in terms of the biblical text. Both are founded on God's initiative and commitment to Israel and God's commitment is unconditional. This is shown in the Sinai/Horeb covenant by texts such as Exodus 19:3-6 where Israel's obedience is the right response to God's initiative in establishing the covenant relationship. It is also shown in Moses' assurance in the Moab covenant that God will not abandon Israel despite its failures (Deut 30:9). God's steadfast love rather than Israel's obedience (which is fragile) is what maintains the relationship. The same goes for the relationship between God and David; he is God's choice and on the basis of this is expected to be loyal. Disloyalty brings retribution in the form of Nathan's prophecy of 2 Samuel 12:10—as it does for Israel in the words of the Torah— but this does not cancel the relationship.[18]

Two further comments can be made. One is that the Former Prophets are not just about interpreting the past; as the name implies they are also prophecy. They provide a challenge for subsequent generations to follow the Torah and so avoid the disasters that beset the preceding generations in the land. As such these books are also a continuation of the Torah's function as catechesis, as instruction. A second is that the story of Israel under the prophets and kings shows that monarchy, as an institution, is no better or worse than judgeship. It is the people operating in them and their relationship with God that matter, not the institution. To put it another way, the institution does not save, God does, for those who are loyal.

---

18. On this point it is worth quoting the words of Krasovec (*Reward, Punishment, & Forgiveness*, 305). 'It can safely be said that both the Sinaitic and Davidic covenants are in principle conditional and unconditional, but not in the same sense. Perhaps we can put it this way: the Sinaitic covenant is ultimately unconditional despite its conditionality, while the Davidic covenant is unconditional by definition. But this is possible only within the unconditionality of the covenant with Israel as a whole'.

Part Three

Divine Righteousness in the Latter Prophets

Introduction

Although a distinct section of the HBOT, the 'Latter Prophets' or 'Writing Prophets' are an integral part of the ongoing story of Israel and of the larger story of humanity and creation that begins in Genesis 1. Most of the books commence with a superscription that locates the particular prophet at a certain point in the storyline. For example, Isaiah 1:1 refers to the vision that Isaiah saw 'in the days of Uzziah, Jotham, Ahaz, and Hezekiah kings of Judah'. Some books of the twelve 'minor prophets' lack this kind of superscription but can nevertheless be located along the storyline either by information within the book itself or by the fact of being included in the collection.[1] A question that arises is why these prophecies or a selection of them are not included in the storyline, as are for example the prophecies of Nathan, Ahijah of Shiloh, Elijah and Elisha. The only case where this occurs is Isaiah 36–39, a version of which appears in 2 Kings 18–20.

One reason for this may be that the amount of material attributed to each of the Latter Prophets, and the predominant literary form of direct speech, made it difficult to incorporate such material in the Former Prophets without considerable distortion of its storyline. Hence the emergence of distinct books but linked in a variety of ways

---

1. The books in question are Joel, Obadiah, Jonah, Nahum, Habakkuk and Malachi. Joel calls for a solemn assembly in Zion/Jerusalem; Obadiah condemns Edom's treatment of 'your brother' Jacob (1:10), presumably a reference to the northern kingdom's demise at the hands of Assyria; the books of Jonah and Nahum are about Nineveh, the capital of the Assyrian empire that overran Israel and threatened Judah in the eighth century BCE; Habakkuk refers to the rise of the Chaldeans (Babylonians) in 1:6; the location of Malachi after Haggai and Zechariah places it in the post-exilic period.

to the storyline. Another may be that those who compiled the Latter Prophets sought to draw attention to perceived relationships between the various books. The variation in the order of these books in the Rabbinic, Masoretic (MT) and Septuagint (LXX) canonical lists indicates that in the course of the tradition a variety of relationships were identified. Whereas the MT and LXX lists commence the 'Major Prophets' with Isaiah, followed by Jeremiah and Ezekiel, the rabbinic list in the Talmud commences with Jeremiah, followed by Ezekiel and Isaiah.[2] The rabbis saw a different order in these books than the chronological one in the MT and LXX lists.[3] As well as this, the MT and the LXX list the twelve 'minor prophets' differently. The MT has Hosea, Joel, Amos, Obadiah, Jonah, Micah, Nahum, Habakkuk, Zephaniah, Haggai, Zechariah, Malachi, while the LXX has Hosea, Amos, Micah, Joel, Obadiah, Jonah, Nahum, Habakkuk, Zephaniah, Haggai, Zechariah, Malachi. There has been considerable debate over the reason(s) for the different order in the list, particularly of the first six books, and how this indicates different perceptions of the relationship between them.[4]

All this suggests that reading the 'Latter Prophets' as part of the HBOT canon can be a complicated business. Not only is there the uniqueness of each book to consider but there is also its relationship to the other books within the collection. Given the variation in the canonical lists it may be more accurate to speak of 'relationships'. Nevertheless there is a thread that links the various prophetic books and their canonical arrangements and that is the Torah. John Barton argues that the arrangement of the prophetic books in the Talmud reveals that the importance of the prophets for the rabbis did not

---

2. See *Baba Batra* 14b–15a (cited by Edgar W Conrad, *Reading the Latter Prophets* [JSOTSup 376; London/New York: T & T Clark International, 2003], 45). For an analysis of the significance of these different orders of books see Greg Goswell, 'The Order of the Books in the Hebrew Bible,' *JETS* 51/4 (2008) 763-88 (especially 678-84).
3. The reason given in *Baba Batra* for the rabbinic order is 'Because the book of Kings ends with a record of destruction and Jeremiah speaks throughout of destruction and Ezekiel commences with destruction and ends with consolation and Isaiah is full of consolation; therefore we put destruction next to destruction and consolation next to consolation' (cited in Conrad, *Reading the Latter Prophets*, 49).
4. For a survey see Paul L Redditt, 'Recent Research on the Book of the Twelve as One Book,' *CR:BS* 9 (2001), 47–80.

lie 'in their accuracy as a record of the past nor in the information they provide about the future, but chiefly in the effectiveness with which they bear witness to God's consistency in remaining true to the character revealed in the Torah—punishing transgression yet never forsaking his covenant with his people'.[5] This can also be said for the MT and LXX lists of the 'prophetic books'. Reinhard Achenbach concludes that although the alignment of prophecy with Torah took considerable time in the post-exilic period and involved debate and disagreement, the outcome was that 'Prophetic *torah* is not needed any longer, except from the prophet Moses. The prophets can only be understood as explaining the meaning of the *torah*'.[6]

The link between the Torah and the Latter Prophets can be seen in the way they appeal to its story of Israel and its instruction or law. The two are closely linked in the prophetic books as in the Torah; one is appealed to in support of the other. This does not mean that each book does this in the same way; rather each forges its own distinctive combination. Moreover, because they are literary works in their own right and in this sense independent of the Former Prophets, the Latter Prophets are able to employ a variety of literary forms (mainly prophetic speech but also narrative and law) to develop the Torah interpretation of Israel's life in the land. They are also able to deal with a number of issues that are only implied or treated briefly in the Former Prophets. One example is social justice; this does not play a major role in the Former Prophets in contrast to their emphasis on exclusive loyalty to God, whereas it plays a more prominent role in the Latter Prophets.[7] Another is their vision of a new era for Israel beyond the loss of the land. Each prophetic combination of the Torah's story and law also serves the overall aim of Torah theology, to instruct Israel and any reader about God and the ways of God. The Bible's *raison d'être* is to enable believers to know that 'I am the Lord' in whom alone lies salvation.

The Latter Prophets are separated from the Torah—Former Prophets/Historical Books sequence in the LXX arrangement

---

5. John Barton, *Oracles of God: Perceptions of Prophecy in Israel after the Exile* (London: Darton, Longman & Todd, 1986), 20.
6. Reinhard Achenbach, 276 in 'The Pentateuch, the Prophets, and the Torah in the Fifth and Fourth Centuries B.C.E.' in *Judah and the Judeans in the Fourth Century B.C.E.* edited by Oded Lipschits, Gary N Knoppers and Rainer Albertz (Winona Lake: Eisenbrauns, 2007), 253–85. See also Birch, *Let Justice Roll Down*, 246.
7. Cf Mann, *The Former Prophets*, 393–95.

by being located after the Writings; this effectively enhances the predictive aspect of prophecy, pointing to things yet to be fulfilled. However it does not weaken the thematic connection between Torah and prophecy; rather it can be seen to draw attention to the prophetic nature of Torah itself and of Moses as the prophet *par excellence* (Deut 18:15-22; 34:10-12). The future the 'Latter Prophets' prophesy will be in accord with the meaning of the Torah and its vision.

It is reasonable to expect that key theological terms in the prophetic corpus such as righteousness, justice, steadfast love and compassion function in an analogous way. That is, their meaning and use within the Latter Prophets are to be understood as an application and interpretation of their meaning in the Torah, even if historically some of the Latter Prophets preached before the formation of the Torah. This is another way in which the Latter Prophets continue and develop the contribution of the Former Prophets. Each book does this in its distinctive way but the fact that each is a constitutive part of the Latter Prophets and the HBOT means that it is part of a larger whole with an overall purpose. It helps to unfold/reveal the meaning of these key terms in the Torah. It is also reasonable to expect that a representative selection from the 'Latter Prophets' will provide a good indication of how this corpus interprets and applies the terms in question. Because the bulk of occurrences are in the book of Isaiah, it is the obvious choice as a 'representative' prophetic book.

My study of the book of Isaiah will focus on its use of righteousness and associated terms in relation to God. The book is also of particular relevance because of the number of relationships that it covers: God's relationship to Israel and Judah, the relationship between these competing kingdoms, the relationship between the Davidic king and God and between the king and people, God's relationship to Zion (understood in a number of ways, as noted below), God's relationship to other nations as well as Israel and Judah's relationship to other nations. And all this is set within the context of God's relationship to creation. The book of Isaiah sees each of these relationships unfolding God's plan/purpose (*'etsah*), the only plan that brings salvation and right order to the world in contrast to the distorted, destructive plans/purposes of human beings. There is a connection here with Deuteronomy 32:28; it states that a/any nation that claims 'Our hand is triumphant' is 'void of sense' (NRSV; literally 'bereft of plan/counsel'). The study of Isaiah will be followed by a briefer discussion of righteousness in Jeremiah, Ezekiel and the book of the 'twelve prophets' (following the MT order). A link between Isaiah, Jeremiah, Ezekiel and the book of the twelve is that each shares a similar basic sequence that unfolds over the course of a book and recurs at various points within a book; the sequence commences with a critique and condemnation of the existing (old) order, this is followed by an announcement of God's resolve to intervene and punish those responsible, it concludes with a promise that God will establish a new order after the purge of the old.[8] This arrangement reflects the prediction made by Moses in the covenant at Moab (Deut 29–30) and in so doing verifies it as a prophecy; Israel will inevitably fail to be loyal to the covenant, God will punish it for its disloyalty, but God will 'again take delight in prospering you' (30:9) when Israel returns to its senses.

---

8. For a more detailed presentation of this sequence, described as various stages of 'prophetic meaning-making' see Louis Stulman and Hyun Chul Paul Kim, *You Are My People. An Introduction to Prophetic Literature* (Nashville: Abingdon Press, 2010), 13–20.

1
Book of Isaiah

As is well known, modern historical critical analysis claims that Isaiah is in fact three books in one: there is a 'First-Isaiah' in chapters 1–39 that contains prophecies of the eighth century BCE prophet Isaiah (cf the superscription in 1:1) as well as later material; there is a 'Second-Isaiah' in chapters 40–55 thought to be the work of one or more authors during the Babylonian exile in the sixth century BCE; and there is 'Third-Isaiah' in chapters 56–66, attributed to a group in the post-exilic period. This theory is based more on perceived differences between parts of the book than connections. Nevertheless the fact that it is a book has prompted some more recent commentators to seek, and find, evidence of similarity and connection between the three postulated sections. Where one approach finds signs of diversity another finds signs of unity. Given that each theory is based on careful critical analysis but that neither can be proved, it is probably best to see the book of Isaiah as a combination of unity and diversity. The 'subjective factor' of which contemporary literary analysis has made us aware means there is unlikely to be agreement over how unified or diverse it is. There is an instinctive tendency when reading a book to focus on signals of unity rather than diversity. As David Carr warns 'excessive confidence in the existence of a more complete unity in biblical texts—and our need to find it—can blind us to the unresolved, rich plurality built into texts like Isaiah'.[1] A critical reading therefore requires the reader to try and give due weight to diversity as well as unity.

---

1. David M Carr, 'Reaching for Unity in Isaiah,' 182 in *The Prophets*, edited by Philip R Davies (The Biblical Seminar 42; Sheffield: Sheffield Academic Press, 1996), 164–83. Also in *JSOT* 57 (1993) 61–80.

A term that seems to epitomise the combination of diversity and unity that is the book of Isaiah is Zion. It is used variously to refer to the city/hill of Jerusalem (1:27; 2:3b; 4:3; 33:5, 20; 37:32; 40:9; 41:27; 52:1; 59:20; 60:14; 62:1); the temple mount itself (18:7; 31:4b); a combination of the city and temple mount (4:3-5; 29:8); the seat of the Davidic king (11:9 [my holy mountain]; 37:35);[2] and God's house/dwelling place (2:3; 8:18; 12:6; 24:23). Zion is also described on a number of occasions as 'daughter Zion' or 'daughter of Zion' (1:8; 10:32; 16:1; 37:22; 52:2; 62:11).[3] This combination exploits the feminine gender of the Hebrew word for city. Zion appears in later passages of the book as a mother bereft of her children but assured that they will return (50:14-21; 54:1-3; 65:8b), as well as God's spouse (54:5-8). The location of these passages lends support to the theory that different hands compiled the book in at least the postulated three stages. Given these passages are in Second- and Third-Isaiah this imagery may be an example of the creative use of the marriage metaphor from the earlier prophet Hosea. There it refers to the relationship between God and Israel (Hosea 1-3), here to the relationship between God and the holy city. One text even identifies Zion with the people (51:16b). Another image of Zion as a female figure is that of a 'whore' in 1:21. The term normally refers to a sexually unfaithful wife, daughter or daughter-in-law. It could be portraying Zion as an unfaithful daughter, which would link it to references to 'daughter Zion', but the context suggests the image of an unfaithful wife is more likely, which would link it to the image of Zion as wife/mother in passages such as 54:5-8 and 62:1-5.[4] In combination with the plural form 'daughters', Zion forms a construct chain to refer to the female inhabitants of the city in 3:16 and 4:4.

---

2. Isa 28:16 is elusive. After considerable discussion of various proposals, Hans Wildberger opts for a metaphorical reading: the 'foundation stone' stands for faith; 'one who trusts will not panic' (*Jesaja. 3. Teilband. Jesaja 28-39. Das Buch, der Prophet und seine Botschaft* [BKAT; Neukirchen-Vluyn: Neukirchener Verlag, 1982], 1075-77).

3. The Hebrew term for daughter (*bat*) is the same in the absolute or construct form; hence the combination could be translated as a genitive (daughter of Zion) as in the Authorised Version, or as an apposition (daughter Zion) as in the NRSV. The term is also used to describe Sidon in Isa 23:12 and 'virgin daughter' Babylon in 47:1.

4. Support for this reading is provided in the more detailed comment on Isa 1 below.

The variation in the imagery of Zion/Jerusalem and its presence throughout the book indicates that it was a point of focus for each stage of composition and it is meant to play a key role in the book as a whole. This impression is underscored by the way Zion—in the various guises outlined—is to the fore at strategic points in the book.[5] This can be seen in the opening and closing chapters (cf 1:8 21-26, 27; 66:23); in the section bounded by 2:1-4 and 4:2-6; in the thanksgiving text in 12:1-6; in the conclusions to the oracles on the nations (cf 23:18 'those who live in the presence of the Lord') and the so-called 'Isaiah apocalypse' (27:13 'the holy mountain in Jerusalem'); and at the end of chapter 35. It also features prominently in the Hezekiah narrative in chs. 36-39; at the beginning (40:1-11) and towards the end (54) of Second-Isaiah; at the beginning (56:1-8; 'my house' and 'my holy mountain') and the end of Third-Isaiah. As Christopher Seitz has argued, the book of Isaiah is very much a vision of 'Zion's final destiny', which is to be the centre of God's universal sovereignty over all nations.[6]

Zion not only binds the various parts of the book together but also provides a link between it and a variety of other figures and terms, thereby enabling their relationships to be explored. The figures of particular importance in the book and for this study are God, the king, the people (inhabitants of Zion) and the nations; the relevant terms are righteousness, justice and torah/law, as well as steadfast love, faithfulness, and compassion. All these have a role in enshrining God's sovereignty in Zion and nowhere is this epitomised better than in Isaiah 1. The universal horizon of the book is signaled in the initial call to the heavens and the earth to hear the Lord's case against his children (Hebrew 'sons' 1:2-3). Their rebellion has had disastrous consequences for daughter Zion via the invasion of 'aliens'

---

5. It is even implied in the superscription that refers to the 'vision of Isaiah', if one accepts Conrad's proposal that the Hebrew term *khazon* (vision) refers to a prophecy received in a temple, as is the case with Samuel in Shiloh (1 Sam 3:1) and Isaiah in Zion (Isa 6) (*Reading the Latter Prophets*, 71-76).
6. Christopher R Seitz, *Zion's Final Destiny. The Development of the Book of Isaiah. A Reassessment of Isaiah 36-39* (Minneapolis: Fortress Press, 1989). See also the structure of Sweeney's commentary *Isaiah 1-39: With an Introduction to Prophetic Literature* (FOTL 16; Grand Rapids: Eerdmans, 1996). Contrary to the historical critical division of the book into three main blocks, Sweeney sees two major divisions, in chapters 1-33 and 34-66.

(1:7-8) and only God's intervention has preserved her from complete destruction (1:9). Even though the text is not explicit, the reader is prompted to ask why this disaster has come about. An answer is implied by 1:18-20; if God can command the sword to 'eat' those who refuse to repent of their rebellion then presumably God is the one who sent the aliens to 'eat' the land. In order to remedy the situation the 'rulers of Sodom' and the 'people of Gomorrah' must 'listen to the Torah of our God' (1:10).[7] The people and rulers are offered the chance of repentance and reform in 1:18-20 but, whichever decision they make, 1:24-26 affirms the resolve of the 'Sovereign, the Lord of hosts/armies, the Mighty One of Israel' to purge Zion and reestablish the 'whore' as a 'city of righteousness'. It will then become a beacon for the nations and so fulfill its role in the establishment of God's universal sovereignty and world order (cf 2:2-4).

This is the dramatic scenario for the first appearance in the book of terms such as justice, righteousness, Torah, and faithfulness (as an adjective in 1:21, 26). A notable feature of the chapter, and of the book of Isaiah, is that justice and righteousness occur as a pair in sequential lines of poetry (cf 1:21b, 27). These are examples of poetic parallelism, a structural feature of Hebrew and much ANE poetry. Within this poetic structure the two terms function as a hendiadys, referring to one reality.[8] According to Weinfeld's detailed study of ANE and Hebrew usage, the hendiadys or word pair 'justice and righteousness' means social justice although not in a judicial or legal sense.[9] In other words, the word pair refers to right order in society, fostered by right or virtuous behaviour. This would suggest that the hendiadys formed by 'righteousness' and 'faithful' in 1:26b evokes a social justice that will endure.

Isaiah 1 provides a good example of the connection between story and instruction. The story component is in the claim that God has been a devoted Father to his children (Israel); they have repaid this loyalty

---

7. Even though 1:10 may derive from a time when the Davidic monarchy no longer ruled Judah, within the context of the book the reference to 'rulers' (and 'princes' in 1:23) can include the king (cf 1:1).
8. Following Thomas L Leclerc, *Yaweh is Exalted in Justice. Solidarity and Conflict in Isaiah* (Minneapolis: Fortress Press, 2001), 10-13. Leclerc notes 'because both terms in a hendiadys have but one referent, the order of the terms can be reversed with no change of meaning' (12), so 'righteousness and justice'.
9. Cf Weinfeld, *Social Justice in Ancient Israel*, 25-44, see especially 35-36.

with rebellion (1:2). Isaiah 1:5-9 conveys the impression that the loyal Father has punished the wayward children by bringing in aliens to devour the land, but in a merciful gesture has left some survivors. As was seen in the Torah and Former Prophets, God's response to an evil practice takes the form of exposure of its perpetrator(s) followed by punishment of the unrepentant.[10] However punishment does not mean the end of God's relationship with Israel, provision is always made (in the text whatever of history) for a future in which Israel can play its part in God's universal purpose (Gen 12:1-3). This reveals the compassionate component of divine righteousness.

A torah or instruction follows in Isaiah 1:10-20. The call to 'listen to the *torah* of our God' in 1:10 can have two levels of meaning. As an address to the people (rulers of Sodom and the people of Gomorrah) it can refer to what follows in vv 11-20. What the people assume is acceptable is intolerable to God: 'I cannot endure solemn assemblies with iniquity'. The reason lies in the opening statement about God as the ever-loyal parent. To assemble in the temple ostensibly to honour the Father while abusing the other 'children'—the oppressed, the orphan and the widow—is a betrayal of the parent-child relationship.[11] The righteous God cannot be portrayed tolerating such a betrayal; hence the condemnation and the teaching about right conduct in 1:16-20.[12] But the term can also be meant to remind the people of a *torah* that they know or should know and which they are disobeying, as 1:11-20 points out. Within the context of the canonical

---

10. Here the punishment may be implied in the description of a devastated land and city in 1:5-9. Do the following verses imply that the people conduct extravagant liturgies seeking deliverance from enemies, but to no avail? Such is their distorted perception of reality they cannot see the reason for this. Hence God sets out, as so often before, to instruct them.
11. Earlier commentators thought that pre-exilic prophets such as Isaiah and Amos condemned cultic worship outright and advocated an ethical religion (social justice). More recent ones think that their criticism is directed not against cultic worship as such but as (corruptly) practiced in their day. A society that seeks social justice will ipso facto worship God as the source and guarantor of it. For a discussion see Hemchand Gossai, *Justice, Righteousness, and the Social Critique of the Eighth Century Prophets* (American University Studies, Series VII; Theology and Religion, 141; New York: Peter Lang, 1993), 254-71.
12. The Hebrew verb translated as 'spoken' in 1:20 has the same consonants (*dbr*) as 'word' in 1:10, suggesting an inclusion.

HBOT this is of course the Torah.¹³ In this regard it is worth noting that the song in Deuteronomy 32 refers, like Isaiah 1, to the people as God's 'degenerate children' (32:5) in whom 'there is no faithfulness' (32:20b), who 'forgot the God who gave you birth' (32:18).

The fact that Isaiah 1:2-20 presents God as Father addressing the children implies that the term 'whore' in 1:21 pictures Zion as a faithless wife and mother. But whereas Hosea accuses Israel of marital infidelity because she takes part in the cult of the fertility god Baal, the Isaiah text accuses Israel of marital infidelity because she condones the social corruption of her children.¹⁴ Isaiah 1:24-26 makes it clear that God is resolved to restore the kind of social justice to Zion that will endure (cf v 26b; 'the city of righteousness/the faithful city'). It will involve a purge of evildoers from the city and the restoration of the right order that existed at its beginning—presumably a reference to how God established or 'married' Zion. As God reared and brought up children who rebelled (1:2), so as a good husband God provided all Zion needed in order to be a good wife and mother (cf judges and counselors) but it has all been corrupted. Such is the situation that it is only through God's intervention that Zion and those in her who repent will be redeemed (1:27). Social justice depends on God's initiative; human beings cannot establish it of themselves. This implies that the command in 1:17 to 'learn to do good/seek justice' means first of all seeking a right relationship with God, repenting of one's sins before God in worship and committing oneself to doing as God does—looking after the oppressed, the orphan and the widow.¹⁵ To put it another way, Torah contains God's right rule for life but it can only be lived by those whom God empowers to do so. These are the ones who 'return to the Lord your God' (Deut 30:2, 10), who

---

13. As Sweeney states, 'Although it is debatable whether the individual authors of Isaiah intended such a comprehensive of *tora* when they wrote the passages in which the term occurs, the meaning of *tora* takes on a hermeneutical life of its own when it is considered in relation to its full literary and interpretative context in the final form of the book of Isaiah' (63 of 'The Book of Isaiah as Prophetic Torah,' in *New Visions of Isaiah*. [edited by Roy F Melugin and Marvin A Sweeney; JSOTSup 214; Sheffield: Sheffield Academic Press, 1996], 50-67).
14. Cf Wildberger, *Jesaja. 1. Teilband. Jesaja 1-12* (BKAT X; Neukirchen-Vluyn: Neukirchener Verlag, 1980), 60.
15. As Leclerc puts it 'The seeking of God is to take place in the temple *and* in the streets: worship finds its legitimacy in the protection of the orphan and the widow' (*Yahweh is Exalted in Justice*, 46).

repent (Isa 1:27). A key motivation for doing so is that, as the Torah teaches, God is completely committed to restoring right relationships. Even though the term is not mentioned, one could therefore say that 1:24–27 reflects God's steadfast love (*khesedh*).

One may invoke the superscription in 1:1 to say that Isaiah 1 presents a vision of God's purpose that will unfold its meaning as one reads the book.[16] The reader is assured in 2:2–4 that in 'the days to come' God's universal sovereignty in Zion will be recognized by all, and from Zion God's Torah/word will go out to judge the nations and establish world order. As one would expect, the initial judgement (3:13) made is of God's chosen people—the house of Jacob (2:6) and Judah and Jerusalem (3:1)—leading to the sanctification of Zion and its inhabitants (4:2–6). This text forms an 'inclusio' with 2:2–4. Isaiah 5 opens a new section of the book that, like 1:2–3, begins with a version of Israel's story. Whereas 1:2–3 employs the imagery of parent–child to claim that God has been a good Father from the beginning and it is the children who have failed, 5:1–2 employs the imagery of a vintner who has devotedly attended his vineyard (the house of Israel) from the beginning, making a choice planting (house of Judah). But instead of good grapes (justice and righteousness in 5:7) only rotten ones have been produced (bloodshed and a cry of distress).

As in 1:21, the word pair 'justice and righteousness' refers to social justice, the right order in society. A series of woe oracles against the injustice of society follows in 5:8–25. Two features are of note. One is the remedy offered in 5:16; it involves transferring the focus of attention from oneself to God by doing what exalts and honours God and, as Leclerc states, 'The exaltation and sanctification of God are accomplished through the enactment of social justice'.[17] The second is the three woe oracles in 5:18–21 that condemn those who reject this remedy. They mock the 'purpose/plan of the Holy One of Israel' and instead follow their own distorted perception that inverts the true

---

16. Cf Sweeney; 'it constitutes the prologue for the entire book of Isaiah' ('The Book of Isaiah as Prophetic Torah,' 55). Isaiah 1 is no doubt based on one or more experiences of trouble and distress in Israel and Judah's history and scholars debate which one(s). My focus here is the chapter's function within the larger book.
17. Leclerc, *Yahweh is Exalted in Justice*, 62. In his judgement, the parallelism is best rendered as '"YHWH of Hosts is exalted, the Holy one is sanctified" (that is, honored as holy)'.

order of things ('who call evil good and good evil').[18] God's anger is kindled against 'his people' (5:25) because they have rejected God's Torah and word.[19] In response to this rejection of God's universal sovereignty and purpose and to demonstrate that it is the only right way, 5:26–30 announces for the first time in the book how the purge or removal of evildoers from Judah and Zion is to take place—God will summon an as yet unnamed nation 'at the ends of the earth'.

Although the people reject the Torah of the Holy One of Israel (5:24c) there is one who doesn't and confesses that 'I am a man of unclean lips, and I live among a people of unclean lips' (6:5). The repentant Isaiah is immediately cleansed and commissioned to preach God's message to the many.[20] In a powerful reversal of the exodus, God announces that the chosen people will now play a role similar to that of Pharaoh. As God hardened the heart of Pharaoh to demonstrate who has real sovereignty over history (and creation), so Isaiah's preaching will effectively harden 'this people' so that they do not turn from their wicked ways and be healed.[21] This will hasten the time of purge and cleansing of the land, an integral part of God's righteous purpose as announced in Isaiah 1. 'This people' in 6:10 is presumably 'his people', the ones who mock, reject and despise the 'Holy one of Israel' (5:18–19). Yet, as the Torah and Former Prophets always have one or some Israelites escape the destruction of the many and so enable the story to continue, so prophecy does much the same. The final line of 6:13 signals a future beyond the prophesied devastation.

God's sovereign rule over history is illustrated in the subsequent account of the Assyrian crisis (Isa 7–8). Within the context of Isaiah 6, the implication is that what looks to be Ahaz's rejection of Isaiah's word and sign (Immanuel) is really God hardening his heart. God's

---

18. Isaiah 5:19b is the first occurrence of the term *'etsah* (plan/purpose/counsel) which plays an important role in the book (cf 5:19; 8:10; 11:2; 14:26; 16:3; 19:3, 11, 17; 25:1; 28:29; 29:15; 30:1; 36:5; 40:13; 44:26; 46:10, 11; 47:13).
19. The combination of the terms Torah and word (*'imrah*) in the parallelism suggests that they constitute a hendiadys, like 'righteousness and justice'.
20. Isaiah here serves as a model of how the people should respond to the presence of the Holy One of Israel in their midst but do not.
21. Following the MT version as translated in the NRSV. The LXX has 'because the mind of this people is dull, and they have stopped their ears and shut their eyes' (cf also Matt 13:15).

plan (cf 5:26) to summon a nation from the ends of the earth to purge Judah and Zion (7:14-25; cf 5:5-6) and to punish a proud and arrogant Jacob/Israel (9:8-10:4) assumes historical reality in the Assyrian invasion. But the divine plan also includes the birth in due course of a royal son who will establish the throne of David in lasting justice and righteousness (9:7 [MT 9:6]).[22] The establishment of this new order depends on 'the zeal of the Lord of hosts' who 'dwells on Mount Zion' (8:18). Contrary to the disordered 'rule' of those who follow their own counsel and do what is right in their own eyes (5:21), this king will have the spirit of the Lord upon him; 'the spirit of wisdom and understanding, the spirit of counsel and might, the spirit of knowledge and the fear of the Lord' (11:2). Another integral part of the divine plan is the return of the remnant of Israel who will, in the course of their punishment, have learned to rely completely on the 'Holy One of Israel' (10:20-23). Once again we see, in keeping with the Torah, the appeal to the authority of God's word to justify the distribution of punishment and compassion.

God's sovereignty and just judgement are further illustrated by prophesies that condemn Assyria for its arrogance and pride—it is as bad as arrogant Israel in 9:8-9—and announce its doom (10:5-34).[23] Isaiah 10:22 explains the reduction of Israel from being 'like the sand of the sea' to a remnant as 'destruction is decreed, overflowing with righteousness'. To borrow imagery from Isaiah 1, the dross of Israel will be removed in order to recover the pure metal (those who repent).[24] It is all part of God's purpose to establish universal world order. As the following verse (10:23) puts it 'God is making a destruction, and a determined one, in the midst of all the earth' (a literal translation). This is not about creating chaos but the elimination of it. This line of thinking is akin to the destruction in the

---

22. As has been noted, a key responsibility of the king in ANE and Israelite society was social justice, understood not so much in a legal or juridical sense but as that of the patron who sees to the welfare of his subjects, particularly the disadvantaged (cf Houston, *Contending for Justice*, 134-35).
23. While the text claims to be rooted in the time of Assyrian threat, the imagery of 10:13-19 and 10:33-34 in particular indicate that it is a symbol of any power that claims sovereignty that belongs to God alone.
24. According to Krasovec Isa 10:22 'montre que la justice de Dieu se révèle surtout dans le jugement des méchants qui ne reviendront pas' (*La Justice [sdq] de Dieu dans La Bible*, 80).

flood story, to Deuteronomy's warning that God will 'destroy' Israel for its infidelity but restore those who 'return' to the Lord, and to the purge of wicked nations in the book of Joshua, except those who confess faith in the Lord (Rahab and the Gibeonites). It is also similar to the distinction in Jeremiah 24 between the good figs (destined to return from exile) and the bad figs (the old order destined to end).

Isaiah 2:2–4 envisages peace and harmony among the nations; the prophecy of the shoot from the royal 'stump of Jesse' complements this with peace and harmony within the animal kingdom as well as between animals and human beings (cf 11:9; 'they will not hurt or destroy on all my holy mountain'). The jealousy and hostility between Israel and Judah will disappear and they will unite to participate in God's victory over hostile nations (11:13–16). The section concludes in 12:1–6 with a promise that in that day 'you' (singular) will thank God whose righteous anger is followed by comfort. This will lead to a resolve to trust God completely. The addressee here may be an individual, the remnant of Israel and those in Zion (10:20–21, 24) or, within the book, 'my people' who are comforted in 40:1. In 12:6 Zion is exhorted to sing because the 'Holy One' in its midst is establishing universal sovereignty.

Having outlined the divine purpose for the people, the king and Zion, the book turns to the nations with a series of oracles in Isaiah 13–23. If Assyria is the epitome of the proud, arrogant nation in the preceding chapters, it is joined in these oracles by Babylon in 13–14 and Egypt in 19–20. At a number of points there are texts that testify God's action against these nations is part of God's purpose for Israel (14:1–3), Zion (14:32; 16:1; 18:7; 23:18), and the Davidic king who will, as stated in 11:4–5, faithfully seek to enact justice and righteousness (16:5). This is the order that will replace the international disorder among the nations. God's war against the pride and arrogance of these nations is thus part of God's plan 'that is planned concerning the whole earth' and 'who will annul it?' (14:26–27; cf also 19:12, 17). God will confound the plans of the Egyptians (19:3) so that the 'wise counselors of Pharaoh give stupid counsel'. In 6:9–10 God gives Isaiah a commission that will close the minds of the rebellious people and thereby ensure their demise; here the text implies that God will ensure that Pharaoh's counselors give stupid advice and thereby seal Egypt's demise. Yet, as in the prophecies about the return of a remnant of

Israel and the survival of Zion here too a remnant is prophesied, five cities in the land of Egypt that 'swear allegiance to the Lord of hosts' (19:18). As with Israel and Zion, the Lord will strike Egypt, 'striking and healing' (19:22); one could also translate this as 'striking and so/thereby healing' (19:22). The extraordinary conclusion to Isaiah 19 foresees a highway between Assyria, Egypt and Israel, a symbol of peaceful coexistence, with Egypt and Assyria sharing in Israel's blessing.

Even though the so-called 'Isaiah Apocalypse' in 24-27 differs in form from 13-23 in that there are no 'oracles' against the nations, the two can be linked because they are about God's war against the wicked inhabitants of the earth. They have polluted it through their transgression of laws (torahs), violation of statutes and breach of the everlasting covenant (24:5).[25] While these terms do not refer directly to the Torah and the Sinai/Horeb covenant one could say that the latter enable one to discern what is true and false, right and wrong in these torahs, statutes and everlasting covenant. There is also an implied connection here between Torah and ANE and Israelite wisdom. While 24:6-13 paints a gloomy picture of a curse that 'devours the earth', vv 14-16a tell of joyful singing from the ends of the earth 'to the Righteous One' who alone can bring about universal world order. The definitive purge of evil on that day will involve punishment for 'the host of heaven' as well as 'the kings of the earth' (24:21). Sun and moon will retreat before the glory of the Lord reigning on 'Mount Zion and in Jerusalem' (24:23; cf 27:13) and 'on this mountain' the Lord will provide a feast for all peoples (25:6). All that demeans human life (the shroud of death, tears, disgrace) will be removed from the earth and all will confess 'this is our God' (25:9). In short, the ultimate purpose of establishing universal sovereignty in Zion is that all may know the Lord is God (cf Exod 6:7; 7:5). Everything depends on and flows from this. Isaiah 26 is a song about the 'righteous nation that keeps faith' and is therefore able to enter the holy city.[26] This is the nation whose citizens know God as the 'Just One' and that it is only 'when

---

25. This is the first occurrence of the term covenant in the book of Isaiah. Leclerc identifies the term here with Noah (*Yahweh is Exalted in Justice*, 196, n. 12). Other occurrences are 28:15 18; 33:8; 42:6; 49:8; 54:10; 55:3; 56:4, 6; 59:21; 61:8.
26. The nation is not explicitly identified but is presumably Israel/Judah (cf the location of the song and the reference to 'a strong city').

your judgements are in the earth' that 'the inhabitants of the world learn righteousness' (26:7-10). They desire that God's righteousness triumph against 'your adversaries', they know that this will bring true peace because 'we acknowledge your name alone' even though they are powerless. On the basis of this 'confession' of faith, the 'righteous nation' is assured 'your dead will live' (26:19) and are urged to 'hide yourselves a little while until the wrath is past'—until God's purge of all the evil inhabitants of the earth is complete (26:20-21).

Isaiah 28-33 resumes key themes from the preceding chapters in order to affirm God's purpose for Zion as wonderful and wise (cf 28:29), as are all God's instructions and counsel, and to condemn those in Ephraim/Israel (28:1) and those in Jerusalem (28:14) who reject it and cling to the existing 'disorder'. To counter the injustice of the drunkards of Ephraim, God will give 'a spirit of justice to the one who sits in judgement' (28:6). Although this verse does not identify the judge, it may refer to the king who is expected to uphold justice and righteousness. The description of Ephraim as drunks recalls Isaiah 5:11, 22. To counter the scoffers in Jerusalem, God is laying 'in Zion a foundation stone' setting it in exactly the right place by the use of justice as a measuring line and righteousness as a plummet (28:16). This architectural imagery is employed to express the same theology as in 1:21-28; justice and righteousness (or social justice) are 'foundational' components of God's purpose for Zion, both as a city and God's dwelling place (8:18). Furthermore, when one links this passage with earlier occurrences of the hendiadys 'justice and righteousness' in 5:16; 9:7 (MT 9:6) then, as Leclerc notes, the expression 'ties together four key Isaianic complexes: Zion as a temple city, the foundation stone of Zion, the exaltation of God, and the royal throne.'[27]

Isaiah 29 warns the city (Ariel) of the distress it is to suffer as part of God's purge but that this will end suddenly when God comes to strike the nations that fight against her (cf 10:24-34). What is distinctive about chapters 28-33 in relation to the preceding chapters is the condemnation of foreign alliances in 30-31; this plan (30:1) to secure the existing 'disorder' is contrary to God's plan for the nations as set down in 13-23 (24-27). It amounts to a repudiation of that plan and its claim of God's universal sovereignty and will therefore

---

27. Leclerc, *Yahweh is Exalted in Justice*, 78.

be brought undone. Within Isaiah 30 itself a distinctive feature is the close association of the terms 'gracious' (verb *khanan*) and 'merciful/compassionate' (verb *rakham*) with justice and righteousness.[28] God is just in punishing those who pursue foreign alliances for their own gain (30:16); equally God is just in being gracious and compassionate to the remnant who will be left 'like a flagstaff on the top of a mountain' (30:17); Again, as Leclerc notes, 'Justice means two things simultaneously: on the one hand, it is a gracious compassion extended toward the widow and orphan, the poor and oppressed; on the other hand, it is punishment and destruction for those who fail to act with that same gracious compassion'.[29] I would add that these two 'arms' of justice have one overall purpose in mind—the establishment of righteousness, or right order in society and creation. Having dismissed foreign alliances as a false plan, the book reasserts the plan of 9:2-7 (MT 9:1-6) and 11:1-5. This is that 'a king will reign in righteousness, and princes will rule with justice' (32:1), that as a result once closed eyes and ears will be opened and the disorder that has 'reigned' will be seen for what it is, folly, iniquity, error, evil, lies, etc (cf 32:2-7). 'You women' (32:11) are warned that the purge about to take place will be painful until 'a spirit from on high is poured upon us' and the transforming power of God's justice and righteousness brings enduring peace, quietness and trust on earth (32:16-18).[30]

This section of the book concludes in 33 with a series of cameos of the main players in the unfolding drama. There is the woe oracle against the destroyer, the enemy nation(s) that has acted treacherously and not in accord with the divine plan (33:1-3). There is the prayer of the faithful remnant in 33:2-6 waiting for the Lord who has filled Zion with justice and righteousness, presumably in preparation for their return. Zion that was once full of justice and righteousness is thus restored (1:21), enabling those things that are marks of right order in society to flourish (33:6). There is also the cry of those who bewail the

---

28. The connection with righteousness may be seen in 30:21 in the instruction to walk in the right way. Even though the word for way/path here is *derek* whereas in 26:7 it is *'orakh*, there is a strong thematic connection. The former portrays God preparing the path for the righteous while the latter has God as a teacher guiding one along the right path.
29. Leclerc, *Yahweh is Exalted in Justice*, 81.
30. The reference to 'a spirit' from on high that brings about justice can be linked to the spirit of justice that will be bestowed on the judge in 28:6.

devastation in the wake of God's climactic battle against evil (33:7-9). This battle marks the exaltation of the Lord as victor whom all should acknowledge, those both far and near. The next group identified is the sinners in Zion who will only be able to live with God's 'devouring fire' by committing themselves to social justice (33:14-16). Verses 15-16 are similar to Psalms 15 and 24 that declare who is worthy to participate in the temple liturgy. This, plus the reference to fire in v 14, may be intended to recall the earlier condemnation of those who engage in extravagant sacrificial liturgies but neglect social justice (cf 1:10-17, 23). The implication is that those who renounce such evil are the ones who will survive God's purge and participate in Zion's restored liturgy.[31]

Isaiah 33:17-19 assures the righteous (singular; cf 33:15-16) that he will see the king reigning over a vast land and the foreign invaders gone, while 33:20-22 urges him to look upon Zion where 'the Lord is our judge, the Lord is our lawgiver, the Lord is our king'. This three-part parallelism brings together key roles necessary for the good order of society and attributes them to God. This is presumably for two reasons, at least. One is that the people to whom these are entrusted have failed and continue to fail, as texts like 1:10; 3:1-3, 13-15; 28:7-8, 14 point out. This leads to the second reason, the acknowledgement that right judgement, lawmaking and rule can only come from God. This leads in turn to the final part of 33:22: 'he will save us'.

There is a good case for taking Isaiah 34-35 as the introduction to the second part of the book.[32] The two chapters look back as well as forward. The universal call in 34:1 to hear God's judgement against the nations recalls the similar one in 1:2-3 to hear God's case against his people. The announcement of God's war against 'all the nations' (34:5) recalls the purge of Zion announced in 1:21-25. Both texts employ the image of the devouring sword of God (1:20; 34:5). Isaiah 63:1-6 would appear to signal the completion of God's war against

---

31. Cf Wildberger, *Jesaja 28-39*, 1302-3.
32. As outlined by Sweeney in *Isaiah 1-39 with an Introduction to Prophetic Literature*, 39-41, but also acknowledging Roy F Melugin's observation that all proposals about the structure and interpretation of texts are constructed/created by interpreters from perceived signals in the text ('The Book of Isaiah and the Construction of Meaning', in *Writing and Reading the Scroll of Isaiah*, 39-55. For his comments on Sweeney's structure, see 47-48).

Edom and Bozrah announced in 34:5-6.[33] Promises made in Isaiah 35 recur in Isaiah 40-55—the transformation of the wilderness (35:1, 6-7), the exhortation 'do not fear' (35:4) followed by the assurance of salvation, the provision of a highway through the wilderness along which the exiles shall return to Zion (35:8-10).

The two chapters are also interconnected: Isaiah 34 proclaims God's war against all the nations as a prelude to the promise in Isaiah 35 that the 'redeemed' and 'ransomed of the Lord' will return to Zion. In one sense this is nothing new because these themes have been aired in the preceding chapters. But Isaiah 34-35 also provides a lead in to 36-39 which illustrates or validates God's commitment to Zion. Isaiah 36-39 in turn provides a raison d'être for the remainder of the book in which God's plan/counsel is unfolded in relation to the fate of the nations, the exiles' return to Zion, and the destiny of Zion.[34] In Isaiah 36-39 Hezekiah is initially cast as a foil to the feckless Ahaz in Isaiah 7. When Jerusalem is (again) threatened by Assyria, Hezekiah trusts in God and prays for deliverance. Because of his loyalty he is assured that Assyria's plans will come to nothing (37:22-29), that the remnant will take root and flourish (37:31-32), and that 'I will defend this city to save it, for my sake and for the sake of my servant David' (37:35). The subsequent narrative recounts how the angel of the Lord strikes the Assyrian army and that Sennacherib is subsequently killed 'with the sword' (37:36-38). When compared with the narrative of Ahaz and the prophecies of Immanuel in 7:14 and 8:8-10, one could gain the impression that Hezekiah is Immanuel.[35] But, if Immanuel is the 'child borne to us' who will inaugurate a rule of 'endless peace' according to 9:1-7 (MT 9:1-6), then it would seem that Hezekiah is not Immanuel, or at least not *that* Immanuel.[36] Whereas Hezekiah initially trusts God when threatened by Assyria, he foolishly trusts the Babylonians in 39:2. Isaiah intervenes to prophesy that they will strip the place bare, as he earlier prophesied to Ahaz what the king of

---

33. The focus on Edom after the tirade against all the nations in 34:2-4 is surprising but may be a case of the general (the nations) being illustrated via the particular (Edom).
34. For a detailed analysis of the relationship between Isa 36-39 and the preceding and following chapters of the book see Seitz, *Zion's Final Destiny*.
35. Advocated by Seitz, *Zion's Final Destiny*, 65, 263-66.
36. Isaiah 37:32b repeats 9:7c (MT 9:6c), 'The zeal of the Lord of hosts will do this'. However it is in relation to the remnant rather than Hezekiah.

Assyria would do (7:20). The 'great light' of 9:1–7 (MT 9:1–6) is yet to shine.

Isaiah 36–39 plays an important role both within the book of Isaiah and within the larger context of the HBOT. It forges links between the first part of the book (1–33) and the second part (40–66), in particular via Isaiah's prophecy in 39:6–7. It deals with key relationships, such as between God and Zion, God and the Davidic dynasty, God and the people, and God and foreign nations (represented here by Assyria). The version in 2 Kings 18–20 (minus Hezekiah's prayer and with the addition of 18:14–16) enhances the connection between the Former and the Latter Prophets—in three key areas. It is widely accepted that the book of Isaiah is a major representative of the David and Zion/Jerusalem traditions. Because of the prominence of David as the foundational figure in the Davidic/royal tradition it could and no doubt did, at times, rival the Moses tradition; the same can be said for Zion and Sinai as mountains of revelation and sites of worship. The presence of 2 Kings 18–20 effectively situates the Davidic and Zion traditions within the Mosaic Torah revealed at Sinai. According to 2 Kings 18:6 Hezekiah 'kept the commandments that the Lord commanded Moses'. According to 1 Kings 8, Zion is the 'place' chosen by God as a dwelling for the divine name (cf Deut 12:11). Jon D Levenson expresses this incorporation of one within the other as follows:

> God's continuing availability is at Zion, not Sinai, but the canonical division of the Pentateuch from the rest of the Hebrew Bible, adumbrated in Deut 34:10, insures that the heir will be eternally subordinate to the testator, Zion to Sinai, David to Moses.[37]

The reflections on Isaiah 1–39 have focused on the word pair righteousness and justice/justice and righteousness. This is a hendiadys that refers to social justice, in particular the failure of the people to implement it according to the Torah (cf 1:10; 5:24c). Isaiah 1:10–20 teaches that Zion's liturgy is worthless when conducted by those who abuse social justice. One could even say the text implies

---

37. Jon D Levenson, *Sinai and Zion. An Entry into the Jewish Bible* (New Voices in Biblical Studies; Minneapolis: Winston Press, 1985), 188.

that such worship of God is another form of social injustice. It also promotes a distorted perception of God and God's ways. For the sake of the divine name (true knowledge of God and God's purpose), the book proclaims that God will intervene and purge the city (1:21-26) and land (6:11-13) of this evil. But, as with the chosen people in the Torah, the book of Isaiah expresses the conviction that God remains committed to Zion despite such failures; the purge will lead to restoration and renewal. In relation to this a number of occurrences of the word pair proclaims that God will establish social justice so that Zion and its people can play their roles in the unfolding of God's purpose (1:27; 32:16-17; 33:5). Also in keeping with the relationship between the one and the many outlined in the Torah, texts such as Isaiah 9:1-7 [MT 9:1-6]; 11:1-9; 32:1-8 proclaim that God will establish a king who will judge the poor in righteousness (11:4) and play a key role in the establishment of right order centered in Zion. It is an integral part of God's plan that Zion becomes the centre of world pilgrimage and worship (2:1-4), and that the nations (represented in 19:23-25 by Assyria and Egypt) share in Israel's blessing (cf Gen 12:3).

In Isaiah 40:1-11 God announces the end of the Babylonian exile prophesied in 39:5-7 and the return of the exiles to Zion.[38] One would expect to find the subsequent chapters to accompany this good news with an announcement of the imminent establishment by God of justice and righteousness in Zion, so as to right the wrongs condemned in Isaiah 1-39. Surprisingly, this word pair does not reappear until 56:1a. Instead, what one finds in the intervening chapters is the word pair righteousness and salvation (45:21 [righteousness as adjective; God as saviour]; 46:13; 51:5, 8) or salvation (*yesha'/ teshu'ah*) and righteousness (45:8; 51:6; 56:1b). After 56:1a the word pair righteousness and justice occurs in 58:2b, 2c; 59:4a, 9a, 14a but is replaced by righteousness and salvation in 59:16b, 17a; 61:10b; 62:1b; 63:1c.[39] What is striking about this distribution of terms is

---

38. Unlike Jeremiah and Ezekiel, the book of Isaiah does not portray the conquest of Judah and the destruction of Zion by the Babylonians. This may be due to convictions about the inviolability of Zion/Jerusalem (cf Psalms 46-48). Whatever the case, there is a gap between 39:5-7 and 40:1 that in a sense Jeremiah and Ezekiel fill.
39. Cf Gregory J Polan, *In the Ways of Justice Toward Salvation: A Rhetorical Analysis of Isaiah 56-59* (American University Studies; Series VII, Theology and Religion; 13; New York: Peter Lang, 1986), 58-60. Cf also Rolf Rendtorff, *Canon and*

that it lends support to the modern historical-critical division of the book into First- Second- and Third-Isaiah (1–39, 40–55 and 56–66). Like any hypothesis this one cannot be proved but the distribution of terminology does justify analysing the use of righteousness according to the historical critical division.

Isaiah 40–55 can be divided into two main sections, one that deals with the liberation of the exiles from Babylon and the other with the restoration of Zion. The division or transition point would appear to be the hymn in 49:13 which praises God who 'has comforted his people' and is followed by Zion's lament and God's response (19:14).[40] Two additional features support this division. One is that the themes of the exiles and Zion match Isaiah 40:1–11 where the good news is announced first to 'my people' (40:1-8) and then to Zion (40:9-11). The second is that the hymn in 49:13 states 'the Lord has comforted his people', a clear echo of 40:1. In effect therefore, there are three parts to Isaiah 40–55; the introduction in 40:1-11 (in two parts); 40:12-49:13 and 49:14-55:13. It is also significant that the so-called servant songs are located toward the beginning and end of each major section: 42:1-4 and 49:1-6 in the first section and 50:4-9 and 52:13-53:11 in the second. In Isaiah 40:12-49:13 considerable attention is paid to Cyrus as God's chosen instrument of Israel's deliverance from Babylon. Neither Cyrus nor Babylon is mentioned in 49:14-55:13. This would suggest that the servant is 'introduced' alongside Cyrus in 40:12-49:13 and then replaces him in 49:14-55:13, while Zion replaces Babylon as the rightful 'mother' of God's children.

Theology. Overtures to an Old Testament Theology (OBT; Minneapolis: Fortress Press, 1993), 162-64, 181-89; and Leclerc, *Yahweh is Exalted in Justice*, 133. See also John N Oswalt, 'Righteousness in Isaiah: A Study of the Function of Chapters 56–66 in the Present Structure of the Book,' in *Writing and Reading the Scroll of Isaiah. Studies in an Interpretive Tradition vol. 1*, edited by Craig C Broyles and Craig A Evans (Supplements to Vetus Testamentum 70,1; Leiden/New York/Cologne: Brill, 1997), 177-91. According to Rendtorff (162, n. 50) there is no difference in meaning between the feminine (45:8; 46:13; 51:6, 8) and masculine forms (45:8; 51:5) of the Hebrew term for righteousness. As with the hendiadys justice and righteousness, the order of the word pair righteousness and salvation does not appear to change the meaning.

40. Following Paul-Henri Plamondon, 'Sur le chemin du salut avec le Deuxième Isaie,' *Nouvelle Revue Theologique* 104/1 (1982): 241-66. He identifies other hymnic passages at strategic points in 42:10-13 and 44:23.

The first occurrence of righteousness in 40–55 is in 41:2 and refers to Cyrus.[41] The unusual use of the masculine noun (*tsedeq*) to describe him rather than the adjective suggests he is a manifestation of God's righteousness because God is the one who 'summons him to his service'. The following verses 'report' the unstoppable march of Cyrus because God is with him. The context thus implies that the emergence of Cyrus as God's victorious servant is the first stage of the revelation of God's righteousness that the book will unfold. What is implicit in the claim about Cyrus in 41:2 becomes explicit in 42:6 ('I have called you in righteousness'). He is part of God's universal purpose/plan about which no one can counsel God (cf 40:13). It is a righteous plan (41:26) because only the God of Israel declared it 'from the beginning/beforehand'. Only this God is in charge of the course of events and has a plan for humanity and creation.

The second occurrence (as an adjective in 41:10) identifies another servant of God in 40–55, Israel/Jacob. If the sense of righteousness in 41:2 and 42:6 is victory or triumph (cf Judg 5:11b), here it is more protection or deliverance: servant Israel/Jacob is not to fear because 'I will uphold you with my righteous (NRSV 'victorious') right hand'. Cyrus's victory spells deliverance for Israel. It is worth noting at this point another difference between Isaiah 1–39 and 40–55. In the former, Jacob/Israel and Judah/Jerusalem tend to be addressed or treated separately. Although there are references in the latter to the 'cities of Judah' the term Judah does not occur by itself.[42] The people are referred to only as Jacob/Israel. The point of this may be to emphasise that 40–55 envisages the disappearance of the old division and animosity (cf 11:11–16) and the two once more one people. A somewhat different sense of righteousness occurs in 42:21 within the context of a dispute with 'my servant/messenger' in 42:18–25. The servant here is not the one introduced in 42:1–4 but Jacob/Israel (42:24) who is blind and deaf (cf 6:9–10). The questions in 42:19 suggest a dispute over who is responsible for the people's situation of exile—God or Jacob/Israel? The answer given is that both are but in different senses. The people are guilty of disobedience to the Torah (42:24c) whereas God has acted in accord with his Torah by sending

---

41. Passages on Cyrus in 40–55 can be identified in 41:2-4, 25-29; 42:5-9; 44:24-28; 45:1-6 (7), 9-13; 46:9-11; 48:12-15.
42. Cf Isa 40:9; 44:26; 48:1 (waters of Judah); also 65:9.

the disobedient into exile. In doing so God has acted 'for the sake of his righteousness' without which there is no salvation (42:21).[43] If the exile cannot be explained in relation to God's purpose for Israel and humanity then how can one have confidence that the rise of Cyrus is part of this same righteous purpose that embraces all creation (cf 45:13, 19)? The text has to state and defend what is effectively a theodicy otherwise the Torah is bankrupt and the understanding of God that it promotes is fraudulent.

Thus far one gains the sense that righteous/righteousness in 40–55 is primarily about God's deliverance of Israel from exile through the agency of Cyrus and that this will be made known to the ends of the earth (41:5). This becomes even clearer in Isaiah 45–47 that spells out God's purpose/plan for Cyrus and the consequences of this for daughter Babylon (47:1) and her gods Bel and Nebo (46:1). In these chapters we find several occurrences of the word pair righteousness and salvation (45:8, 21; 46:13). The first employs agricultural imagery to state that for righteousness and salvation to flourish on earth they need the righteousness that rains 'from above', from God. The final line of the verse claims that God creates or brings all this about just as, according to v 7, God creates light and darkness/peace and evil. This dramatic verse may be a counter to Persian dualism; there can only be one God who apportions reward (peace) and retribution (evil) and does so in a righteous way, the way that advances God's saving purpose for creation. The particular 'case' of Jacob/Israel will not only lead Cyrus, the anointed one, but all nations to acknowledge (know) this (45:1–6).

The argument that the particular validates or demonstrates the universal is reiterated twice more in 45:9–19 and 20–25. According to the first, the rise of Cyrus is an integral part of God's righteous activity in creation. It is a logical contradiction to argue that his rise is contrary to the overall purpose of the one God. He is as much part of it as the Assyrians or Babylonians who are agents of divine punishment of Israel and Judah. The passage concludes with the universal claim 'I the Lord speak righteousness (NRSV 'the truth')/I declare right things (plural noun from *yashar*). As God creates a world of order and not

---

43. For a similar interpretation see Krasovec, *La Justice (sdq) de Dieu*, 89–90. Isaiah 43:26 also challenges the people to accuse God so that 'you can be proved right/righteous'; for a more conciliatory address, cf 48:1, 18.

chaos, a world on which one can rely, so every word that God speaks can be known and relied upon utterly. The second passage makes the link between God as righteous and God as saviour more explicit (45:21c).[44] All are urged to turn to God because God's righteous word will achieve its ultimate goal in universal salvation and there is no stopping it (45:23). The triumph of God's word is then 'demonstrated' in three cases. Those who turn will proclaim the righteousness and power of God's word, those who initially reject it 'shall come to him and be ashamed' (45:24), and all Israel will be made righteous (NRSV 'shall triumph') in the Lord and praise him. Salvation lies in knowing and praising God as God. Isaiah 46:12-13 is in a similar vein, urging those who are far from righteousness (NRSV 'deliverance') to listen because God is bringing righteousness and salvation near. What this text adds is Zion as the locus or centre of God's salvation for Israel.

The remaining occurrences are in the section 49:14-55:13. The first is the verb 'righteous' in 50:8, within the third servant poem (50:4-9). Although surrounded by accusers the servant voices the conviction that God 'who makes me righteous' (NRSV 'vindicates') is near. God will declare him to be in the right and thereby save him; his task is to remain loyal to the word that God has taught him—the torah of 42:4—because it is the right message. In line with 45:21-25, salvation lies in God's word. The next occurrence of righteousness is in Isaiah 51:1-8 which unfolds in three sections, vv 1-3, 4-5 and 7-8. Each commences with a call to listen and each concludes with an assurance of God's salvation. The parallelism in Isaiah 51:1 identifies those who 'pursue righteousness' as those who 'seek the Lord'. How do they find the Lord? By recalling what the Torah says God did for Abraham and Sarah and believing it.[45] Verse 3 assures them (loyal Israelites) that what God did for their ancestors (blessing) God will do for Zion (comfort, cf 40:1 and 49:13). Verses 4-5 inform 'my people' that God's teaching/torah and judgement, with righteousness (NSRV 'deliverance') and salvation, are now to go out for the benefit of all peoples and for all time (v 6c). The parallelisms and the verb 'go/gone out' in vv 4 and 5 indicate a close association between these terms.

---

44. According to Krasovec the terms here are synonymous (*La Justice (sdq) de Dieu*, 96).
45. Reading the text within the immediate context of 51:1-8 with its references to torah in vv 4 and 7, and within the larger context of the book of Isaiah (cf 2:3c) and the Torah.

The third section in vv 7-8 calls on those who know righteousness, which the parallel line identifies as 'my teaching/torah'. These are presumably the ones who accept the torah and judgement that has gone out according to v 4; the assurance in v 6c of a righteousness (NSRV 'deliverance') and salvation that endures forever is now proclaimed for them as well (v 8b).

The final examples in this section are as adjective and verb in the fourth servant poem (52:12–53:13; cf 53:11), and as noun in the address to Zion (54:9–17; cf 54:14, 17). In the former the faithful servant demonstrates his loyalty to God by bearing the burden God has decreed. He is the righteous one who can thereby 'make many righteous'; in other words he can be an effective mediator or agent of God's righteousness to all. The salvific aspect of the term is clear. In the second, God promises Zion that she shall be established 'in righteousness'. The subsequent verses indicate that this righteousness will be evident in two key arenas of life. One is the military arena: Zion will be protected from any threat of violence and chaos (54:14–17a). The other is the judicial arena: Zion will be able to refute anyone who 'rises against you in judgement' (54:17b). The passage concludes by affirming that 'the servants of the Lord' will inherit all this as their righteousness too; the righteousness of Zion and its citizens are one, or the establishment of Zion in righteousness brings about their righteousness. One may sum up this survey of righteousness in Isaiah 40–55 in the words of Rendtorff, 'The "righteousness" of God is here a component in his saving acts for Israel and the nations.'[46]

As noted earlier, a striking feature of Isaiah 56–66 is the distribution of the respective word pairs righteousness/justice and righteousness/salvation. Isa 56:1 contains both but thereafter they occur separately; the former in Isaiah 58:2b, 2c; 59:4a, 9a, 14a and the latter in 59:16b, 17a; 61:10b; 62:1b; 63:1c. This not only lends support to the hypothesis of Isaiah 56–66 as a distinctive section of the book but also indicates that whoever was responsible for these chapters— or at least the ones in which the above terminology occurs—sought to relate them to Isaiah 1–39 and 40–55 where the respective word

---

46. Rendtorff, *Canon and Theology*, 162.

pairs occur separately.[47] How this is done will be the focus of this part of the analysis.

The relationship between the word pairs in Isaiah 1–39 and 40–55 was explained by proposing that in the former righteousness/justice refers primarily to social justice that has been completely corrupted in Judah and Jerusalem/Zion. The latter proclaims that God's righteousness/salvation will establish a new order in the land and in Zion so that a just society that is completely loyal to God can flourish. That God has made this proclamation means its realisation is already under way and 'shall accomplish that which I purpose' (55:11). Moreover, as Isaiah 40–55 states a number of times, this divine purpose is not just for Israel but also for all humanity and creation. This context needs to be kept in mind when reading Isaiah 56–66. Thus, one can interpret 56:1 as an instruction on how to prepare for the imminent realisation of God's righteousness/salvation—it is to keep justice and do righteousness in a manner that is outlined in the following verses (56:2-8).[48] What is striking about these verses is that they do not focus on society—as for example in Isaiah 1 and 5. Instead the focus is on God—keeping 'my sabbaths', doing 'the things that please me', holding fast to 'my covenant'. Right social conduct may well be included in the instruction to refrain 'from doing evil' but the overall focus is on one's relationship to God. Anyone, whether foreigner or eunuch, who is so devoted will share with Israel in the new order.

The references to 'my covenant' in 56:4, 6 and in 59:21 are significant. The term does not occur in the preceding text except for 'my covenant of peace' in 54:10 where the context points to the covenant with Noah (cf Gen 9:1-7). The occurrences in 56:4, 6, in association with references to the Sabbath observance and to the status

---

47. Whether Isa 56–66 was originally the manifesto of a particular party in a dispute about the nature of the post-exilic Persian province of Yehud is beyond the scope of this study. For a recent contribution see AL Grant-Henderson, *Inclusive Voices in Post-Exilic Judah* (Minnesota: The Liturgical Press, 2002). My focus is on the function of these chapters within the book of Isaiah.
48. I have used the same term 'righteousness' in both cases to reflect the Hebrew (*tsedaqah*). However the Hebrew assumes a different nuance in each word pair, as indicated by the NRSV 'right' and 'deliverance'. The LXX captures the difference by translating *dikaiosune* and *eleos* respectively. The Vulgate uses *iustitia* for both occurrences.

of foreigners and eunuchs in the community, signal that the term has in mind the Mosaic covenant and its laws.[49] In relation to this it is also worth noting that the term Torah does not occur in 56–66; one could say that it is subsumed into the term 'my covenant'. The identification of 'my covenant' with the Mosaic covenant raises the question of its relationship to the 'everlasting covenant/my steadfast, sure love for David' in 55:3. This text does not mean that the Davidic promises in Isaiah 9 and 11, or 2 Samuel 7 and Psalm 89, are cancelled, rather that the people will share in its promises.[50] It is therefore not in competition with or contradiction of the Mosaic covenant. According to Exodus 19:5–6 God promises that the (Mosaic) covenant relationship will establish Israel as his treasured possession out of all the peoples, a 'priestly kingdom and a holy nation'. One could say that Isaiah 55:3–5 adds the term 'glorious' to Israel's profile.

The subsequent occurrences of justice/righteousness in 58:2b, 2c and 59:4a testify to the failure of 'my people' (58:1b) to presumably follow the instructions in 56:1. Within this context a striking but complex text is 57:1–2.[51] Verse 1 appears to target corruption of the legal system with the righteous and devout—the innocent—being condemned and 'taken away', presumably to prison. But what the wicked assume is their victory is in reality their defeat because the righteous are thereby delivered from 'the evil to come' (NRSV 'calamity') and enter into peace (v 2a). Although one cannot be certain, given the awkward syntax of the passage, it is reasonable to suggest that it is based on 56:1. That is, the righteous/devout are assured of God's righteousness/salvation; the corollary of this is that those who put them away unjustly will not enjoy salvation. Isaiah 57:1–2 and the surrounding context expose an important difference

---

49. Cf Leclerc, *Yahweh is Exalted in Justice*, 136–36 and the literature cited there in support.
50. John Goldingay and David Payne speak of a democratizing of the Davidic covenant here (*Isaiah 40–55; A Critical and Exegetical Commentary* [International Commentary on the Holy Scriptures of the Old and New Testaments; 2 vols.; London: T & T Clark, 2006] Volume II, 374), accepted with some caution by Joseph Blenkinsopp (*Isaiah 40–66: A New Translation with Introduction and Commentary* [AB 19A; New York: Doubleday, 2002] 370).
51. For a detailed discussion see Polan *In the Ways of Justice*, 119–24. He concludes that 'the righteous know God's blessing in their passage from the presence of evil to peace' (124).

between Isaiah 40–55 and 56–66. There the threat needing to be removed was Babylon; here it is within Israel itself. As was noted in the analysis of the Torah, the greatest threat to God's purpose for Israel and humanity is not an outside enemy but Israel itself.

Although God vows no peace for the wicked in 57:21, the preceding verses 14–19 affirm God's commitment to 'revive the contrite of heart'. God will accuse but not continually (v 16) because God's justice is an integral part of his righteous purpose, to bring about universal salvation (right order). An instruction follows in which the false righteousness of 'my people' (58:1-8) is contrasted with what God requires (58:6-14). A prophetic voice in 59:1-8 affirms God's desire and power to save and contrasts this with the complete lack of righteousness/justice (v 4a) in the community. This in turn leads to a confession of complete failure, presumably by the 'contrite and humble in spirit' of 57:15b. It culminates in the admission that 'Justice is turned back and righteousness stands at a distance' (59:14a). They are like visitors who want to enter a city for its good but are refused admission.

The only one who can save Israel from this situation is God (v 16a), just as in Isaiah 40–55 God is the only one who can summon Cyrus to deliver Israel from its prison. At this point we find the first occurrences in 56–66 of the word pair righteousness and salvation (59:16b-17a). The text employs military imagery, perhaps to evoke or form a parallel with Israel's deliverance from Babylonian power in 40–55. According to the verses that follow (59:18-20) God's war against injustice is universal but its immediate goal is the redemption of Zion and 'those in Jacob who turn from transgression' (59:20).[52] This verse underscores the centrality of Zion in the book of Isaiah's vision of God's universal sovereignty. It also draws on the motif of a faithful remnant from earlier texts of the book (cf Isa 10:20-23; 11:11).

This announcement of impending righteousness and salvation is followed by Isaiah 60–62 that resumes key themes from earlier chapters. Isaiah 60 is addressed to Zion, assuring her that 'I will appoint

---

52. There is debate as to whether Isa 59:18 refers to Israelites as God's enemies or non-Israelites. In favour of the former is Polan (*In the Ways of Justice*, 298-99), of the latter John DW Watts (*Isaiah 34-66 Revised Edition* [WBC 25; Nashville: Thomas Nelson, 2005], 855).

Peace as your overseer, and Righteousness as your taskmaster' (60:17); as a result 'your people shall all be righteous' (60:21).[53] In Isaiah 61 a speaker whose credentials appear to combine those of the servant in 42:4 (cf spirit) and Cyrus in 45:1 (cf anointed), or perhaps David, announces that he has been sent to bring good news to the oppressed, broken-hearted, captives and prisoners. The link with Isaiah 40–55 is clear but the following verses appear to identify these suffering folk with 'all who mourn in Zion'. These could be the ones who confess their sins (59:9-15) and turn from transgression (59:20). They will be transformed into 'oaks of righteousness' (61:3c), a great and enduring sign of God's glory. Isaiah 61:8-9 confirms the Lord's commitment to the establishment of justice and to make 'an everlasting covenant' with these mourners. The speaker then resumes in 61:10, rejoicing because he too will be transformed—like one with new clothes— by God's salvation and righteousness. The final verse of the chapter adds the universal factor: all nations will witness the transformation of mourners in Zion by divine righteousness (cf similar imagery in 61:3c, 11) and the praise of God that this generates. All that God does is meant to lead to the knowledge and acknowledgement of God. Isaiah 62:1-2 guarantees that Zion will also experience the impact of God's righteousness (NRSV 'vindication') and salvation.

The final chapters of the book (63–66) provide an elaborate explanation as to why the restoration of Zion in righteousness and justice, assured in 60–62, is yet to be (fully) realised. It draws on elements of the preceding chapters as well as the Torah and Psalms to present its response, which one may also describe as a theodicy or defense of God and God's ways.[54] The dramatic passage in 63:1-6 claims God is fully engaged, as God always is, in bringing about universal righteousness and salvation (61:1c; NRSV 'vindication'). An essential aspect of this is the conquest of evil; the war against Edom announced in 34:5-17 is now portrayed as having taken place, with God returning in triumph.[55] A speaker in 63:7-14 (the same as

---

53. The Hebrew noun translated in the NRSV as 'taskmaster' derives from a verb that can mean 'urge, drive, exact'. Within the context of 56–66 the sense may be more of righteousness as an exacting master who urges the best from the subject.
54. For a discussion and pertinent literature, as well as a list of parallel texts to 63:7-14 and 64 see Watts, *Isaiah 34–66*, 898.
55. These two texts may reflect the historical demise of Edom in the post-exilic period. Within the context of the book of Isaiah, it becomes an example of God's

in 61:1?) then recounts God's saving deeds on behalf of the 'house of Israel' despite its rebellions (63:10). As God has done in the past through Moses so God is doing now: God is still with Israel despite the rebellions and divisions outlined in the preceding chapters. This is not only a message for the audience portrayed in the book but for any readers. The recital is punctuated by a series of questions ('where' in 63:11b–12); these do not deny its claims but ask where is God in relation to Israel's present situation? The questions prompt a group to lament in 63:15–19, asking why God hardens 'our heart, so that we do not fear you' (v 17). Is this a complaint that the impact of the prophetic message, proclaimed in 6:9–10 and reiterated in 29:10–11 is still in force—unjustly, according to the group? A prayer follows in 64:1–12; presumably the same 'we' confess their sinfulness (cf reversal of 'righteous' in 64:6) and beg God to save them and Zion. The sequence of lament followed by prayer/petition is found in a number of lament psalms and suggests the author(s) of these texts drew on Israel's cultic practice.

One should pray to God when in distress and confess one's sin but one must then wait for God's answer, which may not be what the petitioner asks for. This is hinted at in the final verse of Isaiah 64. God's answer is given in Isaiah 65–66; all divine speech except perhaps for 66:10–11. In brief, the reply states there is no contradiction between God's response to 'this/any' situation and 63:1–6, and indeed any of 'the gracious deeds of the past (63:7–14). God held/holds out 'my hands all day long' only to be rebuffed by a rebellious people. Yet, in an echo of 8:1–4 and 10:20–22 there is a loyal remnant named 'my servants' in 65:8c. For their sake God will not destroy all. These servants are 'my chosen' who will enjoy blessing while 'you', the rebels, will not (65:13–16). The identity of the rebels and the servants is left unspecified; the latter could be the ones who confess their sinfulness in 64:5–12. The reader(s) is invited to decide which group he/she or they belong to, but who would dare claim to be worthy of God's blessing, given that the function of 65:1–16 is to teach that God alone makes such judgements? All one can do is pray, seek justice and righteousness, and trust completely in God. The following announcement of a 'new heavens and a new earth' and the creation of 'Jerusalem as a joy' (65:17–19) provides further assurance that all

---

power over the nations (Sweeney, *Isaiah 1–39*, 434).

that has taken place thus far (in the book) is integral to the fulfillment of God's righteous purpose for Jerusalem/Zion and for all creation. In a resumption of key aspects of the opening chapter, Isaiah 66 affirms that these two key components of God's purpose—favour for the humble and contrite in spirit versus punishment for the wicked (66:2b-6, 18-24), and the restoration of Zion (66:7-16)—continue on until God declares the creation of a new heavens and a new earth complete.

To sum up this analysis of righteousness and justice in Isaiah: in chapters 1-39 social justice is identified as an integral part of a right relationship with God. God has established this relationship for the welfare of God's children (1:2-3) and the 'Father' will not tolerate the children abusing it. Because God's relationship with Israel is also part of God's purpose for all humanity and creation, such abuse not only distorts Israel's perception of God but also the nations' perception of God. As well it turns Zion, the locus of the presence on earth of the 'Holy One of Israel', into an unholy place which is an intolerable situation. But God's purpose will not be thwarted; hence the proclamation that God will purge people and city by summoning a nation from the ends of the earth (Assyria, Babylon). This is followed by the announcements in 40-55 that God will bring back the exiles (the remnant) to a purified Zion. The recurrence of the word pair righteousness and salvation in these chapters emphasises that the establishment of God's righteousness in creation, manifest above all in the right order of society, is an act of salvation or deliverance from its opposite—idolatry and social abuse and the disorder that accompanies them. But the final part of the book (56-66) prophesies that human beings are incapable of maintaining what God establishes; inevitably they fail. But God does not fail and shows unswerving commitment/ steadfast love to Israel and humanity despite its failures.[56] In this sense, the book of Isaiah echoes the theology of the Torah in texts such as Exodus 32-34; Numbers 13-14; Deuteronomy 29-30 and 32. According to Isaiah, the full realisation of God's purpose is yet to come—the book is a vision (*khazon*). This full realisation will presumably also reveal the identities of the Davidic king who is to reign in endless peace (cf 9:1-7; 11:1-9) and the servant who is to redeem the many (52:13-53:12).

---

56. According to Oswalt the book of Isaiah teaches that as deliverance is a gift of God, so is righteous behaviour ('Righteousness in Isaiah,' 190).

2

Books of Jeremiah[1] and Ezekiel

The Book of Jeremiah

The occurrences of righteousness in the book of Jeremiah deal with three key relationships. One is between God and the people, the relevant texts being Jeremiah 3:11 (verb); 51:10 (noun); 4:2 (noun in a unique combination with truth [*'emet*] and justice); and 9:24 (MT 9:23) (noun in another unique combination with steadfast love [*khesedh*] and justice).[2] The second is between God and the Davidic king; being combined with justice as a word pair in 22:3, 13, 15; 23:5; 33:15. The third is between God and the prophet (11:20; 12:1; 20:12).[3] In the prophecies of restoration after the Babylonian exile, Jerusalem is given two new names that employ the term—the 'abode of righteousness' in 31:23 and 'The Lord is our Righteousness' in 33:16. The former is also applied to God in 50:7 (NRSV 'the true pasture') while the latter is applied to the righteous branch for David in 23:6. These indicate that God's righteousness is to be a central feature of the prophesied new order. As in the book of Isaiah, Jeremiah's preaching commences with a recall of Israel's story that emphasises God's loyalty compared with Israel and Judah's disloyalty. Whereas Isaiah 1:2–3 employs the

---

1. Citation of texts in Jeremiah is according to the NRSV, which follows the MT division not the LXX.
2. There are other occurrences of these trios but the terms are combined in a different way. In Isa 59:14 the failure of truth is the reason why 'justice is turned back, and righteousness stands at a distance'. Psalm 33:5 implies that, because the Lord loves justice and righteousness, the 'earth is full of the steadfast love of the Lord'. In 1 Kgs 3:6 David is described as walking before God in truth, righteousness and uprightness (*yishrah*) of heart.
3. There does not appear to be any difference in the meaning of the word pair with the feminine or masculine form (22:13).

parent–child metaphor to describe the relationship, Jeremiah 2:2–3 employs the metaphor of a marriage. It is likely that this is borrowed from the earlier book of Hosea.

After the case against the unfaithful 'wife' has been laid out before the heavens (cf Jer 2:12), the conditions for her return are set out in 4:1–2. According to 3:11 Israel is 'less guilty' than her deceitful sister Judah.[4] The latter saw all that Israel did but still 'played the whore' and only pretended to repent. Hence the prophet is instructed to assure Israel of God's mercy if it 'returns', that is, acknowledges its guilt (cf 3:12–14). The fact that the people of Judah are also called to conversion in 4:3–4 suggests this sequence is designed to impress upon the reader the importance of repentance (return) and the consequences of failing or refusing to repent (cf 4:5–6:26). Whatever the case, the conditions 4:2 lays down are as follows. Israel is to remove its abominations and not waver, and it is to swear '"as the Lord lives!" in truth, in justice, and in righteousness' (NRSV 'uprightness'). The 'abominations' refer to Israel's apostasy rather than to social justice. This suggests that the trio of terms in 4:2 refers to the nature of Israel's oath of exclusive fidelity to God. The swearing of an oath also evokes the court arena where a person swears 'as the Lord lives' to speak the truth.[5] In short, these words are to be a genuine expression of Israel's commitment to the Lord. The final part of 4:2 is structured in the Hebrew as a chiasm with 'nations' in the central position framed by two references to God.[6] The arrangement heightens the focus on the nations and their relationship with God, one of the few places in Jeremiah that touches on Israel's vocation to be a mediator of God's blessing to all the nations. Within the immediate context it adds to the necessity and urgency of Israel's 'return'. Within the larger context

---

4. A literal rendering of 3:11 is 'apostate (turning away) Israel has shown herself righteous from deceitful Judah'. The Hebrew comparative (using the preposition *min* [from]) can be translated as 'more' or 'less' depending on the context. So here the NRSV has 'less guilty'.
5. Cf. William J Holladay, *Jeremiah 1. A Commentary on the Book of the Prophet Jeremiah Chapters 1–25* (Hermeneia; Philadelphia: Fortress Press, 1986), 128. Holladay notes that a better translation may be 'by the life of Yahweh'. Holladay judges that here the three terms mean much the same thing—integrity/sincerity.
6. A literal translation reads: 'and they shall bless themselves/be blessed by him (God) the nations and by/in him they shall glory'. For a discussion see Holladay *Jeremiah 1–25*, 128–29.

it recalls Israel's vocation as enunciated to the ancestors (cf Gen 12:1–3; 22:18; 26:4).

Three further points may be added. One is that Israel is expected to put truth, justice and righteousness into action, otherwise the oath is a sham. The social arena is therefore implied. A second is that this truth, justice and righteousness can only be the kind that God wants, a living of the relationship established by God (expressed in the preceding chapters via the metaphor of a marriage). The third is that the notion of truth and speaking truthfully is an important aspect of the portrait of Jeremiah in the book, as evidenced in such passages as 26:15 (where he asserts that he has been truly sent by God) and 28:9 (his confrontation with the false prophet Hananiah). Jeremiah speaks only what he is commanded by God (1:7c) whereas the other prophets speak falsehood (cf 23:9–40).[7] God planted Israel as a 'true seed' (2:21) but according to 9:5 'no one speaks the truth'. The rhetorical question in 9:12 ('Who is wise enough to understand this?') implies a negative answer and this is given in the following verses: no one has obeyed God's voice (of truth). The true, just and righteous God must therefore intervene to remove those responsible for falsehood and corruption (9:15–16). The call to sing a dirge in 9:17–22 underscores the inevitability of this intervention and its terrible impact.

The unique combination of steadfast love, justice and righteousness in Jeremiah 9:24 (MT 9:23) is to be read within this context. It is preceded in 9:23 (MT 9:22) by another unique combination in the HBOT, a three-fold warning to an unspecified 'him' not to boast in 'his wisdom', 'his might', or 'his wealth'. Within the context, the masculine singular pronoun can refer to any individual or people who think that what has been proclaimed in the preceding text can be avoided. To do so is 'to boast/rely on' a distorted/false perception of things that human beings customarily 'rely on' to ensure security and well-being.[8] The one who truly desires to be wise should

---

7. Modern critical analysis has noted the similarity between Jer 1:7, 9, 17 and Deut 18:18. Whether the passage in Jeremiah goes back to the prophet or not, it signals that he is the fulfillment of the promise of a prophet like Moses in Deut 18:15–22. For a discussion see Peter C Craigie, Page H Kelley, Joel F Drinkard, Jr., *Jeremiah 1–25* (WBC 26; Dallas, Texas: Word Books, 1991) 9, and Georg Fischer, *Jeremia 1–25* (HThKAT; Freiburg im Breisgau: Herder, 2005), 98–99.

8. According to Gail R O'Day, 'Wisdom, might, and riches refer to both distorted

instead boast/rely on knowing that 'I am the Lord'. In this instance, to know the Lord is to acknowledge that the Lord alone is the one who always does (present participle) steadfast love, justice and righteousness. These three positives in 9:24 (MT 9:23) counter the preceding three negatives (wisdom, might, wealth). Gail O'Day catches the relationship between 9:23 and 24 well: 'God's steadfast love, justice, and righteousness are the source of identity and well-being, of security and governance'.[9] But there is also the larger context to consider; it conveys the challenging notion that the destruction of the corrupt order is also a manifestation of steadfast love, justice and righteousness, and that this is something in which God delights. Rather like Isaiah 42:21, Jeremiah 9:24 (MT 9:23) claims that what pleases God above all (what God is committed to) is the establishment of righteousness and justice on earth; of necessity this means the elimination of anything that contradicts it or threatens it.

As noted, the word pair righteousness/justice occurs in Jeremiah in the context of the relationship between God and the king (cf. Jer 22:3, 13, 15; 23:5; 33:15). As in Isaiah and elsewhere it means the implementation of social justice or right order in society. The Davidic kings are supposed to uphold this order that has its origins in God's covenantal word (cf Jer 22:9, 21).[10] In urging the king to 'deliver from the hand of the oppressor' 22:3 shows that it has a salvific dimension (cf also Jer 21:12). As one would expect this dimension is more to the fore in 23:5-6 that prophesies God will raise up a 'righteous branch' for David to execute justice and righteousness, thus bringing God's salvation to Judah and Israel. Jeremiah 23:5-6 is largely repeated in 33:15-16, the only difference being that the name 'the Lord is our righteousness' is applied to the Davidic king in 23:6 and to Jerusalem in 33:16.[11]

---

individual identity and well-being and distorted societal identity and well-being' (p. 261 of 'Jeremiah 9:22-23 and I Corinthians 1:26-31. A Study in Intertextuality', *JBL* 109/2 [1990]: 259-67. According to Fischer and others these were valued in the wisdom tradition; Jer 9:24 (MT 9:23) does not so much replace them as put them in their proper place (*Jeremiah 1-25*, 367-69).

9. O'Day, 'Jeremiah 9:22-23 and I Corinthians 1:26-31', 262.

10. One could say that in the arena of social justice the king is 'primus inter pares', as the temple sermon in Jeremiah 7 indicates. All are called to uphold it. It has been suggested that 22:1-5 is a version of the temple sermon delivered to the king (cf. Craigie, Kelley, Drinkard, *Jeremiah 1-25*, 297).

11. The name is a play on the name of king Zedekiah (YHWH is [my] righteousness);

One may group 11:20; 12:1 and 20:12 together as a trio of a different kind. Each appeals to God as judge/arbitrator. In 11:20 Jeremiah seeks retribution against his enemies. This will be a righteous judgement because Jeremiah has committed his cause to God and so is righteous. In 12:1 however, Jeremiah's complaint is against God: why do the wicked prosper when they, like everything else, are supposed to be under God's guiding hand ('you plant them, and they take root')? It is the classic theodicy question and the answer, for a believer, is anticipated in somewhat ironic fashion in the first line of the verse ('You will be in the right O Lord'). One may complain to God about the awful state of affairs, as the lament psalms testify, but in the end one has to trust that God will resolve things in God's way and that this is the right way. If God is judged untrustworthy then one may seek another provider.[12] The 'confessions of Jeremiah', to which 12:1 belongs, come to a dramatic climax in 20:7-17. In 20:12 he resumes his prayer of 11:20 but prefaces it with an acknowledgement that it is God who decides the distribution of reward and retribution ('you test the righteous'). However, in 20:14-18 he curses the day of his birth and laments his prophetic vocation.[13] There is no response from God to this prayer and curse in the subsequent text, nor any further laments or complaints from Jeremiah: the prophet resolutely carries out his commission. Does this signal that Jeremiah is resolved to live with his questions unanswered or does the remainder of the book provide an answer? It is as if Jeremiah dies to his former 'self' for the sake of preaching and obeying God's word, whatever it may be.[14] Jeremiah's passage from former to latter, from old to new, provides a kind of model or template for that of Israel in the book; within the larger HBOT context it recalls the passing of the failed exodus generation and the emergence of the successful conquest generation in the book of Numbers.

---

cf. Holladay, *Jeremiah 1-25*, 619. Jeremiah 51:10 also brings the salvific aspect of righteousness to the fore; the judgement against Babylon is Israel's righteousness (NRSV: 'vindication').

12. This is effectively the line taken by the women devotees of the queen of heaven in Jer 44:15-19.
13. The reference to his mother's womb recalls 1:5; the curse parallels the one in Job 3.
14. On this see ch. 6 of Louis Stulman, *Order Amid Chaos. Jeremiah as Symbolic Tapestry* (The Biblical Seminar 57; Sheffield: Sheffield Academic Press, 1998). Fischer regards Jeremiah 20 as a turning point in the book (*Jeremia 1-25*, 627).

The Book of Ezekiel

The term righteousness is not used either by God or of God in the book of Ezekiel. It is employed exclusively to describe Israel's conduct and relationship to God: the bulk of occurrences are as adjectives and nouns in three key passages within the book, 3:16-21, 18:1-32 and 33:1-20. The word pair justice and righteousness occurs in the second (18:27) and third passage (33:14, 16), as well as in 45:9 (addressed to the princes). The three passages function as instruction or torah: the first establishes Ezekiel as sentinel to the house of Israel while the second and third are addressed to Israel by its sentinel. Besides these, the adjectival form occurs also in 21:3, 4 and 23:45 (to describe righteous judges), with the masculine noun in 45:10 in reference to right balances and measures—as in Leviticus 19:36. Unlike Isaiah and Jeremiah, Ezekiel's preaching does not commence with a presentation of Israel's story. This comes later, in Ezekiel 16 (via the allegory of the abandoned baby girl), in 20 (via an account of the generations), and in 23 (via the allegory of the two sisters Oholah and Oholibah). These sisters represent the capital cities of the northern kingdom of Israel (Samaria) and her younger (or smaller) sister Jerusalem, the capital of Judah. There is some connection with Isaiah and Jeremiah in the use of female figures to portray the stories of Israel/Samaria and Judah/Jerusalem. Isaiah portrays Zion/Jerusalem as a woman as does Ezekiel 16; Ezekiel 23 compares the actions of Samaria and Jerusalem in a way that is similar to Jeremiah's comparison of Israel and Judah in 3:6-14. Ezekiel is unlike Isaiah and Jeremiah in another sense in that it accuses Israel of being disloyal from its beginnings. Like Isaiah 1:2; 5:1-2 and Jeremiah 2:5-7, Ezekiel 16:1-14 claims that God has done everything right for Israel (the abandoned waif). But there is no acknowledgement of Israel's loyalty in the wilderness period ('the devotion of your youth' as in Jer 2:2; cf. also Hos 2:15b 'when she came out of the land of Egypt'). Once the girl reached puberty ('the age for love/betrothal'; 16:8) she played the whore (16:15). In a similar way Ezekiel 20:18-21 seems to contradict Numbers 27-36 by condemning the 'children in the wilderness' for behaving like their parents (the exodus generation).

The story of Israel as presented in Ezekiel is bleak but its purpose is to promote the theology or teaching of the book. This can be illustrated by some comments on the passages where righteousness occurs. In 3:16-21 Ezekiel is appointed a sentinel or watchman for the house of Israel and a sentinel's normal role is to warn people of danger so that it can be avoided. Yet, according to RR Wilson, Ezekiel's role is not so much to warn as to announce God's sentence 'you shall surely die' (3:18; cf 33:8).[15] The third person singular version of this is the formula for capital punishment in Torah texts such as Exodus 21:12-17 ('he shall surely die'). Paul Joyce sums up the thrust of 3:16-21 as:

> the purpose of this passage is to reinforce the absolute justice of the current judgement, underlining the culpability of Israel for the now inevitable (indeed already present) disaster. Israel has had every warning and is wholly to blame for the crisis that is even now engulfing her.[16]

On this interpretation Ezekiel is instructed to preach a message of repentance that his rebellious audience will not accept. The case of the righteous turning from his righteousness is hypothetical; in reality there are no righteous. There is some similarity with Isaiah 6 here. Despite this bleak prospect, Ezekiel is warned that he must be resolute in his preaching, as the warnings about failure to do so indicate (3:18, 20)—shades of Jeremiah 6:27-30; 15:19-21.

The accuracy of this assessment of the people is verified in Ezekiel 18. It presents competing explanations of the Babylonian exile (the setting of the book; cf 1:1). One is expressed in the bitter proverb 'The parents have eaten sour grapes, and the children's teeth are set on edge' (18:2). That is, the exiles are suffering for the sins of preceding generations. Because this explanation operates within a religious context it presumes the act-consequence connection is the work of God. But the context of Ezekiel 18 shows the proverb is also an accusation that God's way is unjust. This prompts a defense of God's way that exposes the accusation as a classic case of playing the blame game. The term used to describe God's way (*derek*) is *takan* which can be translated as 'fair', 'right' 'just'. It only occurs in the two key instructions or torahs that defend God's way of acting against those

---

15. RR Wilson, 'An Interpretation of Ezekiel's Dumbness,' *VT* 22 (1972), 91-104.
16. Paul M Joyce, *Ezekiel: A Commentary* (Library of Hebrew Bible/Old Testament Studies 482; New York/London: T&T Clark, 2009), 81.

of the people (cf 18:25, 29; 33:17, 20). One could say that it functions as the equivalent of the term righteous to describe God's actions in other books.

At first glance the defense of God as 'fair' in 18:5-24 would seem to advocate individual responsibility as an answer to the accusation, and in the process to contradict the punishment clauses in Exodus 20:5b and Deuteronomy 5:9b. But a number of factors question such a reading. One is that the description of the righteous in Ezekiel 18:5-9 reflects criteria in the law codes of Deuteronomy 12-26 and Leviticus 17-26. The text seems to have the Torah in view. A second is that Deut 24:16 legislates that 'only for their own crimes may persons be put to death'. It would be surprising if this were a contradiction of the template text of 5:9b. A third is that Ezekiel 18:5-24 covers three generations. Does this reflect disagreement with Exodus 20:5b and Deuteronomy 5:9b or an illustration of how the clause 'those who reject/hate me' applies across these generations. A fourth is that a number of commentators judge Ezekiel 18 is not about individual responsibility. The employment of the singular example is a characteristic of priestly law (cf Lev 20:9, 15) and the text uses this 'to convey the true meaning of great historical events, which invariably affected the nation as a whole'.[17] Ezekiel 18 is addressing the nation as a unit as well as each individual within it. A similar phenomenon occurs in the Decalogue, which is in the second person singular but addressed to all Israel.

These reflections help throw some light on the otherwise puzzling 18:19. Here the people (plural), as reported, criticise the argument presented in the preceding verses and hold that the son should suffer for the sins of his father. But this contradicts their earlier complaint that God acts according to the proverb and therefore unjustly. What Ezekiel 18 does is effectively expose them as preferring the theology of the proverb because it suits their evil agenda. To accept the prophetic argument would be to admit they are sinners and that they are being justly punished for their sins and not the sins of their fathers. They are 'those who reject/hate me'. But this would put an end to their blame game whereby they can accuse God of being 'unfair' and cast themselves as innocent victims, righteous ones.[18] As the chapter

---

17. Joyce, *Ezekiel*, 140.
18. Joyce, *Ezekiel*, 142. This feigned or fake righteousness may also be the sense of 21:4.

unfolds their deceit is revealed; they are rebels like their ancestors condemned in the reviews of Ezekiel 16; 20; 23.

Ezekiel 33:1-20 comes just before the turning point in the book, 33:21-22, the report of the fall of Jerusalem. The 'sentinel' passages in 3:16-21 and 33:1-9 form a frame around the intervening material. Ezekiel 33:10-20 recapitulates the arguments in 3:16-21 and 18:1-32. Ezekiel 33:10 might indicate that the people (now) accept responsibility for the exile although their words are more a complaint than an acceptance.[19] However the accusations in vv 17 and 20, that repeat 18:25, 29, confirm the entrenched rebellious attitude of the people. There is no repentance and God's retribution must proceed in accord with the way it is presented in 16; 20; and 23. According to 20:9, 22 God resolves not to destroy Israel because of its sin 'for the sake of my name, that it should not be profaned in the sight of the nations among whom they lived'.[20] Reprieve or grace for Israel is an integral part of the manifestation of God's name among the nations so that all may know 'I am the Lord' (cf 24:27; 25:5, 7, 11, 17, etc; cf Exod 6:7; 7:5). Israel's rebellious conduct conveys a false knowledge of the divine name and for the sake of the name such conduct will be punished. God will not tolerate evil or falsehood. By the same token God is steadfastly committed to establishing a right relationship with all peoples and loyalty is foundational to such a relationship. A sign of this is God's unswerving loyalty to disloyal Israel. God promises to give Israel a new heart and a new spirit so that 'you shall be my people and I will be your God' (Ezek 36:26; cf Deut 30:6 and Jer 31:31-34).

---

19. Joyce argues that the phrase 'our transgressions and our sins' in 33:10 can refer to undeserved punishment rather than acknowledgement of sin (cf. Dan 8:12, 13; 9:24; Zech 14:19) (*Ezekiel*, 191.). Moshe Greenberg however takes it as an expression of responsibility (*Ezekiel 21-37* [AB22A; New York: Doubleday, 1997], 673-77.

20. God's protection of the status of the divine name also recalls the issue of God's reputation among the nations in Exod 32:12 and Num 14:15-16.

3

Book of the Twelve Prophets

As noted in the introduction to this chapter, the MT and LXX list the first six of the twelve so-called 'minor prophets' in different order. For the purposes of this brief survey, the MT order will be followed: it is the one given in most English translations. The book of the twelve intensifies the question of the relationship between unity and diversity in the HBOT: it is one book but within it are twelve books each attributed to a different prophet. Recent scholarship has explored thematic and structural evidence of connections between the books, applying appropriate methodologies, both diachronic and synchronic, in order to identify and test signs of relationship and unity.[1]

This analysis has identified four main thematic connections; the 'Day of the Lord' and similar terms, the fertility of the land, the destiny of the people, and the defense of God (theodicy), expressed in citations or allusions to Exodus 34:6–7 in Joel 2:13; Jon 4:2; Micah 7:18; Nahum 1:2–3.[2] In terms of structure, there is a movement from an initial eighth century BCE setting of the kingdoms of Israel (north) and Judah (south) in the first six books, through a seventh century setting of Judah alone in Nahum, Habakkuk and Zephaniah, to a post-exilic setting in Haggai, Zechariah, and Malachi.[3] Another perceived

---

1. As noted earlier, a thorough review of this scholarship is provided by Redditt, 'Recent Research on The Book of the Twelve as One Book,' 47–80.
2. Cf Redditt, 'Themes in Haggai–Zechariah–Malachi,' *Interpretation* 61/2 (2007): 184–97. The 'Day of the Lord' occurs sixteen times in the HBOT, thirteen of these are in the Book of the Twelve, two in Isa 13:6, 9 and one in Ezek 13:5. Similar phrases are 'on that day' and 'in those days'; these also occur in the Book of the Twelve.
3. Even though Joel is undated it is located between Hosea and Amos, both set in

structural arrangement reflects in a general way the one observed in the Torah and in Isaiah, Jeremiah and Ezekiel: the movement from an initial indictment of the sinful people, to the failure of repentance and God's resolve to destroy the unrepentant via foreign invasion, to the promise of a new righteous order that will replace the wicked old one. Embedded in this arrangement in somewhat different ways in the prophetic books is the claim that foreign nations are as rebellious and unrepentant as Israel. They too will be judged and punished so that they can take part in the new order to be established. All this is part of the Bible's claim that the Lord alone is God and has a purpose that embraces all creation.

A number of the twelve books are structured in this way: for example Hosea, Amos, Micah, Zephaniah. But one can also discern it within the larger Book of the Twelve. The focus of Hosea and Amos is the evil in the northern kingdom of Israel, in particular its apostasy (cf Hosea) and social injustice (cf Amos). These frame the book of Joel which pleads for the kind of penitential liturgy (in Zion) that may lead God to 'turn and relent' from punishment. Amos 8:2 pronounces the end of 'my people Israel' but Obadiah condemns Edom for 'the violence done to your brother Jacob' (v 10). Edom has no divine mandate to punish Israel. Almost as a counter to Israel's intransigence, Jonah proclaims God's mercy to a repentant Nineveh—the Assyrian capital. Micah brings this eighth century setting to a climax by announcing that Judah and Jerusalem are also completely corrupted and destined for destruction (3:12). But it also proclaims that in the days to come (after the punishment) it will become a beacon for all the nations (4:1–4; cf Isa 2:2–4).

The book of Nahum prophesies doom for cruel Nineveh (3:19c) while the book of Zephaniah extends the theme of punishment to embrace not just Israel, Edom, Judah and Assyria but all humans and animals (1:3). The great day of the Lord is imminent when all the nations will be gathered to receive God's judgement (1:14; 3:8): all are unrepentant and it is only when God has purged the evil and left a humble remnant that a new era will be inaugurated. Habakkuk

---

the eighth century. Obadiah is about Edom taking advantage of Israel's demise, and Jonah is about the Assyrian capital Nineveh. Nahum prophesies the end of Nineveh in the seventh century while Habakkuk speaks of God rousing the Chaldeans/Babylonians, who conquered Assyria.

is located between Nahum and Zephaniah as a lament about the perceived lack of evidence of God at work (1:2-4). God answers by pointing to the Chaldeans and provides the prophet with a vision 'for the appointed time' (2:3). The proper response is to wait and trust in faith for the unfolding of the vision (2:4; 3:16b). The final group of books (Haggai-Zechariah-Malachi) 'point toward God's eventual transformation of judgment to glory' for temple, city and people.[4] Human beings will fail—hence the call to faith and obedience particularly in Malachi—but God's love is steadfast. John Watts has also drawn attention to how the Book of the Twelve begins with God's love in Hosea 1-3 and concludes by resuming or reaffirming it in Malachi.[5] The following analysis is restricted to those passages (and contexts) where righteous/righteousness and associated terms are found.

Hosea

Hosea 1-2 encapsulates the structural arrangement of the book of the Twelve in its use of the marriage metaphor: there is the unfaithful wife and her children (Israel/land) in 1:2-9, the husband's intervention in 2:1-13 (MT 2:3-15), and the promise of renewal of the marriage in 2:14-23 (MT 2:16-25). The first occurrence of righteousness is in the promise of renewal (cf 2:19 [MT 2:21]) in company with a list of associated divine attributes: justice (*mishpat*), steadfast love (*khesedh*), mercy/compassion (*rakhem* in the plural), faithfulness (*'emunah*). Within the marriage metaphor these signify the 'bride price' the groom is willing to pay for the bride.[6] More generally they express God's complete commitment to Israel, providing it with the means to form an intimate and loyal relationship. As 2:20 (MT 2:22)

---

4. Cf 129 of Paul R House, 'The Character of God in the Book of the Twelve,' in *Reading and Hearing the Book of the Twelve*, edited by James D Nogalski and Marvin A Sweeney (SBL Symposium Series 15; Atlanta: Society of Biblical Literature, 2000), 125-45.
5. Cf John DW Watts, 'A Frame for the Book of the Twelve: Hosea 1-3 and Malachi,' in *Reading and Hearing the Book of the Twelve*, 209-17. Sweeney notes the related theme of divorce in both Hosea 1-3 and Malachi (*The Twelve Prophets* [vol. 1; Berit Olam; Collegeville MN: The Liturgical Press, 2000], xxviii-xxix).
6. Cf FI Andersen and DN Freedman, *Hosea* (AB 24; New York: Doubleday, 1980), 283.

states, 'you shall know that I am the Lord'. The implication of course is that they also refer to the complete commitment that is expected of Israel. Hosea 2:14-15 (MT 2:16-17) indicates that this will be a renewal of the covenant. Although 2:18 (MT 2:20) is not as specific its promise of a covenant with the animals and the end of war may reflect the hope of cosmic peace and harmony voiced in Isaiah 9:2-7 (MT 9:1-6) and 11:1-9, and even Genesis 9:8-17 (without the 'fear and dread' of 9:2).[7]

Righteousness next occurs in Hosea 10:12 as part of a call to repentance in order to avoid the punishment of (Assyrian) invasion. The call is preceded in 10:11 by a theodicy somewhat like Isaiah 1:2-3; 5:1-2 and Jeremiah 2:2-3. God has done the right thing by the 'trained heifer' Ephraim and so it alone is to blame for the neglected, unplowed land (cf 4:1-3). The imagery shifts from the animal to the agrarian in 10:12: the call to Judah and Jacob to sow righteousness and harvest steadfast love refers to the 'seed' that God has provided—the essential ingredients of the covenant ethos (cf 4:1; 6:6).[8] If they farm as God has instructed then God will bless them with more seed/fruit—righteousness. But the implication is that there is no righteousness to sow or love to reap; the seed bin is empty or, more accurately according to the book, it has been filled with the seed of noxious plants—what her lovers have provided (2:12 [MT 2:14]; 9:1c). It is only when all this is destroyed that Israel will be able to once more know its true lover. The book concludes with the claim that the one who is wise and discerning knows 'these things' (14:9 [MT 14:10]). The parallelism that follows suggests 'these things' are in essence two: 'that the ways of the Lord are right' (plural of *yashar*; cf Deut 32:4) and that 'the righteous (NRSV 'upright') walk in them' while transgressors only stumble.[9] The verse implies that the righteous are able to walk in God's ways (be obedient) because of a foundational factor that enables them to do so—the nature of their relationship with God. The wicked reject this requirement and inevitably stumble.

---

7. For a discussion see J Andrew Dearman, *The Book of Hosea* (NICOT; Grand Rapids Mich: Eerdmans, 2010), 121 (on 2:14) and 135-36 (on 2:18). Andersen and Freedman accept the connection with Isa 11:6-9 but are doubtful about Gen 9:8-11 (*Hosea*, 281).
8. Cf Dearman, *Hosea*, 271.
9. Reading the Hebrew particle '*ki*' which commences the parallelism as 'that' rather than 'for'.

In this way their wickedness is exposed (by God). Ehud Ben Zvi calls the verse 'an interpretative key for the entire book', providing both instruction and hope.[10]

Amos

The word pair righteousness/justice occurs in Amos 5:7, 24; 6:12 and has much the same meaning as the word pair in Isaiah—social justice.[11] These three texts are part of a section of the book that runs from 5:1 to 6:14. It commences with a lamentation that is designed to motivate the 'house of Israel' to seek the Lord and live a just life, instead of abusing justice and righteousness (5:7). The call to repent becomes more specific in 5:15 (justice alone) and 5:24, the second occurrence of the word pair.[12] The final example (6:12) is in a context (6:8–14) where the call to repent is replaced by the announcement of doom. In sum, 5:1–6:14 exposes the complete failure of Israel to change from its abuse of social justice, an abuse made all the worse because at the same time the guilty feign devoted worship of God at the shrines of Bethel and Dan. The language of 5:21-24 is close to that of Isaiah 1:12-17. God must be portrayed repudiating such behaviour because it promotes a deeply distorted perception of God and God's just and right ways. The day of liturgical celebration that the people long for will be replaced by a day of darkness, the Lord's day of destruction (cf 5:18; 8:9).

Micah

This book is located in the middle of the Twelve in the MT list. It commences by effectively endorsing the judgements of Hosea and Amos against the northern kingdom (1:2-7) but then laments that the contagion has infected Judah and reached Jerusalem (1:8-9). The city will be devastated (3:12) but 'in the days to come' will be restored

---

10. Ehud Ben Zvi, *Hosea* (FOTL XXIA/1; Grand Rapids, Mich: Eerdmans, 2005), 317.
11. Amos 2:6 and 5:12 use the adjective alone but also in a social sense, to refer to an innocent victim.
12. The imagery of waters and ever-flowing streams in 5:24 conveys the sense of justice and righteousness as life-giving, dynamic qualities rather than legal terms.

as a beacon for all the nations (4:1–4; cf the version in Isa 2:2–4). The first occurrence of righteousness is in 6:5, within a passage that recalls key moments in the story to refute any reproach that the people may bring against God. The review covers the exodus, the episode of Balaam in Numbers 22–24 and the entry into the land (cf Josh 3–5).[13] Recalling these will or should enable the people to know that God always acts righteously. God delivers from oppression (as in the exodus), from false and evil plans (like those of Balak), and fulfills his purpose (entry into the promised land). The right response to this is 'to do justice, and to love kindness (*khesedh*), and to walk humbly with your God' (6:8). A person who does these things effectively becomes an agent or mediator of God's purpose in establishing right order in society. Micah 6:9–16 shows however, that as in Hosea and Amos, the people are incapable of repentance and change. Righteousness is invoked in only one other passage in the book, in conjunction with justice/judgement in Micah 7:9 (*mishpat*). Here the prophetic figure—presumably representing the community—accepts that he must bear God's just punishment until he 'executes judgment for me'.[14] One has the impression of a prisoner patiently awaiting a court's decision on his release. He will then be brought out of the darkness of prison into the light and will see 'his (that is, God's) righteousness' (NRSV 'his vindication'). His enemy will also see and be ashamed of the taunt 'where is your God?' (7:10). Both parties will realise that the Lord's actions, whether in the dark or in the light, are for the good/salvation of humanity (cf Isa 45:7).

Habakkuk

As noted in the introductory comments, Habakkuk raises the question of theodicy and so can be linked to the passages in Hosea (for example, 10:11–12) and Micah (for example, 6:1–5) that recall God's actions in the past in order to contrast divine loyalty and righteousness with Israel's disloyalty. However, Habakkuk adds an intensity and urgency

---

13. On Mic 6:5c ('Shittim to Gilgal') as referring to the Jordan crossing see Bruce K Waltke, *A Commentary on Micah* (Grand Rapids, Mich.; Eerdmans, 2007), 35–56.
14. Cf Hans-Walter Wolff, *Micah: A Commentary* (Minneapolis: Augsburg, 1990), 221.

to the 'question' in a way that is similar to Jeremiah's confessions or lamentations. There are three occurrences of the adjective righteous in the book; the first two are within questions (1:4 within 1:2-4 and 1:13 within 1:12-14). The first asks why God makes the prophet see evil of an extreme kind—the righteous surrounded by the wicked and justice perverted—and not do anything about it. Why is this so when, according to 1:12-13 and the tradition (from of old), the all holy and pure God cannot bear wrongdoing and always punishes it? From a human perspective it looks as though chaos rules (1:14). The answer is provided by a word of God in 2:4 where the third use of the adjective occurs: 'the righteous live by their faith'. The challenge for the righteous is to hold fast in faith/fidelity ('emunah) even when experience seems to bring only distress and suffering. To bolster this call to faith, the loyal prophet is provided with a vision for 'the appointed time' (cf the day of the Lord). When this appointed time arrives, the righteous ('these' in 2:6a, NRSV 'everyone') will pronounce a song of doom over the proud and arrogant one ('him' in 2:4, 5, 6). The book concludes with the conviction that the 'day of calamity' will be in keeping with God's other great acts of salvation (3:1-19).[15]

Zephaniah

The preceding books refer from time to time to God's universal lordship and that the divine purpose embraces all creation. However, Zephaniah brings this theme to the fore with its opening oracle. God's resolve to sweep away everything on earth, human and animal, as voiced in 1:2-3, is reminiscent of the flood story. Given this cosmic scenario what is the appropriate response? The two occurrences of the term righteousness and their respective contexts provide some clues. The first is in 2:3—in conjunction with justice (NRSV 'his commands') and humble/humility—and the second is in 3:5. Zephaniah 2:3 initially appears to clash with 2:1 where the addressees are 'O shameless nation'. But, as Sweeney notes, this seems to be part of the book's rhetorical strategy, to motivate those in 2:1 to become the humble ones of 2:3: then 'perhaps you may be hidden on the

---

15. For allusions in this chapter to the exodus story and other texts, see the discussion in Sweeney, *The Twelve Prophets*, volume 2, 484-87. There would also appear to be some connections with themes in Isa 63-66.

day of the Lord's wrath'.[16] Here, seeking the Lord is paralleled with seeking righteousness and humility; it is a sign that one desires a right relationship with God. This is the thing to do but the 'perhaps' (*'ulai*) of 2:3 provides no certainty that seekers of righteousness will be spared the day of God's universal wrath. Nevertheless, as in other texts that announce God's wrath, someone or a group (a remnant) has to survive this kind of scenario otherwise evil wins the battle and the story of God's righteous saving plan for humanity and creation runs out of steam.

There is no clear connection between the seekers and the remnant in the book (cf 2:7, 9c; 3:13) and this may be deliberate. It is God who (righteously) decides the composition of the remnant 'on that day'. What every Israelite (and human being) is required to do is acknowledge God's sovereignty by seeking righteousness and trusting God's judgment. The second occurrence in 3:5 states that the righteous God is in the midst of the soiled, defiled city executing justice. As with the notion of the remnant, one needs this presence of God in the midst of a corrupt creation otherwise the implication is that God has given up or is impotent in the face of evil (cf God's concern for the divine reputation or name in Ezekiel as well as Exod 32:12; Num 14:18). According to Zephaniah (set in the reign of Josiah) the presence of God is in Zion whereas in the later Ezekiel God leaves the city and temple but maintains communications with Israel through the prophet. In a different way each book seeks to maintain a theology of God as righteous in a context of pervasive evil.

Zechariah

The trio of Haggai–Zechariah–Malachi is set in the post-exilic Persian period. The destruction of Israel, Judah and Jerusalem has taken place, confirming the words of the 'former prophets' as Zech 1:4 declares. One can read this term as a reference to the preceding books in the Twelve. But, as the 'former prophets' also proclaimed, the day of God's destruction of the old corrupt order is to be followed by the establishment of a new one, which is the concern of these three prophetic books. The focus of Haggai is the divinely authorised rebuilding of the temple, while Zechariah 1–8 covers, via a series of vision reports, various aspects of the promised restoration.

---

16. Sweeney, *Zephaniah: A Commentary* (Hermeneia; Minneapolis: Fortress, 2003), 118.

The first occurrence of righteousness in Zechariah is in combination with faithfulness/truth (*'emet*) in 8:8, part of God's response to a delegation from the northern city of Bethel (7:1–3). The delegation's question is about whether they should continue their mourning and fasting as they had done since the Babylonian exile.[17] The reply invokes the 'former prophets' once more to assert two things. One is to remind the delegation (and the reader) why they are in mourning (7:4–14). The disaster of the exiles took place because the people failed to obey God's command to 'Render true judgements, show kindness and mercy to one another' (7:9)—in other words, to maintain right relationships within the community. The second is to reaffirm God's remedy for this failure (8:1–8), namely that Zion will be re-established as the 'faithful city', that God will bring 'my people' to live there, and that 'they shall be my people and I will be their God, in faithfulness and righteousness' (8:8). This 'theology of grace' clearly echoes the promise of the renewal of the marriage relationship in Hosea 2:19 (MT 2:21; cf also Exod 6:7). Zechariah 8:14–20 assures both Israel and Judah that if they do as God commands, mourning will be turned to rejoicing (in Zion). Apart from this, the adjective righteous (NRSV 'triumphant') is used in combination with the participle of the verb 'to save' (NRSV 'victorious') in 9:9 to describe the king who comes to rule in the restored Zion. The particular form of the Hebrew participle—the niphal—indicates that this king is victorious because he is delivered/saved (by God). Like the royal figure in Isaiah 9:2–7 (MT 9:1–6) this king will bring war to an end and 'command peace to the nations' (9:10b). Righteousness here is closely linked to the realisation of God's universal saving purpose.

Malachi

The book of Malachi sets out to defend God's ways against a barrage of criticism from an unspecified audience ('you' in 1:2) as well as a specified audience (the priests). Like Ezekiel 18 and 33, the book tells of a heated dispute within the community and the apportioning of blame for what is wrong. The text does not specify what triggers 'you'

---

17. Sweeney argues that the months listed in 7:3–5 refer to fasts associated with the destruction of the temple at the Babylonian exile and the assassination of Gedaliah (cf also 8:19) (*The Twelve Prophets*, volume 2, 640, 654).

and the priests to blame God; the aim of the book is to defend God by pointing to the failures of the people and priests. They are like their ancestors condemned in the 'former prophets'. The dispute unfolds in two basic sequences, 1:2–17 and 3:6–15, and each is followed by an announcement of how God will remedy the situation (3:1–5 and 3:16–4:6 [MT 3:16–24]). It is in these texts that righteousness occurs, as a noun in 3:3 and 4:2 (MT 3:20), and as an adjective in 3:18. The first dispute climaxes with the question 'Where is the God of justice?' God's response is given in 3:1–4 with the announcement that 'my messenger' is to come and purge both temple and 'sons of Levi' until they present 'offerings to the Lord in righteousness' (3:3). This endorses the position of preceding books in the Twelve: in the end only God can turn rebellious people or priests into righteous ones. Once this happens the liturgy will be acceptable and, in answer to the question in 2:17, God 'will draw near to you for judgment' (3:5). This does not necessarily mean that God is at present an absent judge but that the perception of the priests and people is so distorted they cannot see where justice lies. It is only when they have been purged that they will weclome God's judgements as the only just ones.

The second shorter dispute is followed by the report of a group 'who revered/feared the Lord'. Its members are not named but they are presumably ones who accept God's indictment of the disputants. A book is written for them: its content is not given but it is best understood as a book of instruction (torah): loyalty to this book is loyalty to God.[18] On the day God acts they will be protected whereas the wicked will be punished: this 'event' will confirm the teaching in the book, enabling them to know the difference between the righteous and the wicked. The parallelism in 3:18 indicates that the righteous is one who serves the Lord. In the context of the book serving the Lord means not only exclusive devotion to the Lord but also to the community, avoiding the social evils exposed in the debates. Malachi 4:1–3 (MT 3:19–21) reveals some details of what will happen on the 'day'; the appearance of God will be like a new dawn (a sun of righteousness) or a soaring bird that will not only heal the loyal ones (cf restoration of a loyal remnant) but empower them to be God's

---

18. Following James D Nogalski, pp. 134–35 of 'Recurring Themes in the Book of the Twelve: Creating Points of Contact for a Theological Reading,' *Interpretation* 61/2 (2007): 125–36. The book is not a record of the names of those who fear God.

agents in the destruction of the wicked (a reversal of the destruction of Israel/Judah by invading armies). Israel will once again play its role in the realisation of God's saving purpose. As the conclusion to the MT prophetic corpus the final verses are significant. Redditt holds that they are a later addition 'casting a backward glance over not simply Malachi or the Twelve, but the entirety of the Torah and the Prophets of the HB. The verses appeal both to the teaching of Moses and to the prophet Elijah.'[19]

It is to be expected that as the HBOT took final form there had to be a decision as to what constituted the foundational revelation or teaching and that this would be associated with a founding figure in the tradition, namely Moses. This also meant that subsequent works that were accepted as having revelatory status could not be in contradiction with the foundational one. Hence the prophetic works that were accepted fall under the umbrella of the Torah teaching. The same move can be seen in the New Testament canon in the relationship between the Gospels and other works. As has been seen in this survey of the Latter Prophets, they invoke the Torah as the foundational teaching, interpreting and applying it to the stage in the storyline with which the respective superscriptions and other 'pointers' in the book associate them. But they also invoke the prophetic aspect of Torah and in two ways. One is that each (selected) example of Israel's fidelity or infidelity is identified as the fulfillment of a Torah prophecy; a second is that they point beyond the particular situation or example to the fulfillment of God's righteous purpose as proclaimed in the Torah.

---

19. Redditt, 'Themes in Haggai–Zechariah–Malachi,' 194.

Part Four

Divine Righteousness in the Writings

Introduction

As noted in the general introduction to the book my analysis of divine righteousness in the Writings section of the Hebrew canon (Wisdom Literature of the Greek canon) focuses on the book of Psalms (or Psalter) and the book of Job. There are several reasons for this. An immediate and obvious one is that a study such as this cannot hope to cover every base and so a selection needs to be made. I hope the following reasons justify the selection made, at least to some degree.

The Psalter provides fertile ground for reflection on divine righteousness for a number of reasons. One is the frequency of references to it. A second is that the references occur in a rich variety of psalm types, as identified by form criticism. The classification of the psalms according to form or type will be outlined in the following chapter. The fact that these various types of psalms are included in the one book of the Psalter raises the question of diversity in unity. How diverse is the use of the terms in the Psalter for divine righteousness and justice, and associated terminology, and does this usage draw on and develop a basic or shared understanding? A third reason that invites focus on the Psalter is that many psalms would appear to record the people's response to the understanding of God as presented in the Torah, Prophets and Writings, as well as their own response to, and reflection on, personal experience. Many psalms were probably composed by sophisticated poets and musicians, members of professional guilds or choirs. But it is reasonable to suppose that such professionals were keen to 'sell' their products to the wider public in the sense of having them sung and performed in the liturgy. This in turn presumes sensitivity on their part to the mood and needs of the people at prayer.

In relation to the more specifically wisdom literature of the Hebrew canon, there are the books of Proverbs, Ecclesiastes (Qoheleth) and Job. While the book of Proverbs contains numerous references to righteous/righteousness and related terminology, they are mainly concerned with right relationships between human beings. But there is a small cluster of texts in Proverbs 8 that convey something of its notion of divine righteousness. As one would expect the book declares that true human righteousness derives from God. According to 8:22 God created Wisdom at the beginning of his way (8:22; NRSV 'work'). The authentic righteousness that leaders decree and judge (8:15-16; *tsedeq*) derives from her. Her teaching is impeccable because 'all the words' that come from her mouth are 'in righteousness' (8:8; *tsedeq*, rendered in the NRSV as 'righteous'). She is the loyal custodian of riches, honour, enduring wealth and righteousness (8:18; *tsedaqah*), and a trustworthy guide because she always walks 'in the way of righteousness' (8:20; *tsedaqah*). In short her relationship with God ensures that the relationships she forms with all, whether they are kings and nobles (8:15-16) or the 'simple' (8:5; 9:4), will be righteous. She will instruct them in the right way and the fruit/yield of her instruction is 'better than gold' or 'choice silver'. Lady Wisdom is the perfect model of divine righteousness and she is completely committed to God's purpose of establishing and restoring right relationships.

There are no specific references to divine righteousness in the book of Ecclesiastes/Qoheleth, but the author's reflection on the lack of, and the abuse of, righteousness in the human arena raises questions about God's governance of the world.[1] According to 3:17 the author 'said in my heart' that God will judge the righteous and the wicked, and the young man is warned about this in 11:9. Yet, as is well known, the author laments on a number of occasions that 'all is vanity (*hevel*)'. This term has generally been translated as 'vanity' but the root meaning of *h-v-l* is 'breath'. This conveys the sense of something that is vital and tangible, yet elusive. As Thomas Krüger notes, the meaning of the term 'seems to vary according to context between the negative: "worthless, futile" and the neutral: "transitory, fleeting"'.[2]

---

1. The relevant texts in Ecclesiastes are a)- on the righteous (*tsadiq*): 3:17; 5:8; 7:15, 16, 20; 9:1, 2; b)- on righteousness (*tsedeq*); 3:16; 5:8; 7:15.
2. Thomas Krüger, *Qoheleth. A Commentary* (Hermeneia; Augsburg: Fortress,

This suggests that the book may be not so much despairing of any meaning in life but warning the reader not to think that he or she can pin down its meaning. God has 'made everything suitable for its time ... yet they cannot find out what God has done from the beginning to the end (3:11; cf also 11:5'). It may be better therefore to speak of Qoheleth's caution about knowing how God rules the world in righteousness rather than skepticism about whether one can discern any righteousness in it at all.[3]

In my judgment, the book of Job commends itself to this study more than the preceding works because, as noted in the general introduction, it mounts a challenge to the Act–Consequence dynamic or connection as a way of explaining evil and maintaining faith in a righteous and just God. Does the book end up denying that God is just, or does it demolish a particular defense of divine righteousness that is upheld by appeal to the Act–Consequence connection, or does it offer another understanding to replace the one that it attacks? The chapter on Job will try to determine whether it provides answers to these questions and, of so, what they might be.

2004) 42.

3. According to Choong-Leong Seow, Qoheleth's use of *hevel* 'does not mean that everything is meaningless, but that everything is beyond human apprehension and comprehension' (*Ecclesiastes: A New Translation with Introduction and Commentary* [AB 18C; New York: Doubleday, 1997] 59).

1

The Psalter

The one hundred and fifty psalms of the Psalter are divided into five books (Psalms 1-41; 42-72; 73-89; 90-106; 107-150), perhaps in imitation of the Pentateuch.[1] Some relationship between the one and the five is indicated not only by the fact that the five are parts of a larger book but also because each book ends with a doxology of praise. Does this signal that the overall purpose of the Psalter is the praise of God and to urge its users to join in that praise? As well as this, within the five books there are collections of psalms with the same superscriptions: for example, the psalms of/to David in 3-41; 51-72, the psalms of Korah in 42-49 and Asaph in 73-89; and the 'songs of ascents' or pilgrim psalms in 120-34. Do the psalms in each collection have a common focus or thematic connection? Other collections have been identified either by tradition—for example, the 'halleluia' psalms (Ps 111-18), or by scholarly analysis for example—the 'Elohistic' psalms (Ps 42-83), so-called because of preference for the term 'Elohim' (God) over 'YHWH' (Lord).[2] The location of the Elohistic psalms in books two and three may suggest something about the nature of these books and their function within the larger Psalter.

Historical critical analysis, in particular form criticism, sought the basis of unity and diversity in the psalms not in the collections or

---

1. The MT numbering of the psalms will be followed throughout, in preference to the LXX. In order to simplify matters I will list only the NRSV verse numbering for each reference. The MT includes the psalm title or superscription in its verse numbering.
2. See J Clinton McCann Jr, 658 of 'The Book of Psalms. Introduction, Commentary, and Reflections', in *The New Interpreter's Bible, Volume Four* (Nashville; Abingdon, 1998), 639-1280.

books but in their classification according to type or genre. According to Hermann Gunkel the principal types are laments, psalms of praise, thanksgiving psalms, royal psalms, psalms celebrating the enthronement of God as king, psalms of Zion/temple, psalms of trust, wisdom psalms, torah psalms, etc.[3] Such classification has proved enormously helpful although, as one might expect, there is ongoing debate and disagreement about some psalms. For example, should Psalm 6 be classified as a lament or as one of the seven penitential psalms as in church tradition (6; 32; 38; 51; 106; 130; 143)?[4] Although there is no mention of sin in Psalm 6 the references to God's rebuke and discipline in v 1 have been seen as implying sin and guilt. Form Criticism has also sought to identify the 'life setting' (*Sitz-im-Leben*) of the various types of psalms. For example, Sigmund Mowinckel proposed the influential thesis of a cultic setting at major feasts of the Israelite liturgical year.[5] It was recognised that while a psalm may have been composed for a particular setting or use its subsequent incorporation into the Psalter probably allowed other options. Under the impetus of rhetorical criticism the focus of attention shifted from psalm classification to the uniqueness of each psalm.[6] What emerged from this was another example of unity within diversity, or the relationship between the one and the many: different psalms share the same or similar imagery and use similar poetic and structural devices (for example Ps 108 combines elements from 57 and 60).

More recently considerable attention has been devoted to the relationship between the various psalms in each of the five books as well as the relationship between the books themselves. Is the Psalter more than the sum of its parts?[7] It has long been recognised

---

3. See Hermann Gunkel, *Introduction to Psalms: The Genres of the Religious Lyric of Israel*, completed by Joachim Begrich; translated by James D Nogalksi (Macon Ga.; Mercer University Press, 1998).
4. Cf McCann, 'The Book of Psalms', 704.
5. Sigmund Mowinckel, *The Psalms in Israel's Worship*, 2 volumes, translated by DR Ap-Thomas; Oxford: Blackwell, 1962).
6. This was partly in response to James Muilenburg's influential essay on the strengths and limitations of Form Criticism ('Form Criticism and Beyond', *JBL* 88 [1969]: 1–28).
7. For a recent discussion of this development and the relevant literature see Howard N Wallace, *Psalms* (Readings: A New Biblical Commentary; Sheffield: Sheffield Phoenix Press, 2009), 3–9. A key study in this development has been Gerald H Wilson's *The Editing of the Hebrew Psalter* (SBLDS 76; Chico, Calif:

that Psalm 1 serves as an introduction to the Psalter: it teaches that the person devoted to 'law of the Lord' is happy/blessed and will be counted among the righteous; in contrast the wicked will perish. One can read the reference to law/torah in two senses: the first links it to the teaching of the Torah and the two ways outlined in Deuteronomy 30:15–20; the second signals that the Psalter itself is a torah or instruction for those who follow it faithfully. The two senses are not in conflict; the one devoted to Torah is a loyal Yahwist and will ipso facto be devoted to the torah of the Psalter and its prayers. Reading or celebrating the psalms will not only recall the Torah but also instruct one as to its meaning and value. It is significant that the fourth book commences with a psalm of Moses (90; the only one so entitled) and that book five contains the longest psalm, 119, which celebrates Torah and is almost a Psalter in its own right. As an instruction on how to read the Psalter, Psalm 1 can also be described as an example of wisdom teaching as found in texts such as Proverbs 1:1–7. Psalm 1 may reflect the identification of wisdom with Torah as expressed in Sirach 24:23. In light of these observations it is probably not accidental that each book of the Psalter commences with wisdom psalms or psalms that contain wisdom motifs (cf 42–43; 73; 90; 107).[8]

A number of commentators propose that Psalm 2 has been linked editorially to Psalm 1 via the warning that kings hostile to the Lord's anointed will perish and the promise that all who take refuge in him are happy/blessed (2:12).[9] A connection between the two is further suggested by the fact that Psalm 2 does not have a title or superscription.[10] Is their association a reflection of Deuteronomy 17:14–20 which enjoins the king to have a copy of the Torah and observe it diligently? Another possible association is with the

---

Scholars Press, 1985); see also 'Shaping the Psalter: A Consideration of Editorial Linkage in the Book of Psalms,' in *The Shape and Shaping of the Psalter*, edited by J Clinton McCann (JSOTSup 159; Sheffield: Sheffield Academic Press, 1993), 72–82.

8. Although Ps 107 is largely a thanksgiving hymn, the concluding vv 42–43 may well have been added to give it a wisdom orientation and thereby align it with the other wisdom psalms that commence books 1–4 of the Psalter.
9. Cf Patrick D Miller 'The Beginning of the Psalter', in *The Shape and Shaping of the Psalter*, 83–92, and the literature cited there. More recently, see Steven S Tuell, 'Between Text & Sermon. Psalm 1', *Interpretation* 63 (2009): 278–80.
10. Similar examples are Psalm 10, which appears to continue 9; Psalm 33, which continues 32; and Psalm 43, which continues 42 (note how 43:5 repeats 42:11).

Former Prophets which commences with the new leader Joshua being urged to meditate on the law day and night (Josh 1:8; same verb for 'meditate' as in Ps 1:2). The connection between Psalms 1 and 2 may also serve as a guide for reading/understanding the larger Psalter. There is a similarity between the assurance in Psalm 1 that the devotee of the Torah will join the 'congregation of the righteous' and the assurance to the king in Psalm 2 that he will triumph over his enemies. In both psalms those who refuse allegiance to the Lord will perish (1:6; 2:12). The two psalms effectively unite king and people in the cause of righteousness and salvation. The king is God's agent in breaking the power of evil and watching 'over the way of the righteous'. The superscription for Psalm 3 identifies the king as David. The connection between David and all who pray the psalms is well expressed by Brevard Childs: 'The psalms are transmitted as the sacred psalms of David, but they testify to all the common troubles and joys of ordinary human life in which all persons participate'.[11]

As with the wisdom or torah psalms, it is presumably not without significance that psalms of David—Davidic dynasty are located at the end of book one (41), book two (72) and book three (89). The last laments the end of the Davidic dynasty's rule at the Babylonian exile. The psalms that follow in book four (90-106), in particular 93, 95-99, shift the focus from the (failed) Davidic rule to the Lord as universal king. However, Psalm 110 in book five would appear in its turn to resume Psalm 2 by 're-enthroning' David as God's earthly representative. As well as this, the final collection of psalms before the concluding hymns of praise in 146-50 is attributed to David (138-45). Does this point to a messianic expectation in the Psalter, a new kind of David who will play his role in the fulfillment of God's purpose?[12] Two additional observations add to a sense of some overall

---

11. Cf Childs, *Introduction to the Old Testament as Scripture* (Philadelphia: Fortress Press, 1979), 521.
12. The function of Psalms 93-99 and the final Davidic collection within the Psalter is debated. Wilson thinks that Psalms 93, 95-99 are the theological heart of the Psalter and signal a de-emphasising of the Davidic dynasty. Others disagree, pointing to the Davidic psalms in Book 5. For a discussion and the relevant literature see J Clinton McCann, 'Righteousness, Justice and Peace: A Contemporary Theology of the Psalms', *HBT* 23 (2001): 111-31, in particular 116-18. For Wilson's most recent reflections see 'King, Messiah, and the Reign of God: Revisiting the Royal Psalms and the Shape of the Psalter', in *The Book*

purpose in the arrangement of the Psalter. One is that lament psalms tend to predominate in the first three books of the Psalter whereas thanksgiving and praise tend to predominate in books four and five. The other is that there is a perceived movement from psalms of the individual to communal and national ones across the Psalter.[13] Does this second observation indicate the Psalter is designed to encourage the faithful to face the various kinds of difficulties (laments) that can lead to division, isolation and hostility? God is the only one able to deliver them from such afflictions and unite them in a community of thanksgiving and praise. The doxologies that conclude each book may be an additional pointer to this as the Psalter's overall purpose, or at least a key purpose.

Norman Whybray has played devil's advocate in this recent development of psalm study. He accepts there is a preponderance of lament in the earlier books and praise in the later books but concludes 'There is no evidence that there was a systematic and purposeful redaction of the whole Psalter in any of the suggested ways'.[14] He also notes that, according to M Millard, there is no evidence in Judaism that the Psalter was read as a unified work for instructional and devotional purposes.[15] Whybray has a point in criticising those who hold that the psalms 'were ordered in such a way as to present a single comprehensive message'.[16] Given the richness and diversity of the psalms this seems unlikely. A more balanced position is that of Jerome Creach who argues that the 'destiny of the righteous is a central organizing subject that provides a fruitful entrée into the Psalter as a whole' and that this is crucial 'for understanding the Psalter's many literary and theological dimensions'.[17] He is not claiming to have discovered *the* single or central organising subject of the Psalter but

---

of Psalms. Composition and Reception, edited by Peter W Flint and Patrick D Miller, Jr (Supplements to Vetus Testamentum 99; Leiden/Boston: Brill, 2005), 391–406.

13. For both proposals see Wilson, 'The Shape of the Book of Psalms', *Interpretation* 46/2 (1992): 129–42, in particular 138–39.
14. Norman Whybray, *Reading the Psalms as a Book* (JSOTSup 222; Sheffield: Sheffield Academic Press, 1996), 119.
15. M Millard, *Die Komposition des Psalters* (FAT 9; Tübingen: Mohr, 1994).
16. Whybray, *Reading the Psalms as a Book*, 118.
17. Jerome FD Creach, *The Destiny of the Righteous in the Psalms* (St. Louis, Missouri: Chalice Press, 2008), 150.

a central one that provides, in his view, reliable access to the riches of the Psalter.

The disagreements about the nature and purpose of the Psalter do not rule out reading it as a book, although they indicate pretty clearly that it is not a book in our modern sense of the term. To read the Psalter as a book is in a sense unavoidable; it is an application of the principle that texts can only be understood within their context, and context varies. There is the context of the original author of the text, the context in which the text comes to be preserved, and the context of the reader(s). The above survey shows how reading a psalm within the context of a collection of psalms, a book of the Psalter, and the Psalter as a whole, affects one's understanding not only of the particular psalm but other psalms as well. The differing interpretations that arise are due at least in part to the limitations of readers' ability to take these various contexts into account and assess them accurately.

The following analysis of the righteousness of God and associated terms in the psalms will employ the contextual approach, commencing with a comment on the meaning of terms in individual psalms and then exploring the implications of reading this within the larger context of the Psalter and the HBOT. There are eighty-eight occurrences in the Psalter of the noun righteousness (masculine and feminine forms) and fifty-two of the adjective righteous (the bulk of these referring to the individual or the community). Jenni and Westermann hold that the Psalter is one place where there is a distinction between the meaning of the masculine and feminine forms of the Hebrew terms for righteousness. The feminine *tsedaqah* tends to refer to a particular action and the masculine *tsedeq* to a condition/state. Righteous actions are a sign of or bring about a state of righteousness, a way of living. For example, in Psalm 40:9-10 the psalmist testifies that 'I have told the glad news of deliverance (*tsedeq*; as a way of living) in the great congregation. I have not hidden your saving help (*tsedaqah*; the particular action) within my heart'. Psalm 72:1-2 prays that God will act in *tsedaqah* toward the king so that he may bring about a state of *tsedeq* in the realm, while Psalm 119:142 proclaims that the communication of the Torah was an act of *tsedaqah* that established an everlasting state of *tsedeq* for Israel.[18] Whether this

---

18. Jenni/Westermann, *Theologisches Handwörterbuch*, II, 518-19.

distinction operates throughout the Psalter may be debatable but it is worth keeping in mind in the following survey.

As noted earlier, Psalm 1:6 states that 'the Lord watches over (Hebrew, 'knows') the way of the righteous'. Within the context of the psalm this 'way' is the torah/Torah of the Lord in v 2.[19] A clever combination of spatial (the way), temporal (day and night) and farming imagery (fruit yielding trees) captures the sense of the torah embracing all aspects of a person's life or way, enabling him/her to arrive at their destiny (the congregation of the righteous). An additional factor that emerges from reading v 2 in conjunction with v. 6 is that to meditate on the torah is to be instructed personally by God. The torah of the Lord is God's word that speaks to the righteous at every point on life's journey. The context of vv 5–6 also adds a dimension to the assertion that the Lord 'knows' the way of the righteous. It is preceded and followed by statements about sinners/wicked, implying that the verb 'know' here signals God's protection of the righteous against the way (threats and temptations?) of the wicked.[20] Although the psalm does not state so explicitly, the clear implication is that God is the source of human righteousness and that it is bestowed so that one's life may be part of God's purpose: that one becomes a member of God's community of righteous ones. A right relationship with God and community is mediated via one's relationship with the torah. The way of the righteous is further highlighted by the contrast with the way of the wicked. At the beginning of the psalm the wicked appear to be part of a community, in contrast to the lone figure meditating on the torah, but theirs is no real community and they are scattered like chaff in the wind. The psalm does not pronounce God's judgment against the wicked; it simply states that their way will perish. Like their illusory community the way of the wicked is in fact not a way at all; it goes nowhere. The focus is on contrasting ways; what ultimately happens to the wicked is left unresolved.

The key components of the psalm may be summarised as follows. Complete devotion to the torah of the Lord is the mark of

---

19. As noted earlier the term torah can refer to the Torah or the torah/teaching that unfolds as one reads/prays the psalms.
20. As McCann notes, 'the psalmist was no naïve optimist and knew about the 'real world' (*A Theological Introduction to the Book of Psalms. The Psalms as Torah* [Nashville: Abingdon Press 1993], 34).

the righteous because it shows that one recognises God and God's word as the origin, guide and goal of life. God is the source of human righteousness as the appropriate way of life, as Psalm 1 implies and as 4:1 makes clear. The righteous may appear to be isolated and alone compared to the wicked but in fact God is the righteous one's constant companion via meditation on the torah and such a one is assured of membership in the only true community—that of the righteous. The presence of the torah makes life a journey that begins with God, has God at every point on the way, and at its goal. This is celebrated in extended form in Psalm 119. In contrast the wicked have no community and are not on the way to life's goal. This trio of God, the righteous (whether one or many) and the wicked (whether one or many) appears in many psalms, especially the ones classified as laments. I will now consider some examples of the lament genre in which the righteousness of God features.

In Psalm 5:8 the feminine term and the context point to righteousness as God's action ('Lead me, O Lord'). However the parallelism implies that divine righteousness is also a way—God's way. The final verses employ the image of God as a warrior with a shield, protecting all those who 'take refuge in you': these are the righteous (v 12). God not only provides the right way but personally protects the righteous from enemies at every step along it. In contrast to Psalm 1 where the focus is on contrasting the ways of the righteous and the wicked, here it is on deliverance from the wicked. The reference to mouths, hearts, throats and tongues in v 9 indicates they are plotting evil against the righteous. In another contrast to Psalm 1, appeal is made to God to punish the wicked. There are two sides of the coin of God's righteousness in action in Psalm 5: deliverance of the righteous means punishment of the wicked—both are elements of God's saving purpose. Salvation or deliverance is quite explicit in Psalm 35:1 ('in your righteousness deliver me'); in Psalm 35:24 the context of the appeal to God's righteousness points to it, as does the resolve to celebrate the manifestation of it in v 28.

The classification of Psalm 85 as a community lament is somewhat disputed but it does contain the appeal to God for intervention accompanied by a series of anguished questions that are a feature of lament psalms (cf vv 5-6). Two things are striking about God's righteousness in this psalm. One is that it is not part of a petition as in the preceding cases. Instead, it is located in the final portion of the psalm that envisages the imminent arrival of God's salvation and glory in the land (vv 10–12). As the verses unfold, righteousness gradually assumes prominence. The imagery in v 10 is of God's personal ambassadors—steadfast love, faithfulness, righteousness and peace—working in perfect unison to prepare the advent of God's glory. In v 11, faithfulness is envisaged springing from the ground like a vigorous crop, an ever-reliable source of life-giving nourishment on earth, while righteousness sees and oversees all things from its heavenly vantage point. God's governance and care embrace heaven and earth. In v 12, righteousness is singled out for the key role of going ahead to carve out a path for God's steps. It is of course a perfectly made path and going in a definite direction; within the context it is to 'your people'. Via this evocative series of images, vv 10–12 link righteousness closely to other key attributes of God but also single out its role in the re-establishment of a right relationship between God and 'your people'.[21] From the context this presumably involves the forgiveness of sin (cf 85:2).

Psalm 88:12 asks whether God's righteousness (feminine), steadfast love and faithfulness are known in the shadowy realm of the dead. The question does not so much doubt their reality or reach as wonder whether the deceased are able to experience (know) them in action. For this psalm as for most of the HBOT, salvation and the realisation of God's purpose takes place in this world (cf Isa 38:18–19). One important reason for this conviction is implied in v 10: no one has risen from the grave to praise God for his righteousness, steadfast love and faithfulness. Ultimately this is why one cries to God for deliverance and why God provides it (cf 22:31; 40:9–10; 100:4–5; 106:47). Psalm 88 is perhaps the bleakest lament psalm in the Psalter and occurs toward the end of book 3, a section of the Psalter with a predominance of lament psalms—most would identify 74; 77; 79; 80; 83; 86; 88 and 89:38–51 as laments. Of these Psalms 77; 86; 88 and 89:38–51 appear to be laments of an individual but, given recent analysis of connections between psalms and a sequential reading of groups or collections of them, the distinction between individual and

---

21. Cf Erhard S Gerstenberger, *Psalms, Part 2, and Lamentations* (FOTL XV; Grand Rapids/Cambridge: Eerdmans, 2001), 130–31. All the occurrences of righteousness in the psalm are masculine.

community laments has become rather blurred. Also, as noted earlier, it is argued that an individual speaker in a psalm, such as David, can stand for or speak for the nation or humanity at large.

Whether individual or national, lament psalms exhibit features that have an impact on the notion of God's righteousness in the Psalter. One is that the appeal for deliverance does not envisage the enemies' repentance and conversion, except for 7:12 (as a warning) and 83:16 that calls for them to be shamed so 'they may seek your name'.[22] In contrast a strong theme in prophetic literature is the participation of all nations in the universal triumph of God's righteous purpose. The horizon of the lament psalms is God's victory over evil in this or that particular battle, however one could argue that they gain a more universal perspective when read within the larger context of the psalms celebrating the Lord as universal king and the psalms of praise in 146-50. A second feature is that only one lament psalm explicitly identifies foreign oppression as God's punishment for sin (79:8-9).[23] Compare this to prophetic literature that prophesies God will hand sinful Israel over to one or more of the four agents of punishment—'sword, famine, wild animals, and pestilence' (cf Ezek 14:21). These execute God's judgement and are an integral part of God's righteous purpose—the removal of an existing evil disorder and the establishment of a new one that is in accord with God's will.

Thus the lament psalms differ from prophecy in their understanding of the relationship between God, Israel and foreign nations. For the former elimination of the enemy is the sure sign of God's salvation, for the latter the inclusion of the enemy is the ultimate sign of God's universal salvation. The former portray Israel as inexplicably ('why O Lord') and even unjustly oppressed whereas the latter portray Israel as justly punished. In the prophetic books punishment is a sign of God's righteousness, in the psalms deliverance from the enemy will be a sign of God's righteousness. For the lament psalms theodicy is a significant issue (the question 'why'), for prophecies of divine punishment the answer to the 'why' is generally clear. Despite

---

22. However, this prayer would seem to be cancelled by the following verse, 83:17.
23. The verse in question is preceded by an appeal that God 'not remember against us the iniquities of our ancestors'. The appeal to 'forgive our sins' follows in v. 9. The psalm accepts some notion of generational punishment as well as 'this generation's' punishment.

their differences what unites these two uses of righteousness is the removal of an existing evil order or situation in favour of what is perceived as the right one. As well as this, the lament psalms share an important element with the Torah in the form of Israel's affliction in Egypt.[24] According to the narrative, Israel's oppression is not due to sin but the action of an evil Pharaoh whose perception of reality is so distorted that he cannot see Israel as the mediator of divine blessing but only as a threat. Israel's undeserved oppression and its cry to God provides the right opportunity for a display of divine power that will lead Israel and Egypt to acknowledge 'I am the Lord (cf Exod 6:7; 7:5). Knowledge of the divine name and praise of the one who bears it is what salvation is ultimately about, according to the HBOT. It is how the Psalter ends (Ps 146–150). Lament psalms enable an individual or the community to identify with afflicted Israel in the exodus stage of its story and thereby rekindle faith and hope.

These features of the lament psalms emerge from reading them as a distinct genre, apart from their Psalter context. However, if one reads them within this context the picture can change quite considerably, as Robert Cole argues for the laments in book 3. Within this context the reasons for affliction and oppression now become clear. For example, he states that 'the wicked of Psalm 73 are members of the chosen nation itself, whose punishment in 74 is thereby explained' (cf 73:10–11).[25] One can extend this contextual reading to link books within the Psalter; thus 'our iniquities' and 'our secret sins' in Psalm 90:8 explain why the situations lamented in book 3 arise. If correct this kind of reading would bring the lament psalms, at least of book 3, more into line with prophetic theology. While it is legitimate and even necessary to read psalms in their present (canonical) context, Cole's interpretation renders the anguished questions 'why' in Psalm 74:1, 11 somewhat superfluous, unless a reader of the canonical sequence is meant to nod knowingly at this point.[26] Given that most psalms were

---

24. It may perhaps also be associated with prophetic texts that condemn a foreign nation for overstepping its divine mandate and trying to destroy Israel (cf Isa 10:5–19). This places the people in a situation from which God vows to deliver them.
25. Robert L Cole *The Shape and Message of Book III (Psalms 73–89)* (JSOTSup 307; Sheffield: Sheffield Academic Press, 2000), 29, cf also 36.
26. His explanation of the 'why' questions seems to me to confuse 'why' with 'how long', the temporal factor (*The Shape and Message*, 32).

composed as independent pieces and only subsequently incorporated into the Psalter, with apparently minimal editing, gauging the level of connection is always going to be a rather subjective matter. In a recent essay, Beat Weber calls for a combination of *lectio repetitiva* (of individual psalms) and *lectio continua* (of psalms in sequence/context) in order to give due weight to the uniqueness of each psalm as well as its place in the Psalter.[27]

God's righteousness (masculine and feminine) occurs frequently in the psalms with the term justice. The combination indicates further nuances in the meaning of both terms. According to Kaiser, Psalm 7 professes faith in God as the righteous judge 'fourfold': as deliverer of the unjustly accused, as the one who ensures the appropriate working of the Act–Consequence connection, as the King who brings order to his people, and as the judge who brings the evildoer to book.[28] The psalmist is confident of being counted/judged among the righteous because of complete trust in God and God's ways ('God is my shield; cf Ps 5:12). Two points may be noted. One is that the role of God as judge here provides the template or model for human judges: their task is to identify the oppressed or unjustly disadvantaged and rule in their favour. In other words, they are to deliver them from their oppressive situation. In doing so they exercise their God-given authority correctly and so are in a right relationship with God as well as the community they serve.[29] The second point is that the psalmist expects a favourable judgement because he/she is righteous ('upright in heart'; cf also 36:10). In contrast, Psalm 143:2 begs God not 'to enter into judgement with your servant, for no one living is righteous before you'. This admission echoes similar ones in Psalm 14:2–3 and 130:3 (cf also Job 4:17; 9:2; 25:4). Either these are contradictory understandings of what it is to be righteous or there is some flexibility and creativity in the use of the term—not unusual in the context of

---

27. Beat Weber, 'Von der Psaltergenese zur Psaltertheologie: Der nächste Schritt der Psalterexegese? Einige grundsätzliche Überlegungen zum Psalter als Buch und Kanonteil', in *The Composition of the Book of Psalms*, edited by Erich Zenger (BETL 238; Leuven: Peeters, 2010), 733–44, see especially 738–41. See also Harry P Nasuti, 'The Interpretive Significance of Sequence and Selection in the Book of Psalms', in *The Book of Psalms. Composition and Reception*, 311–39.
28. Cf Kaiser, *Yahwes Gerechtigkeit*, 242.
29. Cf Carl Graesser 'Righteousness, Human and Divine', *Currents in Theology* 10 (1983): 134–36.

highly rhetorical poetry. For Jerome Creach, the psalms hold that although no one can be righteous before God in the sense of being perfect, a person who acknowledges and seeks to know God's will via the Torah is righteous.[30] Such a one acknowledges sin and asks for forgiveness. As was noted in preceding chapters, both Torah and the Prophets also affirm that no one is completely righteous before God.

The image of God as judge is to the fore in the so-called 'enthronement psalms' or the psalms that celebrate God as universal king (93–99). Psalm 93 commences with the proclamation that 'The Lord is king', one who is robed in majesty and strength, the creator who 'established the world' (93:1c) and who rules over it for ever. Creation, represented by the mighty flood waters, proclaims God's kingship. The psalm concludes by proclaiming that God's decrees (*'edut*) are, like creation, firm or enduring (NRSV 'sure'). Within the context of the psalm this term presumably refers to God's decrees/words that bring into being and order all creation; however it is used in 99:7b to refer to the decrees and statutes entrusted to Moses and Aaron. As observed in the chapter on the Torah, the Sinai covenant laws are an integral part of God's creative word/decree.[31] Although Psalm 94 does not use the term king it calls on God as 'judge of the earth' to rescue 'your people' by giving the proud and wicked what they deserve. The psalmist then reports his/her own experience in order to assure that divine judgement reaches every one of 'your people' (94:16-22).

The following psalms all describe God as king (96; 97; 99 have the refrain 'the Lord is king') and, except for 95, see judging as the predominant feature of the Lord's righteous rule. Psalm 96 proclaims the Lord's universal kingship to the nations and resumes the statement about God as creator in 93:1c to assure the nations that God will judge 'with equity' (96:10c) and 'with righteousness' and 'with truth' (96:13c). For its part 97:2b would appear to combine elements of 89:14 and 93:2 with its statement that 'Righteousness and justice

---

30. Creach. *The Destiny of the Righteous*, 2–5.
31. The intimate connection between creation and the Torah occurs also in Psalm 19, whether or not it is made up of two once independent psalms that were later joined (19:1-6 and 19:7-14). The perfection of the Torah, its decrees (*'edut*), precepts (*piqqudim*), and command (*mitsvah*) mirror the perfect order of creation (cf Creach, *The Destiny of the Righteous*, 143–44).

are the foundation of your throne'.³² As God's throne is established forever in 93:2 so, according to 97:2b, are God's righteousness and justice. This psalm clearly links God's righteousness as creator with deliverance of the oppressed. According to 97:6, 'The heavens proclaims his righteousness; and all the peoples behold his glory'; according to 97:10c-11, 'he rescues them (the faithful) from the hand of the wicked. Light dawns for the righteous'. Deliverance of those unjustly oppressed is an integral part of God's purpose to establish righteousness and justice in the kingdom (cf 94:16-22). For its part Ps 98:9b draws on 96:10c 13:c to affirm that 'He will judge the world with righteousness, and the peoples with equity' (from *yashar* 'right/even'). Psalm 99:4 praises God as a 'Mighty King, lover of justice' who has executed 'justice and righteousness in Jacob'. These psalms may well have been performed during the liturgy in the Jerusalem temple. They express the conviction that, even though there may not be much sign of righteousness on earth at this or that time, God is the everlasting king and is bringing humanity to 'Know that the Lord is God' (100:3), on which all else depends. A visible sign in Israel/Jacob of God's universal kingship is the Davidic dynasty. Psalm 72 asks God to 'give to the king your justice/and your righteousness to a king's son' so that 'he may judge your people with righteousness and your poor with justice'. The psalm prays to God for the grace of right rule because, although all depends on God's initiative, the king is expected to respond with the appropriate human initiative—to be completely loyal to God and God's way (as the king testifies in Ps 18:20-30).

This linking of the particular (the rule of the Davidic king) and the universal (God's rule over all creation) in Psalms 93-99 occurs also in relation to Zion. It is the earthly locus and sign of God's everlasting heavenly throne (cf 93:2 and 97:8; 99:2). The particular and universal symbolism of the temple/Zion appears in a number of earlier psalms (for example, 46; 48; 84; 87; 118:19-28 [the 'gates of righteousness']). It is not without reason that Wilson and others identify Psalms 93-99 as the 'theological heart' or at least a focal point of the Psalter.³³

---

32. Within the context of books 3 and 4, one could argue that Ps 97 reaffirms 89:14 in the wake of the lament in 89:38-51. The latter would appear to accuse God of not being loyal to David (89:49) and so failing to be righteous and just.

33. Cf Wilson, 'King, Messiah, and the Reign of God,' 391-406; McCann, 'Righteousness, Justice and Peace', 116-18, 126; Creach, *The Destiny of the*

Significantly, features that characterise lament psalms in books one to three, namely the questions 'why' and 'how long' (in various forms in Hebrew) and the accusation of failure or neglect on God's part, exemplified in Psalm 89:38–51, do not occur in books four and five except for two instances of the cry 'how long' (90:13 and 94:3). These differences between books four and five and one to three suggest that an overall aim of the Psalter is to instill confidence in the faithful that, despite appearances to the contrary (voiced in the laments of books one to three), God is universal King and is bringing the divine purpose to its fulfillment.

The association of God's righteousness with other related terms, in particular steadfast love (*khesedh*) and faithfulness (*'emet*/*'emunah*), adds further nuances to its meaning. The relevant psalm texts are 33:5; 36:5–6, 10; 40:9–11; 85:10–12; 89:14 and 103:6–8, 17. The parallelism in 33:5 implies that what ensures the earth is (or will be) full of righteousness and justice is God's steadfast love; that is, God's unswerving commitment to establishing right order in creation.[34] In Psalm 36:5–6 the terms steadfast love and faithfulness in v 5 appear to be synonymous as also are righteousness and justice in v 6. While the first pair conveys an assurance that God's commitment is to all creation, rather like 33:5, the second pair appears to remind the reader that God's righteous rule is ultimately beyond human reckoning (like 'the mountains of God/mighty mountains', 'like the deep' (*tehom* the same term as in Gen 1:2, 'darkness on the face of the deep'). The following verse affirms that it is all for the good of humans and animals. If this is a fair reading of 36:5–6, the prayer in v 10 implies that such righteousness (NRSV 'salvation') is not bestowed on the godless/unrighteous but only the 'upright of heart'.

Psalm 40:9–10 lists a number of divine attributes or qualities: righteousness (masculine form in v 9, feminine in v 10), faithfulness/truth (*'emunah*), salvation (*teshu'ah*), steadfast love (*khesedh*), and faithfulness/truth (*'emet*). The context is of thanks to God who has

---

Righteous, 71.

34. For John Goldingay the verse conveys the conviction 'that the whole world experiences Ywh's commitment, along lines suggested by the Noah covenant (Gen. 9)', (*Psalms. Volume 1: Psalms 1–41* [Baker Commentary on the Old Testament Wisdom and Psalms; Grand Rapids, Mich: Baker Academic, 2006], 466)

delivered one who was patient and trusting. The sign of this trust is devotion to the Torah that 'is within my heart/bowels' (v 8). Verses 9 and 10 are structured as two parallelisms ('I have/have not'), the first about righteousness and the second about the other attributes listed. This has the effect of separating the statements about righteousness from the ones about the other attributes. Gerstenberger sees the masculine form *tsedeq* in v 9 referring to 'divine and human righteousness' and as 'the pivotal point of the message'.[35] It may be that the terms listed in v 10 are meant to spell out aspects of *tsedeq* in v 9. Psalm 85:10–12 has already been commented on; as in 40:9–10 righteousness (masculine) is singled out to some degree from steadfast love, faithfulness and peace. It has a universal perspective and so can go before God to carve out a path which points to and leads unerringly to the right goal. Steadfast love and faithfulness express God's unswerving commitment to 'walk' this path and establish peace.

In Psalm 89:14 it is steadfast love and faithfulness that go before God's presence (face), while righteousness and justice are associated with God's throne. The context of this verse is creation, God bringing order out of chaos represented by the raging sea and the monster Rahab (cf vv 9–10). God's throne is founded on the pillars of righteousness and justice, an assurance that right order has definitively replaced primeval chaos—here the terms righteousness and justice are effectively synonymous. The image of steadfast love and faithfulness going before God conveys a sense of God's full and active presence in creation. Psalm 103 links righteousness, justice and steadfast love to the Mosaic/Sinai covenant. Righteousness and justice (here synonymous) are described as God's 'ways/acts' that were made known to Moses and the people (vv 6–7).[36] They are not just for 'you' (vv 3–5) but for 'all who are oppressed'. God's steadfast love is manifest above all in God's merciful (*rakhum*) and gracious (*khanan*) forgiveness of Israel's sins (v 8)—this is a sign of God' complete

---

35. Gerstenberger, *Psalms: Part 1: With an Introduction to Cultic Poetry* (FOTL XIV; Grand Rapids, Mich: Eerdmans, 1988), 171. Cf the proposal by Jenni and Westermann outlined above that the masculine form (*tsedeq*) (with no pronoun suffix) refers to the state or condition of righteousness whereas the feminine form (with pronoun suffix) refers to God's righteous action.
36. Cf Gerstenberger, *Psalms: Part 2*, 217.

commitment. Verse 8 alludes to Exodus 34:6–7, as do Psalms 86:15 and 145:8. Verse 17 emphasises that God's righteousness and steadfast love are not only for those addressed in the psalm ('you') or reciting it ('us') but for all generations.

God's righteousness in the psalms can be summed up by the following comment from McCann; it reflects Schmid's understanding of the term in the larger HBOT:

> the Psalter encourages the reader to understand justice and righteousness less in terms of specific distributive/retributive acts and more in terms of a harmonious world order characterized by the creation and sustenance of conditions that make life possible for all, especially for the poor and needy.[37]

One may not be able to apply this statement to each and every psalm, particularly a number of the lament psalms, but it would seem to be the case, or the biblical claim, as one reads through the Psalter, with the predominance of psalms of praise and thanksgiving in the latter books.

---

37. McCann, 'Righteousness, Justice and Peace', 121.

2

Book of Job

David Clines, who recently completed a massive three-volume commentary on Job, thinks most readers would see 'the major question' of the book as the problem of (innocent) suffering. However Clines himself thinks that it is the 'moral order of the world, of the principles on which it is governed' by the divinity.[1] The two views are in fact related because the reality of innocent suffering questions in what sense, or whether in any sense, God's governance of creation can be called just. The argument or arguments that seek to defend the righteousness/justice of God in the face of such suffering is generally called 'Theodicy'.[2] It employs what is called the Act–Consequence connection or dynamic, a conviction about the order or structure of creation. For ancient societies this order was established by the creator god or gods; from a modern point of view it is seen more as a sociological version of the physical law of cause–effect. For both points of view the connection is difficult to prove in every instance— human perception is limited—and this leads to disputes. Are bad children always the consequence of bad parenting; did the team lose the game because of internal rivalry or was the opposition simply better? Within a religious context the authority of a god is invoked (via prophet, priestly ritual, etc) to try and settle disputes. Good consequences are attributed to the god's reward/blessing for good

---

1. David JA Clines, *Job 1–20* (WBC 17; Dallas, Tx: Word Books, 1989), xxxviii.
2. According to JL Crenshaw 'Theodicy is an articulate response to the anomie of existence, one that goes beyond silence, submission, and rebellion to thoughtful justification of the deity in the face of apparently contradictory evidence. The concept antedates by millennia the origin of the word 'theodicy', a neologism coined by GW Leibnz in 1710'. (*Defending God. Biblical Responses to the Problem of Evil* [Oxford: OUP, 2005], 201, fn 37).

actions and bad consequences to the god's retribution/punishment for bad actions. It is an argument from authority that the faithful will accept as long as the context within which it operates is accepted. Is the book of Job about defending God as just or exposing God as unjust and so demolishing theodicy? Given that it is part of the canon of Scripture it is unlikely the latter is the case. But its purpose may be, and may have been seen to be by those who accepted it as part of Scripture, more subtle and nuanced than a defense of God as righteous and just.

The book provides a reader with what must be the most advantageous perspective of any book in the HBOT. He or she is made privy not only to what takes place between Job and his friends on earth, but also what takes place between God and the satan in heaven (the prologue), as well as between God and Job in 38:1–42:6, and between God and Job's friends in 42:7–9. It is as if a reader is, like God, able to see and hear all that goes on in heaven and on earth. Ironically however, the result is that, as ongoing study of Job seems to indicate, readers are unable to achieve clarity or closure about what the book means.[3] To put this another way; the effect of 'listening in' to the dialogues between the various characters in the book is that readers themselves become participants, debating what the characters in the book are on about, how they contribute to its overall meaning, and whether indeed it has an overall meaning. As Carol Newsom notes, the most common approach in recent scholarship 'makes the dialogical nature of the book the fundamental hermeneutical key' to understanding it.[4] If this is the case then knowledge would seem to be a central feature of the book, because a key aim of dialogue is to enhance one's knowledge, either of the dialogue partner(s) or of the topic under discussion, or both. But engaging in genuine dialogue is also an admission that one's knowledge is limited and will always remain so; in a sense one always needs to learn from the other. God is the key dialogue partner both in the prologue and in 38:1–42:6, and is the topic or central focus of the dialogue between Job and his friends in 3:1–37:24. It is reasonable to conclude therefore that a central concern of the book is knowing God and that God, as the key

---

3. See the review of recent literature on Job by Carol A Newsom, 'Re-considering Job', in *CR:BS*, 5.2 (2007), 155–82.
4. Carol A Newsom, 'Re-considering Job', 157.

dialogue partner, is the one from whom the human participants must learn. Knowledge through dialogue implies of course a relationship, however tenuous. The book of Job may therefore be described as an examination or exploration of what kind of knowledge forms the basis for a real or right relationship with God. This aligns it with what was seen as a primary purpose of the Torah, as formulated for example in Exodus 6:7, 'You shall know that I am the Lord your God'.

The nature of the book means that a reader needs to consider each dialogue at two levels. One is the privileged perspective that the book provides for a reader, the other is that of its characters as they engage in dialogue or debate within their respective realms (God and the satan in the heavenly court; Job and his friends on earth). The book commences with a description of Job as 'blameless and upright' that is endorsed by God in 1:9, who also calls Job 'my servant'. In this way the reader is informed that there is a relationship between Job and God, in which Job knows how to be blameless and upright before God and to act in accord with this knowledge. However the satan believes that Job has acted not out of loyalty to God but for personal gain. Within the context of the first encounter between God and the satan, the question 'Does Job fear God for nothing?' would seem to apply to what the satan considers to be 'his possessions', things that Job has acquired by manipulating the divinity's reward–retribution system (1:10). The satan is confident that if Job's possessions are reduced to nothing he will curse God.[5] But the narrative reveals that the satan misjudges Job who knows that all 'he has' is not his possession but God's gift and what God gives God can take away. He also knows that this does not mean his relationship with God is over because it does not depend on whether or not one receives gifts. Hence he can say 'Blessed be the name of the Lord'.[6]

---

5. A number of commentators have described this as a wager between God and the satan over Job (cf for example 142–43 of Philip Yancey's, 'A Fresh Reading of the Book of Job', in *Sitting With Job. Selected Studies on the Book of Job*, edited by Roy B Zuck (Grand Rapids, MI: Baker, 1992), 141–50. Others, such as Edwin M Good, argue that the satan's prediction that 'he will curse you to your face' implies a self curse ('or else I will be cursed') as an unspoken consequence (*In Turns of Tempest: A Reading of Job, with a Translation* [Stanford, Calif: Stanford University Press, 1990], 194–95).

6. As is well recognised, there is a play on the Hebrew verb *barak* in the prologue; depending on the context it can mean bless (as in 1:21) or curse (as in 1:11). Thus

Job's second trial reduces him to nothing in another sense—covered in sores and an outcast on the ash heap.[7] In response to his wife who urges him to curse (*barak*) God and die, Job asks 'Shall we receive the good at the hand of God, and not receive the bad?' (2:10). As a rhetorical question it expects a positive answer. If Job's first response affirms that God has every right to take away what God gives, his second implied response would seem to be that we are not the arbiters of what God gives or takes away. Whatever it is we should accept it, trusting that God knows what God is doing.

Trusting or having faith in someone presumes a relationship based on some shared knowledge and experience. The prologue does not specify what this is for Job as a character in the book or the impact that his trials may have had on it. The reader is invited to fill the gaps. Thus, his experiences may have challenged his existing understanding, leading to a new or revised one and a deeper commitment to God. On this reading the trials function as a kind of revelation. Alternatively, Job may be hanging on to his existing knowledge (what one may call his 'piety') and struggling to relate the dissonant experiences to it. There may be a hint of this in his question in 2:10. In short Job's responses stimulate reflection in the reader about Job as a character, with the expectation that there will be more to come as the book unfolds. It is the nature of faith to seek understanding, particularly when challenged or troubled. Can a faith relationship be sustained when the search yields no results—is this another and perhaps even the ultimate form of fearing/revering God for nothing?

By being made privy to the debate in heaven between God and the satan, the reader is invited or challenged to reflect on God as a character in the prologue. God is clearly on Job's side and, it would appear, prepared to stake the divine reputation or status on the judgement that Job is 'blameless and upright'. Nevertheless God also allows the satan to afflict Job twice, the first being the destruction of his property and the death of his children, and the second a degrading disease. Is God's conduct blameless and upright and is this the kind of God in whom Job (or the reader) should place complete trust? One's

---

one could say that it will be a blessing for the satan if Job curses God because it will vindicate his judgement, but—following Good (cf preceding note)—it will be a curse for the satan if Job blesses God because it will vindicate God's judgement.

7. Cf Clines, *Job 1–20*, 50.

immediate response may be 'certainly not' but there are a number of factors that need to be taken into account. The first is that an extreme kind of test is needed to show that Job fears God 'for nothing'. The second is Israel's monotheistic belief that the one Lord of creation and history is in charge of all that takes place, otherwise another god is in charge or it is chaos. Both alternatives are unacceptable. The third is the modern critical judgement that this is story, not history, and that the plots of some biblical stories depict people who, in order to advance the plot, are treated by God or others in ways that appear offensive or unrealistic to modern eyes. In short, the background or 'flat' characters (Job's children) are portrayed in this story in a way that reflects its ancient Israelite and biblical context.[8]

The right kind of knowledge is essential for a relationship to be sustained and flourish; when it is not there questions arise that drive a search to fill the void. This is captured dramatically in Job's speech that initiates the dialogue with his friends. In 3:20 Job asks 'Why is light given to one in misery, and life to the bitter in soul' and in 3:23 'Why is light given to one who cannot see the way, whom God has fenced in'? Light in these verses means life.[9] Even though the terms 'misery' and 'bitter' allude to Job's physical plight the repeated question 'why' in 3:20 and 3:23 suggest that they are also to be taken as expressing his inability to 'see the way' and to a sense of being 'fenced in' by God. These refer to two things that appear contradictory in Job's eyes and cause him misery and bitterness. One is the meaninglessness of his life in his eyes. If Job's experience does not point to a relationship with God of some kind then life is not worth living because there is effectively no real life. As Job puts it in 3:11–19, it would be better not to have been born (cf also 6:8–10). The second is the question, why is God nevertheless keeping him alive in his miserable state? God must have some purpose or reason for doing so but Job does not or cannot know it. He likens this situation to being kept in prison (fenced in) or, in the terms of 7:17–19, of being under constant surveillance for no apparent reason.

---

8. On characterisation in biblical narrative, see Alter, *The Art of Biblical Narrative*, 114–30.
9. So Édouard Dhorme, *A Commentary on the Book of Job* (Nashville, Tn: Thomas Nelson, 1967), 37–38, and Clines, *Job 1–20*, 98–99.

The lengthy debate that ensues between Job and his friends has a common denominator. Both appeal for their explanations to experience, as one has to within this world. Eliphaz claims to have seen 'those who plow iniquity and sow trouble reap the same' (4:8). In other words, he has seen the act–consequence connection in action and thereby verified. Bildad invokes the authority of the tradition, the 'bygone generations' who reached the same conclusion (8:8). Job's affliction must therefore be God's just punishment for something that he or his children have done and is designed to bring him to repentance (8:1-7). Eliphaz informs him that his situation is not unique because no one can be righteous before God (cf his rhetorical question in 4:17). In short, Job's situation is part of the common lot of flawed humanity. But Eliphaz cannot of course prove his case; we are unable to monitor or assess all relevant phenomena and so our explanations are limited. The author(s) of the book may be implying that Eliphaz unwittingly admits as much: if humanity is flawed— no one is righteous before God—then it would seem to follow that our perception of things is flawed. From the reader's privileged perspective, the judgements made by Job's friends and Eliphaz are inadequate as explanations of Job's situation. Perhaps the implied message is that we need to be very cautious in making judgements from our limited human perspective.

Job rejects their explanation by also appealing to experience, firstly his own. According to his 'examination of conscience' he is innocent of any wrongdoing (6:30; 9:15-21). In terms of the reward-retribution doctrine as argued by his friends he should be blessed, not afflicted. He also supplies supportive evidence from the experience of the wider world. According to Job this shows that the innocent suffer while the wicked prosper (9:22-24; 21-24). On the basis of this how can his friends be so sure that because he is afflicted he is therefore guilty? It is God who is the guilty party for afflicting him unjustly. For the reader however Job is, so to speak, in the same boat as his friends. His limited perception means that he can no more disprove his friends' argument than prove his own. The reader knows from the prologue that God is Job's defender whereas it is the satan who is his adversary.

Nevertheless there is a difference between Job and his friends, namely his awareness of the limitations of argument. He can rebut his friends' argument but does this prove he is right? His appeal to God for a judgement about his case is a recognition of this limitation and an attempt to overcome it. Even though his own experience and his assessment of the experiences of others lead him to doubt that he will get a fair judgment (cf Job 9–10), it is the only court of appeal that can offer a perspective beyond the earthly one.[10] As well as this, Job's continued existence on this earth means that he is still in a relationship with God, however bewildering and painful it appears to him. Granted that God has some purpose in maintaining this relationship then Job has a right to know about it—otherwise it is not a real relationship. If he is guilty then he should know the charge; if he is innocent then he should know why he is afflicted. Can a relationship continue when one party is not in the know and the other does not communicate? In 13:3b he expresses his desire 'to argue my case with God' and, even though he fears he will be killed, 'I will defend my ways to his face' (13:15b). Armed with this resolve Job addresses God directly, appealing for permission to outline his case and then for God to reply (13:20-22).

A defendant in a lawsuit is unlikely to get far without reliable witnesses to back his or her case.[11] Job believes that he has a witness 'in heaven' (16:19) but the text leaves the reader unsure who this might be. Some commentators propose that it is God but, as Habel points out, Job envisages this witness as the kind who will arbitrate between a mortal (himself) and God. Habel himself favours an angelic figure such as the one that Elihu claims in 33:23 'declares a person upright' (*yashar*).[12] This is possible but Clines's proposal may be the better one, that it is not a person but rather the truth about Job. This 'witness' is already lodged in heaven and will testify for him should he die before being able to argue his case with God. Clines also thinks that this is the most likely meaning of the redeemer in whom Job places his hope for

---

10. Norman C Habel (and others) proposes that the arrangement of the book of Job reflects a legal metaphor replete with legal terminology, and with Job as the litigant (cf *The Book of Job. A Commentary* [OTL; London: SCM Press, 1985], 54–57). Whether one accepts this hypothesis or not, it is difficult to deny that the book draws, at least in part, on legal procedures.
11. According to Deut 17:6; 19:15 two or three witnesses are required; one is not sufficient for any case involving capital punishment (cf also Num 35:30).
12. Cf Habel, *The Book of Job*, 274–75.

final vindication in 19:25-27.[13] Given this is the case, God must know the truth about him. Why then does God not reply to Job's pleas? If God refuses to speak now it will be, in Job's eyes, a further sign that God is unjust and provides no scope for the petitioner. Despite this, according to 23:4-7, Job still hopes to find God and present his case, confident that an upright person—such as he believes he is—'could reason with him, and I should be acquitted forever by my judge' (23:7). In his final discourse in chapters 29-31 Job accuses God of being unjust towards him (30:20-23) and effectively challenges God to strike him if found guilty of any of the sins he names (31:1-34). Job is so confident of his innocence that if his adversary (God) were to write 'a book' about him Job would carry it proudly on his shoulder and 'bind it on me like a crown'. According to Habel this book would be 'a writ of release exonerating Job'.[14] According to Clines it would contain the charges God has against him, but Job is so confident they will appear trivial in comparison to his overall righteousness (cf 27:6) that he would be happy to parade them around as a trophy.[15] On this reading Job assumes that God's account of him will be at the very least close to his own self-assessment; to wit, God will act as Job expects a just judge should.

Job's final speech would seem to portray him almost as certain of his assessment of his situation as his friends are of their assessment. But of course he cannot be sure until God speaks. One also needs to keep in mind his doubts in earlier discourses about the hope of getting a just judgement from God. The friends have been chided by some commentators for speaking about God rather than to God and for their naïve certainty, in contrast to Job. They may be charged with defending a too mechanistic understanding of the reward-retribution doctrine but they are presented as honest brokers—as honest as Job— and with what they see as Job's best interests at heart.[16]

---

13. Cf Clines, *Job 1-20*, 389-90 and 457-60.
14. Cf Habel, *The Book of Job*, 439.
15. Cf Clines, *Job 1-20*, xliv.
16. Newsom has recently argued, against a number of commentators, in favour of a more positive portrayal of the friends in the book—cf *The Book of Job: A Context of Moral Imaginations* (New York: OUP, 2003), 96-127, and 'The Consolations of God: Assessing Job's Friends Across a Cultural Abyss', in *Reading from Right to Left*, edited by JC Exum and HGM Williamson (London/New York: Sheffield Academic Press), 347-58.

The differing perspectives between Job and his friends are reflected to some extent in the different uses of the term righteous/righteousness. Eliphaz asks in 4:17 'Can mortals be righteous before God' (cf also 15:14), and Bildad concludes the friends' discourses in 25:4 with the same question. In 9:2 Job appears to take up this question and answer it by appealing to his personal assessment that he is indeed righteous (9:15, 20), a conviction that he reasserts in 13:18 and describes in 27:6 as 'my righteousness'. Clearly, Job's notion of his righteousness does not tally with his friends' notion as indicated by Bildad's remark in 8:6.[17] The only way to resolve this is Job's proposal in 31:6 that he 'be weighed in a just balance, (literally 'scales of righteousness') and let God know my integrity'. Although Job is sure of his righteousness the verse reveals that he is willing to accept God's verdict and the consequences—this implies an admission or awareness that he cannot be the ultimate judge of his own case. The term rendered here as 'integrity' (*tummah*) carries the sense of being dedicated to the pursuit of the good in all circumstances.[18] The implication is that while Job's conviction about his righteousness is limited it has been made in all honesty—faith seeking authentic understanding. Although Job makes these confident assertions about his righteousness it is not until God has carried out the actual weighing and pronounced the verdict (cf the legal metaphor) that Job and the friends will know.

There is a third use of righteous/righteousness in the book—in relation to God. Bildad asks a leading question in 8:3, 'Does God pervert justice, or does the Almighty pervert righteousness'? As already noted, Job doubts that he can receive a fair judgement from God and even accuses God of being an unjust judge (cf 9:24; 12:17; 19:7; 21). Despite his misgivings and even terror at the prospect (23:15), in the end he is prepared to be weighed in the scales of righteousness by God and therefore judged. This is another indication that the book does not reject the reward–retribution doctrine, rather it questions our ability to prove or disprove the righteousness of God's judgements from within our limited human perspective. In relation to this point, the intervention of Elihu is significant. Like the reader

---

17. A literal translation is 'If you are pure and upright, he would now arouse himself for you and make sure the habitation of your righteousness'.
18. Cf Jenni/Westermann, *Theologisches Handwörterbuch*, II, 1047.

he is privy to the dialogues but only enters the fray after 'the words of Job are ended' (31:40b). He sums up his position by stating 'The Almighty—we cannot find him; he is great in power and justice, and abundant righteousness he will not violate' (37:23). This provides the expected answer to Bildad's rhetorical question in 8:3 but adds the important rider 'we cannot find him'. Human beings cannot 'find God' unless God reveals himself and his purpose. The location of Elihu's speech suggests that this statement serves both as a response to Job and the friends and as a lead in to God's speeches in chapters 38–41. Will these, the reader may well ask, reveal divine righteousness in a way that satisfies Job?

There are two speeches by God (38:1–39:40 and 40:6–41:34) and two replies by Job (40:2–5 and 42:1–6). There is also God's challenge to Job in 40:1 to respond to the first speech. Each of the speeches by God is in two sections. Job 38:1–38 is about the foundational elements of creation while 38:39–39:40 depicts a series of wild and powerful animals. Job 40:6–14 is about the wicked and the proud of the earth while 40:15–41:34 celebrates the two great beasts Behemoth (40:15–24) and Leviathan (41:1–34). The speeches are permeated by questions and Job's replies presumably are meant to relate to these.

God's speeches are clearly a response to Job's insistence on a trial in which he can argue his case before God (cf chapter 13). God gives Job the opportunity to do so but not before the divinity's case (defense) has been outlined. This takes place in two steps. In the first God accuses Job in 38:2 that he has 'darkened counsel (*'etsah*) by words without knowledge'. Job's version of how God governs creation, though honest, is neither complete nor accurate. God then presents the divine case for good governance of creation by parading two forms of incontrovertible evidence before Job (and the reader). The first (38:4–38) portrays God as the only one who has the power to establish all the elements of creation in their right order to perform their designated functions. Furthermore, God alone is able to use elements or powers in creation to right wrongs and punish the wicked—cf 38:12–15, 22–23.[19] This issue is resumed in a more intense

---

19. GR Driver argued that the references to the 'wicked' in 38:13, 15 are veiled allusions to stars and constellations (cited with approval by Clines, *Job 38–42* [WBC 19; Dallas, Tx: Word Books, 2010], 1103–4). Whether or not this is the case is difficult to establish but there can be little doubt that 38:22–23 refers

and challenging way in 40:6–14. If the first kind of evidence is on the cosmic scale the second kind focuses on detail, specifically wild and powerful animals that are effectively beyond human control. Human beings do not have the power or knowledge to control these animals but God does; they are all embraced within God's care of creation. This issue is resumed in 40:15–41:34 with even more dramatic and challenging evidence from the animal world, namely Behemoth and Leviathan.

The catalyst for the second set of speeches is Job's reply to the first set in 40:3–5. Dhorme underestimates its function in the drama by stating that 'Job alone stammers out a few words of humility'.[20] More sensitive to the context is Habel who states that here 'Job does not retract his position, but neither does he renew his earlier challenge'.[21] His complaint that he is a righteous man who has been unjustly treated by God still stands. In his eyes it has not been satisfactorily answered. This prompts a key question from God in 40:8, a literal rendering being 'Will you indeed annul my justice/judgement (*mishpati*), will you condemn me so that you may be righteous (*titsdaq*)?' In short, if Job believes that he is righteous and God is not then he should be able to take God's place as universal judge; he is invited to do so in the rather sarcastic section that follows in 40:10–14. These verses also point out that if Job is going to take God's place as judge then he will not only need the requisite knowledge but also the power over creation to execute his judgements against the proud and wicked. Job may believe he is righteous but as a creature he cannot be the source of universal righteousness or right order in creation. Given that God is this source how can Job claim that he himself is righteous yet accuse God, the source of it, of not being so? Furthermore, as God's question in 40:1 implies, any litigation process that is unable to sift all the evidence cannot judge that God is bad. The inability of Job (and any human being) to judge God prompts the reader to recall the prologue where God judges Job justly and rightly, whereas

---

to God wielding the forces of nature to remove evil (cf Josh 10:11) and so re-establish right order among nations and in creation.
20. Dhorme, *Job*, xiv.
21. Habel, *The Book of Job*, 549. He further notes 'By clapping his hands to his mouth (v. 4b), Job not only cuts off any further claim or refutation on his part (cf. 29:9) but also expresses his amazement at the way Yahweh has responded (cf. 21:5)'.

the 'creature' in the heavenly court, the satan, does not. Job's inability to know creation let alone have any power to order it is further demonstrated by the graphic depiction of Behemoth and Leviathan that follows in 40:15–41:34. Despite their enormous size and power they, just like Job, (40:15) have been created by God and are under God's providential care.

Some commentators think God's speeches set out to demolish the doctrine of reward and retribution as an integral part of God's governance of creation.[22] As a critique of the friends' rather mechanistic application of it this may be true, but one needs to avoid separating the natural or amoral order and the moral order. Against it there is the evidence of 38:12–15, 22–23 that locates the fate of the wicked and the 'day of battle and war' within God's governance of creation. Within the larger context of the HBOT, the analysis of divine righteousness so far has found a strong connection between the natural or created order and the moral order. God's purpose is to establish universal world order and this involves eliminating the evil that human beings do. Leviticus warns that God will withhold the produce of the land from sinful Israel and ultimately expel it so that the land can 'enjoy its sabbath years' and thereby recover from the damaging impact of Israel's transgressions (cf 26:14–35). Furthermore, as Newsom points out, ancient societies in general 'did not distinguish sharply between the realms of the natural order and moral order.'[23]

Job's second reply in 42:1–6 is one of the most debated passages in the book. The *ketiv* (you know)/*qere'* (I know) in v 2 and some difficult Hebrew syntax in v 6 have led to a variety of proposed translations/interpretations; these range from the negative (Job remains unrepentant and hostile to God), to the ambiguous (its meaning is perhaps deliberately left open ended), to the positive (Job repents of his former hostile position).[24] While 42:1–6 in itself may

---

22. See E Greenstein, 'In Job's Face/Facing Job', 311–12 in *The Labour of Reading. Desire, Alienation and Biblical Interpretation,* edited by FC Black, R Boer, and E Runions (Atlanta: Society of Biblical Literature, 1999), 310–17; Matitiahu Tsevat, 'The Meaning of the Book of Job', 211–13 in *Sitting with Job*, 189–218.
23. Newsom, 'Re-considering Job', 170.
24. For a recent survey see Newsom, 'Reconsidering Job', 171–73, and 18–22 of Campbell, 'The Book of Job: Two Questions, One Answer', *AusBR* 51 (2003): 15–25.

be able to sustain a negative translation it does not sit well with the following verse in which God informs the friends that 'you have not spoken of me what is right, as my servant Job has done'. If 42:3-4 establishes clear links—via quotations—with the preceding context then it is reasonable to expect that 42:6 prepares, at least in part, for what follows.[25]

On the basis of this reading one can make the following comments. The first is in relation to the dialogue between Job and his friends. The doctrine of reward and retribution is not dismissed because it is an integral part of God's righteous governance of creation. However, the human being can only monitor creation in a limited way and therefore any formulations about how God's governance works are bound to be inadequate. This applies both to the friends' mechanistic view of how reward and retribution works and to Job's charge that it doesn't work. There is nothing new in this of course, it is the same appeal to the difference between creator and creature, the mystery that is God, that recurs throughout the HBOT. Nevertheless, one can also say that Job has grown in knowledge. Even though God censures him for darkening 'counsel by words without knowledge' he is not accused of any sin for which his affliction is the punishment. Is this an endorsement of the doctrine that, when all else fails, one must follow one's conscience and in doing so one is in the right (cf 27:6 'I hold fast my righteousness, and will not let it go')? God's personal appearance and address to Job also confirm that he is, in some sense at least, in a right relationship with God and that this must have a purpose. Unlike his previous demands to have an explanation of his sufferings, Job is now prepared to wait on God for that purpose to be revealed.[26] Faith in the Other has trumped the desire for personal satisfaction (the

---

25. Job 42:3 refers to the commencement of God's reply in 38:2, while 42:4 refers to it (quoting 38:3b) as well as to the commencement of the second speech (quoting 40:7b).
26. In his first volume on Job, Clines (*Job 1–20*, xlvi) translates 42:6 as 'Therefore I melt in reverence before you, and I have received my comfort, even while sitting in dust and ashes'. The third and final volume contains a more succinct version, 'So, I submit, and I accept consolation for my dust and ashes' (*Job 38–42*, 1205). EJ van Wolde has something similar 'Therefore I turn away from/repudiate and comfort myself/repent of dust and ashes' (250 of 'Job 42:1-6: The Reversal of Job', in *The Book of Job,* edited by WAM Beuken [BETL 114 Leuven: Leuven University/Peeters, 1995], 223–50).

explanation). In terms of the plot of the book, the divine purpose can be said to be revealed in 42:7 where God designates Job as the one to intercede for his friends, which he readily does.

The second comment is in relation to the Prologue. After all the questioning in the dialogues and God's replies is Job any the wiser about why disaster struck him? God does not tell him the reason for it, perhaps because to do so would eliminate or compromise the separation between heaven and earth that is an essential element of the plot of the story. All literary forms are limited, enabling us to be creative but also imposing limitations. The author(s) of Job recognise the limitation imposed by the storyline but overcome it to an extent via the clever ploy of providing the reader access to the debate in the heavenly court. He or she is invited to consider whether the test that proves God's judgement of Job (the human being) is right is worth the cost. To put it another way, is the most important role or function of the human being to stay loyal to God no matter what the cost? While the reader is invited to consider such things, another function of this literary ploy is to remind the reader that this is not reality. In reality, one is always operating from the earthly perspective of Job and his friends.

Another question one may ask is whether God's speeches would or should change Job's responses to the disasters that struck him in the Prologue. His response to the first is to acknowledge that all he has is gifted by God, and what God gives God can take away; his response to the second is to ask his wife that if we accept good from God, should we not also accept evil. The gifts that God takes away are the evil to which Job refers in his question to his wife. Perhaps an implication is that one needs to believe that what God takes away from a loyal servant, which is experienced as an evil, is for a good purpose that cannot be probed from an earthly perspective, but a purpose that is an integral part of God's righteous purpose in creation.

Can one describe the book of Job as a theodicy? If by theodicy one understands the defense of God's justice mounted by the friends the answer is of course negative. What the book does is assert, in particular via the speeches in chapters 38–41, that God is righteous and just in a way that is beyond human comprehension. Even though we only come to know God through personal experience or the experience of others, all such knowledge is limited. The creature cannot know the creator as the creator knows the creature. One believes God is righteous, one cannot prove that this is so. While some commentators hold that Job (and Ecclesiastes) mount a trenchant critique of the theology of wisdom espoused in Proverbs, this is true only in part. There are texts in Proverbs that show an awareness of limitations in the search for wisdom. Proverbs 27:1 advises 'Do not boast about tomorrow, for you do not know what a day may bring'; while 21:30 asserts that 'No wisdom, no understanding, no counsel, can avail against the Lord'.[27]

---

27. Cf Birch, *Let Justice Roll Down*, 339–40.

Concluding Remarks

Like most investigations this one began '*in medias res*', that is, within an already established context of scholarly analysis of righteousness and associated terminology. As pointed out in the Preface recent studies of the term *tsedeq/tsedaqah* favour the view that it refers primarily to right order in relationships; the judicial or legal usage of the terminology is an application of this more basic meaning. Although the term is employed in relation to the covenant with Israel, Schmid and others argue that this operates within the larger context of biblical creation theology. Creation and salvation are not separate entities in the HBOT; God's saving deeds are an integral part of the divine purpose to bring creation to its fulfilment. Right world order is a key manifestation of righteousness that has its origins in and is dependent on divine righteousness—God's right relationship with creation.

The findings of this study endorse this viewpoint; they also support the view of Barton outlined in the Introduction that history is an integral aspect of the biblical view of creation. The history or, perhaps better, story of creation—expressed in a limited, or perhaps selective way in the biblical narrative—is an integral part of God's saving purpose for creation. The 'theology of history' or salvation history identified by von Rad could be reconceptualised in this sense.[1]

Although the HBOT's understanding of righteousness and related terminology no doubt grew out of individual and community experience and was subsequently applied to the divinity, within the canonical context divine righteousness is presented as the foundation and model of all other instances of righteousness or right relationships.

---

1. Cf von Rad, *Old Testament Theology*, volume 1, 106.

Without this foundation how can one, within the context of biblical faith, speak of or assess human righteousness? Given that the Torah is the foundational revelatory document in the HBOT, one would expect to find there the authoritative teaching about divine righteousness. In my judgement however, this does not seem to have been the primary focus of recent studies of righteousness; instead attention has been directed more to Prophecy and the Writings. A likely reason for this is the far more numerous occurrences of the term in these parts of the canon than in the Torah. This study differs to a significant degree from preceding ones by focusing on the Torah.

I have argued that there are several factors that support this approach. One is the already mentioned status of the Torah as the foundational document of the HBOT. A second is the strategic location in the Torah narrative of a number of references to divine righteousness; a key one being Deuteronomy 32:4 which sums up its description of God and all God's ways as righteous (*tsadiq*) and upright (*yashar*). The song of Deuteronomy 32 is to serve as a witness against the people when they are disloyal to the terms of the covenant relationship; the song prophesies that this will inevitably be the case at some stage or stages in the future. As witness the song also testifies accurately to the righteous and upright conduct of God in relation to Israel as presented in the preceding Torah narrative. Deuteronomy 32:4 provides a kind of key to reading the way God is presented in the Torah.

A third factor is the narrative form of the Torah: it tells its story of creation and humanity. A story unfolds a relationship or a series of relationships between its key characters; given that righteousness refers to right order in relationships then the storyline of the Torah provides an appropriate context for unfolding its teaching about righteousness. Given also that God is the key character in the Torah, it can be read as the unfolding of an intricate web of relationships—between God and creation, between God and Israel (both as community and as individuals), between God and the nations, between Israel and the nations, between Israel and creation (the land), and between selected Israelite figures (the ancestors, Moses, etc). The purpose of the Torah storyline is to teach or reveal how God responds to disorder and evil that human beings unleash in creation and how God sets about restoring right relationships or righteousness in all the areas in which it is damaged by sin and disobedience.

As is well recognised, the narrative or story form is a very effective way of teaching or instructing, of doing Torah. Recent studies of biblical narrative have drawn attention to its 'art of reticence', its preference for communicating meaning by implication and allusion rather than by direct and explicit statements. This feature helps to explain why the Torah does not contain numerous references to righteousness and associated terminology, yet is able to present its understanding of them in the way the storyline unfolds.

The story form normally deals with individual characters or a people or community as 'a' character in the story. This enables the Torah to develop another important aspect of righteousness—its dynamic power. The righteousness of one (for example, Noah, Abraham, Moses, the one people of Israel) can bring salvation to the many. That is, it brings right order into the lives of the many—according to the HBOT, this is the only 'real life'. Because all righteousness stems from God, the righteousness of the one touching the many provides a teaching (and a revelation) of how the righteousness of the one God of Israel touches all. It is another way of expressing the relationship between the transcendent and the immanent.

A number of narrative examples of the Torah's teaching on divine righteousness have been explored in the study, with particular attention given to the story of the golden calf apostasy in Exodus chapters 32–34 and the spy story in Numbers 14. What is instructive about these two examples is the different ways in which they distribute divine justice and mercy, reward and punishment. Granted that they are indicative of how the Torah operates, one could say that it does not seek so much to justify or argue for God's righteousness in the way the 'consequences' of good and bad conduct are distributed as to claim that each instance is an example of divine righteousness in action. The righteous God alone is able to decree what is right in each instance and, according to the text's claim, each is in accord with the 'code of divine conduct' or 'template' text of Exodus 20:5b–6 (cf also Deut 5:9b–10).

One has a sense here of biblical authors proclaiming their faith in God and God's ways that cannot be satisfactorily explained in human terms. There are gaps and questions remain. If this is the case there may be a link here with the unanswered questions of the books of Job and Ecclesiastes, and the challenge to maintain faith despite the frustration, pain and even anger that these can cause.

The Torah's teaching on divine righteousness has also been explored in a selection of texts in the Former Prophets/Historical Books. The story of Israel's conquest of the land showcases God's unswerving commitment (*khesedh* or steadfast love) to the goal of establishing right order in creation (the land). If Israel lives in the land according to the terms of the covenant it will be a primary sign and mediator of divine righteousness. But, as the subsequent story unfolds, the infidelity of Israel and its leaders leads ultimately to the loss of the land. Paradoxically, Israel's exile from the land also serves as a sign of God's right relationship with creation and the nations. In keeping with what is proclaimed in the Torah (cf Deut 29:10-28), the land will be purged of the wicked generation, but the 'next generation' as well as the surrounding nations will see this as a sign of God's righteous purpose.

By the same token, texts such as the above one in Deuteronomy signal that God will punish but not abandon Israel. This would contradict the Torah's theology of the divine purpose to establish right relationships with all of humanity and creation. Hence there is the assurance of a 'next generation' that will have a correct perspective on things; the template for this being the dramatic passage from the failed 'exodus generation' to the successful 'conquest generation' in the Torah. Much the same can be said for the Davidic dynasty. As pointed out in the chapter on the Former Prophets, God's relationship with Israel and the Davidic dynasty, as expressed in the respective texts in the Torah and Samuel–Kings, is unconditional. Hence, although the narrative ends with nation and king in exile, this is not the final chapter of their story—the realisation of God's righteous purpose is still in train.

What Israel's role is to be in this is spelled out in various passages in the books of the Latter or Writing Prophets. These books form an integral part of the story of Israel by the way they proclaim and apply the Torah, by the superscription which links a particular book to a point or points in the storyline of the Former Prophets (for example, Isa 1:1), and by information within the books themselves. The study focused on the book of Isaiah because it is here that one finds the most occurrences in any prophetic book of righteousness and associated terminology, and a treatment of these in relation to God's purpose or plan (*'etsah*) for all of creation. The dominant poetic form of books such as Isaiah allows for greater flexibility in the use of theological terminology and imagery. The meaning of righteousness and its relationship to other terms can be presented in a way that is not really possible in the story form with its commitment to unfolding a plot via the interaction of key characters.

The book of Isaiah unfolds a vision of the realisation of God's purpose that involves a purge of the people and the polluted city of Zion. This is the necessary prelude to a reshaping of creation in order to provide a highway for the nations to come and worship with Israel on Zion, God's holy mountain, and there to learn the way of the Torah (cf Isa 2:1-4; 19:23-25; 25:6-10; 66:22-23). As the goal of this universal pilgrimage, Zion will be established 'as the highest of the mountains'. The book of Isaiah employs the terms righteousness and justice in particular in relation to right social conduct—a sign of a right relationship with God. According to the opening verses of the book (1:2-3) God has established this relationship for the welfare of the children (Israel) and cannot therefore tolerate its abuse by the children. In keeping with the Torah, God's relationship with Israel is part of God's universal purpose for humanity and creation; hence its abuse distorts not only Israel's but the nations' perception of God and God's purpose. It also pollutes Zion, the locus of the divine presence on earth. The book announces God's resolve to purge people and city and restore social justice. The purge involves exile of the people from the land until such time God decrees their return—as a people once more in a right relationship with their 'creator'.

This of course can only take place on God's initiative; it is a saving act and, as was noted in the analysis of the so-called 'Second Isaiah' in 40-55, is signalled by the combination of the terms righteousness and salvation. The final chapters of the vision that is the book of Isaiah (56-66) proclaim that the people—and all human beings—will fail to maintain what God initiates. Despite this, and once more in keeping with the Torah, God does not fail the chosen people and shows steadfast love/loyalty to Israel and humanity. The book ends with the assurance that God's plan to establish universal righteousness or right order will triumph (66:22-23), but accompanying this is the sobering note that this will, as it must within the theology of a righteous God, involve the ongoing purge of evil (66:24).

My limited analysis of righteousness and associated terminology in the Psalter led me to concur with McCann's conclusion, which can be restated here:

> the Psalter encourages the reader to understand justice and righteousness less in terms of specific distributive/retributive acts and more in terms of a harmonious world order characterized by the creation and sustenance of conditions that make life possible for all, especially for the poor and needy.[2]

One can see in this statement the close relationship between creation and salvation that McCann discerns in the Psalter's understanding of righteousness. It professes the conviction that God's righteous actions are at once transcendent and immanent: the establishment of universal world order touches each and everyone, especially those most in need of deliverance from the disorder caused by human sin—the poor and the needy.

Consideration of the book of Job provided an opportunity for some limited reflections on the question of theodicy—the defence of God as just in the face of (perceived) evil experiences. Job asks the theodicy questions in 3:20, 23, 'Why is light given to one in misery, and life to the bitter in soul... Why is light given to one who cannot see the way, whom God has fenced in'? In my judgement the book argues that we cannot mount a satisfactory defence of God as righteous and just from our earthly perspective, even one that is enhanced by God's word. In order to pronounce definitively on this question, we would need to see all of creation and its intricate web of relationships from the perspective of the one who creates and sustains it, and the rhetorical questions that permeate the speeches of God in Job 38 – 41 effectively state that this is not available to us. Moreover, our human words would need to be able to express fully the content of the divine word and this is also not possible.

In a telling ironic touch the author(s) of Job 'create' a privileged reader's perspective on the dialogues between the players in the story, especially God and Job, in order to point out that, in reality, we do

---

2. McCann, 'Righteousness, Justice and Peace', 121.

not enjoy such a perspective. We are on earth alongside Job and, in the end, are challenged to echo his replies in 40:3-5 and 42:1-6 or reject them. Despite the uncertain and disputed meaning of the latter, God's statement to the friends in 42:7 ('you have not spoken of me what is right, as my servant Job has') would suggest that it is to be read in a positive rather than a negative sense. That is, Job is prepared to trust that God is righteous and trustworthy even though God does not provide a direct answer to his bitter questions.[3] According to 42:7, and indeed the whole HBOT, this is the right response to make, no matter how bad experience may be and how frustrating our limited human perspective. If one denies righteousness and justice to God, the source of all life, then how can one speak in any sense of human righteousness and justice?

Given the scope and diversity of the HBOT it is difficult and even dangerous to try and sum up its understanding of divine righteousness and its relationship to what is regarded as associated terminology. Nevertheless, I would like to end this study with an attempt to do so, with apologies for some inevitable inadequacy and incompleteness.

Righteousness (*tsedeq/tsedaqah*) may be described as that attribute of the divinity that establishes right (ordered) relationships with all aspects of creation. God's steadfast love or loyalty (*khesedh*) is God's unswerving resolve to do this, despite the disloyalty of human beings in particular and the chaos and disorder they unleash. God's faithfulness/truth (*'emet/'emunah*) ensures that all God's words and actions are reliable and trustworthy. The righteous God executes justice (*mishpat*) by bringing ' evildoers to account and by delivering those unjustly oppressed from affliction. God's punishment of evildoers is designed to stop the chaos and disorder that their actions unleash and to manifest divine sovereignty over all aspects of creation and history. Such punishments also serve as an instruction for the evildoers and/or those who witness their judgement and punishment. God is gracious (*khanan*) to those who are loyal and merciful (*rakham/rakhamim*) to those who sin yet repent, as well as to those who are oppressed and denied right relationships within the

---

3. As Campbell states 'An answer is not given to the question at the core of the second theme' (that is, 3:20). 'Job 42:6 puts an end to the discussion' ('The Book of Job', 25).

community. God's judgments against evildoers and in favour of the oppressed are necessary steps on the way to the restoration of right relationships that, because they originate with God, are dynamic and life giving.[4]

---

4. Readers may like to compare this with Walter Brueggemann's summary in his *Theology of the Old Testament. Testimony, Dispute, Advocacy* (Minneapolis: Fortress Press, 1997), 303; 'Yahwel's righteousness entails governance of the world according to Yahwel's purposes, which are decreed at Sinai and which are assured in the very fabric of creation. The substance of that righteousness is the well-being of the world, so that when Yahweh's righteousness (Yahweh's governance) is fully established in the world, the results are fruitfulnss, prosperity, freedom, justice, peace, security, and well-being (*shalom*)'.

Bibliography of Works Cited

Aberbach, M and L Smolar, 'The Golden Calf Episode in Postbiblical Literature,' *HUCA* 39 (1968): 91–116.

Achenbach, Reinhard, 'The Pentateuch, the Prophets, and the Torah in the Fifth and Fourth Centuries B.C.E.' in *Judah and the Judeans in the Fourth Century B.C.E.*, edited by Oded Lipschits, Gary N Knoppers and Rainer Albertz (Winona Lake: Eisenbrauns, 2007), 253–85.

Adam, Klaus-Peter, 'Saul as a Tragic Hero: Greek Drama and Its Influence on Hebrew Scripture in 1 Samuel 14,26–46 (10,8; 13,7–13a; 10,17–27),' in *For and Against David. Story and History in the Books of Samuel*, edited by A Graeme Auld and Erik Eynikel (BETL 232; Leuven: Peeters, 2010), 123–83.

Amser, Samuel, 'Les documents de la loi et la formation du Pentateuque,' in *Le Pentateuque en question. Les origins et la composition des cinq premiers livres de la Bible à la lumiere des recherches récentes*, edited by Albert de Pury (Le Monde de la Bible; Geneva: Labor et Fides, 1989), 235–57.

Andersen, FI and DN Freedman, *Hosea* (AB 24; New York: Doubleday, 1980).

Arnold, Bill T, *Genesis* (NCBC; Cambridge: Cambridge University Press, 2009).

Alter, Robert, *The Art of Biblical Narrative* (New York: Basic Books 1981).

Auld, A Graeme, *I & II Samuel. A Commentary* (OTL: Louisville: WJK, 2011).

Aurelius, Erik, *Der Fürbitter Israels. Eine Studie zum Mosebild im Alten Testament* (CB 27; Stockholm: Almqvist & Wiksell, 1988).

Baden, Joel S, *The Composition of the Pentateuch. Renewing the Documentary Hypothesis* (New Haven & London: Yale University Press, 2012).

Bailey, Randall C, *David in Love and War. The Pursuit of Power in 2 Samuel 1–12* (JSOTSup 75; Sheffield: JSOT Press, 1990).

Barker, Paul A, *The Triumph of Grace in Deuteronomy* (Paternoster Biblical Monographs; Carlisle, UK/Waynesboro, GA: Paternoster Press, 2004).

Barr, James, *The Semantics of Biblical Language* (Oxford: Oxford University Press, 1961).

Barr, James, *Comparative Philology and the Text of the Old* Testament (Oxford: Clarendon Press, 1968).

Barr, James, *The Concept of Biblical Theology. An Old Testament Perspective* (Minneapolis: Fortress Press, 1999).

Barton, John, *Oracles of God: Perceptions of Prophecy in Israel after the Exile* (London: Darton, Longman & Todd, 1986).

Barton, John, *Ethics and the Old Testament* (London: SCM Press, 1998).

Barton, John, *Reading the Old Testament. Method in Biblical Study* (second edition, London: Darton, Longman and Todd, 1996).

Begg, Christopher, 'The Destruction of the Calf (Exod 32,20/Deut 9,21)', in *Das Deuteronomium: Entstehung, Gestalt und Botschaft: Deuteronomy: Origin, Form and Message*, edited by Norbert Lohfink (BETL 68; Levuen: University Press, 1985), 208–51.

Ben Zvi, Ehud, *Hosea* (FOTL XXIA/1; Grand Rapids, Mich.; Eerdmans, 2005).

Berman, Joshua A, *Created Equal. How the Bible Broke with Ancient Political Thought* (Oxford: Oxford University Press, 2008).

Birch, Bruce C, *Let Justice Roll Down: The Old Testament Ethics, and Christian Life* (Louisville, Ky: Westminster/John Knox, 1991).

Birch, Bruce C, 'The First and Second Books of Samuel. Introduction,

Commentary, and Reflections', in *The New Interpreter's Bible, Volume Two* (Nashville; Abingdon, 1998), 947-1383.

Blenkinsopp, Joseph, *Isaiah 40-66: A New Translation with Introduction and Commentary* (AB 19A; New York: Doubleday, 2002).

Blenkinsopp, Joseph, *Creation, Un-creation, Re-Creation: a discursive commentary on Genesis 1-11* (London/New York: T&T Clark, 2011).

Blum, Erhard, 'The Literary Connection Between the Books of Genesis and Exodus and the End of the Book of Johsua', in *A Farewell to the Yahwist? The Composition of the Pentateuch in Recent European Interpretation*, edited by Thomas B Dozeman and Konrad Schmid (SBL Symposium Series 34; Atlanta: SBL, 2006), 89-106.

Bolin, Thomas M, 'The Role of Exchange in Ancient Mediterranean Religion and Its Implications for Reading Genesis 18-19*,' *JSOT* 29.1 (2004): 37-56.

Booker, Christopher, *The Seven Basic Plots. Why We Tell Stories* (London: Continuum, 2004).

Boorer, Suzanne, 'The Earth/Land ('eretz) in the Priestly Material: The Preservation of the "Good" Earth and the Promised Land of Canaan Throughout the Generations', *AusBR* 49 (2001): 19-33

Brueggemann, Walter, *First and Second Samuel* (Interpretation; Louisville: Westminster John Knox, 1990).

Brueggemann, Walter, *Theology of the Old Testament. Testimony, Dispute, Advocacy* (Minneapolis: Fortress Press, 1997).

Brueggemann, Walter, *Deuteronomy* (Abingdon Old Testament Commentaries; Nashville: Abingdon, 2001).

Campbell, Antony F and Mark A O'Brien, *Sources of the Pentateuch. Texts, Introductions, Annotations* (Minneapolis: Fortress Press, 1993).

Campbell, Antony F and Mark A O'Brien, *Unfolding the Deuteronomistic History: Origins, Upgrades, Present Text* (Minneapolis: Fortress Press, 2000).

Campbell, Antony F, 'The Storyteller's Role: Reported Story and Biblical Text,' *CBQ* 64 (2002): 427-41.

Campbell, Antony F, 'The Book of Job: Two Questions, One Answer,' *AusBR* 51 (2003): 15-25.

Campbell, Antony F, *1 Samuel* (FOTL VII; Grand Rapids/Cambridge: Eerdmans, 2003).

Campbell, Antony F, *2 Samuel* (FOTL VIII; Grand Rapids, MI: Eerdmans, 2005).

Campbell, Antony, F, *Making Sense of the Bible. Difficult Texts and Modern Faith* (New York; Mahwah, NJ: Paulist Press, 2010).

Carr, David M, 'Reaching for Unity in Isaiah,' in *The Prophets*, edited by Philip R Davies (The Biblical Seminar 42; Sheffield: Sheffield Academic Press, 1996), 164–83.

Childs, Brevard S, *The Book of Exodus. A Critical Theological Commentary* (OTL; Philadelphia: Westminster, 1974).

Childs, Brevard S, *Introduction to the Old Testament as Scripture* (Philadelphia: Fortress Press, 1979).

Christensen, Duane, *Deuteronomy 21:10–34:12* (Word Bible Commentary; Nashville: Thomas Nelson Publishers, 2002).

Clines, David JA, *Job 1–20* (WBC 17; Dallas, Tx: Word Books, 1989).

Clines, David JA, *Job 38–42* (WBC 19; Dallas, Tx: Word Books, 2010).

Cole, Robert L, *The Shape and Message of Book III (Psalms 73–89)* (JSOTSup 307; Sheffield: Sheffield Academic Press, 2000).

Conrad, Edgar W, *Reading the Latter Prophets* (JSOTSup 376; London/New York: T&T Clark International, 2003).

Cotter, David, W, *Genesis* (Berit OLman; Collegeville: Liturgical Press, 2003).

Craigie, Peter C, Page H Kelley, Joel F Drinkard, Jr, *Jeremiah 1–25* (WBC 26; Dallas, Texas: Word Books, 1991).

Creach, Jerome F D *The Destiny of the Righteous in the Psalms* (St Louis: Chalice, 2008).

Crenshaw, James L, *Defending God. Biblical Responses to the Problem of Evil* (Oxford: OUP, 2005).

Dearman, J Andrew, *The Book of Hosea* (NICOT; Grand Rapids Mich.; Eerdmans, 2010).

Dhorme, Édouard, *A Commentary on the Book of Job* (Nashville, Tn: Thomas Nelson, 1967).

Di Lella, Alexander A, *The Wisdom of Ben Sira. A New Translation with Notes By Patrick W. Skehan. Introduction and Commentary by Alexander A. Di Lella, O.F.M.* (AB 39; New York: Doubleday, 1987).

Douglas, Mary, *Purity and Danger* (London: Routledge & Kegan Paul, 1966).

Douglas, Mary, *Leviticus as Literature* (Oxford: Oxford University Press, 1999).

Dozeman, Thomas B, *Commentary on Exodus* (Eerdmans Critical Commentary; Grand Rapids MI: Eerdmans, 2009).

Duncker, Christina, *Der andere Salomo. Eine synchrone Untersuchung zur Ironie in der Salomo-Komposition 1 Könige 1-11* (Frankfurt: Peter Lang, 2010).

Earl, Douglas S, *Reading Joshua as Christian Scripture* (Journal of Theological Interpretation Supplements 2; Winona Lake, Ind: Eisenbrauns 2010).

Fischer, Georg, *Jeremia 1-25* (HThKAT; Freiburg im Breisgau: Herder, 2005).

Fishbane, Michael, *Biblical Interpretation in Ancient Israel* (Oxford: OUP, 1985).

Franz, Matthias, *Der barmherzige und gnädige Gott. Die Gnadenrede vom Sinai (Exodus 34, 6-7) und ihre Parallelen im Alten Testament und seiner Umwelt* (BWANT 160; Stuttgart: Kohlammer, 2003).

Frolov, Serge, *The Turn of the Cycle. 1 Samuel 1-8 in Synchronic and Diachronic Perspectives* (BZAW 342; Berlin/New York: Walter de Gruyter, 2004).

García López, F, 'La place du Lévitique et des Nombres dans la formation du Pentateuque,' in *The Books of Leviticus and Numbers*. Edited by Thomas Römer (BETL 215 (Leuven; Dudley, MA: Peeters, 2008), 75-98.

Gerstenberger, Erhard S, *Psalms: Part 1: With an Introduction to Cultic Poetry* (FOTL XIV; Grand Rapids, Mich: Eerdmans, 1988).

Gerstenberger, Erhard S, *Psalms: Part 2, and Lamentations* (FOTL XV; Grand Rapids/Cambridge: Eerdmans, 2001).

Goldingay, John, *Psalms. Volume 1: Psalms 1–41* (Baker Commentary on the Old Testament Wisdom and Psalms; Grand Rapids, Mich: Baker Academic, 2006).

Goldingay, John and David Payne, *Isaiah 40–55 Volume II; A Critical and Exegetical Commentary* (International Commentary on the Holy Scriptures of the Old and New Testaments; London: T&T Clark, 2006).

Good, Edwin M, *In Turns of Tempest: A Reading of Job, with a Translation* (Stanford, Calif: Stanford University Press, 1990).

Gordon, R P, *I & II Samuel* (Exeter: Paternoster, 1986).

Gossai, Hemchand, *Justice, Righteousness, and the Social Critique of the Eighth Century Prophets* (American University Studies, Series VII; Theology and Religion, 141; New York: Peter Lang, 1993).

Goswell, Greg, 'The Order of the Books in the Hebrew Bible,' *JETS* 51/4 (2008): 763–88

Grant-Henderson, AL, *Inclusive Voices in Post-Exilic Judah* (Minnesota: The Liturgical Press, 2002).

Graesser, Carl Jr, 'Righteousness, Human and Divine,' *Currents in Theology and Mission* 10 (1983): 134–41.

Greenberg, Moshe, *Ezekiel 21–37* (AB22A; New York: Doubleday, 1997).

Greenstein, Edward L, 'In Job's Face/Facing Job,' in *The Labour of Reading. Desire, Alienation and Biblical Interpretation*, edited by FC Black, R Boer, and E Runions (Atlanta: Society of Biblical Literature, 1999), 310–17.

Gunkel, Hermann, *Introduction to Psalms: The Genres of the Religious Lyric of Israel* (completed by Joachim Begrich; translated by James D Nogalksi; Macon Ga; Mercer University Press, 1998).

Gunn, David N, 'Narrative Criticism', in *To Each Its Own Meaning. An Introduction to Biblical Criticisms and Their Application*, edited by Steven L McKenzie and Stephen R Haynes (Louisville, Ky: Westminster/John Knox, 1993), 171–95.

Habel, Norman C, *The Book of Job. A Commentary* (OTL; London: SCM Press, 1985).

Heschel, Abraham J, *Heavenly Torah As Refracted through the Generations* (London: Continuum, 2005).

Ho, Ahuva, *Tsedeq and Tsedaqah in the Hebrew Bible* (American University Studies Series VII, Theology and Religion 78; New York: Peter Lang, 1991).

Holladay, William J, *Jeremiah 1. A Commentary on the Book of the Prophet Jeremiah Chapters 1–25* (Hermeneia; Philadelphia: Fortress Press, 1986).

House, Paul R, 'The Character of God in the Book of the Twelve,' in *Reading and Hearing the Book of the Twelve*, edited by James D Nogalski and Marvin A Sweeney (SBL Symposium Series 15; Atlanta: Society of Biblical Literature, 2000), 125–45.

Houston, Walter J, *Contending for Justice. Ideologies and Theologies of Social Justice in the Old Testament* (Library of Hebrew Bible/Old Testament Studies 428; London: T&T Clark, 2007).

Hurvitz, A, *The Transition Period in Biblical Hebrew: A Study in Post-Exilic Hebrew and Its Implications for the Dating of Psalms* (Hebrew University: Jerusalem, 1972).

Jenni, Ernst and ClausWestermann, *Theologisches Handwörterbuch zum Alten Testament* (Band, II; Munich: Kaiser Verlag/Zürich: Theolgischer Verlag, 1984).

Jobling, David, *1 Samuel* (Berit Olam. Studies in Hebrew Narrative & Poetry; Collegeville, Mn.: The Liturgical Press, 1998).

Joosten, Jan, 'A Note on the Text of Deuteronomy xxxii 8*,' *VT* 57 (2007): 548–55.

Joyce, Paul M, *Ezekiel: A Commentary* (Library of Hebrew Bible/Old Testament Studies 482; New York/London: T&T Clark, 2009).

Kaiser, Otto, *Der Gott des Alten Testaments: Theologie des Alten Testaments 3. Yahwes Gerechtigkeit* (UTB für Wissenschaft; Göttingen: Vandenhoeck & Ruprecht, 2003).

Kaiser, Walter C Jr, *Toward Old Testament Ethics* (Grand Rapids: Zondervan Publishing House, 1983).

Keys, Gillian, *The Wages of Sin. A Reappraisal of the 'Succession Narrative'* (JSOTSup 221; Sheffield: Sheffield Academic Press, 1996).

Koch, Klaus, 'Is There a Doctrine of Retribution in the Old Testament?', in *Theodicy in the Old Testament*, edited by James L Crenshaw (Issues in Religion and Theology 4; Philadelphia: Fortress Press, 1983), 57–87.

Klein, Daniel A, 'Who Counted Righteousness to Whom? Two Clashing Views by Shadal on Gen 15:6,' in *Jewish Biblical Quarterly* 36 (2008): 28–32.

Klein, Ralph W, *1 Samuel* (2nd ed.; WBC 10; Nashville, Tenn.: Thomas Nelson, 2008).

Knauf, Ernst Axel, *Josua* (Zürcher Bibel Kommentare AT 6; Zürich: Theologischer Verlag, 2008).

Knierim, R, *The Task of Old Testament Theology: Substance, Method and Cases* (Grand Rapids: Eerdmans, 1995).

Kooij, Arie van der, 'A Kingdom of Priests: Comment on Exodus 19:6,' in 'A Kingdom of Priests: Comment on Exodus 19:6,' in *The Interpretation of Exodus: Studies in Honour of Cornelis Houtman*, edited by Riemer Roukema (Contributions to Biblical Exegesis and Theology 44; Leuven/Paris/Dudley, MA: Peeters, 2006), 171–79.

Krasovec, Joze, *La Justice de Dieu dans La Bible Hébraique et L'Interpretation Juive et Chrétienne* (OBO 76; Göttingen: Vandenhoeck & Ruprecht, 1988).

Krasovec, Joze, *Reward, Punishment, & Forgiveness. The Thinking & Beliefs of Ancient Israel in the Light of Greek and Modern Views* (Supplements to Vetus Testamentum 78; Leiden: Brill, 1999).

Knight, George AF, *The Song of Moses. A Theological Quarry* (Grand Rapids: Eerdmans, 1995).

Krüger, Thomas, *Qoheleth. A Commentary* (Hermeneia; Augsburg: Fortress, 2004).

Labuschagne, Casper, 'The Song of Moses: Its Framework and Structure,' in *De Fructu Oris Sui: Essays in Honor of Adrianus van Selms*, edited by IH Eybers, CJ Fensham, CJ Labuschagne, WC van Wyk, and AH van Zyl (Leiden: EJ Brill, 1971), 85-98.

Lamb, David T, 'The "Eternal" Curse: Seven Deuteronomistic Judgement Oracles against the House of David,' in *For and Against David. Story and History in the Books of Samuel*, edited by A Graeme Auld and Erik Eynikel (BETL 232; Leuven: Peeters, 2010), 315-25.

Laato, Antti, and Johannes C de Moor, editors, *Theodicy in the World of the Bible* (Leiden: Brill, 2003).

Leclerc, Thomas L, *Yaweh is Exalted in Justice. Solidarity and Conflict in Isaiah* (Minneapolis: Fortress Press, 2001).

Lee, Won W, *Punishment and Forgiveness in Israel's Migratory Campaign* (Grand Rapids, MI.: Eerdmans, 2003).

Leuchter, Mark, 'Why is the Song of Moses in the Book of Deuteronomy?' *VT* 57 (2007): 295-317.

Levenson, Jon D, *Sinai and Zion. An Entry into the Jewish Bible* (New Voices in Biblical Studies; Minneapolis: Winston Press, 1985).

Levenson, Jon D, *Creation and the Persistence of Evil: The Jewish Drama of Divine Omnipotence* (San Francisco: Harper & Row, 1988).

Levenson, Jon D, *The Hebrew Bible, the Old Testament, and Historical Criticism. Jews and Christians in Biblical Studies* (Louisville: Westminster/John Knox Press, 1993).

Levin, Christoph, 'Gerechtigkeit Gottes in der Genesis,' in *Studies in the Book of Genesis. Literature, Redaction and History*, edited by A Wénin (BETL 155; Leuven: Leuven University Press/Peeters, 2001), 347-57.

Levine, Baruch A, *Numbers 1-20. A New Translation with Introduction and Commentary* (AB 4A; New York: Doubleday, 1993).

Levinson, Bernard M, *Legal Revision and Religious Renewal in Ancient Israel* (New York: Cambridge University Press, 2008).

Lohfink, Norbert, 'Darstellungskunst und Theologie in Dtn 1,6-3,29'. *Biblica* 41 (1960): 105-34.

Lohfink, Norbert, 'The Strata of the Pentateuch and the Question of War,' in *Theology of the Pentateuch. Themes of the Priestly Narrative and Deuteronomy*. Translated by Linda M Maloney (Edinburgh: T&T Clark, 1994), 173–226.

Lohfink, Norbert, 'Prolegomena zu einer Rechtshermeneutik des Pentateuch' in *Das Deuteronomium*, edited by Georg Braulik (Österreichische Biblische Studien 23; Frankfurt: Peter Lang, 2003), 11–55.

Long, Burke O, 'Framing Repetitions in Biblical Historiography,' *JBL* 106 (1987): 385–99.

Lundbom, Jack R, *The Hebrew Prophets. An Introduction* (Minneapolis: Fortress, 2010).

Luyten J, 'Primeval and Eschatological Overtones in the Song of Moses (Dt 32,1–43),' in *Das Deuteronomium. Entstehung Gestalt und Botschaft*, edited by Norbert Lohfink (BETL LXVIII; Leuven: Leuven University Press, 1985), 341–47.

Mann, Thomas W, *The Book of the Torah. The Narrative Integrity of the Pentateuch* (Atlanta: John Knox Press, 1988).

Mann Thomas W, *The Book of the Former Prophets* (Eugene, Or: Cascade Books, 2011).

McCann, J Clinton, *A Theological Introduction to the Book of Psalms. The Psalms as Torah* (Nashville: Abingdon Press, 1993).

McCann, J Clinton, 'The Book of Psalms. Introduction, Commentary, and Reflections,' in *The New Interpreter's Bible, Volume Four* (Nashville; Abingdon, 1998), 639–1280.

McCann, J Clinton, 'Righteousness, Justice and Peace: A Contemporary Theology of the Psalms,' *HBT* 23 (2001): 111–31.

McConville, J Gordon, *Deuteronomy* (Apollos Old Testament Commentary 5; Leicester: Apollos/Downers Grove: InterVarsity Press, 2002).

McConville, J Gordon & Stephen N Williams, *Joshua* (The Two Horizons Old Testament Commentary; Grand Rapids, Michigan: Eerdmans, 2010).

McKenzie, Steven L, '*Ledavid (for David)*! "Except in the Matter of Uriah the Hittite"', in *For and Against David. Story and History in the Books of Samuel*, edited by A Graeme Auld and Erik Eynikel (BETL 232; Leuven: Peeters, 2010), 307-15.

Melugin, Roy F, 'The Book of Isaiah and the Construction of Meaning', in *Writing and Reading the Scroll of Isaiah. Studies in an Interpretive Tradition*, edited by Craig C Broyles and Craig A Evans (volume 1; Supplements to Vetus Testamentum 70,1; Leiden/New York/Cologne: Brill, 1997), 39-55.

Milgrom, Jacob, *Leviticus. A Book of Ritual and Ethics* (A Continental Commentary; Minneapolis: Fortress Press, 2004).

Millard, M, *Die Komposition des Psalters* (FAT 9; Tübingen: Mohr, 1994).

Miller, Patrick D, 'The Beginning of the Psalter', in *The Shape and Shaping of the Psalter*. Edited by J Clinton McCann (JSOTSup 159; Sheffield: Sheffield Academic Press, 1993), 83-92.

Mowinckel, Sigmund, *The Psalms in Israel's Worship* (2 vols.; translated by DR Ap-Thomas; Oxford: Blackwell, 1962).

Mueller, E Aydeet, *The Micah Story: A Morality Tale in the Book of Judges* (Studies in Biblical Literature; New York: Lang, 2001).

Muilenberg, James, 'Form Criticism and Beyond,' *JBL* 88 (1969): 1-28.

Muilenburg, James, 'The Intercession of the Covenant Mediator (Exodus 31:1a, 12-17)', in *Hearing and Speaking the Word: Selections from the Works of James Muilenburg*, edited by TF Best (Scholars Press Homage Series; Chico, Calif.: Scholars Press, 1984), 170-92.

Mullen, E Theodore Jr, *Narrative History and Ethnic Boundaries. The Deuteronomistic Historian and the Creation of Israelite National Identity* (SBL Semeia Studies; Atlanta Georgia: Scholars Press, 1993).

Murphy, Francesca Aran, *The Comedy of Revelation. Paradise Lost and Regained in Biblical Narrative* (Edinburgh: T&T Clark, 2000).

Murray, Stephen Butler, *Reclaiming Divine Wrath. A History of a Christian Doctrine and Its Interpretation* (Bern: Peter Lang, 2011).

Nasuti, Harry P, 'The Interpretive Significance of Sequence and Selection in the Book of Psalms,' in *The Book of Psalms. Composition and Reception*, edited by Peter W Flint and Patrick D Miller, Jr (Supplements to Vetus Testamentum 99; Leiden/Boston: Brill, 2005), 311-39.

Nelson, Richard D, *Joshua* (Interpretation; Louisville, Ky.: Westminster John Knox, 1997).

Newsom, Carol A, *The Book of Job: A Context of Moral Imaginations* (New York: OUP, 2003).

Newsom, Carol A, 'The Consolations of God: Assessing Job's Friends Across a Cultural Abyss,' in *Reading from Right to Left*, edited by JC Exum and HGM Williamson (London/New York: Sheffield Academic Press), 347-58.

Newsom, Carol A, 'Re-considering Job', in *CR:BS* 5.2 (2007): 155-82.

Niditch, Susan, *War in the Hebrew Bible. A Study in the Ethics of Violence* (Oxford: Oxford University Press, 1993).

Niditch, Susan, *Judges* (OTL; Louisville/London: Westminster John Knox, 2008).

Nihan, Christophe, 'L'injustice des fils de Samuel, au tournant d'une époque. (Quelques remarques sur la fonction de 1 Samuel 8,1-5 dans son context littéraire),' *BN* 94 (1998): 26-32.

Nogalski, James D, 'Recurring Themes in the Book of the Twelve: Creating Points of Contact for a Theological Reading,' *Interpretation* 61/2 (2007): 125-36.

Noth, Martin, *Exodus* (Philadelphia: Westminster Press, 1962).

Noth, Martin, *The Deuteronomistic History* (JSOTSup 15. second edition; Sheffield: JSOT Press, 1981/1991).

O'Brien, Mark A, 'The Contribution of Judah's Speech, Genesis 44:18-34, to the Characterization of Joseph,' *CBQ* 59 (1997): 429-47.

O'Brien, Mark A, 'Deuteronomy 16.18-18.22; Meeting the Challenge of Towns and Nations,' *JSOT* 33.2 (2008): 155-72.

O'Brien, Mark A, 'The Dynamics of the Golden Calf Story (Exodus 32-34),' *AusBR* 60 (2012): 18-31.

O'Day, Gail R, 'Jeremiah 9:22-23 and I Corinthians 1:26-31. A Study in Intertextuality,' *JBL* 109/2 (1990): 259-67.

Olson, Denis T, *The Death of the Old and the Birth of the New. The Framework of the Book of Numbers and the Pentateuch* (Brown Judaic Studies 71; Chico, CA.: Scholars Press, 1985).

Olson, Denis T, *Deuteronomy and the Death of Moses* (OBT; Eugene, Or: Wipf & Stock, 1994).

Olson, Denis T, *Numbers* (Interpretation; Louisville: John Knox Press, 1996).

Oswalt, John N, 'Righteousness in Isaiah: A Study of the Function of Chapters 56-66 in the Present Structure of the Book,' in *Writing and Reading the Scroll of Isaiah. Studies in an Interpretive Tradition*, edited by Craig C Broyles and Craig A Evans (vol. 1; Supplements to Vetus Testamentum 70,1; Leiden/New York/Cologne: Brill, 1997), 177-91.

Otto, Eckart, *Theologische Ethik des Alten Testaments* (Theologische Wissenschaft 3,2; Stuttgart: Kohlhammer, 1994).

Otto, Eckart, 'Moses Abschiedslied in Deuteronomium 32. Ein Zeugnis der Kanonsbildung in der Hebräischen Bibel,' in *Die Torah: Studien zum Pentateuch: Gesammelte Aufsätze* (BZABR 9; Wiesbaden: Harrasowitz, 2009), 641-78.

Peckham, JB, *History and Prophecy* (New York: Doubleday, 1993).

Perdue, Leo G, *The Collapse of History: Reconstructing Old Testament Theology* (OBT; Augsburg: Fortress Press, 1994).

Perdue, Leo G, *Reconstructing Old Testament Theology: After the Collapse of History* (OBT; Minneapolis: Fortress, 2005).

Phillips, Anthony, *Lower than the Angels. Questions Raised by Genesis 1-11* (Oxford: Bocardo & Church Army Press, 1983).

Plamondon, Paul-Henri, 'Sur le chemin du salut avec le Deuxième Isaie,' *Nouvelle Revue Theologique* 104/1 (1982): 241-66.

Polak, Franz, 'Theophany and Mediator: The Unfolding of a Theme in the Book of Exodus,' in *Studies in the Book of Exodus. Redaction Reception Interpretation*, edited by Marc Vervenne (BETL 126; Leuven: Leuven University Press/Peeters, 1996), 113-47.

Polan, Gregory J, *In the Ways of Justice Toward Salvation: A Rhetorical Analysis of Isaiah 56–59* (American University Studies; Series VII, Theology and Religion; 13; New York: Peter Lang, 1986).

Polzin, Robert, *Samuel and the Deuteronomist. A Literary Study of the Deuteronomistic History. Part Two. 1 Samuel* (San Francisco: Harper & Row, 1989).

Redditt, Paul M, 'Recent Research on The Book of the Twelve as One Book.' *CR:BS* 9 (2001): 47–80.

Redditt, Paul, 'Themes in Haggai–Zechariah–Malachi.' *Interpretation* 61/2 (2007): 184–97.

Rendtorff, Rolf, *Canon and Theology. Overtures to an Old Testament Theology* (OBT; Minneapolis: Fortress Press, 1993).

Ricoeur, Paul, *The Symbolism of Evil* (Boston: Beacon Press, 1969).

Rudnig, Thilo Alexander, '"Ausser in der Sache mit Uria, dem Hethiter" (1 Reg 15, 5): Jahwes und Davids Gerechtigkeit in 2 Sam 10–12,' in *For and Against David. Story and History in the Books of Samuel*, edited by A Graeme Auld and Erik Eynikel (BETL 232; Leuven: Peeters, 2010), 273–92.

Sakenfeld, Katharine Doob, *Faithfulness in Action: Loyalty in Biblical Perspective* (OBT; Philadelphia: Fortress Press, 1985).

Sakenfeld, Katharine Doob, 'Love in the OT', in *The New Interpreter's Dictionary of the Bible I–Ma Volume 3*, general editor Katharine Doob Sakenfeld (Nashville: Abingdon Press, 2008), 713–18.

Sanders, Paul, *The Provenance of Deuteronomy 32* (Oudtestamentische Studiën 37; Leiden/New York: Brill, 1996).

Schipper, Jeremy, 'Hezekiah, Manasseh, and Dynastic or Transgenerational Punishment,' in *Soundings in Kings. Perspectives and Methods in Contemporary Scholarship*, edited by Mark Leuchter and Peter-Klaus Adam (Minneapolis: Fortress Press, 2010), 81–105.

Schmid, Hans Heinrich, *Wesen und Geschichte der Weisheit* (BZAW 101; Berlin: Walter de Gruyter, 1966).

Schmid, Hans Heinrich, *Gerechtigkeit als Weltordnung: Hintergrund und Geschichte der alttestamentlichen Gerechtigkeitsbegriffes* (Tübingen: Mohr (Siebeck), 1968)

Schmid, Hans Heinrich, 'Creation, Righteousness, and Salvation: "Creation Theology" as the Broad Horizon of Biblical Theology,' in *Creation in the Old Testament*, edited by Bernard Anderson (Philadelphia: Fortress Press, 1984), 102-17. German original, 'Schöpfung, Gerechtigkeit und Heil', in *Zeitschrift für Theologie und Kirche* 70 (1973) 1-19.

Schmid, Hans Heinrich, *Altorientalische Welt in der alttestamentlichen Theologie* (Zurich: Theologischer Verlag, 1974).

Seibert, Eric A, *Subversive Scribes and the Solomonic Narrative. A Rereading of 1 Kings 1-11* (Library of Hebrew Bible/Old Testament Studies 36; New York/London: T&T Clark, 2006).

Seifrid, Mark A, 'Righteousness Language in the Hebrew Scriptures and Early Judaism.' In *Justification and Variegated Nomism, vol. 1. The Complexities of Second Temple Judaism*, edited by DA Carson, Peter T O'Brien, and Mark A Seifrid (WUNT 2/140: Tübingen: Mohr Siebeck/ Grand Rapids MI: Baker Academic, 2001), 415-42.

Seitz, Christopher R, *Zion's Final Destiny. The Development of the Book of Isaiah. A Reassessment of Isaiah 36-39* (Minneapolis: Fortress Press, 1989).

Sénéchal, Vincent, *Retribution et intercession dans le Deuteronome* (BZAW 408; Berlin/New York: Walter de Gruyter, 2009).

Seow, Choong-Leong, *Ecclesiastes: A New Translation with Introduction and Commentary* (AB 18C; New York: Doubleday, 1997).

Ska, Jean-Louis, *Introduction to Reading the Pentateuch* (Winona Lake, Ind.: Eisenbrauns, 2006).

Ska, Jean-Louis, 'Josh 8:30-35: Israel Officially Takes Possession of the Land,' in *'Gerechtigkeit und Recht zu üben' (Gen 18, 19): Studien zur altorientalischen und biblischen Rechtsgeschichte, zur Religionsgeschichte Israels und zur Religionssoziologie. Festschrift für Eckart Otto zum 65. Geburtstag,* edited by Reinhard Achenbach and Martin Arneth (BZABR 13; Wiesbaden: Harrassowitz, 2010), 308-16.

Skehan, Patrick W, 'The Structure of the Song of Moses in Deuteronomy (32:1-43),' in *A Song of Power and the Power of Song*, edited by Duane L Christensen (Winona Lakes: Eisenbrauns, 1993): 156-68.

Smith, Richard G, *The Fate of Justice and Righteousness During David's Reign: Rereading the Court History and its Ethics according to 2 Samuel 8:15b–20:26* (Library of Hebrew/Old Testament Studies 508; New York: T&T Clark, 2009).

Smith, Mark, *The Priestly Vision of Genesis 1* (Minneapolis: Fortress Press, 2010)

Stulman, Louis, *Order Amid Chaos. Jeremiah as Symbolic Tapestry* (The Biblical Seminar 57; Sheffield: Sheffield Academic Press, 1998).

Stulman, Louis and Hyun Chul Paul Kim, *You Are My People. An Introduction to Prophetic Literature* (Nashville: Abingdon Press, 2010).

Sweeney, Marvin A, *Isaiah 1–39, with and Introduction to Prophetic Literature* (FOTL XVI, Grand Rapids: Eerdmans, 1996).

Sweeney, Marvin A, 'The Book of Isaiah as Prophetic Torah,' in *New Visions of Isaiah*, edited by Roy F Melugin and Marvin A Sweeney (JSOTSup 214; Sheffield: Sheffield Academic Press, 1996), 50–67.

Sweeney, Marvin A, *The Twelve Prophets* (volumes 1 and 2; Berit Olam; Collegeville MN: The Liturgical Press, 2000).

Sweeney, Marvin A, *Zephaniah: A Commentary* (Hermeneia; Minneapolis: Fortress, 2003).

Sweeney, Marvin A, *I & II Kings. A Commentary* (Louisville/London: Westminster John Knox Press, 2007).

Tigay, Jeffrey, *Deuteronomy* (JPS Commentary; Philadelphia: Jewish Publication Society, 1996).

Trible, Phyllis, *Texts of Terror: Literary Feminist Readings of Biblical Narratives* (OBT, 13; Philadelphia: Fortress Press, 1984).

Tsumura, David Toshio, *The First Book of Samuel* (NICOTI; Grand Rapids, Mich: Eerdmans, 2007).

Tuell, Steven S, 'Between Text & Sermon. Psalm 1,' *Interpretation* 63 (2009): 278–80.

Turner, Laurence A, *Genesis* (Readings: A New Biblical Commentary; Sheffield: Sheffield Academic Press, 2000).

Tsevat, Matitiahu, 'The Meaning of the Book of Job,' in *Sitting with Job: Selected Studies on the Book of Job*, edited by Roy B Zuck (Grand Rapids, MI.: Baker Book House, 1992), 189-218.

Van Seters, John, *The Life of Moses. The Yahwist as Historian in Exodus-Numbers* (Louisville: Westminster/John Knox, 1994).

Wallace, Howard N, *Psalms* (Readings: A New Biblical Commentary; Sheffield: Sheffield Phoenix Press, 2009).

Waltke, Bruce K, *A Commentary on Micah* (Grand Rapids, Mich.; Eerdmans, 2007).

Watts, James W, *Reading Law. The Rhetorical Shaping of the Pentateuch* (The Biblical Seminar 59; Sheffield: Sheffield Academic Press, 1999).

Watts, John D W, 'A Frame for the Book of the Twelve: Hosea 1-3 and Malachi,' in *Reading and Hearing the Book of the Twelve*, edited by James D Nogalski and Marvin A Sweeney (SBL Symposium Series 15; Atlanta: Society of Biblical Literature, 2000), 209-17.

Watts, John D W, *Isaiah 34-66 Revised Edition* (WBC 25; Nashville: Thomas Nelson, 2005).

Webb, Barry, *The Book of the Judges. An Integrated Reading* (Eugene, Oregon: Wipf & Stock, 2008).

Weber, Beat, 'Von der Psaltergenese zur Psaltertheologie: Der nächste Schritt der Psalterexegese? Einige grundsätzliche Überlegungen zum Psalter als Buch und Kanonteil,' in *The Composition of the Book of Psalms*, edited by Erich Zenger (BETL 238; Leuven: Peeters, 2010), 733-44.

Wenham, Gordon J, *Story as Torah. Reading the Old Testament Ethically* (Old Testament Studies; Edinburgh: T&T Clark, 2000).

Weinfeld, Moshe, *Social Justice in Ancient Israel and in the Ancient Near East* (Minneapolis: Fortress Press, 1995).

Weinfeld, Moshe, 'Justice and Righteousness f¡DÚpVvIm The Expression and its Meaning,' in *Justice and Righteousness. Biblical Themes and their Influence*, edited by Henning Graf Reventlow and Yair Hoffmann (JSOTSup 137; Sheffield: Academic Press, 1992), 228-46.

Wénin, André, 'Le précepte d'Adonai Dieu en Genèse 2, 16–17. Narration et anthropologie,' *RSR* 82/3 (2008): 303–18.

Wénin, André, La question de l'humain et l'unité du livre de la Genèse, in Studies in the Book of Genesis, edited by A Wénin (BETL 155; Leuven: Leuven University Press/Peeters, 2001), 3–34.

Westermann, Claus, *Genesis 1–11. A Commentary* (London: SPCK, 1984).

Whybray, Norman, *Reading the Psalms as a Book* (JSOTSup 222; Sheffield: Sheffield Academic Press, 1996).

Widmer, Michael, *Moses, God and the Dynamics of Intercessory Prayer* (FAT 2/8; Tübingen: Mohr Siebeck, 2004).

Wildberger, Hans, *Jesaja. 1. Teilband. Jesaja 1-12* (BKAT X; Neukirchen-Vluyn: Neukirchener Verlag, 1980).

Wildberger, Hans, *Jesaja. 3. Teilband. Jesaja 28–39. Das Buch, der Prophet und seine Botschaft* (BKAT X/3; Neukirchen-Vluyn: Neukirchener Verlag, 1982).

Wilson, Gerald H, *The Editing of the Hebrew Psalter* (SBLDS 76; Chico, Calif: Scholars Press, 1985).

Wilson, Gerald H, 'The Shape of the Book of Psalms,' *Interpretation* 46/2 (1992): 129–42.

Wilson, Gerald H, 'Shaping the Psalter: A Consideration of Editorial Linkage in the Book of Psalms,' in *The Shape and Shaping of the Psalter*, edited by J Clinton McCann (JSOTSup 159; Sheffield: Sheffield Academic Press, 1993), 72–82.

Wilson, Gerald H, 'King, Messiah, and the Reign of God: Revisiting the Royal Psalms and the Shape of the Psalter,' in *The Book of Psalms. Composition and Reception*, edited by Peter W Flint and Patrick D Miller, Jr (Supplements to Vetus Testamentum 99; Leiden/Boston: Brill, 2005), 391–406.

Wilson, R R, 'An Interpretation of Ezekiel's Dumbness,' *VT* 22 (1972): 91–104.

Wolde, EJ van, 'Job 42:1-6: The Reversal of Job,' in *The Book of Job*, edited by WAM Beuken (BETL 114 Leuven: Leuven University/Peeters, 1995), 223-50.

Wolff, Hans-Walter, *Micah: A Commentary* (Minneapolis: Augsburg, 1990).

Wong, Gregory TK, *Compositional Strategy of the Book of Judges: An Inductive, Rhetorical Study* (Supplements to Vetus Testamentum 111; Leiden/Boston: Brill, 2006).

Yancey, Philip, 'A Fresh Reading of the Book of Job,' in *Sitting With Job. Selected Studies on the Book of Job*, edited by Roy B Zuck (Grand Rapids, MI: Baker, 1992), 141-50.

Young, Ian, 'Is the Prose Tale of Job in Late Biblical Hebrew?' *VT* 59 (2009): 606-29.

Zenger, Eric, 'Le theme de la 'sortie d'Egypte' et la naissance du Pentateuque,' in *Le Pentateuque en question. Les origins et la composition des cinq premiers livres de la Bible à la lumiere des recherches récentes*, edited by Albert de Pury (Le Monde de la Bible; Geneva: Labor et Fides, 1989), 301-31.

Indicies

Index of Names, Subjects and Places

A
Abraham, 3, 4, 5, 10, 44n, 45n, 46, 47–50, 59, 60, 75, 112, 115, 123, 124, 126, 130, 153n, 197, 267.

Act-Consequence, 7, 8, 9, 39, 211, 229, 242, 249, 254.

B
Balak, 115, 220.

C
Creation, xi, xii, xiii, 2, 4, 5, 7–11, 13, 14, 21, 22, 24, 25, 26, 28, 29, 31, 35–42, 44, 46, 53, 55, 57, 60, 64–68, 74, 82, 85, 86, 89, 91, 92, 93, 96, 103, 107, 114, 115, 117, 119, 125, 137, 138, 171, 174, 184, 189, 195, 196, 199, 203, 204, 216, 221, 222, 243, 244–247, 249, 253, 258–262, 265, 266, 268–271.

Compassion, xiv, 9, 29, 31, 32, 40, 41, 43, 44, 48, 69, 82n, 83, 109, 112, 117, 132, 139, 145, 146, 169, 174, 179, 181, 185, 189, 217.

D
David, 7, 135, 138, 150, 151n, 152–156, 157–170, 174, 178, 180n, 185, 186, 191, 192, 200, 202, 204, 205, 208, 231, 234, 240, 244, 268.

Distorted Perception, 39, 50, 54, 56, 61, 63, 72, 74, 91, 98, 100, 101, 102, 134, 139, 149, 167, 181n, 184, 193, 207, 219, 225, 241.

F
Falsehood, 71, 207, 213.

Forgiveness, 40n, 71, 75, 78, 83, 84, 94n, 98n, 172n, 239, 243, 246.

J
Jerusalem/Zion, 7, 70n, 105, 108n,

129n, 152, 153, 158n, 161, 162, 164, 165, 166, 169n, 171n, 178, 179, 183, 187, 188, 191, 192, 193n, 195, 199, 203n, 204, 205, 208, 210, 213, 216, 219, 222, 224.

Just, xiii, xiv, 4, 21, 22, 23, 27, 28, 30, 31, 32, 40, 41, 44, 49, 60, 68, 73, 79, 91, 98, 108, 109, 121n, 131, 132, 137, 150, 154, 157, 160, 161, 163, 169, 170, 188, 189, 192, 199, 201, 219, 221, 224, 228, 244n, 249, 250, 254, 255, 256.

Justice, vii, ix, xii, xiii, xiv, xv, 1, 3, 4, 10n, 23, 24, 27, 29, 46, 48, 69, 91, 94, 108, 113, 132, 152, 155, 156, 173, 174, 179, 180, 182, 183, 184n, 185n, 186, 187n, 189, 190, 192, 193n, 198–202, 204–208, 210, 211, 217, 219–222, 224, 227, 234n, 242, 244–247, 249, 256, 258, 259, 262, 267, 269, 270, 271.

Judge, xiii, 3, 8, 11, 12, 27, 31, 38n, 40, 43, 44, 60, 69, 79, 83, 105, 108, 120, 138, 139, 140, 142, 143, 146, 148, 150, 154, 162, 164, 167, 182, 183, 188, 190, 193, 206n, 209, 210, 212, 224, 228, 243, 244, 256, 259,

Judging/judgeship, 73, 142, 150, 170.

Judgment, 2, 8, 23n, 28, 29, 42, 47, 48, 69, 79, 91, 97, 99, 100, 145, 146, 149, 150, 154, 156, 161, 168, 184, 188, 190, 197, 198, 203, 209, 219, 220, 223, 224, 227, 243, 252–256, 259, 262, 266.

Justify, 72, 185, 194, 211, 216, 240, 267.270, 271.

Justification, xn, 72, 249n.

Justified, 41, 73.

K

Kindness, 159, 220, 223.

Knowledge, xv, 11, 14, 27, 28, 38, 39, 40, 46, 54, 55, 56, 57, 60, 61, 64, 65, 68n, 73, 80, 82, 84, 96, 101, 114, 135, 138, 139, 148, 159, 185, 192, 202, 213, 241, 250, 251, 252, 253, 258, 259, 261.

L

Land, 3, 5, 6, 10, 21, 23, 26, 27, 32, 35, 37, 45, 46, 53, 54, 65, 66, 68, 71, 73, 75, 79, 80, 86, 89, 91, 92, 94, 96, 98, 100–103, 105–115, 117, 119, 112, 123, 124n, 125n, 126, 127, 128, 129, 131n, 132, 140, 144, 152, 154, 158, 161, 163, 165, 169, 170, 173, 180, 181, 184, 187, 190, 193, 199, 210, 215, 217, 218, 220, 239, 260, 266, 268, 269.

Law, the, xii, xiii, xv, 3, 6, 7, 8, 12, 21, 22, 23, 31, 32, 33, 39, 43, 44, 49, 65, 66, 68, 69, 71, 85, 94, 96, 105, 106, 108, 112, 116, 119, 122, 126, 127, 128, 157, 158, 159, 163, 166, 169, 173, 179, 187, 190, 200, 212, 233, 234, 243, 249.

Love, xiv, 9, 58, 67, 68, 82n, 85, 98, 108, 113, 117, 153, 159, 169, 170, 174, 179, 183, 200, 204, 207, 208, 210, 217, 218, 220, 239, 244–247, 268, 271.

M

Mercy, xiv, 41, 68, 82n, 83, 84, 95, 132, 149, 168, 206, 216, 217, 223, 267.

Moses, 4, 5, 6, 8, 21, 22, 23n, 24n, 25n, 26n, 28n, 30, 32, 47n, 49, 53, 55, 56, 57, 60–64, 67n, 70-86, 90, 95–100, 102, 103, 105–113, 115, 116, 119, 120, 126, 128, 130, 131, 141, 150, 154, 157, 158, 159, 161, 163, 166, 169, 170, 173, 174, 192, 203, 207n, 225, 233, 243, 246, 266.

N

Narrative, 9, 11, 12, 13, 21, 22, 26, 31, 32, 33, 35, 36, 37, 40, 43, 44, 47, 48, 54, 55, 56, 59, 61–66, 70, 71, 73–76, 78, 82, 85, 89, 92, 95, 100, 101, 102, 105, 106, 109, 113, 116, 120, 122n, 123, 124, 125, 127, 131, 132, 134n, 137n, 141–145, 147, 148n, 149, 150, 155n, 156, 157, 159, 160, 161, 162, 166, 167, 168, 173, 179, 191, 241, 251, 253n, 265, 266, 267, 268,

O

One and the many, 24, 44, 48, 64, 77, 129, 232.

Order, xi, xii, xiii, 2, 5, 6, 7, 10, 11, 12, 26, 31, 35, 36, 37, 39, 40, 41, 44, 46, 48, 53, 56, 58, 67, 68n, 73, 79, 93, 100, 102, 112, 113, 117, 119, 121n, 122, 132, 140, 151, 159, 172, 174, 180, 182–187, 189, 190, 193, 194, 196, 199, 201, 204, 205, 208, 215, 216, 220, 222, 241, 242, 243, 245, 246, 247, 249, 258, 259, 260, 265-271.

P

Plan (Divine), 9, 28, 37, 46, 55, 59, 61, 64, 74, 75, 76, 78, 81, 96, 113, 116, 152, 153, 154, 158, 159, 174, 184, 186, 188, 189, 190, 193, 195, 196, 221, 222, 261, 268, 269.

Poetry, xv, 12, 26, 180, 243.

Prophecy, 2, 4, 6, 8, 9, 12n, 13, 26, 31, 40, 57, 58, 59, 84, 112, 113, 115, 117, 120, 122,

131n, 138, 139, 151, 157, 160–166, 168, 169, 170, 173, 174, 175, 179n, 184, 186, 192, 225, 240, 266.

R

Rebellion, 84, 94, 95, 100, 102, 110, 111, 112, 146, 161, 180, 181, 203, 249n.

Relationship, xi, xii, xiii, xiv, 1–7, 10, 12, 23–31, 36, 37, 39, 40, 41, 43, 44–48, 50, 51, 53, 54, 56, 60, 61, 64, 65, 66, 69, 70, 71, 73–82, 85, 89–97, 99–103, 107, 108, 111, 114, 117, 120, 122–125, 128–132, 134, 138, 139–141, 143, 145–149, 151, 152, 154, 157, 159n, 160, 166, 168, 170, 172, 174, 178, 179, 181, 182, 183, 191n, 192, 193, 199, 200, 204, 205, 206, 207, 208, 210, 213, 215, 217, 222, 223, 225, 228, 231, 237, 239, 240, 242, 251, 252, 253, 255, 261, 265, 266, 267, 269, 270, 271, 272.

Reward and Retribution,

Right, 4, 5, 7, 10, 11, 24, 29–31, 36, 37, 39, 40, 41, 44, 45, 47, 51, 53, 54, 57, 59, 60, 64, 67, 69, 70, 77–79, 80, 87, 90, 93, 101, 111, 117, 122, 124, 125, 129, 132, 133, 134, 137, 143n, 146, 149, 151, 152, 153, 162, 170, 173, 174, 180–185, 189, 190, 193, 195, 196, 198, 199, 201, 204, 211, 213, 218, 219, 221–223, 228, 233, 238, 239, 241, 242, 244, 245, 246, 250, 252, 253, 255, 258, 261, 262, 265–269, 271, 272.

Rights, 95, 97, 125, 142, 146,

Righteous/Righteousness, viii, x, xi, xii, xii, xiv, 1–4, 5, 6, 8–11, 21, 23, 24, 26, 27, 29–32, 36, 40, 43, 44, 45, 47–49, 51, 53, 54, 57–59, 62, 65, 67–69, 75, 77, 81, 83, 89, 90, 91,93, 97, 103, 106, 108, 110, 112, 117, 121, 122, 126,130, 131, 133, 135, 146, 148, 152, 154, 156, 159, 160, 161n, 163, 164, 168, 169, 174, 175, 179–190, 192, 194–204, 205–212, 216–225, 227–229, 233–247, 249, 251, 254–261, 262, 265–271.

S

Salvation, xi, xii, xiii, xiv, 1n, 2, 9, 10, 44, 53, 59, 60, 67, 74, 75, 77, 81, 113, 116, 151, 158, 173, 174, 191, 193, 194n, 196–202, 204, 208, 210, 211, 234, 238–241, 245, 265, 267, 269, 270.

Salvation History/History of Salvation, 9, 11, 265.

Sin/sinful, 37, 50, 59, 72, 73, 75–79, 83–85, 92, 93, 97, 99, 109, 111, 117, 130, 132, 137, 139–142, 144–150, 154, 155,

Index of Names, Subjects and Places

160, 162, 163–165, 167, 168, 190, 202, 211–213, 216, 232, 237, 239–241, 243, 246, 256, 260, 261, 270, 271.

Sinai, xiv, 3, 26, 31, 37, 38, 42, 43, 44, 53, 63, 64, 65, 66, 68, 70, 71, 76, 80, 81, 82n, 83n, 86, 93, 95, 96, 164, 170, 187, 192, 243, 246. 272n.

T

Torah, the, xv, 2, 4–14, 21-24, 26, 27, 29, 30, 31, 32, 35, 36, 37, 40–45, 47-49, 5355, 57n, 58, 59, 60n, 65, 68–72, 82, 84, 89, 91–98, 100, 101, 103, 105–108, 111–113, 115–117, 119, 120, 122–125, 127–135, 140, 141, 144, 149–153, 155, 157–159, 161–167, 169, 170, 172, 173, 174, 180–185, 187, 192, 193, 195–197, 200–202, 204, 211, 212, 216, 225, 227, 232–234, 236, 237, 241, 243, 246, 251, 266, 267–269.

Truth, xiv, 31, 55, 57, 67, 71, 79, 138, 169, 196, 205, 206, 207, 223, 243, 245, 255, 256, 271.

U

Upright, the, 4, 21, 23, 24, 32, 252, 255, 256, 266,

Index of Biblical References

Genesis
1–11	3, 42n, 50	3:16–19	40
1:1–24a	3, 35, 36	3:16	46
1:2	36, 245	3:21	41, 102
1:10	46	4:26	44n
1:26	31	6–9	41
1:28–29	93	6:5–7	42, 84
1:28	43	6:5	45
1:31	82, 85n, 96	6:7	42, 43n
2–11	117	6:8	42, 81
2:1	85n	6:9	2, 2n, 43, 44
2:2	85n	6:11–12	42
2:3	85n	6:22	43
2:4a	35	7:1–2	2
2:4b–3:24	35, 37	7:1	43, 44, 81
2:4b–25	3	7:11	2n
2:4b	35	7:12	42
2:16–17	38	7:24	42
2:17	38, 40, 41	8:1	60
2:24	90	8:20	44
3:1–19	41	8:21	44, 84
3:5	50	9:1–7	43
3:12	61	9:1–5	92
3:14–19	39	9:2	218
3:14	40, 112	9:8–17	218
3:15	40	9:15	60
		9:16	60

9:20–27	45	19:29	48, 60
9:26	44n, 60	20	32, 49
12–25	45	20:4	2n, 49
12	32	20:7	50
12:1–3	3, 45, 46, 113, 153n	20:17	50
		22	45, 46, 50
12:1	123	22:3	49
12:2	123, 153	22:14	123
12:3	3, 50, 115, 123	22:15–18	45
12:10–20	46, 49, 50	22:17–18	113
12:22	50	22:17	123
13:5	123	22:18	125
13:13	47	23	50
13:16	123	25:18	123n
14	3	26	32
15	46	26:4	123
15:1–6	45	26:5	126
15:5	153n	27:29	123
15:6	45, 48	27:29c	123
15:13	59	28:13	123
15:18	123	28:14	123
16	46	37–50	50
17:20–22	123n	38:26	2n
18–19	2	39	50
18	75	39:9	50
18:16–33	45, 46,	44:16	2n
18:16–19	46	46:3	123
18:18	46, 113, 123		
18:19	46	**Exodus**	
18:20	47	1–15	56
18:23	2n, 47, 49	1:8	54
18:24	2n	1:15–20	62
18:25	2n, 47, 101n	1:21	59
18:25b	48	2:1–10	62
18:26	2n	2:11–22	60
18:28	2n	2:13–14	61n

2:23	60, 145	9:5	2n
2:24	59, 60	9:6	2n
3–4	60, 64	9:12	56n
3:7–15	29	9:14	55n, 152
3:7	53n	9:27	2n, 3, 53, 57, 58
3:8	123	9:29	55n
3:15	82	9:30	57
3:19–20	58	10:2	55n, 56n
4:14–17	76	10:27	56n
4:21	55, 56n	11:10	56n
4:22	73	12:23	58
4:24–26	62	12:25	123
4:26–26	62	12:29–32	58
5:1–9	61n	13:11–16	60
5:2	55, 57	13:11	123
5:22–23	61	13:15	56n
5:22	61	14:4	58, 152
6:7	27, 30, 55, 73, 213, 223, 241, 251	14:5	58
		14:10–14	95
6:8	123	14:10–12	53n, 63
6:14–25	77	14:10	58
6:25	2n	14:18	152
7:3	28, 55, 56n	14:25	58
7:5	27, 30, 55, 56, 58, 152, 213, 241	14:28	58
		14:30–31	63
7:13	56n	14:31	58, 150
7:17	55n	15:1–18	53
7:22	56n	15:3	29
7:31	28	15:6	2n
8:10	55n	15:13	58
8:11	152	15:16	63
8:15	56n	15:18	58, 65n
8:19	56n	15:22–26	63, 95
8:22	55n	16	44
8:32	56n	17:1–7	63
9:4	2n	17:8–16	53, 63

17:18	63	21–23	66
18:10–11	63	21:12–17	38n, 211
18:17–18	62	21:12	154
18:19	2n	21:22–23:33	95
18:23–33	75n	22:20–22	65n
19–24	64, 147	22:21–24	68, 69, 83
19	70	22:24	68n
19:1–9	86	22:27	68, 69
19:3–6	64, 66, 95	23:2–33	66
19:4	65	23:6–8	68, 69
19:5–6	200	23:7	2n, 3, 69
19:5	64	23:12b	80
19:20–22	86	23:17	65
19:23	86	23:20–33	68, 71, 78, 80, 95, 123
19:24	76		
19:29	75	23:20–22	126
20:1–17	65, 95	24	70
20:1	79	24:10	82n
20:2–17	85	24:12–14	72
20:2–6	66	24:13–14	76
20:2–3	29	24:13	2n
20:2	66	24:14	76n
20:3–5a	66	24:15–18	81
20:5a	67, 98	24:17	72
20:5b–6	66, 68, 73, 78, 82, 83, 84, 95, 98, 110, 267	25–31	37, 76n, 86
		25:8	70
		28–29	76
20:5b	66, 67, 71, 73, 78, 79, 84, 99, 212	28:8	2n
		30:33	2n
20:6	66, 67, 82, 83	31:1a	80n
20:7	83	31:12–17	80n
20:8–11	44	31:16–17	85
20:17	65n	32–34	27, 28, 49, 70, 71, 72, 94, 103, 112, 204
20:18–20	149n		
20:20–21	66n		
20:22–23:33	85	32	70n

32:1	96	33:1–3	79
32:1–6	72	33:1	123
32:2–4	73	33:2	80, 81
32:3	76, 77, 79	33:3	56
32:4	163	33:4–6	79
32:5	76	33:5	56, 79, 81
32:7–14	72, 73, 75, 78	33:6	79, 84
32:7–10	79, 154	33:7–11	72
32:7	72, 73	33:9	80
32:8	75	33:11	82n
32:9	56	33:12–23	72, 80
32:10	73, 74, 78, 97, 161	33:12–17	80
32:11–14	74	33:13	81
32:12–13	81	33:14	81
32:12	213n, 222	33:16	81
32:13	123	33:18–23	80
32:14	74, 76, 78, 95	33:18	81, 82
32:15–29	75	33:19	78, 82, 83, 83n, 84, 85, 98
32:17–18	75		
32:17	81	33:20	82
32:20	77n	33:21	2n
32:21–24	76	33:23	83
32:25–29	76, 77	34	70n, 85n
32:25	76	34:1–4	72, 82
32:29	76	34:4–7	78
32:30–34:9	75	34:5–9	72
32:30–34	72, 77, 78	34:5–7	82, 85
32:30	77	34:5	83n, 85
32:32–33	77	34:6–7	xiv, 29, 68, 70n, 82, 83n, 84, 85n, 98, 99, 110, 215, 247
32:33	77, 78, 82, 83n, 84, 98		
32:34	78, 79, 80, 123		
32:35	79	34:6–7a	83
33–34	147	34:6	83, 83n
33	70n	34:7	84, 154
33:1–6	72	34:8–9	84

34:10–28	72	**Numbers**	
34:11–26	82, 85, 98	1–25	94
34:14	98	5:11–31	77
34:29–35	72	5:14	67
34:32	72, 82	11–12	97
35–40	37, 54, 76n, 85, 86	11:1–3	95
35:2–3	85	11:4–35	95
36:1–2	85	11:18	99
36:26	213	12	95
39:32	85n	13–14	28, 49, 53, 72n, 94, 95, 110, 111n, 112, 204
39:43	85n		
40:33	85n		
40:34–38	86	13:30	96
41:38–39	50	13:32	96
41:57	54	14	84
44:18–34	51	14:1–4	101
44:22	51	14:2–3	96
50:20	51	14:2	101
		14:3	101, 102
Leviticus		14:4	96
1–7	86	14:7	96
6:9	90	14:8–9	96, 126
16	86	14:11–35	96
16:3	91	14:11–25	97n
16:5	91	14:11–12	100
16:30	93	14:11	97, 99
17–26	69n, 212,	14:12	97, 98, 100, 161
18:24–28	125n	14:13–19	98
19	90	14:13–16	98n, 99, 102
19:15	2n, 91	14:15–16	213n
19:17–18	69n	14:15	100
19:33–34	69n	14:16	98
19:36	2n, 91, 210	14:17	125
20:22	125n	14:18	68, 98, 99, 100, 102, 222

14:19	98n	**Deuteronomy**	
14:20	99, 103	1–4	120
14:21–35	99, 100, 101, 102	1:1–5	106
14:21	99, 152	1:5	106
14:22	100	1:6–4:40	106
14:23	100	1:8	113
14:24	101, 126	1:10	123
14:26–35	101	1:16	2n
14:26	101n	1:19–46	109, 110, 111n
14:28	99	1:19–45	107
14:29	94	1:21	113
14:31	102	1:22–25	111
14:33	102	1:26–29	111
14:34	101, 102	1:35	113
14:36–38	49	1:37	110, 111
14:38	101n	1:38	111
14:39–45	102	2–3	128
16	49, 91	2	123n
20:2–13	111n	2:10–14	107
20:5	212	3:23–28	154
20:9	212	3:25	112
21	101	3:26	110, 111
21:2–3	68	3:28	111
21:10	154n	4:1	113
22–24	62, 220	4:6	109, 114, 116
24:9	113, 115, 116, 123	4:8	2n, 3, 108
25	124	4:21	110
26–36	94	4:24	110
26	94	4:25–31	131
27–36	210	4:25–28	112
27:12–14	111n	4:25	131n
31	124	4:26	71n
31:18	125	4:27–28	114, 116
32	102	4:29–30	131
33:55	130n	4:29	113
35:30	255n	4:31	113

4:32	131	9:7–10:11	107
4:41–43	106	9:7–10	70n
4:44–5:1a	106	9:7–10:11	110
5:1b–26:19	106	9:8–10:11	27
5:6–21	106	9:13	56
5:6–7	2	9:16	56
5:9b–10	68, 110, 266	9:18	110
5:9b	212	9:21	77n
5:21	65n	9:25	110
5:31	108	9:27	111
6:1–3	126	10:6–9	107
6:4–9	32	10:9	108
6:5	157	10:10	109, 110
6:6–7	32	10:11	70n
6:10	113	10:16	125n
6:12–25	8, 12n	10:17–18	108
6:14	125n	10:19	108
6:15	110	11:8–9	126
6:18	113, 126	11:12	108
6:23	113	11:13–15	108
7:1–2	123	11:21	126
7:2–3	125b	11:22–25	126
7:2–6	114	11:29–30	127
7:2–5	129	12–26	212
7:2	68	12:8–10	123
7:3	160	12:10–12	108
7:4	71b	12:10	153, 158
7:6	91	12:11	153
7:8	113	12:12–26	106
7:9–10	110	13:5	29n
7:9	125n	13:1–18	125n
7:25–26	128	15:18	65n
7:26	68	16:18–20	108
8:1	31	16:18	2n
8:18	113	16:20	2n
9:4–6	112	16:19	2n

17:4	145	29:1	106, 107
17:6	255n	29:2–30:20	106
17:7	29n	29:6	108
17:14–20	132, 135, 144, 145, 150, 160, 233	29:9	108
		29:10–28	268
17:17	160	29:13	113
17:18–20	144n	29:15	107
18:15–22	6, 111, 207n	29:19	56
18:18	207n	29:24	116
19:11–13	154	29:25	113, 114
19:15	255n	29:26–28	114
20:2–13	110	29:29	112
21:10–34:12	23	30:1	114
21:18–21	27	30:2	113
22:20–22	65n	30:6	113, 157, 213
22:20–21	27	30:7	114
22:21	29n	30:10	157
22:22	29n, 49, 154n	30:11–14	128
22:24	29n	30:15–20	8, 233
23	120	30:19–20	5
24:6	212	31–34	106
24:13	108	31:9–12	111
25:1	2n	31:9	66n
25:15	2n	31:26–29	141
26	113	32	4, 6, 54, 106, 116, 137, 204, 266
26:5–9	12n, 113		
26:12–15	113	32:1–43	21, 22, 106
27	106	32:1–3	24, 24n
27:1–26	127	32:3	30
27:2	127n	32:4–9	24n
28	106	32:4–6a	24
28:33–34	114	32:4a	27, 28
28:48–57	114	32:4	4, 2n, 21, 23, 24, 25, 30, 266
28:49–52	116		
29–30	6, 107, 147, 158, 204	32:5a	24
		32:5b	25

32:6b–14	24, 26, 27	32:44–46	23
32:6b–9	25	32:46–47	32
32:6b	27	32:47	31
32:8–33	27	32:48–52	110n, 111n
32:8–9	25, 115	33	106
32:10–14	24n, 26	33:19	2n
32:13–14	26	34:1–12	106
32:15–18	24, 24n, 27	34:1	112
32:15	24	34:10	6
32:18	24		
32:19–27	24, 27	**Joshua**	
32:19–25	24n	1:5	122
32:19	27	1:6	122
32:26–35	24n	1:7	119, 126
32:26–27	27	1:8	122, 234
32:27	31	1:16	126
32:28–33	24, 27, 28	2	116, 124
32:28–29	28	2:2–3	123
32:28	28	2:8–11	123
32:30	24	5:2	126
32:31	24	6:10	122
32:32–33	28	6:17–18	68
32:34–35	24, 28	6:17	125
32:34–38	28	6:18	128
32:35	28, 29, 30n	6:21	68
32:36–38	24, 28	7:6–26	128
32:36–43	24n	7:11	128
32:36	43n	8:27	125
32:37–38	29	8:30–35	126, 127
32:39–42	24, 29	8:32	126
32:39	25, 29n, 41	8:34	126
32:39b	29	9	123, 130
32:40	27	9:2–3	123
32:41	29, 30n	9:2	126
32:43	24, 30	9:4	124
32:43bcde	30	9:6	126

9:9–11	123	2:1–5	129, 130
9:14–15	124	2:1b	131
9:18–19	124	2:2	129, 130
9:18	124	2:3	131
9:23	124n	2:4–5	130
9:24	123, 124	2:6–10	130
10–11	68	2:7	113n, 126
10:11	259n	2:10	130, 134
12:8	122	2:11–3:6	130
13:2–6	152	2:11–19	120
13:13	129n	2:11–13	130
15:63	129n	2:14–15	130
16:10	129n	2:14	131
21:43–45	122, 159	2:17	131
21:43	122	2:19	130
21:44	122	2:20–22	131
21:45	122	2:20–21	131n
23:4–5	129, 152	2:21–22	131
23:13	130n	2:22	131n
24	147	3:1–2	131
24:2–13	12n	3:4	131
24:14	127	3:5–6	131
24:19	127	3:7–16:31	129
24:28–31	130	3:9	132
24:31	113n, 126, 127, 129	3:15	132
		4:3	132
		4:4–10	133
Judges		5:6–7	132
1:1–3:6	129	5:11	132
1:1–36	129, 131	5:13	132
1:1–2.5	130	6:6	132
1:2	131	8:27	133
1:19	131	9	132, 135
1:21	129n	10:5–19	132
1:22	131	10:10–16	132
1:29	129n	10:10	132

11:12–28	12n, 115n	2:21b	138
11:30–40	133	2:22–25	138
12	132	2:25	138n, 142
13:1–7	128	2:26	138
13:1	132, 135	2:27–36	138
13:3–7	137	2:35	138
17–21	133, 134, 135	2:36	139
17–18	133	3:1	138
17:1	133, 137	3:11–18	139
17:6	133, 134, 135	3:20	139
17:13	133	4–7	139
18:1	133, 135	4:3	140
18:21	133	4:11	139
18:30–31	134	4:18	139
19–21	133, 134, 135	6	140
19:1	133, 135, 137	6:1–9	144n
19:4–5	133	6:19	140n
21:3	134	6:13–7:2	140
21:19–21	134	7	133
21:22	134	7:1	142
21:25	133, 134, 135	7:3	140
		7:4–6	140

1 Samuel

1:6	137	7:13	140, 144
1:11	137	7:15	140
2:2	137	8–12	150
2:3b	138	8	141, 143, 145, 147
2:6	138	8:1	143n
2:8c	138	8:1–5	142
2:9	138	8:4–6	143
2:10	138n	8:3	145n
2:10b	138, 153	8:4	143n
2:10c	138	8:5	145
2:11	138	8:6	143
2:12–17	138	8:7–8	141, 142, 143, 144, 145, 146, 148, 149, 151n
2:17	138		

8:11–17	145, 146	13:13	150
8:18	145	14:24	151
8:19	145	14:26–46	151n
8:22	142, 143	14:32	151
10:1	152	15	68, 151
10:8	150, 151n	15:10–11	151
10:17–27	151n	15:22–23	151n
10:17–25	141	15:23	151
10:17–19	141, 144, 148, 149, 151n	15:26	151
		15:35	151
10:23–24	146	17:46	152
10:24	146	22:6–19	139
10:26–27	146	27:8–12	153n
11:1–12	146		
11:14–12:25	141	**2 Samuel**	
12	120, 146, 147, 148, 150	5:1–5	152
		5:11	152
12:1–5	148	6	152n
12:1–3	146	6:6–7	140n, 152
12:4–5	146	6:12	153
12:6–17	146	7	152, 153, 157, 158, 200
12:6–11	148		
12:6–8	12n	7:1–2	152n
12:9–12	151n	7:1	152
12:9–11	147, 148	7:9b–17	153
12:10	148	7:14–15	155
12:12	147, 148	7:23	153
12:17–18	149	7:26	153
12:18–19	146, 147	8:9–10	152
12:18	149n, 150	8:11–17	153
12:20–25	146	8:15	xiii, 152, 159
12:20	149	8:15b–20–26	155
12:22	149	8:15b	155, 156
12:23	150	11–12	153, 156
12:24	149	11:4	153
13:7–13a	151n	11:23–25	154

11:25	155n	8:25	158, 160
12:9–10	156	8:41–43	159
12:10–12	155	8:56	159
12:10	155n, 157	9:1–3	164
12:11–12	154	9:3	164
12:11	155	9:4–5	158, 160
12:13b	154	9:5	158
12:20–23	153, 154	9:8–9	170
13–20	155	9:10–14	160
15:24–29	156	9:15–22	160
22	138	10	160
23:3	155	10:6–10	159
		10:9	158, 159

1 Kings

		10:14–29	160
2:1–9	157	11	148
2:1–4	157, 158, 159, 164	11:1–2	160
2:4	157, 158, 160	11:12	160
2:5–9	157, 159	11:14–25	161
2:13–25	159	11:29–39	160
2:27	139	11:31–39	120
2:35	139	11:31–38	160
3:6	205n	11:33–34	161
4:20–21	113n	11:38	161
4:21–34	158	12	158, 161
4:25	113n	12:10	158
5:1–12	164	12:26–32	70n, 73
5:1–6	108n, 158	12:38–30	63
5:7–12	159	14:7–14	163
7	158	21:20–24	120
7:15	158		
8	120, 192	**2 Kings**	
8:1–11	159, 164	16:3	163
8:7–9	164	17	109, 119n
8:9	164	17:7–23	120, 163, 166
8:14–53	164	17:17	163
8:20	158	17:19	163

17:25	119	25	5, 119n
18–20	171, 192	25:21b	165
18:6	192		
18:14–16	192	**2 Chronicles**	
18:15	168	30:9	84
19	120	33	165, 167
19:1–6	243		
19:7–14	243	**Nehemiah**	
20:12–19	168	9:17	84
21:1–18	164	9:31	84
21:6	163		
21:7–9	169	**Job**	
21:9	169	1:9	251
21:7b–9	164	1:11	251n
21:10–15	166	1:21	251n
21:20	167	2:10	252
22:2	168	3:1–37:24	250
22:8	119	3	209n
22:15–20	120	3:11–19	253
22:16	119	3:20	270
22:17	166	3:23	270
22:19	169	4:8	254
23:3	169	4:17	242, 254, 257
23:5	139n	6:8–10	253
23:9	139n	6:30	254
23:10	163	7:17–19	253
23:21–23	169	8:1–7	254
23:25	168	8:3	257.258
23:26–27	166	8:6	257
23:27b	166	8:8	254
23:29	168	9–10	255
23:32	167	9:2	242, 257
24:2b–3	166	9:15–21	254
24:12	165	9:15	257
24:19	167	9:20	257
24:20	169	9:21–24	254

9:22–24	254	38:15	258n
9:24	257	38:22–23	259, 260
12:17	257	38:39–39:4	259
13	259	40:6–41:34	258
13:3b	255	40:6–14	258, 259
13:8	257	40:2–5	258
13:15b	255	40:3–5	259, 271
13:20–22	255	40:7b	261n
15:4	257	40:8	259
16:19	254	40:10–14	259
19:17	257	40:15–41:34	258, 259, 260
19:21	257	40:15	260
19:25–27	256	41:1–34	258
21:15	259n	42:1–6	258, 260, 271
23:4–7	256	42:2	260
23:7	256	42:3–4	261
23:15	257	42:4	261n
25:4	242	42:6	261
26:14–35	260	42:7–9	250
27:6	256, 257, 261	42:7	262, 271
29–31	256		
29:9	259n	**Psalms**	
30:20–23	256	1–41	231
31:1–34	256	1	8, 233, 234, 238
31:6	257	1:1–7	233
31:40b	258	1:2	8, 32, 234, 237
33:23	255	1:5–6	237,
37:23	258	1:6	234, 237
38:1–42:6	250	2	234
38–41	258, 262, 270	2:12	233, 234
38:1–39:40	258	3–41	231
38:1–38	258	3	234
38:2	259, 261n	4:1	238
38:4–38	258	5:8	238
38:12–15	259, 260	5:9	238
38:13	258n	5:12	238, 242

6	232	51–72	231
6:1	232	51	232
7:12	240	57	232
9	233	60	232
10	233	69:28	78n
14:2–3	242	72	23n, 234, 244
15	190	72:1–2	152n, 236
18	23n	73:10–11	241
18:20–30	244	73–89	231
19:1–6	243	73	233, 241
22:31	239	74	23n, 239, 241
24	190	74:1	241
32	232, 233	77	239
33	233	78	12n, 23n
33:5	205, 245	78:8–9	240
35:1	238	80	239
35:24	238	82	23n
35:28	238	83	239
36:5–6	245	83:16	240
36:5	245	83:17	240n
36:6	245	84	244
38	232	85	238
40:8	246	85:2	239
40:9–10	239, 245, 246	85:5–6	238
40:9	245, 246	85:10–12	239, 246
40:10	245, 246	85:10	239
41	234	85:11	239
42–83	231	86	239
42–72	231	86:15	84, 247
42–43	233	87	244
42	233	88	239
42:11	233	88:12	239
43	233	88:38–51	239
43:5	233	89	200, 234
46	244	89:9–10	246
48	244	89:14	243, 244n, 246

89:38–51	239, 244n	106	12n, 233
89:40	244n	106:47	239
89:49	244n	107–150	231
90–106	231, 234	107	233
90	233	107:42–43	233
90:13	245	108	232
93–99	234n, 243, 244	111–118	231
93	234, 243	111:4	84
93:1c	243	112:4	84
93:2	243, 244	116:5	84
94	243	118:19–28	244
94:3	245	119	233
94:16–22	243, 244	130	232
95–99	234n	130:3	242
95:8–11	100n	138–145	234s
96	243	143	232
96:1–2	100n	143:2	81n, 135, 242
96:10c	243, 244	145:8	84, 247
96:13c	243, 244	145:17	247
97	243, 244n	146–150	234, 241
97:2b	243, 244		
97:6	244	**Proverbs**	
97:8	244	5:12	99
98:9b	244	8	23n, 228
99	243	8:5	228
99:2	244	8:8	228
99:4	244	8:15–16	228
99:7b	243	8:20	228
100:3	244	8:22	228
100:4–5	239	9:4	228
103	246	10–30	9
103:6–8	245	21:30	263
103:6–7	246	27:1	263
103:8	84, 246		
103:17	245	**Ecclesiastes**	
105	12n	3:11	228

3:17	228	1:21b	180
11:5	228	1:23	190
11:9	228	1:24–27	183
		1:24–26	180, 182
Sirach		1:26	180
24	6	1:26b	180, 182
24:33	233	1:27	178, 179, 180, 182, 183, 193
Isaiah		2:1–4	179, 193, 269
1–39	177, 192, 193, 194, 195, 198, 199, 204	2:2–4	93, 116, 180, 183, 186, 216, 220
		2:3	178
1–33	192	2:3b	178
1	23, 23n, 199	3:1–3	190
1:1	177, 268	3:1	183
1:2–20	182	3:13–15	190
1:2–3	180, 190, 204, 205, 269	3:13	183
		3:16	179
1:2	24, 182, 210	4:2–6	94, 179, 183
1:5–9	180	4:3–5	178
1:7–8	180	4:3	178
1:8	178, 179	4:4	179
1:9	180	5	183, 199
1:10–20	181, 192	5:1–2	183
1:10–17	190	5:5–6	185
1:10	180, 190, 192	5:7	183
1:11–20	181, 182	5:8–25	183
1:12–17	219	5:11	188
1:16–20	181	5:12	210
1:17	182	5:16	183, 188
1:18–20	180	5:18–21	183
1:20	190	5:18–19	184
1:21–28	188	5:21	185
1:21–26	179, 193	5:22	188
1:21–25	190	5:24c	184, 192
1:21	180, 182, 189	5:25	184

5:26–30	116, 184	11:2	185
5:26	184	11:4	193
6:5	184	11:8	40
6:9–10	186, 203	11:9	178, 186
6:9	195	11:11–16	195
6:10	184	11:11	201
6:11–13	193	11:13–16	186
6:13	184	12:1–6	186
7–8	184	12:6	178
7:14–25	185	13–23	186, 187, 188
7:14	191	13–14	186
7:20	192	13:6	215n
8:1–4	203	13:9	215n
8:8–10	191	14:1–3	186
8:18	178, 185, 188	14:26–27	186
9	200	14:32	186
9:1–7	191, 192, 193, 204	15:7	220
9:2–7	189, 218, 223	16:1	178, 186
9:7	185, 188	16:5	186
9:8–10:4	185	18:7	178, 186
9:8–9	185	19–20	186
9:10b	223	19:3	186
10:5–34	185	19:12	186
10:5–19	116, 241n	19:17	186
10:5–11	114n	19:18	187
10:20–23	185, 201	19:22	187
10:20–22	203	19:23–25	193, 269
10:20–21	186	23:18	179, 186
10:22	185	24–27	187, 188
10:23	185	24:5	187
10:24–34	188	24:6–13	187
10:24	186	24:14–16a	187
10:32	178	24:21	187
11	200	24:23	187
11:1–5	189	25:6–10	269
11:1–9	193, 204, 218	25:6	187

25:9	187	33:17–19	190
26	187	33:20–22	190
26:7–10	188	33:20	178
26:20–21	188	33:22	190
27:13	179, 187	34–35	190, 191
28–33	188	34	191
28:1	188	34:1	190
28:6	188, 189n	34:5–17	202
28:7–8	190	34:5–6	29, 191
28:14	188, 190	34:5	190
28:15	187n	35	179, 191
28:18	187	35:1	191
28:29	188	35:6–7	191
29	188	35:8–10	191
29:8	178	36–39	171, 179, 191, 192
29:10–11	203	37:22–29	114n, 191
30–31	188	37:22	178
30:1	188	37:31–32	191
30:16	189	37:32	178
30:17	189	37:32b	191n
31:4b	178	37:35	178, 191
32:1–8	193	37:36–38	191
32:1	189	38:19–19	239
32:2–7	189	39:2	191
32:11	189	39:5–7	193, 193n
32:16–18	189	39:6–7	192
32:16–17	193	40–66	192
33	189	40–55	171, 191, 194, 195, 196, 198, 199, 200, 201, 202, 204, 269
33:1–3	189		
33:2–6	189		
33:5	178, 193		
33:6	190	40:1–11	179, 193, 194
33:7–9	190	40:1–8	194
33:8	187n	40:1	193n, 194, 197
33:14–16	190	40:9–11	194
33:15–16	190	40:9	178, 195n

40:12–49:13	194	45:20–25	196
40:13	195	45:13	196
41:2–4	195n	45:19	196
41:2	195	45:21–25	197
41:5	196	45:21	193, 196
41:8–10	12n	45:21c	197
41:10	195	45:23	197
41:25–29	195n	45:24	197
41:26	195	46:1	196
41:27	178	46:9–11	195n
42:1–4	59, 194, 195	46:12–13	197
42:4	202	46:13	193, 194n, 196
42:5–9	195n	47:1	196
42:6	187n, 195	48:1	195n
42:9	100n	48:12–15	195n
42:10–13	194n	49:1–6	59, 194
42:18–25	195	49:3	59
42:19	195	49:8	187n
42:21	195, 196, 208	49:13	194, 197
42:24	195	49:14–55:13	194, 197
42:24c	195	49:14	194
43:10	25, 29	50:4–9	59, 194, 197
43:13	25, 29	50:8	197
43:25	25, 29	50:14–21	178
44:6	29	51:1–8	197
44:8	29	51:1–3	197
44:23	194n	51:4–5	197
44:24–28	195n	51:4	198
44:26	195n	51:5	193, 194n
45–47	196	51:6	193, 194n
45:1–6 (7)	195n, 196	51:6c	197, 198
45:1	202	51:7–8	198
45:7	29, 41	51:7–8	197
45:8	193, 194n, 196	51:8	193, 194n
45:9–19	196	51:8b	198
45:9–13	195n	52:1	178

52:2	178	58:2b	193, 198, 200
52:13–53:12	204	58:2c	193, 200
52:13–53	59	58:6–14	201
53:11	59, 198	59:1–8	201
53:12–53:13	198	59:4a	193, 198, 200, 201
53:12	59	59:9a	193
54:1–3	178	59:9–15	202
54:5–8	178	59:14	205n
54:7–10	42n	59:14a	193, 198, 201
54:9–17	198	59:16a	201
54:10	187n, 199	59:16b–17a	201
54:14	198	59:16b	193, 198
54:17	198	59:17a	193, 198
54:17b	198	59:20	178, 201, 202
55:3–5	200	59:21	187n, 199
55:3	187n, 200	60–62	201, 202
55:11	199	60	201
56–66	177, 194, 198, 199, 200, 201, 202n, 204, 269	60:14	178
		60:17	201
		60:21	202
56:1–8	179	61:8	187n
56:1	198, 199, 200	61	202
56:1a	193	61:1	203
56:1b	193	61:1c	202
56:2–8	199	61:3c	202
56:4	187n, 199	61:8–9	202
56:6	187n, 199	61:10b	193, 198
57:1–2	200	61:10	202
57:1	200	61:11	202
57:2a	200	62:1–2	202
57:14–19	201	62:1	178
57:15b	201	62:1b	193, 198
57:16	201	62:11	178
57:21	201	63–66	202, 221n
58:1–8	201	63:1–6	29, 190, 203
58:1b	200	63:1c	193, 198

63:7–19	12n	2:21	207
63:7–14	202, 203	3:1	205
63:10	203	3:11	206n
63:11b–12	203	3:12–14	205
63:15–19	203	4:1–2	205
63:17	203	4:2	205, 206
64	202n, 203	4:5–6:26	205
64:1–12	203	4:34	20
64:5–12	203	5:1	48
64:6	203	5:15–17	116
65–66	203	6:27–30	211
65:1–6	203	9:12	207
65:8b	178	9:15–16	207
65:8c	203	9:17–24	207
65:9	195n	9:22–23	208n
65:13–16	203	9:23	207, 208
65:17–19	203	9:24	207, 208
66:2b–6	204	11:20	205, 209,
66:7–16	204	12:1–3	207
66:10–11	203	12:1	205, 209
66:18–24	204	15:19-21	211
66:22–23	269	20	209n
66:23	179	20:7–17	209
66:24	269	20:12	205
		20:14–18	209
Jeremiah		21:12	208
1–25	206n	22:3	205, 208
1:7	207n	22:21	208
1:7c	207	22:13	205, 208
1:9	207n	22:15	205, 208
2:2–3	206, 218	22:18	207
2:2	210	22:19	208
2:4–8	12n	23:5–6	208
2:5–7	210	23:6	205, 208
2:12	206	23:9–40	207

24	186	18:1–32	210, 213
26:4	207	18:2	211
26:15	207	18:5–24	212
28:9	207	18:5–9	212
31:23	205	18:25	212, 213
31:29–30	8	18:27	210
31:31–34	213	18:29	212, 213
31:31–33	100n	20	12n, 210, 213
33:15–16	208	20:5b	212
33:15	205, 208	20:9	213
33:16	208	20:18–21	210
47:6–7	29	20:22	213
50:7	205	21:3	210
50:11–20	114n	21:4	210, 212n
51:10	205, 209n	23	210, 213
		23:45	210
Daniel		24:27	213
8:12	213n	25:5	213
8:13	213n	25:7	213
9:24	213n	25:11	213
		25:17	213
Ezekiel		27	114n
1:1	210	33	223
3:6–14	210	33:1–20	210, 213
3:16–21	210, 211, 213	33:1–19	213
3:18	211	33:8	210
5:9b	212	33:10–20	213
8	18	33:10	213
13:5	215n	33:14	210
14:12–20	49	33:16	210
14:21	240	33:17	212, 213
16	210, 213	33:20	212, 213
16:1–14	210	37	100n
16:8	210	40–48	94
16:15	210	43:12	94
18	211, 212, 223	45:9	210

Hosea
1–3	178, 217n
1–2	217
1:2–9	217
1:2–3	218
2:1–13	217
2:12	216
2:14–23	217
2:14-15	218
2:15b	210
2:18	218
2:19	217, 223
2:20	217
2:23	100n
4:1–3	218
4:1	216
5:1–2	218
6:6	216
10:11–12	220
10:11	218
10:12	218
14:9	216

Joel
2:13	84, 215

Amos
2:6	219n
3:9	24
5:1–6:14	219
5:7	219
5:12	219n
5:15	219
5:21–24	219
5:24	219
6:12	219
8:2	216
8:9	219s

Obadiah
3:12	216
4:1–4	216
8:10	216

Jonah
4:2	84, 215

Micah
1:2–7	219
1:2	24
1:8–9	219
3:12	220
4:1–4	220
4:1–4	116
5	23n
6:1–5	220
6:3–5	12n
6:5	220
6:5c	220n
6:9–16	220
7:9	220
7:10	220
7:18	215

Nahum
1:2–4	217
1:2–3	215
1:3	84, 216
1:14	216
2:3	217

3:16b	217		4:1–3	223
3:8	216		4:2	223
3:19c	216		4:4	6
			4:5	6

Habakkuk

Zephaniah

1:2–4	221		1:2–3	221
1:4	221		2:1	221
1:12–14	221		2:3	221, 222
1:12–13	221		2:7	222
1:13	221		2:96	222
1:14	221		3:5	221, 222
2:4	221		3:13	222
2:5	221			
2:6	221			
2:6a	221		**Zechariah**	
3:1–19	221		1–8	222
			1:4	222

Malachi

			7:1–3	223
1:2–17	224		7:9	223
1:2	223		8:1–8	223
2:17	223		8:8	223
3:1–4	223		8:14–20	223
3:1–3	223		9:19	223
3:3	223		10:7–9	100n
3:5	223		14:19	213n
3:6–15	223		18	223
3:16–4:6	223		33	223
3:18	223			

Lightning Source UK Ltd.
Milton Keynes UK
UKOW01f0443070218
317473UK00002B/158/P